HISTORY OF LINCOLNSHIRE

Edited by

MAURICE BARLEY

VOLUME VII

SEVENTEENTH-CENTURY LINCOLNSHIRE

by

CLIVE HOLMES

THE HISTORY OF LINCOLNSHIRE COMMITTEE

THIS project for a History of Lincolnshire was begun in 1965 under the chairmanship of Dr Alan Rogers, then of the University of Nottingham and now Professor in Continuing Education in the New University of Ulster. The first volume appeared in 1970. The Committee planned a total of twelve volumes, of which six have already appeared. The present volume is the seventh and the remaining five are in advanced stages of preparation.

Lincolnshire is not one of the favoured counties of England. It has never had its own history produced by an industrious eighteenth- or nineteenth-century antiquary. It is not that there have been few students of Lincolnshire history; rather the size of the county, among other factors, presented problems in bringing together all the material. The Victoria County History proceeded no further than one volume.

The first steps were taken by the Lincolnshire Local History Society, now the Society for Lincolnshire History and Archaeology, with which the Committee still works in close collaboration. The aim was to publish volumes by specialists already engaged in work on particular periods and subjects, aimed at the general reader as well as the scholar. The series will provide a more or less comprehensive account from prehistoric times down to the second half of the present century.

The series was fortunate in having as its first general editor Dr Joan Thirsk of St Hilda's College, Oxford, but commitments obliged her to relinquish this task. Maurice Barley, Professor Emeritus of Archaeology in the University of Nottingham, has taken her place and the Committee is deeply indebted to him for all his work.

An initial financial basis was provided by the Pilgrim Trust, the Seven Pillars of Wisdom Trust, the Marc Fitch Fund, the Lincolnshire Association and the Willoughby Memorial Trust. Help in other ways has been given by the Lincolnshire Association, the Lincoln City and County Library and Museum Services, the Society for Lincolnshire History and Archaeology, the Community Council of Lincolnshire, and the Departments of Adult Education and Geography of the University of Nottingham.

This volume and volume X could not have been published without a financial guarantee generously offered by the Lincolnshire County Council; and we are most grateful to them for this help.

Paul Everson has been production editor for this volume, and in particular has helped in the acquisition of illustrations. The Committee also wishes to thank Elizabeth Everson who does so much work on the distribution of the books, and is grateful to many others who have assisted in so many ways.

DENNIS MILLS
Chairman

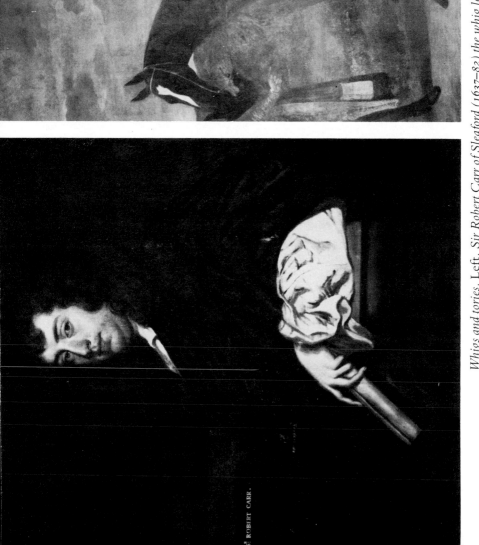

S.ᵣ ROBERT CARR.

Whigs and tories. Left, Sir Robert Carr of Sleaford (1637–82) the whig leader in Lincolnshire during the Exclusion crisis: right, his tory opponent, Robert Bertie, third earl of Lindsey (c.1630–1701). Lindsey chose to be portrayed on his famous racehorse 'the Willoughby Bay', but both men wore layers of the turf

HISTORY OF LINCOLNSHIRE
VII

Seventeenth-Century Lincolnshire

by

CLIVE HOLMES, M.A., Ph.D.

Associate Professor of History, Cornell University

LINCOLN

HISTORY OF LINCOLNSHIRE COMMITTEE

for the Society for Lincolnshire History and Archaeology

1980

PUBLISHED BY

THE HISTORY OF LINCOLNSHIRE COMMITTEE

86 NEWLAND, LINCOLN

© THE HISTORY OF LINCOLNSHIRE COMMITTEE

ISBN 0 902668 06 4

PRINTED IN ENGLAND BY

W. S. MANEY AND SON LTD, HUDSON ROAD LEEDS LS9 7DL

FOR JACK PLUMB

CONTENTS

PART II   NARRATIVE

LIST OF PLATES

Frontispiece: Sir Robert Carr of Sleaford, and Robert Bertie,
third earl of Lindsey

Acknowledgements

The frontispiece of Sir Robert Carr is reproduced by kind
permission of the National Trust; that of the third earl of Lindsey,
by kind permission of the earl of Ancaster, courtesy of the
Courtauld Institute of Art. Plates I and II (copyright M. Barley),
VI, VII, XI, XII and XIII are reproduced by kind permission of the
National Monuments Record; plates VIII and IX are copyright
British Museum. Plate III was taken by Gordon Turnill, and is
reproduced by courtesy of his widow. Plates IV, V and X were
photographed by Paul Everson. Plate XIV is reproduced by
kind permission of the Trustees of Sir John Soane's Museum,
courtesy of the Courtauld Institute of Art. Plate XV is reproduced
by permission of J. N. Heneage, courtesy of the Lincolnshire
Archives Office. To all these individuals and institutions, to Terence
Leach, John Chandler and Group Capt. Basil de Iongh who helped
me locate illustrations, and to Neil French and Geoff Young who
gave assistance in processing photographs, I should like to express
my sincere thanks.

LIST OF TEXT FIGURES

I am very grateful to Mr C. Lewis and the cartographic staff of the Department of Geography, Nottingham University, who drew figures 1, 3, 4 and 6. Figure 2 is reproduced by kind permission of the earl of Ancaster; courtesy of the Lincolnshire Archives Office.

ACKNOWLEDGEMENTS

WRITING a history of seventeenth-century Lincolnshire from a base in up-state New York has not been the easiest task. Its successful completion has only been made possible by the generous assistance of many people, whom I should like to thank.

From its inception the work has had two patrons — the History of Lincolnshire Committee, who commissioned the volume, and my university, Cornell. The Committee, through its chairmen, Alan Rogers and Dennis Mills, have been supportive and patient throughout. Since the completion of the manuscript, I have enjoyed working with the Committee's editor and sub-editor, Maurice Barley and Paul Everson: the former's sensitivity to points of style has enhanced the clarity and readability of the book, while both men have worked tirelessly on the technical side of its production. Cornell has backed my work in many ways. It has provided grants to enable me to travel to England and a fellowship at the Society for the Humanities which freed me from my normal teaching load and enabled me to test ideas and to write in a most congenial atmosphere. The university, through its work-study scheme, has also funded a number of students who have assisted in the collection of materials: the tedious and often grimy labours of Fran Ciardullo, Lisa Fine, Leslie Wilson and, especially, Marjorie Rath, in the 'Dryasdust' compilations, calendars and indexes provided the skeleton around which this study was formed. Cornell is also blessed with an excellent library: its staff, particularly Janet Draper, have successfully secured copies of a series of obscure and ancient antiquarian and topographical studies.

Other American libraries and institutions have been equally supportive. The librarians of Haverford College, Union Theological Seminary and the American Baptist Historical Society have given me a great deal of help with the tracts generated by the religious controversies of the period; the Huntington Library sent me copies of papers from the Ellesmere collection; Maija Cole of the Yale University Parliamentary Diaries project allowed me to use transcripts of the diaries of the 1624 and 1626 parliaments. In England the staffs of the Bodleian Library, the British Library, Cambridge University Library and the Public Record Office have been most generous with their assistance; so, too, have the town clerks of Boston, Grantham and Stamford, the incumbent of Helpringham and Mrs E. Farmery of Croft who gave me access to borough and parochial records in their custody. I am equally grateful to the owners of manuscripts deposited in the Lincolnshire Archives Office, particularly to the Rt Hon. the earl of Ancaster and the Rt Hon. Lord Monson whose family papers have furnished so much information. The staff of the Lincolnshire Archives Office have, of course, done much more than merely produce documents: they have suggested new lines of inquiry, checked points of detail and recommended illustrations; to them all, particularly Mary Finch and Michael Lloyd, my especial thanks.

Maurice Barley and John Morrill have read the entire manuscript; Felicity Heal and Mark Kennedy have criticized, respectively, the sections on the clergy and on fen drainage. The work has benefited from their suggestions. I must also acknowledge a debt, if a less direct one, to other scholars: to the late Sir Francis Hill and to Joan Thirsk whose pioneer studies on aspects of the history of Lincolnshire in this period gave me a superb foundation upon which to build. My thanks also to my colleagues at Cornell, and in the Conference on British Studies with whom I have debated and refined my views on the nature of seventeenth-century society and politics — views which were originally formed in discussion with my graduate teacher, Jack Plumb, to whom I dedicate this book.

Institutions, libraries and archives; scholars; finally, friends. I have made many in my trips to Lincolnshire, but I must thank, in particular, Lis and Ray Wright of Donington in Holland for their hospitality and their compelling enthusiasm for their native county. My wife helped with the index and with proof-reading — and with more besides.

Brighton   C.H.
May 1980

LIST OF ABBREVIATIONS

Abbreviation	Full Title
AASR	Associated Architectural and Archaeological Societies' Reports and Papers
AHR	Agricultural History Review
APC	Acts of the Privy Council of England, London, 1890–1964
Arch.	Archaeologia
Archaeol. J.	Archaeological Journal
BL	British Library
BL Add.	Additional Manuscripts in the British Library
BL Harl.	Harleian Manuscripts in the British Library
Brace, ed., Minutes of the Gainsborough Monthly Meeting	The First Minute Book of the Gainsborough Monthly Meeting of the Society of Friends, 1669–1719, ed. H. W. Brace, LRS, vols 38, 40, 44, Lincoln, 1948, 1949, 1951
Bull. IHR	Bulletin of the Institute of Historical Research
C	Chancery Records in the Public Record Office
CJ	Journals of the House of Commons, i-xiii, London, 1803
CSPD	Calendar of State Papers, Domestic Series, London, 1870–1972
CSPVen.	Calendar of State Papers and Manuscripts relating to English Affairs existing in the Archives of Venice, London, 1871–84
CTB	Calendar of Treasury Books, i-xxxii, London 1904–62
Cole, ed., Speculum	Speculum Diœceseos Lincolniensis, 1705–23, ed. R. E. G. Cole, LRS, vol. 4, Lincoln, 1913
DL	Duchy of Lancaster Records in the Public Record Office
DNB	Dictionary of National Biography
E	Exchequer Records in the Public Record Office
EHR	English Historical Review
EcHR	Economic History Review
Foster, ed., State of the Church	The State of the Church in the Reigns of Queen Elizabeth and King James as illustrated by documents relating to the Diocese of Lincoln, ed. C. W. Foster, LRS, vol. 23, Lincoln, 1926
Grey, ed., Commons Debates	Debates in the House of Commons from the year 1667 to the year 1694, ed. A. Grey, 10 vols, London, 1763
H of LMP	Main Papers collection in the House of Lords Record Office
HMC	Historical Manuscripts Commission
Hill, Tudor and Stuart Lincoln	J. W. F. Hill, Tudor and Stuart Lincoln, Cambridge, 1956
Hist. J.	Historical Journal
J. Eccles. Hist.	Journal of Ecclesiastical History
Jacobson, ed., Works of Sanderson	The Works of Robert Sanderson, ed. W. Jacobson, 6 vols, Oxford, 1854
LAAS	Lincolnshire Architectural and Archaeological Society's Reports and Papers
LAO	Lincolnshire Archives Office
LAOR	LAO Archivists' Reports
LH	Lincolnshire Historian

LHA	*Lincolnshire History and Archaeology*
LJ	*Journals of the House of Lords*, II–XVI, London, no date
LNQ	*Lincolnshire Notes and Queries*
LR	Records of the Exchequer Office of the Auditors of Land Revenue in the Public Record Office
LRS	Lincolnshire Record Society's Publications
NQ	*Notes and Queries*
Nalson MS	This collection, originally in the possession of the dukes of Portland at Welbeck Abbey, has been deposited in the Bodleian Library, Oxford, where its reference numbers are MS Dep. C. 152–76. I have used the Nalson reference as it facilitates consultation of the calendar of the collection, in HMC *Portland*, 1
PC	Registers of the Privy Council in the Public Record Office
Peyton, ed., *Minutes of Quarter Sessions for Kesteven*	*Minutes of Proceedings in Quarter Sessions held for the Parts of Kesteven in the County of Lincoln*, 1 and 11, ed. S. A. Peyton, LRS, vols 25, 26, Lincoln, 1931
RO	Record Office
SP	State Papers in the Public Record Office
STAC	Records of the Court of Star Chamber in the Public Record Office
Trans.Royal Hist.Soc.	*Transactions of the Royal Historical Society*
VCH	Victoria County History
Wood, ed., *Memorials of the Holles Family*	*Memorials of the Holles Family 1493–1656, by Gervase Holles*, ed. A. C. Wood, Camden Soc., 3rd series 55, 1937

Books and tracts published in the seventeenth century are cited in the form given in A. W. Pollard and G. R. Redgrave, *Short title catalogue of books printed in England, Scotland and Ireland, and of English books printed abroad, 1475–1640*, London, 1926, and D. Wing, *Short title catalogue . . . 1641–1700*, 3 vols, New York, 1972.

FOREWORD

THIS contribution to the history of Lincolnshire will have a twofold appeal. For Lincolnshire readers it will be the first general account, and a fascinating one at that, of the crises and conflicts, disputes and even warfare, in a century that experienced more turmoil than any other in modern times. If there was more turmoil than we are used to, the seventeenth century seems real because the issues are still familiar from personal experience: tensions between church and chapel; arguments over changes in land use and conditions of employment in farming; the relations between classes. The contrast between that age and ours is that we express our differences in a more discreet or mealy-mouthed fashion.

The realities of local life and the vigour and feeling of their expression come across, because Dr Holmes knows so well the contemporary sources, printed and manuscript, and quotes them so effectively. Real persons emerge, such as Bishop Williams or the saintly rector of Boothby Pagnell, Robert Sanderson; familiar characters such as Cornelius Vermuyden are seen in a fresh and critical light.

Readers more detached from the county and its people are offered an interpretation of local history which will certainly prove to be important and of enduring value. Dr Holmes enjoys controversy and challenges widely-held views about the character of the local community. He also writes from a base of familiarity with the social sciences and the work and attitudes of American historians. Lincolnshire is thus presented with an outstandingly lively and original contribution to its history, in which the town and the village, in all the complexities of their structure, are seen with a new clarity.

MAURICE BARLEY
General Editor

CHAPTER 1

INTRODUCTION — LOCAL HISTORY AND COMMUNITY

T HE study of English local history has never been a cloistered academic pursuit. The student is invariably motivated by a sentimental attachment to the area which he investigates, by a sense of its special quality for him. That sense may be a matter of birth or residence: for me, a Hampshireman now living in up-state New York, it was Lincolnshire's varied beauty and its people which I came to appreciate in my earlier work on the eastern counties that made me undertake this book. However, if the impulse for the study of local history is unchanging, linking the current investigator to distinguished predecessors — to Richard Butcher, Francis Peck, or W. O. Massingberd in my case — the product has become considerably more sophisticated in the years since the war. The improvement reflects a number of developments. Some are broad-ranging: changes in social structure and in education ensure that local history can no longer be 'a history of the upper classes by the upper classes for the upper classes'.[1] Others, such as the increased availability of records and the use of new analytical and quantitative techniques, are more narrowly technical. There has also been an important conceptual reformulation: a redefinition of the purpose of local history and of the function of the local historian.

Central to the reconceptualizaton of the discipline has been the suggestion that the focus of local study must be the community. In 1952 in separate works the two founders of the Department of Local History at Leicester University, with which, in a professional and institutional sense, the modern study of local history has been chiefly associated, defined the mission of the local historian in virtually identical terms. For W. G. Hoskins 'the fundamental problem, surely, is the origin and growth of the local community

[1] L. Stone, 'English and United States Local History', *Daedalus* (Winter 1971), p. 128: see also W. G. Hoskins, *English Local History: the Past and the Future*, Leicester, 1966, pp. 5, 9.

I

. . . [and] in rural districts, at least, . . . the process by which this local, and largely self-contained community has disintegrated'; for H. P. R. Finberg the historian's task was 'to re-enact in his own mind . . . the Origin, Growth, Decline and Fall of a Local Community'.[2] Since then the inaugural lectures of the succession of professors of English Local History at Leicester have reiterated the emphasis on the study of communities.[3] The latter has been no mere programmatic abstraction, however. The best *vade mecum* for the novice local historian is organized about the idea that the community is the proper unit of investigation, while a number of studies of individual villages acknowledge an intellectual debt to the Leicester school and its community orientation.[4] So too do a number of studies of social units geographically more extensive than the village. In his work on the civil war in Kent, Alan Everitt suggested that the English counties in the seventeenth century should be conceived as communities 'each with its own distinct ethos and loyalty', and his approach has been duplicated by Anthony Fletcher and J. S. Morrill in studies of, respectively, Sussex and Cheshire in the early Stuart period.[5]

What, then, is a community? Professor Finberg provided a definition: 'a community is a set of people occupying an area with defined territorial limits and so far united in thought and action as to feel a sense of belonging together, in contradistinction from many outsiders who do not belong'. A community entails geographical contiguity and, more important, a collective consciousness. It is the latter, Finberg argued, which legitimizes the local historian's study, and raises it above mere antiquarianism or the dependent status of handmaid to national history. Local history involves the study of a social unit, the community, which had as much, indeed more,

---

[2] H. P. R. Finberg, *The Local Historian and his Theme*, Leicester, 1954, p. 9; W. G. Hoskins, 'The Writing of Local History', *History Today*, 2 (1952), p. 490.
[3] H. P. R. Finberg, *Local History in the University*, Leicester, 1964, p. 7; Hoskins, *English Local History*, pp. 20, 21; A. Everitt, *New Avenues in English Local History*, Leicester, 1970, pp. 6, 22.
[4] A. Rogers, *This was their world: approaches to local history*, London, 1972, especially pp. 2, 7, 133: D. G. Hey, *An English Rural Community: Myddle under the Tudors and Stuarts*, Leicester, 1974; M. Spufford, *Contrasting Communities: English Villages in the Sixteenth and Seventeenth Centuries*, Cambridge, 1974, especially p. xix.
[5] A. Everitt, *The Community of Kent and the Great Rebellion*, Leicester, 1966, p. 13; A. Fletcher, *A County Community in Peace and War*, London, 1975; J. S. Morrill, *Cheshire 1630–60: County Government and Society during the English Revolution*, Oxford, 1974, especially p. 333.

significance for its members than those groups — nations, classes — which are the staples of traditional historiography.[6]

In 1962 the definition of community seemed a simple enough task, and Finberg gently mocked those social scientists whose use of the term had produced only a babel — some ninety-four distinguishable definitions. However, while historians have been less fecund in devising and debating alternative concepts of community than their sociologist peers, the emergence of some problems in their employment of the term would suggest that the question of definition 'might perplex us' more than Finberg supposed two decades ago. At worst some investigators implicitly presume that the territorial propinquity of a population will necessarily entail the existence of a meaningful consciousness; no endeavour is made, except the employment of the shibboleth 'community', to demonstrate the existence of any such corporate sensibility or awareness. The community of Middletown then becomes no more than a long-winded synonym for Middletown. Those scholars who have used the term with greater sophistication have been obliged to confront a number of conceptual difficulties. Dr Hey wrestles with the problem of whether a community can be said to exist given the kaleidoscopic mobility of a major part of the population of an area; Mrs Spufford similarly suggests the limitations of an approach which treats the village as a closed social system and argues that '"neighbourhoods" or "social areas" each extending over a group of parishes within approximately an eight-mile radius of a focal village centre' may be more meaningful units of study.[7] An examination of these and related practical and theoretical problems has led Alan Macfarlane to propose abandoning the community as a basic organizing concept of historical investigation.[8]

Such iconoclasm seems extreme. The concept of community remains useful provided that the historian remembers that it is *consciousness* that is being studied, a consciousness which will vary from place to place, and will ebb and flow in time in response to a variety of pressures. In 1962 Professor Finberg suggested an approach along these lines. The local historian, he argued, should engage in the comparative study of communities. He also emphasized that an individual was a member of other social groups besides the local community, for example the family and the state, to which

[6] H. P. R. Finberg, 'Local History' in *Approaches to History*, ed. H. P. R. Finberg, London, 1962, pp. 116–17.

[7] Hey, *Myddle*, pp. 2, 4; Spufford, *Contrasting Communities*, p. 57.

[8] A. Macfarlane, 'History, anthropology and the study of communities', *Social History*, 5 (1977), pp. 631–52.

he owed allegiance, and that loyalties to these entities might in certain circumstances outweigh his emotional ties to the local unit.[9] Yet while some excellent work designed to devise a typology of local units based primarily on patterns of land utilization and social structure has appeared, Finberg's suggestions concerning variations on consciousness have not been consistently pursued, largely, I think, because local historians are reluctant to admit that the village community may not be the fundamental unit of identification, and thus the essential unit of study. This reluctance seems equally compounded of a measure of defensiveness about their discipline, and the engaging romanticism which Professor Stone has remarked.[10] Local historians are still inordinately sensitive to the 'well-meaning condescension' of their nationally-oriented colleagues; perhaps it is believed that an acknowledgement that the local unit was not always the centre of the universe to its population may resurrect the charges of antiquarianism or relegate their status to that of 'drudges . . . providing footnotes for somebody else's History of England'.[11] In addition, several influential exponents of local history subscribe to a vision of the past in which an unpalatable modern world is viewed as the disastrous product of the catastrophe of the industrial revolution. In the antediluvian world men lived in communities: the latter are now 'hollow shells from which the heart and spirit have been leached out by the acids of the nineteenth century'.[12] This cataclysmic account, and the related nostalgia for a vanished rural past and suspicion of the metropolis and all its works, is scarcely conducive to an appreciation of shifts in community consciousness in the pre-industrial period.

This study of seventeenth-century Lincolnshire will also be concerned with the theme of community consciousness. However, I do not propose to treat the latter, to use the language of mathematics, as either a given or a constant. Rather, I intend to investigate changes in the perceptions of social relationships in the course of the period and in particular the shifting balance between loyalties to the locality and those to other groupings. One would hardly expect that the local unit would remain the unmoving centre of the universe in a period usually characterized even by elementary textbooks as one of revolution or crisis.

[9] Finberg, 'Local History', pp. 119, 123.
[10] Stone, 'English and United States Local History', p. 130.
[11] Everitt, *New Avenues*, p. 3; Finberg, *Local History in the University*, p. 14.
[12] Hoskins, 'The Writing of Local History', p. 490; see also A. Everitt, *Change in the Provinces: the Seventeenth Century*, Leicester, 1969, pp. 52–53.

In the first part of the work we will examine aspects of the structure of Lincolnshire society, beginning with the basic local units, village and town. It will be argued that changes in economic function and social structure, though they did not act uniformly throughout the county, weakened the sense of group identity in these units, and that the rise of alternative voluntaristic communities, particularly the nonconformist sects which provided alternative foci of corporate sentiment, may be a reaction to this erosion. We will then study the professional cadres of lawyers and clerics, and the gentry: groups which acted as 'brokers', channelling the products of the national culture into the localities, thus further undercutting local isolation.

The discussion of the role of the gentry will oblige us to confront the argument that, for this class in the seventeenth century, the county itself was a community, and that the political horizons of the gentry were circumscribed by the boundaries of their 'county commonwealths', their 'countries'. At this point, after examining such factors as the education, marriage alliances, origins, and wealth of the gentry, we will abandon the structural analysis employed in the first part of the book. Further analysis of the question of community sentiment requires an examination of the flux of events. Accordingly the second part of this study provides a chronological survey of the political and religious history of the county with particular emphasis upon the interaction of the centre and the locality, that is, upon the responses which the demands of the national governments elicited in the localities, and upon the reactions of the various régimes to local concerns. In conclusion it will be suggested that while change was neither rapid, nor linear, nor universal, the period was marked by the erosion of local loyalties and by a growing awareness of national issues.

From this synopsis it may seem that I am employing seventeenth-century Lincolnshire as a convenient testing ground for certain historiographical concepts. No: the stress upon community is not in the service of an arcane academic controversy, but because it provides the best framework around which to organize a structured yet dynamic account of the experience and ideals of the men and women who lived in the county in our period. Like the great seventeenth-century historian, Gervase Holles of Grimsby, my intention has also been 'to set the right stamp and value upon every person'.[13] The conceptual apparatus is employed to further that end: it is not an end in itself.

---

[13] Wood, ed., *Memorials of the Holles Family*, p. 2.

PART I:
STRUCTURE

CHAPTER 2

GRASS-ROOTS COMMUNITIES: THE VILLAGE

MANY of us, denizens of an industrialized, urbanized society, are tempted to suppose that the village was the repository of human values conspicuously absent in our fast-paced, fluid and atomistic world. The village is associated with isolation and stability; an emotional awareness of group identity, forged in kinship, shared experience and co-operation, is ascribed to its inhabitants. The village, we feel, was an organic community. This vision, for all its romantic idealization, has received some backing from scholars. Anthropologists have announced the discovery, in the remoter corners of the globe, of communities possessing the qualities we attribute to the rustic village. Local historians, the most recent of them borrowing the conceptual apparatus and vocabulary of their colleagues in the social sciences, have argued their existence in the pre-industrial past. Thus Professor Lockridge describes seventeenth-century Dedham, Massachusetts as a 'closed corporate peasant community'. The salient features of the latter are that it 'restricts its membership, retains ultimate authority over the alienation of land, seeks to guarantee its members equal access to resources, and maintains its internal order by enforcing common standards of behaviour'.[1]

THE CLOSED CORPORATE PEASANT COMMUNITY

It is tempting to employ this concept with respect to seventeenth-century Lincolnshire villages. All of the elements which led Lockridge to his characterization of colonial Dedham are to be found in the Lincolnshire evidence. The village community could be restrictive. At Frampton in 1653 the villagers sought to prevent the marriage of an outsider, 'a very poore man . . . lately crept

[1] K. Lockridge, *A New England Town: the First Hundred Years*, New York, 1970, pp. 18–19: for a general discussion, see A. Macfarlane, 'History, anthropology and the study of communities', *Social History*, 5 (1977), pp. 631–52.

into' the town, to a local girl; at Ashby a four-year-old child, deserted by his parents, was dumped at Spalding by the parish officers; at the end of the 1680s a number of Kesteven villages sought to eject those poor squatters who had failed to observe the technicalities of the Acts of Settlement.[2] While no Lincolnshire village retained ultimate authority over land transactions, the community in the manor court, as at Barrow, Hibaldstow or Scotter, could supervise the transfer of copyhold land: the court also organized the agricultural routine of the open fields and the communal utilization of pasture and meadow, and punished those who failed to observe the customs and regulations.[3]

The manor court might also act against minor peccadilloes not related to the agricultural round, but the central institution in the maintenance of the village's internal order was the parish church. The minister, in pulpit and in practice, would hymn the virtues of neighbourliness and charity.[4] Those who failed to observe these norms — drunkards, brawlers, backbiters, adulterers: men like Christopher Barber of Roughton, 'a malicious, contentious and uncharitable person, and one that hath sought and doth seeke the unjust vexation of thy neighbours' — risked prosecution in the ecclesiastical courts. There the determination of guilt or innocence lay, by virtue of the process of purgation, in the hands of the neighbours of the accused. Guilt was punished by a humiliating public confession in the parish church or by excommunication, the ultimate penalty which cut those so penalized from the community: as the vicar of Helpringham solemnly intoned in 1663, 'I . . . inhibitt you . . . my parishioners . . . from all manner of converse . . . with them or any of them [i.e. those excommunicated] by buying, selling, eating, drinkeing, conversing or talkeing with them'.[5]

[2] *LNQ*, 1 (1889), pp. 109–10; LAO, LQS Minute Book 1665–78, p. 134; Peyton, ed., *Minutes of Quarter Sessions for Kesteven*, pp. 271, 272, 276, 283, 342, 350, 351.
[3] E. Peacock, 'Notes from the Court Rolls of the Manor of Scotter', *Arch.*, 46 (1881), p. 388; E. Peacock, 'The Court Rolls of the Manor of Hibaldstow', *Archaeol. J.*, 44 (1887), pp. 285–86; M. W. Barley, 'The Barrow-on-Humber Town Book', *LAAS*, 2 (1940–41), pp. 13–33; R. C. Dudding, *History of the Parish and Manors of Alford with Rigby and Ailby*, Horncastle, 1930, pp. 180–202. For villagers organizing the utilization of common in a non-manorial context, see H. E. Hallam, 'The fen bylaws of Spalding and Pinchbeck', *LAAS*, 10 (1963–64), pp. 40–55.
[4] Jacobson, ed., *Works of Sanderson*, VI, pp. 291–95.
[5] LAO, Court Papers 58/2/72: for purgation, 58/4/8; CH/P 10, no. 53: for penance, Foster, ed., *State of the Church*, pp. lxvi, civ: for excommunication, LAO, Helpringham Vestry Book, *sub* 1663.

The church was the focus of the village community not only as a function of the explicit affirmation of the neighbourly values in its religious ideology, but as the most common and the best attended meeting place of the entire population. Gathered in the church, often in a seating arrangement which reflected the village's internal hierarchy, the parishioners collectively participated in the weekly services and in the christenings, weddings and funerals of their fellow villagers. These rites of passage were marked not only by corporate religious, but also secular ceremonies, like the wake at Sutterton in 1642 when the bereaved neighbours of Miles Silvers downed some three stone of cheese and ten gallons of ale.[6] Other secular activities, often dimly related to forgotten religious festivals, spilled out from the church: the Ascension Day procession around the fields of Coleby, the Haxey Hood fair.[7] The church was often the political centre of the village. At Frampton the accounts of the retiring parish officers were reviewed, and their successors elected, at an annual meeting in the chancel. At Haxey the fourteenth-century Mowbray deed, which the commoners believed to be a bar to further dominal exploitation of the fen, was kept in the church. It was enshrined in an iron-bound chest beneath a stained-glass window 'wherein was the portraiture of Mowbray set . . . holding in his hand a writing, which was commonly reputed to be an embleme of the deed'.[8]

We may suggest the addition of a further characteristic of the closed corporate peasant community to the list advanced by Lockridge. It seeks to defend its individual members and its corporate autonomy from external interventions. The community might endeavour to protect its members from fiscal burdens. Taxation could be avoided by foisting a disproportionately heavy proportion of the levy onto the inhabitants of affiliated hamlets or, better yet, onto non-resident landowners. The maintenance of an illegitimate child could be shunted onto another parish by inventing a specious paternity claim.[9] The prospect of expense was not the only external pressure which activated the community's mechanisms of self-defence. The community might insulate its individual members from legal proceedings by concealing their offences: when Robert Parke, churchwarden of Ancaster denounced his

[6] LAO, Court Papers 69/1/38; Resp. Pers. 9/45, 66; AD. AC 28, f. 43.
[7] STAC 8 277/11; W. B. Stonehouse, *The History and Topography of the Isle of Axholme*, London, 1839, p. 291.
[8] LAO, Frampton Vestry Book; Daniel Noddell, *To the Parliament of the Commonwealth of England*, London, 1654, p. 5 (mispagination for p. 9).
[9] E 178 4041; E 134 1 James I Mich. 4; LAO, LQS File 1634, no. 169.

brother to the ecclesiastical court for engaging in pre-marital sex, 'which falt I present . . . to the discharge of myne owne place and office', he was displaying a conscientious regard for his sworn duty seldom emulated by his less scrupulous peers.[10] Perhaps the integrity of the village community emerges most clearly in its response to challenges to its enjoyment of corporate rights. Attempts by adjacent villages or landowners to take advantage of a community's common; the infringement of rights of way; a lord's enclosure schemes: all would be resisted by lawsuits, often supported by a common fund, or by violence.[11] For the first two decades of the seventeenth century the men of Revesby sparred with Sir John Aylmer and his henchmen — thugs, suborned witnesses, shady lawyers — figuratively in the courts, literally on the village streets and even in the church, as they sought to repel his attempts to enclose common land and to establish dominal rights of jurisdiction over them. On Ascension Day 1616 the vicar of Coleby led his flock from the church in the traditional perambulation of the fields: in the course of the procession they levelled the hedges recently erected by the lord of the manor on part of their common.[12]

There is, then, a good deal of evidence of behaviour which Professor Lockridge would consider characteristic of the closed corporate peasant community, yet a blanket application of this description to the villages of seventeenth-century Lincolnshire would entail the neglect of a considerable volume of countervailing evidence.

INTERACTION: AGRICULTURE AND THE MARKET TOWN

One of the offences within the cognizance of the ecclesiastical courts was slander involving imputations of immorality: when John Thompson of Killingholme said 'thou . . . swivest other men's wives . . . [and] . . . hast as many whores and concubines as Solomon had', the indignant Thomas Pennell, an East Halton yeoman, promptly sought redress for the injury to his good name at Lincoln. About a quarter of a sample of such defamation cases in the diocesan records, like that of Pennell *versus* Thompson, involved parties from different villages. Similar cross-village contacts emerge from a study of the bastardy cases determined by the Kesteven quarter sessions. Thirty-two maintenance orders were

[10] LAO, CH/P 10, no. 73: for the failures of the churchwardens to present offences in 1604, for example, see Vj 18, pp. 5, 6, 68, 69, 79, 89, 115, 175.
[11] STAC 8 42/11; 108/8; 145/20; 253/77; 296/10; 308/13.
[12] Ibid., 39/4, 5; 137/16; 186/27; 212/5, 11 (Revesby); 163/30 (Coleby).

issued from 1674 to 1695: in ten of these cases the putative father was not a resident of the same village as his paramour.[13]

We can presume that cases of defamation and fornication did not represent isolated and unique contacts. They presume wider-ranging social and cultural intercourse between villagers. How did this occur?

First, the basic agricultural routine of many villages involved considerable co-operation with others. Intercommoning was a frequent practice in seventeenth-century Lincolnshire, most notably in the fens of the Isle of Axholme and the south-eastern quarter of the county, but also on the uplands of the Wold and the Cliff. The relations generated between intercommoning villagers were not necessarily over-friendly. There was endless litigation between the men of Misterton in Nottinghamshire and those of Epworth concerning the rights enjoyed by the former in Haxey Carr, and frequent quarrels between the villagers of the Hales and Helpringham with the Hollanders, from Donington, Bicker and Swineshead, who shared common in the fen which lay between them.[14] Yet any attempt by foreigners — other villages, enclosing landlords, fen drainers — to intrude and to disrupt the traditional arrangements would generate co-operative resistance. A common fund to finance litigation might be established; rioters gathered from the affected villages would smash fences, fill ditches, burn crops and drive off or maim animals.[15]

Secondly, the inhabitants of different villages interacted in the local market towns, of which there were thirty-seven in seventeenth-century Lincolnshire.[16] While these varied widely both in size and complexity of function, it is possible to provide a general account of their social role (see plates IV and V).

In the middle ages four of the Lincolnshire towns had been deeply involved in the international trade in wool and cloth: the ports, Boston and Grimsby; Lincoln and Stamford as cloth manufacturing centres and marts for wool. None of the four sustained its medieval eminence. Grimsby's decline was most marked. The silting up of its haven had left it stranded, the decaying carcase of a once-great

---

[13] The defamation cases are in LAO, Resp. Pers. 9; Court Papers 58/4; 59/1, 3; 62/2: the maintenance orders are from Peyton, ed., *Minutes of Quarter Sessions for Kesteven*, passim.

[14] J. Thirsk, 'The Isle of Axholme before Vermuyden', *AHR*, I (1953), pp. 24–25; STAC 8 168/15; LAO, Helpringham Vestry Book, *sub* 1606.

[15] STAC 8 15/3; 113/11; 125/3; 129/13; 145/20.

[16] *The Agrarian History of England and Wales*, IV, ed. J. Thirsk, Cambridge, 1967, pp. 473–74.

port. Reference to poverty and decay echo through the accounts of visitors to the town: Holles wrote, elegiacally, 'the haven hath bin heretofore commodious, now decayed; the traffique good, now gone: the place rich and populous, the houses now meane and stragling by reason of depopulation, and the towne very poor'. Eleven ships and 171 mariners had sailed from Grimsby to join Edward III at the siege of Calais: three centuries later only 'one poore coale ship' plied from the port. The same government survey, in 1629, found a scant eleven vessels based on Boston, and only five of those of more than fifty tons burden. In 1666 it was reported that no ship had been built at Boston for over twenty years. Lincoln and Stamford, like the ports, had also fallen on hard times and were the shells of the great commercial centres they had once been. Lincoln's decline in population, memorialized by unused and dilapidated churches, was particularly marked, and gave the lie to the rosy description of the city in the preamble to the 1628 charter as 'one of the chiefest seats of our whole kingdom . . . for the staple and public market of wool sellers and merchant strangers meeting together'.[17]

The currents of international trade had turned into other channels, but the four towns were still important *local* centres. Dr Hinton, analysing the port books, has argued that we should not take too seriously Boston's continual lamentations of miserable poverty, the usual response to the government's requests for taxes or loans. The town was a centre for the export of produce from its hinterland and the importation of goods for local consumption. Boston's shipping boomed in the 1630s and its merchant-factors were busy men. As Hinton concludes, the port was not unprosperous, 'except by comparison with the wonderful affluence of its legendary past'. The town also provided specialized services for the surrounding countryside — a harpsichord tuner; doctors. In 1662 John Barnaby, a Boston apothecary, received a testimonial from, amongst others, the vicars of Moulton, Kirton and Friskney; they praised the abilities and diligence which had made him 'very serviceable both in the towne and country adjacent'.[18]

Stamford was an important market centre, with a small group of craftsmen, particularly in the leather trades, working the raw

[17] *Lincolnshire Church Notes made by Gervase Holles*, ed. R. E. G. Cole, LRS, vol. 1, 1911, pp. 1–2; SP 16/138/60; *CSPD 1665–66*, p. 209; T. Allen, *The History of the County of Lincoln*, 1, London, 1833, p. 118.
[18] *The Port Books of Boston, 1601–40*, ed. R. W. K. Hinton, LRS, vol. 50, 1956, pp. xxxiv–xliii; LAO, MG 5/2/1, f. 24v; LAO, LTD 1662, testimonial for John Barnaby.

materials produced in the area. After 1660 the town experienced an economic resurgence. The Welland navigation improved the town's prosperity, but more significant was the development of overland transportation and thus of the coaching trade. Grantham which alone of the five Lincolnshire boroughs lacked a glorious past against which to contrast its current condition, also profited from the growth of road transport. Defoe remarked its busy market, the 'very good trade' of its inhabitants, and the fact that 'lying on the great northern road [it] is famous . . . for abundance of very good inns, some of them fit to entertain persons of very greate quality and their retinues, and it is a very great advantage to the place'.[19]

Lincoln's markets had a local importance, but the city's prime function was as the religious and political centre of the county. A number of lawyers, common and ecclesiastical, resided in the city, where several county gentlemen maintained town houses occupied during the assizes. The city provided a number of services for this clientele: an excellent school, where, in the 1620s the distinguished John Clarke provided the scions of the gentry with a fine classical training, and a veteran from the Dutch army instructed them in 'military postures and in assaults and defences'; a fencing academy; facilities for horse racing.[20] Grimsby duplicated Lincoln's role in microcosm. It was an administrative centre for the surrounding villages and a gathering place for the local squirearchy. A number of gentlemen of quality settled in the borough, and a few became officers of the corporation which, in consequence, became an odd hybrid of gentlemen and 'mean and mechanicke fellowes'.[21]

The Lincolnshire corporations no longer played key roles in international trade. They were geared, like the other, unincorporated market towns, to the needs of their locality. The towns were local entrepôts marketing the produce of their immediate hinterlands and providing the latter with specialized goods and services: the justices' orders during the 1630–31 dearth and in 1636 when the plague raged in Boston and Grantham indicate the market towns' essential functions as outlets for local production and as sources for

[19] J. Thirsk, 'Stamford in the Sixteenth and Seventeenth Centuries' in The Making of Stamford, ed. A. Rogers, Leicester, 1965, pp. 58–76; Daniel Defoe, A Tour through the whole Island of Great Britain, II, London, 1962, p. 103.
[20] H of LMP 22 Dec. 1641, the poll tax return for Lincoln; E. Venables, 'A survey of the houses in the minster close of Lincoln', AASR, 19 (1887–88), pp. 43–75; C. Garton, John Clarke's Orationes et Declamationes, Buffalo, 1972, pp. 21–36; The progresses, processions and magnificent festivities of King James I, III, ed. J. Nichols, London, 1828, pp. 260–66.
[21] Wood, ed., Memorials of the Holles Family, pp. 196–97, 217; E. Gillett, A History of Grimsby, London, 1970, pp. 104, 120–22, 139.

goods, even subsistence items, unavailable in the villages.[22] The towns provided markets; they were also administrative and political centres. Business, public or private, brought men to Lincoln assizes, to the ten towns where quarter sessions met regularly, to towns like Burton Stather or Corby where the local justices met in informal petty sessions. In the 1650s the inhabitants of the surrounding villages trudged into Grimsby to be married by the mayor in accordance with the novel form prescribed by the commonwealth régime.[23] The regular convergence of villagers upon the neighbouring market town must have been one of the basic rhythms of rural life in seventeenth-century Lincolnshire: the cavaliers sought to take advantage of this in June 1643 when an attempt to surprise the parliamentary garrison of Lincoln was spearheaded by a force of sixty men disguised as rustics.[24]

For the villagers, drawn by its economic and administrative functions, the town became a social centre. In the market, or in the town's alehouses, peasants would become acquainted with their peers from other parishes.[25] The degree to which the town was a magnet and a social centre for its rural hinterland was recognized in the establishment of market-day lectureships in certain towns, and by those benefactors, who, endowing schools at towns like Sleaford or Kirton-in-Lindsey, made specific arrangements that places should be available for able boys from the neighbouring villages.[26] Lectures and grammar schools suggest that the town's role in the expansion of the social horizons of the peasantry went beyond the construction of lateral systems of inter-village relations to the establishment of some popular awareness of the wider national culture. Certainly the market towns were centres for the dissemination and discussion of information about current affairs: in the 1690s, when the curate of Broughton wanted 'to hear what news there was stirring' he rode to Brigg or Caistor.[27]

Peasants from different villages interacted with one another: in some parts of Lincolnshire the form of agricultural organization forged interconnection, while the market town was an important

[22] SP 16/189/58; 192/40; *LNQ*, 3 (1898), pp. 113, 114, 116, 117.
[23] SP 16/192/30; 349/123; A. C. Sinclair, *A history of Beelsby*, London, 1947, pp. 50–51.
[24] John Vicars, *Jehovah-Jireh*, London, 1644, pp. 372–73.
[25] LAO, Court Papers 58/2/75; Resp. Pers. 9/65.
[26] E. Venables, 'The primary visitation of the diocese of Lincoln by Bishop Neile, AD 1614', *AASR*, 16 (1881–82), pp. 44–47; E 134 16 Charles I Easter 21; LAO, ANDR 6, ff. 8–9, 12–15; *LNQ*, 11 (1911), pp. 6–15.
[27] *The diary of Abraham de la Pryme*, ed. C. Jackson, Surtees Soc., 54, 1870, pp. 60, 97–98, 122.

social centre for the 'countrymen' from its rural catchment-area. Such relationships were hardly peculiar to the seventeenth century, and their existence must make us question the applicability of the notion of the isolation of the village in any period. The geographical mobility of the rural population, which we must now discuss, may also have been more common in medieval society than is usually recognized: but it was certainly an important social fact in the seventeenth century.

GEOGRAPHICAL MOBILITY

We may distinguish several forms of mobility. There was some seasonal ebb and flow of agricultural labour: so we find the young men and maids of Laughton and Osbournby working in the fields together (and exchanging ribald jests) during the haymaking season.[28] The common practice, whereby adolescents, often from well-to-do yeoman families, were placed in service for a few years resulted in another kind of geographical mobility: Sent Wells of Tattershall and Margaret Featherstone of Hough were servants at, respectively, Tumby and Brant Broughton, when marriage was proposed to them.[29] There were also vagrants wandering the countryside and living by begging and petty theft. They were liable to arrest, whipping, and extradition to their place of birth or legal settlement, and in the early 1630s when dearth in the localities and government directives galvanized the local magistrates to unusual assiduity, the records are full of accounts of 'privy searches' to round up transients, and smug statistics of their fearsome punishment.[30]

Rural migration and subsequent resettlement was probably more significant for inter-village relationships than either vagrancy or temporary seasonal and generational mobility. Rural craftsmen — carpenters, smiths, masons, weavers, and the like — seem to have been a particularly mobile group. Few of them could rival the pilgrimage of the smith, Robert Knight, who was born at Wellingore and worked in Cambridge, Boston, and four marshland villages before settling at Bratoft at the age of fifty; yet in a group of twelve rural craftsmen whose careers can be traced, only one worked in the village of his birth.[31] Peasants, as well as rural

[28] LAO, Court Papers 69/2/1.
[29] Ibid., 62/2/18; Resp. Pers. 10, no. 14.
[30] For example, SP 16/272/23; 294/12, 31–35; 315/19.
[31] Knight's career, and those of the other craftsmen, are set out in their statements to the ecclesiastical courts: these are in the series LAO, Resp. Pers. 10 and Court Papers 69/2.

C

craftsmen, migrated. The extent of this phenomenon is impossible to determine precisely, but the analysis of certain (admittedly limited) indicators and consideration of the general direction of population trends in the county suggest that it was considerable.

Let us examine the latter point, the demographic history of Lincolnshire, first. Between 1563 and 1723 the population of the archdeaconry of Lincoln, which covered all the county save the

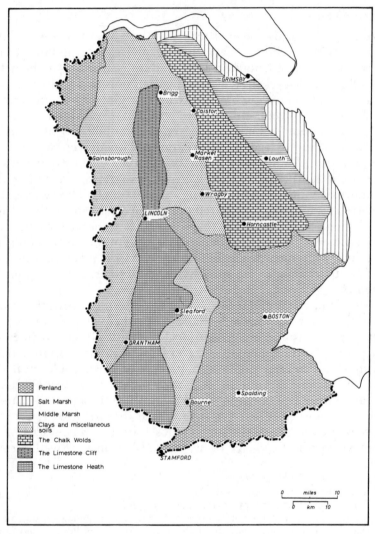

Figure 1   *Major agricultural regions in the county*

north-west quadrant, increased about fourteen per cent.[32] A cursory analysis of a small number of parish registers suggests that the rate of increase was not constant.[33] The birth-rate was high in the period 1600–40, although the growth of population was retarded by catastrophic years when the death-rate leaped, usually as a function of the classic combination of dearth and plague, as in 1610–13 and 1629–32.[34] After the civil war the birth-rate appears to have fallen and population growth slowed.

The population of Lincolnshire expanded from 1563 to 1723 as analysis of parish registers would lead us to expect. Yet if we examine, not the general figure for the county, but those which can be calculated for the broad agricultural regions within it (see figure 1), a more complex pattern emerges. In the greater part of the county, population stagnated through the course of the seventeenth century; it fell sharply, by a quarter, in the southern Wolds. Conversely, population increase was considerable in the towns: all the boroughs save moribund Grimsby experienced population increases of more than fifty per cent, and expansion of a similar magnitude occurred in the unincorporated market towns like Sleaford, Horncastle and Spilsby. Population also rose in the Holland fens: less in the already densely settled towns of north Holland and southern Lindsey which shared common in the fens above Boston than in the townships in Elloe and in eastern Kesteven which had access to the fens of south Holland. The latter area had been lightly settled in 1563; its population nearly doubled in the ensuing century and a half. The pattern in north-western Lincolnshire would appear to be similar. Between 1603 and 1676 the number of communicants in the archdeaconry of Stow fell very slightly: but the general figure conceals a rise in the population of Gainsborough (+32%), and of the fen towns on the Isle of

---

[32] The figure is reached by comparing the 1563 survey, printed in G. A. J. Hodgett, *Tudor Lincolnshire*, Lincoln, 1975, pp. 189–99, with the survey of 1723, in Cole, ed., *Speculum*, passim. The discussion relies heavily on J. Thirsk, *English Peasant Farming*, London, 1957, pp. 8, 10, 51–54, 93–95, 140–46, 155, 167–70, 180–87, 200–4.

[33] I have used *The Parish Registers of Alford and Rigsby*, ed. R. C. Dudding, Horncastle, 1917; *The Registers of Doddington-Pigot*, ed. R. E. G. Cole, London, 1898. Obviously much more work should be done in the parish registers.

[34] For years of dearth, see W. G. Hoskins, 'Harvest fluctuations and English economic history', *AHR*, 12 (1964), pp. 28–43; 16 (1968), pp. 15–31; for the plague, R. C. Dudding, *History of the manor and parish of Saleby with Thoresthorpe*, Horncastle, 1922, pp. 176–78; Dudding, *History of the parish and manors of Alford with Rigsby and Ailby*, Horncastle, 1930, pp. 209–10.

Axholme (+15%).[35] Natural increase cannot have caused the growth in the population of either the towns or the fen. At Alford between 1668 and 1681 the death-rate was considerably higher than the birth-rate, while the fens were considered particularly unhealthy: 'the naturall borne countrye folkes are so fast consumed as there could not be inhabitants if people of other places should not come thether to dwell', argued the men of Spalding.[36] The suggestion that the fen villages and the towns grew by virtue of the influx of people from the areas of population stagnation is supported by contemporary commentary: in 1675 it was reported that 'multitudes of the poor sort from all the countries adjacent' were settling in the Isle of Axholme, while in 1635 the 'great confluence and resort of poore people from forraigne partes' into Grantham was noted.[37]

The movement of population into the fens and the towns can be inferred from a general survey of the demographic history of Lincolnshire in the seventeenth century. Another source, the short biographies of witnesses in the ecclesiastical courts, provides a more positive demonstration that migration was commonplace.[38] In a group of forty-eight deponents who were involved in the agricultural sector, only a fifth were settled in their place of birth. Two additional details emerge from an analysis of this evidence. First, it demonstrates that migration occurred *within* the area of static or declining population, not merely out of it to the towns or fenland. Second, a differentiation emerges related to occupational status. Agricultural labourers moved almost as frequently as did the rural craftsmen, although the area over which they ranged was more constricted: John Kirton (aged 32) had lived for short periods in seven villages, but all in north-west Kesteven; John Barwell (aged 35) had made nine moves, but all in the southern Wolds and the adjacent marshland parishes. The farmers were a more stable group than their labourers. But even among this group only twenty-eight per cent were working land in their birth-places: the majority had moved at least twice.

Why did men migrate? To find jobs, as in the towns, or better yet, to find land. The fens were particularly attractive because, by virtue of the unusual survival of generous common rights of all

---

[35] Based on a comparison of the 1603 return of communicants, printed in Foster, ed., *State of the Church*, pp. 337–53, with the 1676 Compton census, in *LNQ*, 16 (1921), pp. 47–49.
[36] LAO, SS 460/5/65–66.
[37] Thirsk, *Peasant Farming*, p. 201; Grantham Hall Book I, ff. 18–20.
[38] For sources, see above note 31.

inhabitants, with the attendant opportunities for fishing, fowling and turf- or reed-cutting, they guaranteed the settler a reasonable subsistence and a modicum of independence.[39] Men were in part compelled to seek such new opportunities because the traditional agricultural settlements of the clays and the uplands could no longer support their swelling populations. The inhabitants of Eagle, describing the miserable state of the town in 1656, explicitly stated that their land as it was currently utilized could not support the population — a population which had increased by half since 1563. We may see similar pressures at work when villages ordered the restriction of the number of animals that any inhabitant might keep on the commons.[40] But the existence of a mobile, landless, surplus population was not solely a creation of the demographic upswing, of a growing pressure on insufficient resources. The problems created by the latter were compounded by changes in agriculture.

Consider the case of the village of Rowston, which supported thirty-three families in 1563. In 1608 the landlord, Edward King, was accused of converting arable to pasture; he admitted the charge, claiming that the lack of grazing on his Ashby-de-la-Launde estate obliged him to use land in the neighbouring village for that purpose. The government's investigation did not halt the progress of King's enclosure schemes, and by 1723 only twelve families were left in Rowston.[41] In 1603 Richard Rossiter, the lord of Somerby, sought permission to demolish the steeple and chancel of the parish church and so 'be eased of the intollerable burden of so huge, vast and needless' a building: 'needless' because the decaying church, 'hable to receave manie hundreds of people', was now required to house less than fifty. The decimation of Somerby's population had occurred in the sixteenth century but Rossiter was busily reducing the neighbouring parishes of Searby-cum-Owmby and Great Limber to a similar situation by enclosure. As in the case of Edward King, prosecution had negligible effect, and by 1676 the population of the four northern Wold villages where Rossiter held land had shrunk by eighteen per cent.[42] S. A. Johnson has listed twenty-nine Lindsey villages where the glebe terriers demonstrate a seventeenth-century enclosure: the population of this group fell sixteen per cent between 1563 and 1723.[43]

[39] Thirsk, *Peasant Farming*, pp. 140–41, 201.
[40] VCH, *Lincolnshire*, II, p. 334; LAO, CRAGG 5/62.
[41] Thirsk, *Peasant Farming*, p. 183; STAC 8 10/4.
[42] LAO, Court Papers 69/1/43; STAC 8 14/2; 128/5; SP 16/206/71.
[43] S. A. Johnson, 'Some aspects of enclosure and changing agricultural landscapes in Lindsey', *LAAS*, 9 (1961–62), pp. 134–50.

Enclosure, fulminated the great preacher, Robert Sanderson of Boothby Pagnell, resulted in 'unpeopling towns and creating beggars'. Enclosure, echoed his clerical colleague William Worship of Croft, 'unpeoples the countrey'.[44] It *might* do so, as we have seen. But there was not a necessary correlation. Of the twenty-nine enclosed Lindsey villages studied by Johnson, six *gained* population between 1563 and 1723, and population increases were also registered in some of the enclosed villages in the extreme north-western corner of Kesteven.[45] The explanation of this divergence in the population histories of enclosed villages lies in the changing purpose of enclosure. In the sixteenth century landlords enclosed in order to convert arable to sheep pasture and reap the profits of wool production. Depopulation was the usual concomitant of this transformation — hence Sir Thomas More's bitter jibe about man-eating sheep. But in the seventeenth century a relative fall in wool prices and a rise in the prices commanded by arable produce ensured that sheep farming was a less attractive proposition, except on the thin soils of the uplands. Enclosure was now undertaken not to grass over the ploughed lands, but to establish efficient and profitable units of arable production where new husbandry techniques could be employed as they could not in the constricting régime of the open fields.[46]

An enclosure scheme designed to reorganize the utilization of the arable, to practise 'up and down' husbandry as did John Bluett at Harlaxton or Sir Thomas Coney at North Stoke, did not force men from the village. In the absence of mechanization the same number of hands were still required to perform the basic routines of the farming calendar. However, enclosure of this order did enhance the mobility which we have seen to be characteristic of the agricultural labourer, because it usually destroyed the ability of the poorer villagers to employ the common for keeping stock. The cottager who did not own land in the fields and thus had no legal title to use the common would be fortunate to receive a four-acre allotment, as at Fulbeck, when the parish was enclosed.[47] So small a plot was too little to live on, and the labourer was forced to rely on his wages, and to be ready to move in search of work.

[44] Jacobson, ed., *Works of Sanderson*, II, p. 204; William Worship, *The Christian's Mourning Garment*, London, 1615, pp. 130–31.
[45] D. R. Mills, 'Enclosure in Kesteven', *AHR*, 7 (1959), pp. 83–87.
[46] Thirsk, *Peasant Farming*, pp. 159–67; E. Kerridge, *The Agricultural Revolution*, London, 1967, pp. 181–221.
[47] LAO, FANE 1/2/1.

We have examined the degree to which the lateral mobility of the population, fostered by demographic pressure and by enclosure, ensured that villages were not 'closed' in the seventeenth century. However, enclosure did more than enhance mobility. In conjunction with other techniques favoured by enterprising landlords, it assailed other elements which are central to the concept of the closed corporate peasant community.

AGRICULTURAL IMPROVEMENT AND THE SOCIAL STRUCTURE OF THE VILLAGE

Sanderson and his fellow ministers who sought to uphold the traditional Christian and neighbourly virtues reserved their harshest denunciation for the depopulations associated with the ravenous sheep. Yet they recognized that other methods of exploitation, besides conversion to pasture, were available to contemporary Ahabs bent on crushing poor Naboth: engrossing — 'joyning house to house and field to field': 'overthrowing . . . tenures' and 'the unconscionable racking of rents'. All were corrosive of the values they preached.[48]

In his answer to the complaint lodged against him in Star Chamber in 1608 by the attorney general, Sir Henry Ayscough complacently asserted that the population of Blyborough had not been reduced by his enclosure. But he did admit that he had reorganized the farming units on his estate: two farmhouses had been reduced to the status of cottages and the lands previously attached to them divided up among his other farms. This was 'engrossing'. Examples of it can be found throughout the county. Richard Rossiter had consolidated the lands of four farms at Searby to form three new units. At Culverthorpe Sir Edmund Bussey combined the lands of two farms with his demesne and leased the entire unit to a single farmer.[49] Engrossing, as at Blyborough, did not necessarily reduce the size of a village, but it did change its social composition. Creating fewer and larger farms involved displacing some families from the land they farmed; they swelled the already brimming pool of mobile agricultural wage labour. Conversely, the process produced a small élite of substantial tenant farmers. John Faile, the wealthy Newton yeoman who farmed over a thousand acres rented from a number of Kesteven landlords in 1608, would have been an exceptional figure at any time in the

---

[48] Jacobson, ed., *Works of Sanderson*, I, p. 122; II, pp. 186, 192, 314, 344, 352; John Hoskin, *A sermon preached upon the parable of the King that taketh an accompt of his servants*, London, 1609, sig. A2v.
[49] STAC 8 10/4; 14/2.

seventeenth century, but the general well-being of this peasant élite is apparent in the steady increase in the size of their personal fortunes and of their farmhouses during the century (see plates I and II).[50]

Lockridge argues that the closed corporate peasant community endeavoured to guarantee its members equal access to resources. Engrossing eroded equality. Small subsistence farms were amalgamated to form more profitable units for market production, and, in consequence, the village was subjected to social differentiation. Two other changes in agricultural practice were equally detrimental to the social and organizational base of village corporatism: enclosure and the changed attitude to land tenure.

The reorganization of land to establish a number of unitary farms obviated the need for the communal control of the agricultural year. This had been essential when an individual holding consisted of arable strips scattered in the two or three open fields and the village flocks grazed the common. But a farmer in one of the new units made his husbandry decisions alone, and the medieval machinery for collective determination withered. The 'overthrowing . . . tenures', denounced by Sanderson, also weakened the corporate community. In the early seventeenth century a Lincolnshire peasant might be a freeholder, owning land which he could alienate or devise or which would descend to his heirs according to established rules of succession. He might be a leaseholder, renting land according to an agreement with the landlord set out in a contractual instrument. Or the peasant might be a copyholder. The terms on which the latter held his land would be dictated by the custom of the manor — the rent to be paid to the lord, whether or not the land might be alienated, whether it descended upon the death of the tenant. Some customs, as at Spalding and Moulton, gave the copyholder virtually all the advantages of a freehold estate.[51] In other manors, where there was no right of inheritance, or where the rents and fines were not fixed by custom, the lord could easily transmute the copyhold tenures into leaseholds. To the landlord, copyhold was an archaic nuisance, leaving him with a fixed rent in a time of rising prices and restricting his ability to reorganize the utilization and exploitation of his estates. Accord-

---

[50] Ibid., 10/4; M. W. Barley, 'The Lincolnshire village and its buildings', *LH*, 1 (1947–53), pp. 252–72; Barley, 'Farmhouses and cottages, 1550–1725', *EcHR*, n.s. 7 (1954–55), pp. 291–306.
[51] For Spalding and Moulton, see LR 2/284, ff. 218–21; 286, ff. 195–96: for the number of copyholders and freeholders on a sample of manors, see Thirsk, *Peasant Farming*, p. 43.

ingly copyhold tenure was whittled away on all save royal manors in the course of the seventeenth century. Some copyholders were able to obtain freehold estates by purchase, as at Caythorpe, or by sanctioning their lord's enclosure and improvement, as at Swinderby.[52] Elsewhere copyholds were relegated to leasehold either by the lord's purchase of the title or by his strict application of manorial custom to his own advantage. Copyhold survived on royal manors in Lincolnshire in the absence of determined management: the copyholders not only embezzled royal demesne lands, but invented customs which gave them unassailable security of tenure.[53] A progressive landlord would not only seek to foreclose copyhold tenures: he would also purchase the titles to freehold lands which intermingled with his estate, as this would facilitate the enclosure and improvement of the latter. So Sir Charles Hussey bought out the three freeholders at Honington prior to enclosing the estate, and Sir Edward Carr leaned heavily upon a freeholder of Wilsford, a village he planned to enclose, to blackmail him into selling up.[54]

Such developments meant that the peasantry increasingly worked land leased from a rentier. The latter favoured short-term leases as they enabled him to adjust his rents to the maximum the market would bear — Sanderson's 'unconscionable racking of rents'. Land became a commodity, and the landlord-tenant relationship was fundamentally governed by considerations of mutual profit. This may explain the geographical mobility which as we have seen typified even the wealthy farmers. Prior to the civil war it appears that leasehold lands were seldom held by an individual or family for an extended period,[55] and during the agricultural depression of the 1680s the movement of the tenants was extremely rapid: sixteen tenants leased land at Osgodby in 1680; in the next seven years seven of them abandoned their holdings.[56] In the same period a number of Sir John Newton's tenants acted on their threats to quit unless they received rent abatements.[57]

[52] W. H. Hosford, 'An eye-witness account of a seventeenth-century enclosure', EcHR, n.s. 4 (1951–52), p. 215; Mills, 'Enclosure in Kesteven', p. 86.
[53] See John Norden's survey of the manors in the soke of Kirton (SP 14/111/138; Cambridge Univ. Lib., Ff 4 30), and the surveys of the honour of Bolingbroke (DL 42 119) and the manor of Barrow (LR 2/287, f. 214).
[54] STAC 8 17/24; 279/8: see also LAOR, 12, p. 28; 20, p. 68; M. W. Barley and P. E. Russell, 'Notes on the Agrarian History of Owersby and Burgh-le-Marsh', LH, 1 (1947–53), pp. 396–97.
[55] LAO, ANC VI/B/10 (Kirkby Underwood); Holywell 97/2 (Fulstow and Marshchapel).
[56] LAO, ANC VI/A/5: see also TYR 1/1; MON 10/3/1.
[57] LAO, MON 7/12, nos 41, 58, 69, 70, 75.

The new policies governing land management — enclosure, the development of larger units of production — and the changed attitude whereby land was treated as a marketable commodity, could transform the structure of village society. The effects of the new landlordism were most conspicuous in the marshland villages. In the sixteenth century the marshes were farmed by a prosperous middling yeomanry: there were no extremes of wealth and poverty in the area, and the average marsh farmer was better off than his contemporaries in any other part of Lincolnshire. By the early eighteenth century the marshland farmer was the poorest in the county. Coastal erosion and the crown's claim to land won from the sea did not help, but the fundamental reason for the transmutation was the leasing policies pursued by landowners in the area. Marshland pasture was leased in large blocks at very high rents to wealthy farmers from the upland for stock-fattening. Non-residents took the land, and the villagers of the marsh parishes grew poorer.[58] In the fens the peasantry successfully resisted the attempts to exploit the region by a radical transformation of its ecology and husbandry through drainage. In consequence the traditional social pattern survived, marked by the absence of either a wage-dependent rural proletariat or a wealthy yeomanry. Yet, paradoxically, the defence of the relatively egalitarian social structure of the fens reduced the isolation of the villages of the area. The unprecedented threat to their economy posed by the drainers obliged fenmen to co-operate, and created a consciousness of membership of a group whose interest transcended parish boundaries. Fen villages had acted together in the past against those who sought to intrude into their commons but the 1630s and 1640s saw the mobilization of collective violence on an unprecedented scale: in May 1642 sheriff Heron confessed his utter inability to protect the drainage works in the Lindsey Level and the West Fen against rioters brought together 'by a generall combination . . . of that parte of the cuntrey'. More important, the fenmen were obliged to become acquainted with the intricacies of the central government and legal system. In 1650 this political education made the men of Axholme accept both the leadership of the Leveller leaders, Lilburne and Wildman, and their theories, to the extent of planning to join forces with other victims of exploitation. In 1721 the vicar of Market Deeping provided his superiors with a most unflattering collective characterization of 'the people inhabiting these fen towns' — cunning, stupid, surly, selfish, 'opinionative in religious

[58] Thirsk, *Peasant Farming*, pp. 54–57, 142–58: for erosion, see A. E. B. Owen, 'Coastal erosion in East Lincolnshire', *LH*, 1 (1947–53), pp. 330–41.

matters'. Yet we may think that their pride in themselves and in a countryside which others found so uncongenial, and their suspicions of outsiders and of authority, was not unrelated to the fact that many would have been immigrants who had found shelter and a livelihood in the fen, and who had been engaged in the successful defence of these benefits against the expropriatory designs of the drainers.[59]

Commenting on the story of Ahab and Naboth, Sanderson remarked bitterly 'many a petty lord of a hamlet with us would think himself disparaged in a treaty of inclosure, to descend to such low capitulations with one of his poor neighbours as the great king of Israel then did . . . and to sin but as modestly as Ahab yet did'.[60] We have followed the social commentary offered by the divines, and attributed agricultural transformation and its social consequences to the landowners's search for higher returns, a relentless search in which they deployed all their 'great revenues, power and authoritie'.[61] Yet landords' avarice, though important, is not the whole story. The agricultural crises which punctuated the century, particularly those of 1617–23 and of the 1680s, compelled many small producers to sell up. Nor was it only the landlords who favoured agricultural reorganization, and displayed minimal concern for the rights and welfare of the poor. Tax assessments demonstrate that the process of social differentiation was already under way in the early sixteenth century, and the peasant élite was often the group responsible for the enclosure and reorganization of a village's lands, as at Caythorpe, rather than a product of those developments.[62] The development of new modes of agricultural exploitation was neither a purely seventeenth-century phenomenon, nor can it be attributed exclusively to the avarice of great men. Yet it was transforming the structure of rural society.

Professor Lockridge, with whose model we began this chapter, argued that the emotional awareness of group identity which was a central feature of the New England community was a product of a particular social structure and organization. We have seen that in seventeenth-century Lincolnshire this structure was being eroded by population growth and changing agricultural practice. Mobility

---

[59] H of LMP 23 May 1642, certificate of Sir Edward Heron; *CSPD 1652–53*, pp. 374–75; Cole, ed., *Speculum*, pp. 184–85: for the social structure of the fen villages, see Thirsk, *Peasant Farming*, pp. 108–29, 134–35.
[60] Jacobson, ed., *Works of Sanderson*, I, p. 122.
[61] STAC 8 279/8.
[62] Thirsk, *Peasant Farming*, pp. 192–96; Hosford, 'Eye-witness account', pp. 215–16.

was a commonplace; the co-operative organization of husbandry was giving way to a régime of individual unitary farms; the simultaneous development of a peasant élite and a group of wage-dependent labourers was occurring at the expense of the middling peasantry. This is not to argue that the seventeenth century saw the rapid transformation of entities answering Professor Lockridge's description. Interactions in the fields and the market-place had always intruded into the isolation of the village; the rise of population and the process of agricultural innovation had begun in the sixteenth century. Conversely, the open-field system persisted into the eighteenth century in many villages. Yet, if change was neither cataclysmic nor uniform, its general direction is clear.

Did these changes in the structure of rural society and village organization result in a breakdown of the values of community? The chorus of complaints of petty oppression and unneighbourly behaviour suggest that it did. Wealthy yeomen were often prepared to use their economic power to depress the position of their poorer neighbours yet further. At Luddington Joseph Sledmore, who rented three farms, monopolized the common pasture and silenced the attempts of his fellow-villagers to restrain his aggrandizement with abuse and threats of ruinous lawsuits. Suits for every petty trespass were threatened by the wealthy freeholders of Caythorpe as they sought to blackmail their poorer neighbours into contributing to the legal costs of a scheme for the reorganization of the village's lands, even though the poor would be substantially the losers by their scheme. At Willoughton John Chapman headed a clique of rich men who shifted the bulk of the tax and tithe burden onto the poor; the latter dared 'not crosse him nor controll him for feare of his hard usage'. Similarly, at Market Rasen 'the most considerable farmers and tenants' devised an assessment by which taxes were paid predominantly by the tradesmen and the poor, who were 'most shamefully oppressed'.[63] The decay of the fabric and furniture of parish churches may also be indicative of the decay of community sensibility. At Spanby in 1664 the church walls needed replastering and the communion table was worm-infested; the church lacked a pulpit, a chalice, a book of homilies: the immediate necessity was a cover for the font, which was exposed 'to defilement by the excrement of owles, jackdawes, pidgeons, and the like'. Abraham de la Pryme, in his travels in the Humber coast

63 LAO, LQS File 1655, articles against Sledmore; Hosford, 'Eye-witness account', pp. 215–16; LAO, Court Papers 90, depositions concerning Willoughton; Court Papers 62/4/5.

area at the end of the century, recorded a similar picture of the decay of the parish church, once the focus of the community.[64]

Villages, said the attorney general in 1608 as he commenced his prosecution of those Lincolnshire gentlemen accused of depopulation, are 'the first societyes after propagation of familyes wherein people are united . . . in . . . the mutuall comforts of neighbourhood and intercourse one with another'.[65] By the end of the seventeenth century his idealistic description would have been less appropriate: the village was neither so fundamental nor so natural a social unit. It was not composed of families which had interacted within its boundaries for generations; its increasingly mobile population was less often held together by the co-operative organization of agricultural routine. The village was less an organic corporate community than a temporary agglomeration of individual, mobile family units: 'potatoes in a sack', to adapt Marx's epigrammatic description of the nineteenth-century French peasantry.[66]

[64] LAO, Court Papers 61/3/16; Diary of de la Pryme, pp. 138–40.
[65] STAC 8 14/2.
[66] K. Marx, The Eighteenth Brumaire of Louis Bonaparte, New York, 1963, p. 124.

CHAPTER 3

GRASS-ROOTS COMMUNITIES: THE TOWN

I N our previous discussion, towns have appeared as agencies
corroding the closed corporatism of the agricultural village.
For the peasantry they were centres of interaction, exchange
and migration. Yet it can be argued that the towns were corporate
communities. Professor MacCaffrey states that early modern
Exeter was a 'tightly knit and self-contained society', whose
'average inhabitant . . . found his prime social identification in the
community of Exeter'.[1] Is this model applicable to Lincolnshire's
market towns? Before endeavouring to answer this question we
must distinguish between the five boroughs — Boston, Grantham,
Grimsby, Lincoln and Stamford — which, as a consequence of
medieval prosperity, had acquired a substantial measure of
autonomy through incorporation, and the other, unincorporated,
towns.

Many bustling centres stood in the same formal relationship to
the national authorities as did purely agricultural villages, and their
internal government was ostensibly cast in the same manorial
mould. Strong communal sentiment might flourish even in these
little market towns. At Alford local pride focused upon the free
school, which benefited from the gifts and legacies of a number of
yeomen and tradesmen. Men of the same class formed the school's
board of trustees, which ultimately came to exercise an unofficial
authority as the town's government. At Louth a similar process
received royal sanction when, in 1605, the warden and assistants
who controlled the endowment of the free school were granted
minor judicial authority within the town.[2] Yet, lacking a formal

---

[1] W. T. MacCaffrey, *Exeter, 1540–1640*, Cambridge Mass., 1958, pp. 1–2,
203–4.
[2] For Alford, see R. C. Dudding, *History of the parish and manors of Alford with
Rigsby and Ailby*, Horncastle, 1930, p. 117–44: for Louth, see STAC 8 246/6; SP
14/21/10.

institutional structure, the unincorporated towns found it difficult
to resist pressures destructive of their nascent communal aspirations. First, the destitute flocked into them in the hope of finding
employment or a reliable source of poor relief. In 1609 Gainsborough complained that families which became an immediate
charge on the poor rate were occupying shacks on the town
wasteland. The influx was encouraged for his own profit by the
lord of the manor.[3] This was the second threat: enhanced dominal
exploitation, as the local gentry sought a larger cut of the market
revenues from the towns. In some cases the assault was successfully
repulsed and the townsmen were able to enjoy some economic
independence: the men of Spalding fought off the crown's attempt
to enhance its rent-roll, and clubbed together to purchase the long
lease of the tolls of their market and fair from the courtiers to whom
Elizabeth had granted it. But Sleaford's attempts to avoid their
manorial lord's monopoly of milling and the collection of higher
market tolls were successfully resisted by the Carr family. Gainsborough's tranquil enjoyment of a period of prosperity and growth
ended when at the turn of the sixteenth century Lord Burgh, the
town's lenient and non-resident landlord, sold up to Sir William
Hickman. Hickman immediately engaged in the most aggressive
extension and exploitation of his manorial rights. He enclosed part
of the common field and sanctioned the erection of pauper cottages
on the waste; he appropriated revenues designed for the maintenance of the town's streets; he pulled down parts of the parish
church and refused to contribute to the upkeep of the remainder; he
laid claim to all the houses in the town, rejecting the inhabitants'
arguments that they held in free socage. Perhaps his most vigour-
ous efforts went to cash in on Gainsborough's *entrepôt* function. He
levied tolls on corn passing by the town on the Trent; he tried to
extend his market privileges into the neighbouring village of
Morton; he transmuted a benevolence paid from sales of corn in the
market, and intended for the maintenance of the latter, into a heavy
mulct; he had the stalls demolished which tradesmen erected in
front of their shops in the market-place. Worst, from the perspective of the local retailers, he sought to extend the biennial fair and to
encourage 'the resort of the Londoners', who undersold the
Gainsborough merchants. Those of the latter who endeavoured to
resist Hickman's policies risked assault by his henchmen or
prosecution by their lord's crooked manipulation of his authority as
a justice of the peace. The townsmen were not without allies,

[3] STAC 8 167/13.

however. Hickman's dealings and his social pretensions offended the local magisterial élite, not only ancient gentry like Sir John Thorold, who viewed him as a parvenu of mean origins, 'a threadbare fellow', but the eminent lawyer and member of the Council of the North, Sir Richard Williamson. With such powerful patrons, the townsmen met affrays with affrays and suits with counter-suits throughout the first decade of the seventeenth century. But if Hickman did not sustain all his dominal claims, he was successful in his efforts to profit from the town's burgeoning trade: the tolls which Lord Burgh had leased for £10 p.a. were valued at £250 p.a. by 1640.[4]

Enmeshed in a web of lawsuits, his property assailed by thugs, threatened with the stocks, and even imprisoned for a short period on a fabricated felony charge, John Noble, the Gainsborough mercer who led the town's resistance to Hickman, must have looked enviously at those incorporated Lincolnshire towns whose privileges, enshrined in royal charters — their 'title deeds of . . . independence'[5] — to all appearances secured them from the rapacity or jealousy of landlords and magnates.

Grantham's privileges, set out in royal charters which also laid out the basic rules of the town's constitution, are not untypical of those enjoyed by the five Lincolnshire boroughs. The corporation enjoyed the legal status of a collective personality — the power to sue and be sued, to acquire and alienate property, to make bye-laws for the administration of the town. The borough was freed from the interference of the sheriff and other royal functionaries, as its officers acted as magistrates. Within the borough's liberties the latter were also responsible for the execution of royal writs, and from 1604 were empowered to hold a weekly court of record with jurisdiction in civil actions worth less than £40. Grantham was permitted to hold two annual fairs and a weekly market and it returned two burgesses to parliament.[6]

In law the corporations were distinct from the villages and towns subject to the normal routines of county government. They were islands of independence, cut off from the body of the county by their charters. The integrity of these communities, their self-contained corporate status, appears not only in the legal forms but

---

[4] LAO, SS 460/5/65–6; HMC *Cecil*, XVI, pp. 343, 353; E 134 23 Charles II Easter 33 (Spalding): E 134 11 Charles I Mich. 41; 12 Charles I Easter 26 (Sleaford): E 134 9 James I Hil. 14; STAC 8 167/4, 13; 222/13; 293/20; 303/24; SP 23/175, pp. 280–87 (Gainsborough).
[5] G. H. Martin, *The Royal Charters of Grantham*, Leicester, 1963, p. 9.
[6] Ibid., pp. 9–23, 113, 115.

in the operations of the mechanisms of self-government. Every enactment of the governing body concerned with the day-to-day administration of the town affirmed the latter's semi-autonomous status. Some of the orders and bye-laws are particularly indicative of the townsmen's perceptions of their participation in a corporate community: orders for municipal improvements or the upkeep and beautification of public buildings, for instance, or for the due performance of the solemn formalities which emphasized the worship of the town's governors and for the punishment of those who failed to show sufficient respect to the latter. So, too, are those regulations designed to secure the town's continued economic well-being: to keep out interloping tradesmen; to uphold proper standards of quality; to maintain and discipline the town's poor, and to halt the influx of vagrants from the countryside.[7]

Corporate independence had to be defended by perpetual vigilance. All the boroughs dreamed of future grandeur. So in 1641 the corporation of Stamford, inspired by the jumble of myths propagated by their town clerk and amateur local historian, Richard Butcher — that Stamford had been founded in 863 BC by an immediate descendant of Trojan Brutus; that it had been a university town in the seventh century — petitioned their members of parliament to secure a number of substantial benefits, including the making of the Welland navigable, and the promotion of Stamford as the capital of a new county to be formed from Rutland, the hundred of Ness, and the soke of Peterborough.[8] The city fathers of Lincoln invested hopes and money in the Fosse Dyke project as the panacea for the town's economic ills, and even the petty tradesmen who governed decayed Grimsby were fired by the prospect of dredging their clogged haven.[9] These were visions. In reality the defence of existing political and economic privileges was a far more immediate concern. So in Boston litigation was in progress throughout the seventeenth century to defend the town's admiralty jurisdiction; attempts to establish a market at Swineshead and of some Skirbeck men to trade in coals were repelled; the county deputy lieutenants were requested to observe the town's

[7] For such actions, see Grantham Hall Book I, ff. 6v, 7v, 19v–20, 94v, 192, 192v, 210, 212v, 252v, 264, 291v, 293, 296v, 297, 341v, 361. Similar examples abound in the records of the corporations of Boston and Stamford.

[8] See Butcher's *Survey and antiquities of the towne of Stamford*, 1660, pp. 1–2 (reprinted in F. Peck, *Academica tertia anglicana*, London, 1727); Stamford Hall Book I, f. 406, see also ff. 328v, 329v, 331v, 332v, 339v, 342.

[9] Hill, *Tudor and Stuart Lincoln*, pp. 128–34, 206–10; E. Gillett, *A History of Grimsby*, London, 1970, pp. 120, 139–42.

privileges with respect to militia musters; foreign bailiffs who tried to operate within Boston's liberties were arrested.[10]

The necessity of defending existing privileges and urban autonomy had always exercised the towns' rulers. But the assault grew fiercer in the seventeenth century; rights and independence were attacked not just by Skirbeck coal merchants but by the central government and by the gentry élite. Charters were royal gifts, and the crown might employ its legal authority to bring the towns under closer tutelage. In 1628 Charles I's new charter abrogated the popular election — 'by the general voices of the vulgar people' — of Lincoln's magistrates. Promotion to the governing body was to be by co-option, and the senior alderman who had not already undertaken the office was to be 'elected' mayor. The king claimed that the system would prevent factional fighting and popular tumults, but it was clearly part of a more general policy to transmute the governing bodies of towns into closed groups which would be more amenable to royal pressure.[11] The boroughs' dependence upon the central government was equally apparent in the purge of royalists in 1647–48, and the counter-purge under the aegis of the commissioners for regulating corporations in 1662. In the 1680s Charles II and his brother, in an effort to ensure parliamentary election returns favourable to the crown, issued a series of new charters to the Lincolnshire boroughs, which placed the urban governors under direct royal control.[12]

More insidious, and continuing after the reversal of the interventionist policies of James II in 1689, was the growing interest of local magnates in the affairs of the boroughs. The protection of an influential peer or gentleman who could pull strings in high places when the town's interests were at stake was a valuable commodity. Yet there was a *quid pro quo*. Throughout the seventeenth century a borough's patron might seek to nominate freemen; the town's legal officers, schoolmasters, or ministers; its representatives in parliament. This last concern predominated after 1660 as the desirability of a place in the house of commons became ever more apparent to those with political ambitions. The eagerness of county magnates to assist the boroughs with their corporate debt or to repair public buildings increased, as did their gifts of game and plate (see plate

[10] Pishey Thompson, *The History and Antiquities of Boston*, Boston, 1856, p. 67; Boston Common Council Minute Book 2, ff. 63v, 206; 3, ff. 368, 464; 4, ff. 21, 34v, 37.
[11] T. Allen, *The History of the County of Lincoln*, I, London, 1833, pp. 118–27; STAC 8 98/9.
[12] See below, pp. 247–48.

III). The Newton family had designs on a parliamentary seat at Grantham; their agent reminded them of the forthcoming aldermanic feast, and advised a contribution 'in regard of what is past and what may be for the future'.[13] There were tangible benefits for the boroughs in the magnates' pursuit of parliamentary seats. Yet the corporations lost a measure of their autonomy. The choice of freemen and of urban officers was increasingly determined by the political interests of powerful outsiders.

The pattern suggested in the previous discussion, namely the towns' unsuccessful resistance to increasing levels of interference by the county gentry, does not hold for two Lincolnshire boroughs. At Grimsby the economic prosperity upon which the borough's privileged position had been erected had long disappeared leaving only the empty shell of political form, and the decaying town was unable to resist outside pressure. The 'mean and mechanicke fellowes' who formed the town's magistracy were delighted to invite the local gentry to share the burden of government, while parliamentary elections became a major economic activity. By the end of the seventeenth century agents of the Grimsby electorate were peddling control of the borough's representation in London 'to such as would give most money'.[14]

At Stamford there was no increase in the pressure exercised by the powerful upon the borough. It was intense from the beginning of the century as a consequence of the interest displayed in the town by its over-powerful neighbours, the Cecils of Burghley House. Elizabeth's great minister, Lord Burghley, had bought the manor, fee farm and tolls of Stamford from the crown, ostensibly for the benefit of his native town but in fact for the aggrandizement of his personal estate. His purchases gave him a preponderant position in Stamford which he and his heirs exercised with a ruthlessness reminiscent of the Hickmans' bludgeoning of unincorporated Gainsborough. The Cecils were not content to nominate the town's members of parliament, its legal officers and its schoolmasters — one of whom was dismissed only after six years tenure marked by 'groase negligence . . . to the very great damage and hindrance of the towne'. In 1637 the earl of Exeter claimed a monopoly of milling in Stamford and provided water power for his new mills by making a cut through the common pasture; in 1641 the Cecils asserted a novel right to take toll from the freemen of Stamford for

---

[13] Grantham Hall Book I, ff. 207, 341v, 347, 384v, 392–3, 614v, 649v, 662; LAO, MON 7/12/82.
[14] Wood, ed., *Memorials of the Holles Family*, pp. 196–97, 217; Gillett, *Grimsby*, pp. 126, 131–53.

their stalls in the market. The Cecils' high-handed treatment of the town was resented but those who dared to challenge the power of the earl of Exeter and his agents in the 1630s found themselves summoned before the Privy Council, forced to make a humiliating submission, and dismissed from the corporation. In Butcher's expressive phrase, the Cecils 'tossed the best burgesses out of their gownes'.[15]

Stamford's struggle to escape becoming a mere pawn of the Cecils was not fought by a unanimous town government: sharp divisions fissured the latter. While some of the urban élite resisted the Cecils and were crushed for their temerity, others sold out: Richard Butcher, the town's historian and a leader of the anti-Cecil group, reserved his most scathing comments for those elected officials who had ransacked the town's muniments and purloined documents, 'only to advance their owne private designes, together with the designes of the towne's common enemy'. There was some relaxation of Cecil pressure on Stamford during the lifetime of Earl Thomas (1598–1623), who was, to quote Butcher's heavy irony, 'a right pious and charitable person . . . fixed in his generation, as our Saviour Christ was in his passion, betwixt two *etc.*'. In the 1670s the townsmen again escaped Cecil tutelage when they were able to appeal to the earl of Lindsey and Lord Camden, both lured by Stamford's status as a parliamentary borough, against the earl of Exeter. But the brief renaissance of independence soon ended. Lindsey and Exeter agreed to split the borough's seats, and by the early eighteenth century Stamford was a pocket borough completely under the thumbs of its noble patrons.[16]

The autonomy of the corporate boroughs was eroded in the seventeenth century. Increasingly the political forms and the rhetoric and iconography of independence concealed the reality of magnate manipulation. The ability of the gentry to bend the boroughs to their will was enhanced, however, by two developments within the towns: pauperism and faction. Consideration of both should make us chary of attributing a communalist corporatism to the boroughs even at the outset of our period.

[15] Butcher, *Stamford*, pp. 6, 20, 23, 25; Stamford Hall Book I, ff. 331v, 390, 403v, 406; *NQ*, 6th ser. 11 (1885), pp. 226–27; *CSPD 1631–33*, pp. 194, 195; *1633–34*, pp. 300, 467; PC 2/41, pp. 257, 286, 536–38, 549; 42, pp. 535, 549; 43, pp. 481–82; 51, p. 674.
[16] Butcher, *Stamford*, p. 20; *CSPD 1676–77*, pp. 473, 491; *1682*, pp. 589–90; A. Weston, 'Lincolnshire Politics in the Age of Queen Anne: part 2, the boroughs', *LHA*, 6 (1971), pp. 84–85.

Historians frequently argue that increasing population is an indicator of economic advance. The equation would have surprised the governors of Grantham. In 1635 they procured an order from the judges of assize permitting them to punish those who took in lodgers or leased cottages without their consent, to proscribe the building of cottages on the waste or the conversion of stables and barns to dwelling-houses, and to remove all persons who had entered the town in the previous two years. The problem they sought to remedy was the 'great confluence and resort of poore people from forraigne partes' into the borough, where they had become a charge on the poor rate. That the situation was not peculiar to Grantham appears in the request from the mayor of Lincoln for a copy of the order. The circumstances alleged to warrant the order, and the appeal to the judges, demonstrates that the towns' internal mechanisms for preventing unwanted immigration were ineffective. And it is clear that despite the judges' order the influx of paupers continued through the century. The attempt to alleviate poverty, in particular the attempt to establish a manufactury in Grantham where the indigent could find employment, placed a heavy burden on the already overstrained finances of the borough. In 1649 the corporation solicited charitable donations from the county gentry to relieve the poor, and further gifts were sought after the war. Contributions were forthcoming: Sir Edmund Turnor gave £20 p.a. to the poor; Sir Robert Carr loaned £1,000 interest-free to the corporation. But the gentry who contributed thus expected a solid return on their investment: a controlling voice in the parliamentary elections.[17]

The inability of the Lincolnshire boroughs in the seventeenth century to staunch the influx of 'poore people from forraigne partes' should lead us to question their status as communities as defined by Professor MacCaffrey. So should consideration of the examples of internecine bickering among the urban magistracy. The Cecils' smash-and-grab raid on the corporate privileges of Stamford was certainly aided by the disputes among the borough's élite which were engendered by the ministry of the Puritan extremist, John Vicars.[18] Another godly zealot, John Smith, played a role in the divisions at Lincoln, which concluded with Charles I's issue in 1628 of a new charter to the city curtailing

[17] Grantham Hall Book I, ff. 19–21, 192, 192v, 341v, 627v, 662. For the electoral history of Grantham, see below pp. 241–43.
[18] Butcher, *Stamford*, pp. 7, 23–24; *CSPD 1634–35*, p. 15; *Reports of Cases in the Court of Star Chamber and High Commission*, ed. S. R. Gardiner, Camden Soc., n.s. 39, 1886, pp. 198–238; SP 16/119/152.

its democratic constitution. But the Smith fracas was only a skirmish in an extended campaign, beginning in the 1580s, between groups formed around powerful personalities which fought to monopolize the city's revenue and its patronage. The Lincoln governors, while incanting the slogans of corporatism, were prepared to invite the intervention of the central government to secure personal and factional interests which were bound up with controlling civic appointments and the city's property.[19]

Pauperism and factionalism could be directly related. It was claimed that the deployment of Lincoln's corporate funds in the suits and counter-suits generated by internal bickering resulted in the collapse of a public employment scheme, so that the poor were obliged 'to begge, roge up and downe, and lyve idlelie'. Both were certainly indicative of the limitations of corporate communalism in early seventeenth-century Lincolnshire. Both played into the process whereby, after the civil war, the gentry came to exercise a dominant role in the boroughs.

[19] Hill, *Tudor and Stuart Lincoln*, pp. 110–12, 227–32; E. Henderson, *Foundations of English Administrative Law*, Cambridge Mass., 1963, pp. 60–61, 75; STAC 8 98/9; 121/12; HMC *14th Report*, App. 8, pp. 82–89.

CHAPTER 4

GRASS-ROOTS COMMUNITIES: RELIGIOUS ALTERNATIVES

IT has been argued that the seventeenth century witnessed the erosion of the traditional communal values as the social foundations upon which they were reared were undercut. That men were aware of this development and regretted it may be indicated by the readiness of some to affiliate with voluntaristic communities based not on geographical propinquity but on religious compatibility. Catholicism and the Protestant sects provided more than alternative christologies or theories of justification; they offered a strongly corporate social milieu.

CATHOLICS

In 1605 William Smith, an Edlington husbandman, was in trouble with the authorities. He was rowdy in church, refused to pay tithes, and had commenced a series of vexatious suits against his minister. In the course of an alehouse dispute in Lincoln he had argued for transubstantiation and, supporting free will and good works, had denounced Calvin's doctrine of justification as a diabolical heresy. Worse, he had refused to participate in the festivities for 5 November, and had maintained that two priests executed at Lincoln 'dyed not for treason, but for there conscience'.[1]

Smith represented a type of aggressive, popular Catholicism which was virtually to disappear in the course of the seventeenth century. Catholicism increasingly became a seigneurial movement: the Catholic population 'coagulated into local groups', each centred upon a gentleman's house. In 1676 some hundred and fifty Catholics were reported from Kesteven: fifty-six lived at Irnham, the home of the recusant Thimbleby family. Other centres, though none rivalled Irnham, existed at Hough and Little Ponton where Catholic branches of the extensive Thorold clan had settled; at Blankney, Lord Widdrington's estate; at Canwick, Nocton and Scopwick, each of which was the home of a recusant gentry family.

[1] Foster, ed., *State of the Church*, pp. xciii–xciv; LAO, CH/P 10, nos 7, 8; Court Papers 61/1/26.

39

These islands of Catholic worship, formed by a gentleman, his family, servants and tenants, were bound into a national community by the itinerant priests who moved from estate to estate, and by ties of marriage. The recusant gentry of Lincolnshire intermarried with their co-religionists of equal rank — with Treshams of Northamptonshire, Savages of Cheshire, Petres of Essex — seldom with their immediate neighbours. The Lincolnshire Catholics were a fraction of a national religious group which was dominated by an inbred cousinage of landed families.[2]

The militant zeal displayed by Smith in 1605 was also untypical of seventeenth-century Catholicism in Lincolnshire. The dreams of England's reversion to papal jurisdiction faded and quietism prevailed. The Catholic gentry did not rush to arms on behalf of Charles I in 1642: in a list of twenty-nine Lincolnshire recusant landowners, only eight had fought for the king and one of those, Sir Philip Constable of Rasen, claimed that he joined the royalist army only after his house had been plundered by the mob. The majority, like Sir John Thimbleby who conveyed his estate to trustees and lived abroad or in London, lay low for the duration of the war. Again, between 1685 and 1688, while they relished the freedom to practise their religion openly and to engage in modest proselytizing, few of the Catholic gentry whom James II put in commission chose to serve in local government in Lincolnshire. Nor, despite the government's fears, did the Lincolnshire recusants rise in defence of their royal patron after the revolution: there was some belligerent talk, drink-inspired; little more.[3]

The quietism and the limited political and religious ambitions of the Catholic community were rewarded. The plots of the fanatic minority, real or imaginary, could raise the old spectre of militant popery and provoke government action or, as in 1642 and 1688 in Lincolnshire, unleash popular fury. But in general, with the exception of the civil war period when two-thirds of the income from recusants' estates was sequestered, the Lincolnshire Catholics were not subjected to the formidable array of statutory penalties to which they were liable. Because they were no longer thought to pose a threat to society the central government did not press for action, while among the local magistrates 'noe man will become an accuser of his neighbours unles he be verie malicious'. Similar sentiments or fear of reprisals kept the parochial officers from

[2] J. Bossy, *The English Catholic Community*, New York, 1976, pp. 74, 175; T. B. Trappes-Lomax, 'The Owners of Irnham Hall', *LAAS*, 9 (1961–62), pp. 164–77.
[3] SP 23/75, f. 614; 122, p. 391; 254, ff. 235–36: for 1685–89, see below, pp. 249–51 and *CSPD 1689–90*, p. 272; BL Egerton 3337, ff. 175–81b.

reporting Catholic gentry: 'one single popish gentle woman scarres a whole flocke of church wardens'.[4] The Catholics who clustered about the manor houses of their seigneurial leaders at Irnham, Blankney or Hough in the late seventeenth century had rejected traditional community ties for membership of a closed group, self-contained and inbred. They had cut themselves off from local society, which increasingly treated them with benevolent neglect.

PROTESTANT SECTARIES

The Catholics were a tiny minority, 0.7% of the population in 1676. Their identification with the Marian fires of Smithfield and with foreign absolutisms, Spanish or French, would have limited their missionary effectiveness even if they had chosen to proselytize vigorously. The Protestant sects were not so encumbered.

'In Lincolne', Laud learned in 1634, 'there are many Anabaptists'. The archbishop's informant was unduly alarmist. In 1641 the collectors of the poll tax in the city listed only fourteen 'Anabaptist recusants'; all except a wealthy baker and the wife of an alderman were of the poorest class. Ecclesiastical visitations in the 1630s record a smaller cell of about ten sectaries at Scotter and some fourteen Anabaptists and Brownists at Gainsborough — the group whose meetings were attended by Hanserd Knollys, when he was a schoolmaster in the town, and 'with whom I had conference and very good counsel'. But even if we allow that their influence was quite disproportionate to their numbers, it is clear that there were few people prior to the civil war who elected to separate absolutely from the established church and to form alternative and voluntary communities, founded upon religious compatibility, upon godliness.[5]

However, while it is impossible to estimate its size, we must recognize the existence of a larger body made up of those who, while still technically adhering to the Anglican church, established *informal* religious groups. The latter were based upon the same principles and exemplified many of the same social characteristics as the sects.

[4] Foster, ed., *State of the Church*, pp. lxxxviii–lxxxix; William Worship, *The Christian's Mourning Garment*, London, 1615, pp. 31–32: for reprisals by Catholic gentry against those who informed against them, see LAO, Court Papers 68/1/2; STAC 8 21/15.
[5] SP 16/274/12; H of LMP 22 Dec. 1641, Lincoln poll money certificate; LAO, Viij 1, ff. 21, 71; 2, ff. 4, 12v; 3, ff. 46, 52; Brace, ed., *Minutes of the Gainsborough Monthly Meeting*, 1, p. x.

Historians have doubted the possibility of distinguishing Angli-
cans from Puritans in the early seventeenth century. Robert
Sanderson (see plate VIII), the Jacobean rector of Boothby Pagnell,
had no such scholarly qualms. For Sanderson the Puritans were
essentially differentiated by their attitudes to authority and by their
'partiality'. The Puritans, argued Sanderson, illegitimately sought
to appropriate

titles of distinction, to difference some few in the church . . . from the rest,
singling out unto themselves and those that favour them certain proper
appellations, of 'brethren', and 'good men', and 'professors'; as if none had
brotherhood in Christ, none had interest in goodness, none made
profession of the Gospel, but themselves.

Sanderson was content to affirm a central paradox of Calvin's
theology. God's elect were the true church, God's elect deserved
the highest position in our esteem and affections: yet the identity of
God's elect was hidden. No man could 'judge infallibly of the state
of his brother's soul',

judge we neither way peremptorily nor definitively whatsoever probabilities we see either way, sith we know not how far a sanctified believer
may fall into the snares of sin, nor how far a graceless hypocrite may go in
the show of godliness.

Since 'the fan is not in our hand to winnow the chaff from the
wheat', the proper attitude was not one of partiality but of an
ecumenical charity and concern for 'the whole society of Christian
men, the system and body of the whole visible church'.[6]

Theologically this was impeccable; psychologically it was a
difficult position to sustain. To John Vicars, the Puritan zealot at
Stamford St Mary's, the probabilities were perfectly clear. Many of
his parishioners were depraved sinners: drunkards, 'frequenters of
innes', usurers, 'swearers and prophaners of the holy name of God',
sensualists who feasted riotously at Christmas and enjoyed stage
plays, which they attended 'accompanied with painted Jezebels,
wanton Imaheb, and whorish Dalilas'. A minority of his flock,
conversely, were devout and conscientious Christians who refused
to work for ungodly employers, who rebuked the town's magistrates when they failed to share Vicars's sabbatarian concerns and
who clubbed together to improve their prophet's maintenance. Of
course Vicars 'made notes of distinction between the godly and
wicked'. He damned the worldly in fiery sermons. He cleaved to

[6] Jacobson, ed., *Works of Sanderson*, I, pp. 71, 78–80, 216; II, pp. 30–32; III, pp. 7,
10, 12; J. Sears McGee, *The Godly Man in Stuart England*, New Haven, 1976, pp.
212, 214–15, 224–29.

the godly, 'his owne family and his children as he calleth them'. Private meetings, attended by persons from parishes as far distant as Oundle, were held for prayer, fasting and exhortation; Vicars and 'those he termeth his children begotten in the Lord' entered into a covenant 'to doe whatsoever God commandeth'. Vicars's actions were duplicated by several Puritan ministers in Lincolnshire. At the beginning of James's reign Richard Bernard, the vicar of Worksop, and about a hundred of his followers, many from Lincolnshire, covenanted together to stop attending services conducted by non-preaching ministers and to watch over and admonish one another. At Boston in the 1620s John Cotton gathered a tight-knit inner group of the pious who covenanted 'to follow after the Lord in the purity of his worship'.[7]

Prior to the civil war Puritan separatism was a more considerable phenomenon than appears if we focus solely upon the tiny covens of hunted sectaries. In addition to the Anabaptists and Brownists, there were groups whose refusal to make an outright breach with the established church should not blind us to their fundamentally separatist attitudes. We find examples of the 'congregation within the congregation', the godly cadre interlocked by actual subscription to a covenant. A larger group consisted of those whose religious exercises were informal, yet who recognized themselves as 'brethren, professors, good men', distinct from the unregenerate herd. Like the sectaries, these groupings of the godly, whether covenanted or informal, rejected traditional village and parochial ties, and formed alternative communities which dictated social norms and behaviour. Bernard's followers watched over and admonished each other; Cotton's choice of a wife was guided by his brethren, particularly 'holy Mr Baynes'; some of Vicars's female devotees, known sardonically as 'the newe nunnery of Stamford', refused to accept employment with masters of insufficient godliness.[8]

Sanderson argued that, if pursued to its logical conclusion, the Puritans' partiality would 'necessarily . . . enforce an utter separation' from the established church. Cotton's removal to Massachusetts, or John Smith's spiritual pilgrimage — town

---

[7] SP 16/119/52; *Reports of Cases in the Courts of Star Chamber and High Commission*, ed. S. R. Gardiner, Camden Soc., n.s. 39, 1886, pp. 198–238; *The Works of John Smythe*, ed. W. T. Whitley, Cambridge, 1915, pp. 331-34; L. Ziff, *The Career of John Cotton: Puritanism and the American Experience*, Princeton, 1962, p. 49; John Cotton, *The Way of the Congregational Churches Cleared*, London, 1648, p. 20.

[8] *Cases in Star Chamber and High Commission*, p. 205; Cotton Mather, *Magnalia Christi Americana*, ed. T. Robbins, Hartford, 1855, p. 258.

preacher at Lincoln, then minister of a separatist congregation in the Gainsborough area, finally flight with the bulk of his followers to the more tolerant atmosphere of Amsterdam — gave force to Sanderson's reasoning.[9] Yet in 1640 the majority of the Puritans had not formally broken from the national church. Their informal coteries subsisted uneasily within an establishment which they still hoped to colonize.

The explosion of religious experimentation during the civil war and interregnum, followed by the Cavalier Parliament's narrowly restrictive ecclesiastical settlement, ensured that after 1661 a substantial number of people opted out of the established church and combined in religious communities formally distinct from the parochial structure. In 1676 2,594 adults were reported as nonconformists in Lincolnshire, some three per cent of the population. The social characteristics of these groups were qualitatively similar to those of their pre-war antecedents. The sectarian corporatism of the Quakers was most extreme (see plate XI). They deliberately distinguished themselves from 'the world' by their dress, by their use of the archaic second person singular, by their refusal to observe the traditional recognitions accorded to social superiors — such 'vain ceremonies . . . [as] . . . uncovering the head and bowing the knee' — or even to abide by the norms of neighbourly intercourse. John Whitehead, the dominant local influence on the first generation of Lincolnshire Quakerism, excoriated 'the ignorant people's customs and manners, in saying "God eve" and "God morrow"' and was untroubled by a critic's charge that the Quakers treated their fellow villagers as they would 'a hog or a cow': their exclusiveness had been the practice, he argued, of 'Christ's ancient disciples'. Marriage with outsiders — with 'the world's people', those 'out of the Truth' — was also bitterly denounced. Differentiated from the larger society and seeking to minimize contacts with it, the Quakers in their own tightly organized and disciplined communities provided a number of alternative social services such as poor relief and arbitration tribunals to prevent differences between Friends being fought out in the public forum of a court of law 'to the great scandall of Truth'. Like the Catholics, the Quakers were bonded into a national community, though less by family connection than by the centralized structure established by Fox.[10]

The other dissenting groups could not rival the formal organization of the Quakers but the community of the godly was still a

[9] W. H. Burgess, *John Smith the Se-Baptist*, London, 1911, pp. 65–80.
[10] John Whitehead, *The Written Gospel-Labours*, London, 1704, pp. 142–46; Brace, ed., *Minutes of the Gainsborough Monthly Meeting*, I, pp. xviii–xx, 70, 115, 116.

central social reference point for individuals. Gervase Disney of Swinderby was raised in a family 'constantly under a religious discipline'. Gervase noted that his parents were 'careful and circumspect in the disposing of us [i.e., their children] in marriage and imployments, to such as feared God', and his three sisters married men 'all very eminent for holiness'. His own marriage was dominated by religious concerns: he commenced his suit to his future wife upon the recommendation of a godly minister; he first met her at family prayers; the marriage was agreed upon only after a day of religious exercises when the parties 'sought God solemnly'. The couple then settled at Nottingham. The town was chosen because Gervase was a stranger there and felt that he could build up a circle of Christian acquaintances freed from the memories of 'my old bad companions at Lincoln' (the ghosts of an unregenerate adolescence). The town met his expectations. Disney rejected a number of favourable opportunities for economic advancement which would have involved moving from Nottingham, where he enjoyed 'the Gospel and the society of good, quickening Christians'.[11]

'The society of good, quickening Christians': whether regimented in the Quaker meetings, or less rigidly associated in the pre-civil war groups and the post-1661 Presbyterian and Congregationalist sects, the godly asserted the primacy of a community based not upon ties of geography or status but on spiritual kinship. Deeply suspicious of 'the world's people' with whom they were transitorily associated, the godly formed exclusive communities within which they established the bulk of their social relationships.

Of course, we cannot reduce the motives that impelled men and women to affiliate with these voluntaristic religious societies to a simple yearning for corporate ties no longer provided by the village or the town. But that this may have been a consideration can be argued from the post-restoration geographical distribution of dissenters. In 1664 the earl of Lindsey reported that the greatest number of 'Quakers, Anabaptists and other sectaries' were from 'the Isle of Axholme and the Marish'. The early eighteenth-century ecclesiastical surveys bear out his analysis. Nonconformists formed six per cent of the population of these areas, more than double the average for the county as a whole: an equally high proportion of dissenters was reported from the Holland fens.[12] The fens and the

[11] D. Disney, *Some remarkable passages in the Holy Life and Death of Gervase Disney, Esq.*, London, 1692, pp. 22, 23, 53, 64.
[12] Bodleian Lib., Clarendon MS 92, no. 143: the early eighteenth-century figures are calculated from Cole, ed., *Speculum*, passim.

marsh, then, were the strongholds of dissent and these were the areas of a growing population and a rapidly changing pattern of agricultural production, which may have been corrosive of the traditional village ties. The suggestions that dissent proved attractive because it provided a strong corporate bonding in areas where old communal affiliations were being undercut must remain tentative, however. Nonconformity may have flourished in the fen and the marsh because in the absence of a resident gentry it was difficult to suppress, or because the fenmen chose to thumb their noses at the religious policies of a central government which had displayed so scant a respect for their traditional economy and legal rights. We are on stronger grounds in arguing that, whether or not it originated in dissatisfaction with the waning of corporatism of the village community, the growth of religious separatism could only erode still further the neighbourly values of the natural community.[13]

[13] For a discussion of this, see M. Spufford, *Contrasting Communities: English Villages in the Sixteenth and Seventeenth Centuries*, Cambridge, 1974, pp. 344–49.

CHAPTER 5

'BROKERS':
THE PROFESSIONS

So far we have discussed the erosion of the closed corporatism of the village and the borough as a response to a series of impersonal forces — geographical mobility, demographic upswing, new patterns of agricultural exploitation. In this section I propose to examine a number of the social groups which acted as 'brokers', to employ a terminology developed by anthropologists.[1] Brokers are the 'intermediaries between local life and wider life', channelling, often selectively, the products of the national culture into the village and representing the villagers in their dealings with the national system. Three such groups will be examined: first, the professional cadres of lawyers and of clergymen; then the gentry. I will argue that changes in the structure, or training, or role-definition of these groups occurred in the seventeenth century, with effects which were as corrosive of the closed corporate peasant community as were the general processes of social change already analysed.

LAWYERS

At an assize sermon preached in 1614 William Worship, the vicar of Croft, considered the misfortunes of the rustic who had been persuaded to sue in the central courts at Westminster, and, in consequence, had fallen into the toils of the 'unconscionable' lawyer and was ensnared in 'a maze of trouble',

a motion today, tomorrow crost; execution suspended and cald in question by a writ of errour. 'I hope,' saies the plodding weather-beaten soule, 'I shall have an end of my sute the next tearme.' Nay, nor the next tearme, nor the next: nay, nor the next yeere, nor the next.

---

[1] For a short discussion, see R. Redfield, *Peasant Societies and Culture*, Chicago, 1960, pp. 36–38; G. W. Skinner, 'Marketing and social structure in rural China', *J. of Asian Studies*, 24 (1964–65), pp. 41–42.

Worship's satire is a variation on a common seventeenth-century theme, favoured not only by divines but by lay social commentators. Litigation at Westminster, fired by the greed of the legal profession, was waxing and was invariably ruinous to the parties. It was also corrosive of the traditional communal values of neighbourliness and Christian charity.[2]

Any attempt to test statistically the contemporary assumption that Lincolnshiremen were increasingly engaged in litigation at Westminster would be a herculean task, yet the growth of the local legal profession in the course of the century, and a change in its structure in the direction of enhanced specialization, suggest that an increase in business did occur. The career of Sergeant Robert Callis appears to follow a typical pattern for an eminent lawyer in the early seventeenth century. At a special session arranged by the earl of Lincoln in his interminable feud with Sir Edward Dymock, Callis, the latter's legal counsel, challenged the justice of the proceedings and suggested (correctly) that the jury had been packed. For his temerity he was threatened and insulted — 'boy' — by the irascible peer. Subsequently Lincoln was required to explain his actions in Star Chamber. He was unrepentant. Callis was 'a base persone's sonne whose father was tennant in some of . . . [his] . . . townes'; he had no business attempting 'to controle his betters sitting on the bench'. The earl of Lincoln's scorn for Callis's lowly origins was well founded: the lawyer's elder brother, William — 'yeoman' — continued to farm at Little Hale. But undistinguished ancestry did not retard an eminent legal career. Callis had been called to the bar in 1601; in 1617 he was elected to the governing body of Gray's Inn, and was 1622 was appointed reader; in 1627 his professional distinction was recognized in his appointment as sergeant-at-law. In 1622, in the prefatory remarks to his reading, he spoke with affection of his twenty-six years 'continuance' at Gray's Inn and the companionship he had enjoyed there: his 'most worthy fellows and companions of this noble and renowned society' were 'the best companions of my forepast and present life'.[3]

Callis, then, was a most distinguished practitioner in the courts at Westminster. Yet he never lost contact with his native Lincoln-

[2] William Worship, *The Christian's Mourning Garment*, London, 1615, pp. 131–32: in general, see J. S. Cockburn, *A History of the English Assizes, 1558–1714*, Cambridge, 1972, pp. 145–49 and C. W. Brooks, 'Litigants and Attorneys in the King's Bench and Common Pleas, 1560–1640' in *Legal Records and the Historian*, ed. J. H. Baker, London, 1978, pp. 41–59.
[3] STAC 8 91/18; 98/9; 126/19; *The Reading of the famous and learned Robert Callis . . . upon the Statute of Sewers*, ed. W. J. Broderip, London, 1824, p. 25.

shire. In 1604 he was counsel for Sir Edward Dymock; in 1609 and 1610 he represented his Little Hale relatives in disputes over rights of common in the fen with their fellow villagers and with the men of Swineshead; in the latter year he fought the rapacious and unscrupulous Sir Edward Carr on behalf of a yeoman of Wilsford who stood in the way of one of Carr's nefarious enclosure schemes. In 1612 Callis was appointed deputy recorder of Lincoln. Although he soon lost this position when his patron, George Anton, fell victim to the internal disputes which racked the city, Callis later represented one of the factions in their attempt to prosecute their civic rivals in Star Chamber. During James's reign Callis frequently attended Lincoln assizes, was appointed to the commission of the peace, and also to the commission of sewers for the shire. Under Charles, Callis was one of the commissioners who supported the Lindsey Level drainage scheme; he was an active on the bench and in that capacity he was frequently given special responsibilities by the Privy Council; he continued to represent local litigants in the central courts and his advice was valued by the corporation of Grantham.

Robert Callis moved easily between his practice at Westminster and his involvement in the politics and administration of his native county. His 'learned reading' in 1622 symbolizes his double world. He chose to elucidate, for the illumination of his 'fellows and friends of this most famous and renowned inn of court', the Statute of Sewers (23 Henry VIII, c. 5): his interest had been aroused when, as a local commissioner, 'I found that these laws were dark and intricate, and came not usually within the reach and understanding of such as were not well seen and studied in the laws'.[4]

Callis's double life was paralleled in the careers of many lawyers in the period before 1640. Sergeant Heron was counsel for the earl of Lincoln during the Dymock feud; Sir Richard Williamson, 'one of the king's counsel in ordinary attendant at York', vigorously supported the townsmen of Gainsborough in their dispute with the Hickman family. Anthony Irby and Leonard Bawtree were contemporaries at Lincoln's Inn and progressed together through its internal hierarchy of office; both were distinguished legal practitioners — Irby a master in Chancery; Bawtree, from 1614, a sergeant-at-law. Yet both men were vitally involved in the life of Boston, of which Irby was deputy recorder. In 1609 they supported

[4] STAC 8 98/9; 168/15; 279/8; C 2 James I, T 11/32; *Callis on Sewers*, pp. 33, 154–55; C 193/13/1; LAO, SS 503/45; SP 16/148/96; *APC 1628–29*, p. 171; PC 2/48, pp. 67–68; Hill, *Tudor and Stuart Lincoln*, p. 37; LAO, MON 7/11/17; Grantham Hall Book I, f. 31v.

the corporation's attempt to get the county to contribute to the repair of the sluice; in 1614 they represented the borough in parliament; in 1621, instructed by the Privy Council to investigate the cutting of the crosses from the mayoral mace by Puritan zealots, they co-operated in the cover-up of the incident.[5]

In the 1670s Sergeant Francis Wingfield participated actively in Lincolnshire politics on the tory side; he was, the earl of Lindsey remarked approvingly, 'a great card . . . in these parts to play in all affairs of importance'. But he was an anomaly: after the civil war the leaders of the legal profession increasingly divorced themselves from local affairs. Careers like those of Callis, Bawtree and Irby, involving a continuous interplay of local and central concerns, were no longer the norm. We should not suppose, however, that a complete hiatus developed between provincial society and the legal establishment. The luminaries were able to limit themselves to practice at the central courts, with occasional forays into the localities to attend the assizes, as a consequence of a developing division of labour within the profession: the necessary preparative work, the basic mechanics of litigation, was performed by the burgeoning class of local attorneys and solicitors. The new pattern emerges in Sir John Brownlow's suit in 1671 concerning the tithes of Temple Bruer. Four eminent sergeants, none of whom had any local ties, were engaged to argue Sir John's case for him in the Common Pleas. But the spadework was undertaken by his personal legal agent and man of affairs.[6]

It is not easy to delineate the characteristics or to chart the growth of this group of local legal handymen. There was not, as for those who practised at Westminster, close professional supervision founded upon a formal (and tedious) educational routine. Some local lawyers may have studied at one of the inns of Chancery, while others learned their skills from an established practitioner, often a close relative: Robert Smith, clerk of the peace for Lindsey, was the son of Richard the attorney for the city of Lincoln; the son of Edmund Shuttleworth, Lincoln's town clerk, acted as under-

    [5] STAC 8 91/18; 303/24; *The records of the Honourable Society of Lincoln's Inn: the Black Books*, II, ed. W. P. Baildon, London, 1897–1902, pp. 15–168; Boston Common Council Minute Book 2, ff. 73, 189; LAO, SS 503/37; G. B. Blenkin, 'Boston, England, and John Cotton in 1621', *New England Historical and Genealogical Register*, 28 (1874), pp. 126–28.
    [6] HMC *14th Report*, App. 9, p. 384; E. Cust, *Records of the Cust Family . . . the Brownlows of Belton*, London, 1909, p. 101; in general, see J. H. Baker, 'Counsellors and Barristers: an historical study', *Cambridge Law J.*, 27 (1969), pp. 221–23.

sheriff for the county. Some lawyers had negligible training. Robert Popplewell, the influential and ultimately affluent solicitor who at the close of the century was responsible for handling the plethora of litigation on behalf of the Axholme fenmen against the drainers, was the son of a poor farmer and had no academic education beyond that available at 'a common country school'; he gained practical experience as Lady Granville's steward before taking up his responsibilities as the commoners' agent.

Nor was there a uniform career pattern for provincial legal practitioners. Many of the opportunities for employment available to a local lawyer appear in the *curriculum vitae* of John Anderson of Boston, an attorney of the Common Pleas. At various times he acted as under-sheriff of Lincolnshire, as the steward of several manorial courts and as town clerk of Boston. Rewards varied too. Popplewell flourished; so did Anderson, who rose to become mayor of Boston. Other lawyers were far less successful: the poverty of William Taylor of Lincoln excused him from paying the higher assessment imposed upon attorneys in the 1641 poll tax.[7]

This expanding group of local legal professionals did not enjoy a very savoury reputation. They were charged with chicanery, particularly the forging of writs and warrants; with perjury and the manufacture of evidence; with the embezzlement of distrained goods; with taking extortionate fees; with fomenting litigation and 'frivellous suites'.[8] Yet they played an important intermedial role, articulating provincial society into the national system of administration and law. This emerges spectacularly in certain incidents involving local attorneys. Richard Smith of Lincoln advised those displaced from their offices during the factional fights in the city to seek reinstatement by appealing to the Court of King's Bench; Posthumous Priestman of Bourne encouraged the 1641 rioters in the fens by challenging the legality of an order issued by the house of lords on behalf of the earl of Lindsey; Daniel Noddel persuaded the Leveller activists, Lilburne and Wildman, to lead the Axholme men in their battle with the drainers.[9] Yet, if less spectacular, the attorneys' self-interested encouragement of litigation at Westminster was the most important aspect of their intermedial role. It

[7] W. B. Stonehouse, *The History and Topography of the Isle of Axholme*, London, 1839, pp. 340–41; STAC 8 42/8; 118/12; H of LMP 22 Dec. 1641, city of Lincoln poll tax assessment.
[8] STAC 8 51/24; 132/2; 140/18; 257/31.
[9] E. Henderson, *Foundations of English Administrative Law*, Cambridge Mass., 1963, pp. 61–62; H of LMP 4 June 1641, petition of Matthew Cooke; *CSPD 1652–53*, p. 374.

short-circuited the traditional mechanisms for settling disputes based on neighbourly arbitration, and thus undermined local corporatism. This was the opinion of Robert Sanderson, the saintly rector of Boothby Pagnell (see plate VIII). For Sanderson going to law was on a moral par with 'swearing, . . . gaming for money, and dancing and recreation upon the sabbath', and he employed his skills as an arbitrator and casuist 'in reconciling differences and preventing law suits, both in his parish and the neighberhood'.[10]

Robert Sanderson, not content with keeping the legal vultures from his flock, sought to uphold traditional community standards in other ways. He aided the sick and the poor. When a rich landlord insisted that his poor tenant pay the full agreed rent for a pasture the latter had hired, even though heavy rain had destroyed the crop and the poor man faced ruin, Sanderson visited the landlord and persuaded him to forgive the debt. Yet, paradoxically, Sanderson was himself a broker whose ministerial function was potentially as subversive of village corporatism as that of the lawyers whom he decried. The paradox essentially stems from the redefinition of the role of the parochial minister at the Reformation.

THE PROTESTANT MINISTER

Protestant thinkers never tired of deriding the contrast between the want of education, the immorality, and the incompetence all too frequently displayed by the Catholic priest and the privileged status that the Roman hierarchy arrogated to its clergy as a consequence of their unique intercessory and quasi-magical sacramental roles. The Reformation shattered this theological foundation, and reduced to a shadow the institutional structure and associated privileges that had been reared upon it in the middle ages. Yet the Protestant minister's role was still mediatory, though shorn of the supernatural pretensions of the Catholic church. The minister was to guide his flock to a knowledge of the operation of God's saving grace, to inspire them to a personal quest for that grace, and to sustain and encourage them in their Christian commitment as they wrestled with the inward doubts and the worldly concerns that marked their transitory pilgrimage.

Central to this role was preaching (see plates VI and VII). 'The first impediment' to individual repentance was 'the want of the word preached', claimed William Worship. The great Puritan divine, John Cotton, bemoaned the fate of a parish where the minister was not a preacher: 'the people are as ignorant as those that

[10] Jacobson, ed., *Works of Sanderson*, II, pp. 55–56, 308–9; VI, pp. 291–95.

never heard of the name of Christ; as empty of faith, and of the knowledge of Christ, and of every grace of His, as those that never heard of Him'. Cotton argued that an incumbent who did not preach, 'such an one as God might set over His people in His anger and heavy displeasure, but not in mercy', was not a 'lawfull minister'.

No one could deny the legality of Cotton's ministerial calling on such grounds. He was indefatigable in the preaching of the word to his Boston parishioners. He exhausted them. A hostile observer noted that by the conclusion of Cotton's Sunday afternoon exercise — a two-hour sermon, followed by the catechism of the youth, then a further two-hour explication of the catechism — 'there was as many sleepers as wakers, scarse any man but sometime was forced to winke or nod'.[11] Cotton's efforts were not merely reserved for the sabbath. Each Thursday afternoon he gave a public lecture; early on Wednesday and Thursday mornings, and on Saturday at 3 p.m., he gave a series of informal sermons — these to replace a daily exercise at his own house which had to be abandoned when his audience grew too large. Cotton also preached at the corporation's solemn functions and at the 'funerals of the abler sort that died'.[12]

The Anglican apologist, Robert Sanderson, was reluctant to condemn all non-preaching incumbents, while his own efforts at rustic Boothby Pagnell were necessarily less herculean than those of his contemporary at Boston. Yet Sanderson, too, emphasized the centrality of the effective preaching of the word. And the *sine qua non* of the latter, he argued, in an age 'wherein learning aboundeth even to wantonness . . . and the world is full of . . . controversies, and novelities, and niceties in religion', was an *educated* ministry. Both Cotton and Sanderson were superbly trained. Both were precocious scholars and linguists who had enjoyed distinguished university careers: Sanderson, a fellow of Lincoln College, Oxford, and reader in logic, enjoyed a brilliant reputation as a lecturer; Cotton was a fellow of Emmanuel College, Cambridge, noted for his oratorical skills and 'academical dexterity'. Both, Cotton when he was 28, Sanderson at 31, abandoned cloistered Oxbridge and

---

[11] Worship, *The Christian's Mourning Garment*, pp. 18, 44; John Cotton, *Christ the Fountain of Life*, London, 1651, pp. 181–84; E. Venables, 'The primary visitation of the diocese of Lincoln by Bishop Neile, 1614', *AASR*, 16 (1881–82), pp. 50–52.
[12] Ibid.; L. Ziff, *The Career of John Cotton: Puritanism and the American experience*, Princeton, 1962, pp. 41, 50; *Chronicles of the First Planters*, ed. A. Young, Boston Mass., 1846, p. 425; Cotton Mather, *Magnalia Christi Americana*, ed. T. Robbins, Hartford, 1855, p. 260.

dedicated their learning to parochial duties.[13] Such academic distinction was necessarily atypical, but a university education was increasingly the rule for the Lincolnshire ministry. In 1603 thirty-seven per cent of the clergy had a university degree; in a sample of the clergy from the 1640s only five per cent *lacked* the qualification.[14]

This statistic indicates the degree to which the universities were training the educated ministry demanded by Protestant ideology. Indeed, by the early seventeenth century Oxbridge was turning out graduates in excess of the number of available ecclesiastical livings. The surplus graduates frequently took positions in a profession, teaching, which also developed in response to Protestant concerns: John Wesled's legacy of 26s. 8d. p.a. for the maintenance of a schoolmaster at Bratoft was designed 'for the bringinge up of youthe in the feare of god in the said parish'. In 1607 schoolmasters, supported by small legacies, subscriptions or fees, were teaching in sixty-two villages in the county. These village schools, lacking the reputations or the formal endowments of the established grammar schools of the market towns, were often ephemeral. But they did provide a level of education above that of the dame-schools, run by such pedagogues as the wife of the Newton family's gardener.[15] In 1641 eighteen per cent of the adult male inhabitants of eleven marshland villages in the vicinity of Louth could sign their names: at Skidbrooke, the only one of the eleven with a resident schoolmaster in the 1630s, nearly thirty-two per cent of the men signed.[16]

The Protestant ideal of the ministerial calling, as expressed by Cotton or Sanderson, embodies a redefinition of the cleric's hinge role. The medieval priest, supervising rituals primarily designed to guarantee immediate local benefits and rooted in local superstition, was displaced by the 'painful' teacher and preacher. The latter was to deploy his oratorical skills and his learning to exhort his parishioners and to educate them, in sermons, the catechism or the classroom, in the values of the national religious culture. This was

[13] Jacobson, ed., *Works of Sanderson*, II, pp. 86–87; VI, pp. 286–88; Ziff, *John Cotton*, pp. 27–29; *Memoir of John Cotton by John Norton*, ed. E. Pond, Boston Mass., 1834, p. 28.

[14] The 1603 figure is from Foster, ed., *State of the Church*, p. 454; the figure for the 1640s is calculated from A. G. Matthews, *Walker Revised*, Oxford, 1948, pp. 247–59.

[15] *Lincolnshire Wills, 1600–17*, ed. A. R. Maddison, Lincoln, 1891, pp. 11–13; Foster, ed., *State of the Church*, pp. 397–414; LAO, MON 7/12/68.

[16] H of LMP March 1641/2, the protestation return from the wapentake of Louthesk; LAO, Vj 30, f. 85.

the ideal. Before examining it in greater detail, it must be noted that, despite the marked improvement in clerical educational standards, the ideal was not universally realized.

MINISTERIAL DEFICIENCIES

Sanderson, in emphasizing the desirability of an educated ministry, was scarcely original; he echoed the opinions of ecclesiastical reformers, Protestant or humanist, who had proclaimed education as the infallible panacea for clerical deficiencies since the early sixteenth century. The nature of the sample from the 1640s, from which it appears that ninety-five per cent of the clergy had received university education, demonstrates how vain these hopes were, for it consists of those clerics displaced from their livings by parliament for, *inter alia*, immorality and incompetence. William Underwood of Hareby was a Cambridge B.A., yet he was thought to be a poor scholar, 'noe waies furnished with guiftes for the discharge of such a place'; he purchased no books, even borrowing a bible to perform his official duties, and spent most of his day in the village alehouse. Drunkenness was not uncommon and was often associated with sexual irregularities. John Leake of Frodingham was spectacularly immoral: he tempted one woman to his bed by promising a favourable deal on tithes; another woman was solicited with the argument that her consent could not endanger her soul as women had no souls to lose. On this last occasion he was drunk — a frequent occurrence; in his cups he would indulge his taste for 'bawdy songs'. He held an M.A. degree from Cambridge.[17]

Education did not guarantee a committed, godly ministry. Indeed, it could be argued that the university was a poor prelude to the routine duties of a country parson. John Cotton noted how easy it was for young scholars, fresh from the parnassian heights of intellectual life, to resent their exile to some forgotten backwater and to 'despise the people and think themselves unmeet to condescend to peasants'.[18] Susannah Wesley, at the close of the century, bewailed her husband's appointment at Epworth. It was, she wrote, 'a thousand pities that a man of his brightness and rare endowments of learning and useful knowledge . . . should be confined to an obscure corner of the country where his talents are buried'.[19]

---

[17] 'The Royalist Clergy of Lincolnshire', ed. J. W. F. Hill, *LAAS*, 2 (1940), pp. 66, 101–5.
[18] Ziff, *John Cotton*, p. 38.
[19] Stonehouse, *Axholme*, p. 182.

The sense of disappointment and frustration generated among some of the highly trained clerics consigned to

a mean cot composed of reeds and clay
Wasting in sighs the uncomfortable day

(Samuel Wesley's own description of his lot at South Ormsby), must have been enhanced by the inadequate financial rewards — 'hogsheard's wages' — for their chosen profession.[20] At the end of Elizabeth's reign it was suggested that a stipend of £30–£50 p.a. would provide a barely adequate maintenance for a cleric; scarcely a third of the livings in the five deaneries for which the 1603 valuation survives exceeded the £30 cut-off, and forty-four per cent of them were worth less than £15 p.a. The situation did not improve in the course of the century. In 1704 only one-fifth of the livings in the same area achieved the £80 p.a. income which was then considered the minimum for a competent livelihood.[21] Poverty, contemporaries argued, could of itself engender contempt for the clergy among the laity; it also meant than an incumbent would lack books, would have little surplus for charity, and might be forced into a sycophantic dependence upon the local gentlemen or his congregation. He might also be obliged to take on other jobs to make ends meet. At the end of the sixteenth century most Lincolnshire parsons were practising farmers: 'not the Smithfield butcher more skilfull then some of them in handling a fat beast', was William Worship's sarcastic comment. Others did a thriving trade in clandestine marriages, while in the first decade of the seventeenth century the curate of Skellingthorpe doubled as a gardener and the curate of Cranwell as a quack doctor and magician, skilled in determing the sex of unborn children and in finding stolen goods. Vincent Brampton, a grocer's apprentice by training, who received £4 p.a. as curate of Asgarby, became clerk of Partney market and ran an alehouse to make ends meet. When the justices remarked the incongruity of his dual career, he replied 'that he got more by his ale then the alter' and would rather resign his ecclesiastical post than abandon his tavern.[22]

[20] A. Clarke, *Memoirs of the Wesley Family*, New York, 1859, p. 156: for 'hogsheard's wages', see 'Royalist clergy', ed. Hill, p. 74.
[21] The 1603 figure is calculated from Foster, ed., *State of the Church*, pp. 355–62: the 1704 figure is from Cole, ed., *Speculum*, passim. For discussion of the optimum income from livings, see A. Savidge, *The foundation and early years of Queen Anne's Bounty*, London, 1955, pp. 6–9.
[22] C. Hill, *The Economic Problems of the Church*, Oxford, 1963, p. 205; 'Royalist clergy', ed. Hill, pp. 75–76; LAO, Court Papers 58/2/3, 70; R. E. G. Cole, 'Notes on the ecclesiastical history of the deanery of Graffoe', *AASR*, 25 (1899–1900), p. 256; SP 16/379/10, f. 11.

At the end of the seventeenth century some attempt was made to deal with clerical poverty by the official tolerance of pluralism, whereby a cleric was permitted to hold several livings simultaneously and thus to attain an adequate subsistence. This solved one problem only to create another — inadequate supervision at the parochial level. As Bishop Reynolds wrote of Lincolnshire in 1724, 'the clergy thereabouts were obliged to undertake three, or four, or five churches a man to piece out a scanty subsistence, under the uneasy reflection all along that neither the public worship, nor any other part of the pastoral charge could in these parishes have a due attendance'. Lady Thorold noted the same problem. 'The livings are so poor that two or three will not make £50 a year'; in consequence 'most of the parisshes are so neglected that the people are almost heathens'.[23]

Not only was the income available to the bulk of the parochial clergy insufficient, its basic source, tithe, made it difficult to increase as it was a fertile source of friction between the minister and his parishioners. Hounding the latter for tithe on 'onyons, leekes, garlicke, cabbyges, raddiges and other rootes' was not calculated to facilitate the minister's effectiveness in his intermedial role, and could lead to bitter conflict.[24]

For many clergymen, however, the problem was not of increasing income from tithe but of sustaining its real value in a period of rising prices. A number of ministers found themselves the victims of a *modus decimandi*, a composition whereby an agreed sum was paid in lieu of tithes in kind, negotiated by their predecessors years before. So in the reign of Henry VI an agreement had been reached whereby the rector of East Torrington accepted 10s. p.a. and pasturage for two horses in lieu of tithe on certain meadows. In 1616 the rector challenged the composition but was defeated at law and the fifteenth-century settlement upheld. Sir George Heneage of Hainton, the owner of the meadows, in fact paid only a derisory 5s., but he cautioned his son that should the rector demand the full 10s. and pasturage 'it will be the best course to yield thereunto'.[25] Others had more success at law, particularly where the alleged

---

[23] N. Sykes, *Church and State in England in the XVIIIth Century*, Cambridge, 1934, p. 213; Savidge, *Queen Anne's Bounty*, pp. 11–12.
[24] LAO, Court Papers 59/1/42. The parson of North Scarle was arrested on a malicious charge of high treason lodged by his opponents in a tithe dispute (*CSPD 1619–23*, pp. 92–93).
[25] 'Sir George Heneage's estate book, 1625', ed. J. W. F. Hill, *LAAS*, 1 (1938–39), pp. 73–74. For a general discussion of the problems caused by tithe compositions, see Hill, *Economic Problems*, chapters 5, 6.

composition was a matter of 'aunchient custome' rather than formal agreement. But victory could be ruinously expensive, as one of Sanderson's predecessors at Boothby Pagnell discovered. He prosecuted and ended succesfullie for the church, a tedious suite against Mr Pannell, then lord of the towne, in which he recovered the tythes in kinde of the demeanes . . . which, under pretence of a custom to pay onlie £4 p.a. for them, were longe detayned and almost lost from the church. This suite was followed . . . with his extreame chardges, and to the empoverishinge of his state, not longe before his death.[26]

This case embodies both the factors that might deter a minister from pursuing a legal right: dilatory and expensive proceedings; the antipathy of a powerful local gentleman.[27] Not only was the incumbent's financial position in danger of erosion by rising prices, it could also be adversely affected by changes in land utilization. The situation was most serious in the fen and salt marsh where the conversion of pasture to arable upon drainage and enclosure could reduce the value of the small tithes which provided the basic income for the vicars of impropriate livings: at Somercotes St Mary (North Somercotes) the vicar's income fell from £60 to £8 p.a. upon the embanking of the marsh and its redeployment in arable production.[28] But enclosure for pasture also presented problems for incumbents: the disappearance of their glebe, the inappropriateness of an ancient *modus decimandi* for the new agricultural régime, a general reduction in the value of tithes.[29]

We have reviewed a number of the reasons, in particular the inadequate financial rewards, whereby the high ideals of ministerial office expressed by and embodied in Cotton or Sanderson were not universally realized. But that many parishes had to endure the ministrations of the incompetent and the immoral, or of non-resident pluralists, may also be attributed to a structural weakness in the church. The ministers of Lincolnshire were organized as a separate order answerable to the bishop of the diocese of Lincoln; the latter exercised a supervisory and disciplinary authority over the parochial clergy, and was thus immediately responsible for its quality.

---

[26] LAO, Court Papers 68/2/14.
[27] For the opportunities for legal delay, see STAC 8 145/25: for a patron's hostility aroused by a challenge to a tithe composition, and leading to local violence, see STAC 8 247/15; 284/25; 305/18.
[28] SP 16/302/139. See also *CSPD 1637*, p. 28.
[29] *CSPD 1633–34*, p. 309; *1635*, p. 125; LAO, Court Papers 62/3/1; Resp. Pers. 12/193; Bodleian Lib., Clarendon MS 77, no. 157.

Strong and determined episcopal leadership was largely absent in the seventeenth century. The size of the sprawling diocese was partly responsible; so was the fact that Lincoln was frequently a stepping stone to higher preferment in the church, and in consequence there was a rapid turnover among its bishops: six of the eleven men who occupied the see in the seventeenth century did so for less than five years. It was difficult to make any impact in so short a period. Not that longer tenure necessarily produced a vigorous administration. Bishop Thomas Barlow (1675–91) never once visited Lincoln Cathedral, and was commonly referred to as the bishop of Buckden — the episcopal palace in Huntingdonshire where he resided. John Williams (1621–41) was more active but for his first four years as bishop, until his fall from court favour and loss of the office of lord keeper, he 'was not in condition, through the great burthen of other imployments, to appear among his clergy'. In the 1630s his feud with Archbishop Laud, which was to conclude in his suspension from office and imprisonment in the Tower, seriously weakened his administration of the diocese.[30]

Yet even the most concerned bishop could do little to ensure that only the well-qualified would secure ecclesiastical livings. With Williams he might examine prospective ordinands carefully; he might give the livings at his disposal only to the able and the learned. But he could not be sure that his episcopal colleagues would be equally strict, while the number of livings of which he was patron were relatively few. Laymen disposed of over half of the livings in Lincolnshire, and it was virtually impossible for the bishop to reject a patron's candidate for institution provided he had received proper ordination, whatever his personal doubts as to the nominee's fitness for the post.[31]

While little could be done to guarantee that only suitable candidates would secure parochial charges, the bishops might have done more to exhort and discipline existing incumbents. Or, at least, to insist upon vigour and diligence in the officers who exercised the disciplinary authority upon their behalf. The machinery was in place. Visitations were undertaken regularly — the triennial visitation of the entire diocese by the bishop, the more frequent visitations within the various archdeaconries — and the

[30] For Barlow, see DNB: for Williams, see John Hacket, Scrinia Reserata, II, London, 1693, p. 28.
[31] See R. O'Day, 'The law of patronage in early modern England', J. Eccles. Hist., 26 (1975), pp. 247–60. For Williams's exercise of his patronage, see Hacket, Scrinia Reserata, II, pp. 32, 41–42. For the relative strengths of episcopal (6.6%) and lay (56.5%) patronage of livings, see Foster, ed., State of the Church, p. lvi.

church wardens were formally enjoined to report the deficiencies of their incumbent. Yet it seems that little effort was made to encourage such charges, or to investigate them intensively. The fault lay in part with the limited powers at the disposal of the courts, and their institutional structure. If the accused denied the charge he had only to purge himself upon his oath, backed by his neighbours or fellow clergymen; penance was the usual penalty, and might be commuted for cash — 'I will goe to Lincoln and buie out my pennance', the scandalous vicar of Aby (another Cambridge graduate) jeered at his parishioners when they threatened to denounce him for swearing, drunkenness and adultery. Further, for anyone prepared to expend 'muche money', the possibility of appeal within the hierarchy of ecclesiastical courts provided almost endless opportunity for delaying the final determination of a suit.[32] Yet considerable responsibility rests with the officers who staffed the ecclesiastical judicial structure. Many had purchased their offices, and they appear to have been more concerned with recouping their investment with the fees and douceurs that could be extracted from their positions than with the moral improvement of the laity and the disciplining of the clergy for which they were formally responsible.[33] Most popular odium fell upon the lesser officials, the proctors and apparitors, whose reputations had improved little since Chaucer's day.[34] But the leading officers were also tainted with graft and corruption. In 1625 the grand jury of the hundred of Well indicted Thimbleby Holden, the official of the archdeaconry of Stow, and his registrar for demanding excessive fees. John Pregion, Bishop Williams's registrar, was also accused of extortion, and, in a lurid cause célèbre, of begetting a bastard. Dr Farmery, the chancellor of the diocese in the 1630s, employed his authority in a heavy-handed blackmail attempt against the unfortunate French and Dutch Protestant refugees who had settled in Axholme. The latter were threatened into the purchase of privileges and immunities which never materialized, but for which they paid heavily.[35]

---

[32] LAO, Resp. Pers. 9/65; Court Papers 69/1/23.
[33] For the purchase of office in the ecclesiastical courts, see CSPD 1689–90, p. 113; SP 23/214, pp. 371–75.
[34] For the popular reputation of the officers, see LAO, Court Papers 58/2/76; 58/3/3; Resp. Pers. 9/68; 10/16, 265; LQS File 1642 unfol., articles v. John East.
[35] LAO, LQS File 1625, no. 55; Hacket, Scrinia Reserata, II, pp. 94, 118, 123–24, 128; H of LMP 10 Dec. 1640, the petition of James de Con, John le Houg and Gilly Rey.

Bishop Williams is credited with an attempt to make his officers 'live by honest gains; to moderate their fees; to wash their hands of bribes'.[36] Clearly, he failed. The ecclesiastical courts were ramshackle and corrupt institutions, incapable of exercising the disciplinary authority which, in theory, the bishop held over his clergy. That clerical immorality and incompetence were rife owed much to the deficient execution of disciplinary jurisdiction by the tainted entourage of officers of the ecclesiastical courts of the diocese of Lincoln.

Deficiencies in the structure of the church, then, ensured that many parishes were subjected to the ministrations of clerics who had little commitment to the educational mission outlined by Cotton, and consequently played a negligible intermedial role. Some, like Samuel Wesley, dedicated their energies to toadying to the influential in the hopes of securing a more remunerative benefice; others, like William Underwood, sank into intellectual torpor as pillars of their village alehouse.

Yet we should not overemphasize the bleak side. The ideal was realized, and not just by men of national stature like Sanderson and Cotton. In 1605 Grainthorpe was worth a miserable £15 a year. Yet the minister, John Maltby, was a paragon:

a greate friende to the poore and very charitable to all: a painfull peace maker amongst all men: cyvill and sober in his conversation, wyse in government, of a very honest lyfe and cariage, and of his small stipend hath ever from his necessary maintenance mayd such husbandly sparinge for provydinge good bookes the better to further him in his vocation that he therein is not inferior to many in his callinge, and doth soe well bestow himself in his studye . . . whereby wee receyve great comfort daylie from him . . . In comfortinge the sick both poore and riche very paynfull: doinge alwaies what good he can to all: hurtinge none, worthy to be beloved, and is in our towne and countrye very well beloved.[37]

THE MINISTER AND THE VILLAGE COMMUNITY

The Maltby testimonial presents a paradox which is more apparent in Sanderson's career. Both men were preachers of the word, educators, brokers presenting the national religious culture to their rustic audience. Yet both sought to uphold traditional communal values. Maltby was 'a painfull peace maker'; Sanderson was tireless in 'reconciling differences, and preventing lawsuits', and was particularly insistent that landlord-tenant relations be governed by Christian charity rather than the profit motive. Sanderson's dislike

[36] Hacket, *Scrinia Reserata*, II, p. 44.
[37] LAO, LTD 1605 — testimonial on behalf of John Maltby.

of lawyers stemmed from his concern for communal values: the lawyers polarized men whose differences could have been ironed out by the traditional settlement of disputes by neighbourly arbitration.[38]

The attempt to sustain traditional community values, whilst simultaneously performing the exhortatory and educational role demanded by the Protestant ideal, was a juggling act that only men of Sanderson's human sensitivity could hope to perform. Some ministers in their zeal for reformation were less concerned than was Sanderson to display the caution and discretion which he believed essential to the maintenance of corporate religious life in the parish.[39] They lashed out at the vicious, the torpid, the prophane in their parishes, which were split by their diatribes. John Smith during his two tempestuous years as a city preacher at Lincoln engaged in 'personal preaching', flimsily veiled by innuendo, against those civic leaders who opposed his appointment and ministry. James Ashton of Moulton was more direct; having attacked certain vices in his sermon he would at its conclusion point to one or another of his parishioners and say 'you are the man I ment'.[40] In a status-conscious society such temerity could prove dangerous; William Storre of Market Rasen was murdered by a gentleman infuriated by some 'sharpe and nipping reprehensions' delivered in the minister's preaching.[41] This was an isolated case; personal preaching was more frequently fatal to the corporate religious life of the afflicted parish. The prosecution in 1631 of John Vicars of Stamford before the Court of Ecclesiastical High Commission demonstrates the degree to which a ministry could divide a town.[42] Vicars was an arrogant prig whose zeal admitted of no compromise, and who would unhesitatingly threaten those who were unable to meet his exacting standards of personal and religious conduct with 'the arrows of God's vengeance' or, alternatively, 'the thunderbolts of God's wrath'. His pulpit became a 'cockpit of contention' from which he excoriated his opponents, reserving his most apocalyptic invective for the deficiencies of the town's governors. Vicars is an extreme example, but in his sermons we can

---

[38] Jacobson, ed., *Works of Sanderson*, VI, pp. 291–93.
[39] Ibid., I, p. 118.
[40] Hill, *Tudor and Stuart Lincoln*, pp. 110–12; STAC 8 84/5.
[41] See E. Gillett, 'The Hearty Repentance of Francis Cartwright', *LH*, 2 no. 10 (1963), pp. 30–33 and the contemporary tracts cited there. For a similar, non-lethal assault, see STAC 8 192/6.
[42] SP 16/119/52; *Cases in the Courts of Star Chamber and High Commission*, ed. S. R. Gardiner, Camden Soc., n.s. 39, 1886, pp. 198–238; *CSPD 1623–25*, p. 426.

see the range of material covered by a minister with a high sense of his educational mission and none of Sanderson's discretion or concern for neighbourly values. Vicars not only preached the Calvinist theory of justification and a narrow morality from his pulpit; he also analysed the functions and duties of town governors, criticized the national religious establishment and commented on Charles's policies — bewailing England's lukewarm concern for the embattled Protestant cause on the continent; gloating over the assassination of the duke of Buckingham.

We have examined the roles of two profession cadres in the seventeenth century, with particular reference to their interactions with the peasant village. The lawyers' functions had always been subversive of traditional communal mechanisms for settling disputes. It was the growth of the profession and the increased opportunity and encouragement this provided for men to sue in the central courts which troubled clergymen, like Sanderson, who sought to sustain the old neighbourly values. Yet the clergy, too, were subversive of the closed, corporate communitarian ideal, in this case by virtue of the Protestant redefinition of the ministerial function. The parochial clergy were to be educators with the sermon as their prime pedagogical device. They were expected to instruct their parishioners in the values of the national religious culture. They might, like John Vicars, also employ their pulpits to reflect on national issues and policies.

CHAPTER 6

'BROKERS': THE GENTRY

WE have examined two professional groups which played intermedial, hinge roles in seventeenth-century Lincolnshire, transmitting the institutional services and ideological products of the national culture to the smallest units of local society. Changes in both groups in the course of the century — the sheer growth of the legal profession, the improved educational standards of the clergy — ensured that local awareness of the outside world would be enhanced. Paradoxically, the clergymen who damned lawyers for destroying traditional ideals of neighbourliness by encouraging recourse to external mechanisms for settling disputes were, in their employment of the pulpit as a vehicle for the dissemination of information or propaganda, equally corrosive of the old, indigenous values.

Can we examine the gentry in terms of a similar model, as an intermedial group of brokers? The gentry, as the patrons of ecclesiastical livings, dominated the appointment of the local clergy; the gentry were the trustees of schools. Most important, they functioned as the local administrative and judicial agents of the central government. Yet the applicability of the model to the gentry is open to question.

Strangely, given the pertinacious concern for matters of hierarchy and precedence displayed by the élite (a concern which impelled Sir Edward Hussey to expend 20s. to discover which Lincolnshire men had purchased baronetcies after him, and would thus rank beneath him[1]), gentility was an ambiguous and elastic concept in the seventeenth century. The coveted suffix 'gentleman' was accorded to and more frequently claimed by men who were, in other respects, indistinguishable from the better class of farmers, tradesmen or professionals. Even if we reserve the term for those whose wealth, background and life-style guaranteed them both

[1] *LNQ*, 4 (1896), p. 141; Bodleian Lib., MS Top. Lincs. c 3, ff. 5, 10, 11: see also LAO, MON 7/14/9.

uncontested recognition as gentlemen by their contemporaries, and a position in local government, we face a yet more formidable challenge posed by a number of local historians who have argued that any conception of the seventeenth-century gentry as a *national* class is an analytical abstraction devoid of social reality. The shire, it is suggested, was the pre-eminent sphere of activity for the gentry and it became the cynosure of their loyalties: when a gentleman spoke of 'my country' he meant Kent, or Sussex, or Cheshire — not England. The gentry were not engaged in the dissemination of national norms into the localities: their own political, social and cultural horizons were bounded by their county's boundaries, and they viewed national events through a haze of ignorance and mistrust. England, in this account, was a federation of counties, each headed by a tight-knit, introverted group of gentlemen who, acting in what they believed to be the best interests of their shires, filtered, circumvented or flatly disregarded the *fiats* of central government. Professor Alan Everitt, the progenitor of this view of seventeenth-century politics and social organization, coined the term for this dominant caucus of local gentlemen: the 'county community'.

I do not find this emphasis upon the gentry's insularity or their local corporatism wholly convincing. Yet a detailed articulation and critical analysis of the arguments Professor Everitt employs to sustain these conclusions will be a useful way to approach more general questions concerning the gentry of seventeenth-century Lincolnshire, questions of their social values and experience, of their role in local government, of their localism and their awareness of and involvement in national concerns.[2] Professor Everitt's argument for the insularity of the gentry is two-pronged. He examines, first, their social experience; then their involvement in the expanding agencies of local government, the development of which recognized, interacted with, and reinforced the pattern of social relationships.

THE SOCIAL MILIEU OF THE GENTRY

In his paradigmatic study of Kent, Professor Everitt argued that the gentry were *rooted* in their localities. Their income was exclusively derived from estates upon which their families had been settled for generations. He also suggested that the patterns of friendship and hospitality among the local gentry and their marriage alliances were

---

[2] For the historiographical point discussed here, see my article 'The "County Community" in Stuart Historiography', *J. British Studies*, 19 no. 2 (1980), pp. 54–73.

formed largely within the county. Antiquity of settlement, the local agrarian basis of their wealth, endogamous marriage and social relations: introversion was the consequence of this social experience. Let us examine the various elements in this calculation: first, lineage.

John Ferne of Temple Belwood on the Isle of Axholme, writing *The Blazon of Gentrie*, a work of unadulterated snobbery, at the end of the sixteenth century, insisted upon 'bloud', ancient lineage, as the *sine qua non* of gentle status. Our Lord's descent from Shem ensured that he was 'a gentleman of bloud . . . by the part of his mother . . . and might, if he had esteemed to the vayneglory of this worlde . . . have borne coat-armour. The apostles also . . . were gentlemen of bloud, many of them descended from that worthy conqueror Iudas Machabeus'. Blood was supposedly the essential prerequisite of 'the bright estate of noblenesse'; yet the ideal was seldom realized. Gervase Holles noted, after rehearsing with a nice balance of scholarly doubt and family piety the claim of his clan to medieval eminence, that the real 'foundation and groundworks for that greatness our family is now arrived att' should be attributed to a Tudor lord mayor of London.[3] Most Lincolnshire gentry families should have winced in uneasy recognition had they read this ingenuous confession: only seventeen per cent of them, as against three-quarters of their Kentish contemporaries, had been settled on their estates before 1500.[4]

Despite the emphasis upon family antiquity and continuity which is enshrined upon armigerous tombs and emblazoned in what Holles called 'forged, spurious and insignificant genealogies' (see plate XV), and which fired the incessant efforts of subtle lawyers to devise estate settlements that would protect family property from the most improvident heirs, the Lincolnshire gentry was in a state of continuous flux in the seventeenth, as in the previous, century. Families slipped from gentle status and their places were taken by newcomers. Some families disappeared through bad genetic luck. Sir Vincent Fulnetby's lineage is trumpeted in the twenty-three coats of arms that decorate his tomb in Rand church: his estate was divided among three daughters. Sir George St Paul of Snarford (see plate XII) could boast that he was

[3] John Ferne, *The Blazon of Gentrie*, London, 1586, pp. 3, 10–11, 97; Wood, ed., *Memorials of the Holles Family*, pp. 11–12.
[4] The figures for Kent are from A. Everitt, *The Community of Kent and the Great Rebellion*, Leicester, 1966, pp. 36, 328. Those for marriage alliances and antiquity of settlement in Lincolnshire are calculated from *Lincolnshire Pedigrees*, ed. A. R. Maddison, 4 vols, London, 1903–6.

'the ninth heire male by linealle discent that hath possessed this house and manor'; but *he* was childless and was reduced to devising the bulk of his estate to a Yorkshire man who though he possessed the same name was of the most distant relationship, if any, to his benefactor. Sir George was one of the fourteen members of the county's élite to purchase baronetcies from the crown before 1642. His title and those of five other families had become extinct by 1700; only two had passed in direct descent to their holders at the end of the century.[5] Other families fell into debt and were forced to sell up: that was the fate of the Dallisons of Laughton, the Skipwiths of Ormsby and the Tirwhitts of Kettleby, families that could boast of impeccable medieval antecedents in the shire.

New families filled the shoes of those that died out or decayed, moving into their estates and taking their local offices and positions in the hierarchy. Some were families of some antiquity but undistinguished until they rose to prominence, as did the Massingberds of Gunby and Ormsby, through marriage to heiresses, the profits of law and careful estate management. Some were newcomers, investing the profits of trade: Sir Edward Barkham, who had begun his mercantile career peddling hobby-horses in the streets of London and had risen to become lord mayor of that city, purchased an estate at Wainfleet. Other estates fell to those enriched by the practice of law: Richard Brownlow, who bought heavily in Kesteven in the early seventeenth century and who, in the opinion of the irascible and heavily indebted earl of Lincoln, was a 'villayne' who 'purchased land every day from under his nose and . . . would purchase Sempringham House if he were suffered', was chief prothonotary of the Court of Common Pleas and a distinguished law reporter. Some of the newcomers were officers of state: Sir Edmund Turnor acquired Stoke Rochford by marriage, but his posts as commissioner of the alienation office, surveyor general of the outports, and customs farmer produced the capital that bought his other substantial Lincolnshire estates.[6]

Even yeomen, the 'churle's brood' to whom Ferne denied 'all honor, dignitie, or preheminence amongst us', could, by the

[5] Lawrence Stone uses the phrase 'bad genetic luck' of the Manners family in *Family and Fortune*, Oxford, 1973, pp. 201–5: for St Paul, see T. Allen, *The history of the county of Lincoln*, II, London, 1834, p. 55; STAC 8 245/18.

[6] M. Prestwich, *Cranfield: Politics and Profits under the early Stuarts*, Oxford, 1966, pp. 394–400 (Dallison); W. O. Massingberd, *History of Ormsby*, Lincoln, 1893, pp. 104–87 (Skipwith and Massingberd); *LAOR*, 20, p. 15 (Tirwhitt); A. E. B. Owen, 'The Barkhams of Wainfleet and their estates', *LH*, 2 no. 8 (1961), pp. 1–9 (Barkham); STAC 8 257/27; Lincoln Public Library MS 504; LAO, 3 ANC 3/1/3/7 (Brownlow); *LAOR*, 12, pp. 45–46 (Turnor).

judicious investment of the profits of agriculture in land or usury, move into the county élite. William Trollope, yeoman of Bourne, began buying lands in the Spalding area in 1594: his son, who continued to make land purchases, was known successively as 'Thomas Trollope gent.', then 'esquire'; upon the purchase of a baronetcy in 1642 he became 'Sir Thomas Trollope of Casewick'. Richard Hickson staked the modest inheritance he received from his grandfather, a Londonthorpe yeoman, in money-lending and land speculation, until it became a considerable estate. With it came the office of high sheriff in 1622, and status: Richard Hickson, esquire.[7]

The purist Ferne had argued that mere riches could not create gentility: if so, 'then pyrats and theeves, bankers and brothels, with the lyke, shall challenge nobility'. Yet consideration of the rise of the Trollopes and the fall of the Skipwiths demonstrates a reality far different: wealth could purchase the attributes of gentle status and was essential for their maintenance. The claims of antiquity were put in their proper perspective by Sir George Heneage of Hainton: 'Gentility', he advised his son, 'being nothing but ancient riches, . . . if the foundations do sink, the buildings must needs consequently follow'.[8] Sir George's cool assessment provides an excellent prologue to a discussion of the wealth of the gentry.

It was not easy to be a gentleman on the cheap. Frescheville Holles, endowed with only a small income during the lifetime of his father, became heavily indebted 'that he might the better live according to his quality': Sir Charles Hussey claimed that he enclosed Honington so that his estate would be sufficient to maintain 'the port' of his 'place'. Both men, that is, sought to uphold a costly life-style. What was that life-style? Taste and fashions, of course, changed in the course of the seventeenth century, a point easily appreciated visually by comparing, say, Doddington Hall (1597–1600) with Belton House, built a century later, or the funeral monuments of Sir George St Paul at Snarford (1613) and the fifth earl of Exeter at Stamford (1703) (see plates XII and XIII). But some elements remained constant.

A stylish country house was desirable (see plate XIV), and buildings costs, as Gervase Holles noted ruefully of the renovations he undertook at Grimsby, could easily lead to a heavy burden of debt. The house should be a centre of hospitality: Frescheville

[7] M. Campbell, *The English Yeoman*, London, 1960, pp. 37–38. For Hickson and Trollope, see *LAOR*, 6, pp. 33–34; 9, p. 62.
[8] 'Sir George Heneage's estate book, 1625', ed. J. W. F. Hill, *LAAS*, 1 (1938–39), p. 73.

Holles would 'never set down to meales unless he had some of his friendes or neighbours with him'. Both Holles and the second earl of Lindsey, who felt 'in honour obliged' to keep 'a noble house', found that this too could represent a considerable expense. A gentleman should engage in the favourite leisure pastimes of the Lincolnshire gentry, hunting and horse-racing. It was incumbent upon a gentleman to dress in the mode: Gervase Holles's grand-fathers, Sir Gervase (d. 1627) and John Kingston (d. 1617) both revelled in 'costly apparell', and the 79-year-old Sir Gervase spent £30 on the embroidery of a satin suit.

So a gentleman had to support fine buildings and a hospitable household, 'field pleasures' and fashionable clothing. His estate also had to provide the wherewithal to finance an increasingly formal education for his heir, to make adequate provision for his younger sons, to provide dowries sufficient to guarantee good marriages for his daughters, to cover the charges of a funeral appropriate to his station. No wonder Sir Charles Hussey enclosed Honington.[9]

Hussey's action indicates the basic mode by which a seventeenth-century gentry family could sustain or increase its income: by the exploitation of its land-holdings. Yet there were other ways. We have seen the Carrs and the Hickmans aggressively insisting upon their manorial rights in order to increase their rake-off from the trade of Sleaford and Gainsborough. The earls of Rutland smelted iron ore found on the Yorkshire estates. Other gentlemen chose to invest surplus cash. Sir Thomas Grantham and Sir Anthony Irby were shareholders in the Virginia Company; Sir Ralph Maddison lent money and invested in coal mining. Sir Ralph was also an improving landlord and an acknowledged expert upon abstruse questions of international currency manipulation and the balance of trade: since the Maddisons had been seated at Fonaby since the fifteenth century his biography should give us pause before accept-ing any simple equation of antiquity of settlement with parochial attitudes.[10]

Both investment and the exploitation of non-agricultural assets brought gentlemen into contact with the wider world of com-merce. A few of the Lincolnshire gentry with a taste for gambling sought riches in an arena even further divorced from the locality: at

[9] Wood, ed., Memorials of the Holles Family, pp. 61, 125, 127, 201, 218, 223, 228; LAO, 2 ANC 8/54; STAC 8 17/24 — answer of Sir Charles Hussey.
[10] Stone, Family and Fortune, pp. 190–94; T. K. Rabb, Enterprise and Empire, Cambridge Mass., 1967, pp. 301, 321; E. Maddison, 'The making and unmaking of a Lincolnshire estate', AASR, 27 (1903–4), p. 353; STAC 8 83/13: for Gainsborough and Sleaford, see above, pp. 31–32.

the royal court. Whitehall was a lottery with a few spectacular prizes — fabulous opportunities for advancement and enrichment displayed *par excellence* in the meteoric rise of Edward Villiers, a poor Leicestershire squire, to the dukedom of Buckingham. More usually financial difficulties, even ruin — the product of the expenses that attended high living at court and the neglect of the domestic estate — mocked the courtier's hopes. Most of the Lincolnshire men who played court roulette were losers. Sir Roger Dallison, master of the Ordnance, subsidized his court-acquired extravagances by embezzling some £13,000 of the crown's revenue which passed through his hands; discovery spelled ruin and not even a series of shady business deals, legal chicanery and the crudest exploitation of his tenants could save his Laughton estates, valued at £1,500 p.a., from the clutches of his creditors. Sir Thomas Monson's family estates survived his involvement in the court, but he experienced heavy losses. In the early years of James's reign he had accumulated a series of offices — master of the Armoury of the Tower, steward of the Duchy of Lancaster, master falconer. The fall of his Howard patrons, his own tangential involvement in the Overbury scandal (for his part in which another Lincolnshire courtier, Sir Gervase Elwes of Worlaby, was executed) and an attempt by his nephew, William Monson, to emulate the career of Buckingham by supplanting the favourite in the king's affections — a process involving 'washing his face every day with posset-curd' — terminated his career. He lost his court posts and, until 1640, unsuccessfully petitioned the crown for a series of profitable grants 'in regard of my ancient service and in recompense of my many sufferings'. The experiences of the first earl of Lindsey and, later, Sir Robert Carr, duplicate Monson's: Lady Lindsey's note concerning her husband's trip to Newmarket with the court to attend the races may stand as a comment on his entire career as a courtier; 'it will cost his purse, and that he stands little need of'.[11]

However, the bulk of the Lincolnshire gentry derived their income, as did their Kentish counterparts, from the rents and products of their lands. Thus far we must agree with Professor Everitt. What of his argument that the gentry's localistic introversion was in part a function of their vital involvement in the management of their ancestral lands, a management informed by a

[11] For Dallison's fall, see Prestwich, *Cranfield*, pp. 218, 392–400; STAC 8 181/17; LAO, MON 10/1/22: for Monson, Prestwich, loc. cit.; L. Stone, *The Crisis of the Aristocracy*, Oxford, 1964, pp. 108–9: for Lindsey, LAO, 10 ANC 341/1; HMC *Montagu of Beaulieu*, p. 114: for Carr, LAO, ANDR 6, ff. 10–102.

sense that their holdings were a trust and by a concomitant paternalism towards their tenants?

During the first half of the sevententh century the inflation that had characterized the sixteenth century was maintained, and prices commanded by agricultural products continued to outpace the cost of other goods or the wages of labour. In the abstract, the landed gentry should have been able to tap the surplus, either by direct production for the market or as rentiers. Yet rising prices, changing market opportunities and developing agricultural technique called for unremitting and skilled management. Not surprisingly, it was a contemporary commonplace that if a gentleman failed to be involved in the operation of his estate he risked ruin. John Kingston of Grimsby spent heavily on his 'field pleasures', on his wardrobe, on his mistresses, in maintaining his feuds: but, in the opinion of his grandson, it was 'negligence . . . in managing his estate' which 'hurt more than all the rest'. This 'brought his estate into a deep consumption' and led to sales of land in which, through his ignorance, he was defrauded by a servant. Henry Ayscough of Blyborough was another 'inexperienced gentleman . . . that regarded more his pleasure than his profitt'. While he drank, wrestled and quarrelled with his neighbours, his estate became enmeshed in a web of debt and lawsuits. Anthony Meres, 'unskilful' and 'ignorant of his own estate', was tricked by his lawyer into leasing Scotton for eighty years for £100 p.a.: when the lease was made the estate was worth £430 p.a.; £630 when the lease terminated — itself an interesting comment on the problems of a fixed income in a period of price rise. [12]

Involvement in estate management was essential, but, increasingly in the seventeenth century, it might be vicarious. John Guevara, in a letter of advice to Robert, twelfth Lord Willoughby of Eresby (earl of Lindsey from 1627), argued that a landlord must 'understand' his estate, 'for more have been undonn by blindfold expence then by youthfull courses', yet he recognized that the lord's 'more noble occasions' might well prove more attractive than estate management. Besides, a peer should not be 'so serviley observant in things of that nature'. His proposed resolution of this quandary was the employment of a skilled staff under the direction of a lawyer acting as steward and solicitor and an accountant who would be the general receiver of rents: it was, however, incumbent upon Willoughby to act as his own auditor. The development of a

[12] Wood, ed., *Memorials of the Holles Family*, pp. 215, 217, 223 (Kingston); STAC 8 129/9 (Ayscough); LAO, MON 2/75/9; 10/1/22 (Meres).

class of experts in estate management was a seventeenth-century phenomenon. Lord Willoughby, following Guevara's advice, took full advantage of it. In 1609, 1615–17 and 1627 his estates were carefully surveyed. With a record of precise acreages and the terms of existing leases, comments on the quality of the soil and descriptions of the farmhouses, the earl or his agents could make the appropriate managerial decisions: which small outlying estates would be more profitable to sell; where suits should be commenced against those tenants who had concealed the lord's lands or wasted their tenements; where enclosure might be a remunerative pro-position; and, principally, where rents might be raised.[13] So professional estate managers and agents could play an important role in bridging the gap between the need for meticulous manage-ment and the sense that such assiduity was a demeaning bore, beneath the landowner's 'noble occasions'. Intelligent involvement in the management of the estate was essential to financial survival in the seventeenth century, but, increasingly among the wealthier gentry, skilled deputies performed the routines. The existence of this class of professional estate managers should also make us question the assertion that the gentry viewed landownership as a *trust*, and that they were continuously aware of their patriarchal responsibilities to their tenantry.

At one point in Ferne's *Blazon*, Columell, a rustic, interrupts the discussion with complaints of the oppression of his new landlord: 'many are . . . cleaped gentill', he protests, 'that deale full ungently with their tennants'. Although this rank insubordination is quickly squashed — 'what scandalous speech is this . . . from the mouth of a contemptible peasant' — Columell was expressing a common belief: that land ownership entailed social responsibilities. The ideal, in a Christian context, was embodied by Sir George St Paul: he was hospitable; he was charitable to the poor and to poor scholars and ministers; he loaned money without taking interest; he was merciful to his tenants – 'whoever knew him to take the forfeiture of any lease, or when fines or rents were unpaid at times agreed on, to use any extremity to get the same?' Yet behaviour the very reverse of this ideal, behaviour lashed by Sanderson as 'racking

---

[13] LAO, 2 ANC 14/7. The best account of estate management in the period is provided by Stone, *Crisis*, pp. 273–334. In his *Family and Fortune*, pp. 184–90, Stone examines the more antiquated managerial techniques favoured by the Manners family. For Willoughby's surveys, see 5 ANC 4/A/1, 7–9, 13, 14.

the backs and grinding the faces of the poor', was a more secure route to economic success.[14]

Sanderson denounced 'the unconscionable racking of rents'. Yet Lord Willoughby, with his new estate surveys before him, might be tempted to extract a full economic rent from his properties, particularly as the surveys revealed the degree to which the Berties' tenants had benefited from the generosity or ignorance of his predecessor. Friskney, valued at £55 p.a. had been rented for £15 p.a.; at Marshchapel an estate valued at £48 p.a. had been leased for a £50 fine and £6 16s. 5d. a year.[15] Sanderson excoriated those gentlemen engaged in 'overthrowing . . . tenures'. Yet destroying antiquated copyholds with their uneconomic fixed fines and rents, or breaking beneficial leases made by an improvident ancestor, as did Lord Willoughby of Parham at Bardney and replacing both by short term leases was sound managerial practice.[16] Sanderson's most vehement invective was reserved for those engaged in 'pulling down houses and setting up hedges . . . unpeopling towns and creating beggars'. Yet enclosure and engrossing, whether for pasture or to free arable husbandry from the dead hand of the open field regimen, was *profitable*. In 1611 Sir John Hatcher indignantly denied enclosing Careby for pasture and depopulating the village, but added wistfully that if he *had* done so his rents would have increased from £13 to £100 p.a.: Sir Daniel Deligne's rent roll doubled after the enclosure of Harlaxton in 1627; in 1698 the Carr estate at Hale was enclosed, and rents nearly trebled.[17] It is clear from the development of enclosure in the county in the first half of the seventeenth century that, despite legal prohibitions and the censures of moralists, many gentlemen succumbed to the temptations of profit. Sir Charles Hussey was one: finding that his Honington estate, with its poor soil, decayed buildings, feckless tenants, and low rents was 'scarce able to maintaine the port of this defendant's place and service in his countrey', he converted four hundred acres to sheep pasture and demolished eleven farmhouses.[18] Yet, although gentlemen increasingly viewed their estates in terms of market opportunities, and their relations with

---

[14] Ferne, *Blazon*, pp. 21–22; John Chadwick, *A sermon preached at Snarford . . . at the funerals of Sir George Sanct-Paule*, London, 1616, pp. 21–23: for Sanderson's social commentary, see Jacobson, ed., *Works of Sanderson*, II, pp. 191, 204, 314, 344, 352.
[15] LAO, 5 ANC 4/A/1, ff. 8–12, 52, 59–62v.
[16] STAC 8 308/13.
[17] Ibid., 10/4; LAO, PG 11/1/3; LAO, AND 6, ff. 2v, 7.
[18] STAC 8 17/24 — the answer of Sir Charles Hussey.

Figure 2 *Part of the map which accompanies the survey of the manor of Toynton, 1614. The surveyor, Henry Valentine, was employed by Robert, twelfth Lord Willoughby of Eresby, who conducted a series of detailed investigations into his estates in this period. (LAO, 5 ANC H/A/14, p.58A)*

their tenants in terms of the cash nexus, the old ideal of the landlord's social responsibility was not altogether abrogated by economic realities in the seventeenth century. It surfaces in some incongruous places. Edward Hussey, grandson of the man who had enclosed Honington, refused to be a party to a similar scheme at Caythorpe as he believed that enclosers had been pursued by the judgements of a wrathful providence. The Carr family were improving landlords with a vengeance. In 1608 they were prosecuted for converting over six hundred acres of arable and pulling down sixteen farmhouses in the Sleaford area. They had not scrupled to employ their 'great revenues, power and authoritie' to crush those who stood in the way of their projects. Yet in 1627 the Carr's bailiff, having suggested some moderate rent increases upon the tenants, did not think it incongruous to suggest to his master that 'it is hoped you will deale honourablie with them as all your ancestors heretofore have done and that you will be pleased to let them hould there farms so as they maie be able . . . to dischardge such duties to the church and king and countrey as shall hereafter bee imposed uppon them'. Thus the tenants 'wilbe alwaies readie at your call to do you service'. He also advised lowering some rents imposed by the lessee of a Carr property in Gosberton upon his subtenants, 'and so the tenants may not onelie be the better able to pay their rentes, but also they shall have cause to speake honourable of you for your kyndnesse towards them'. The ideal of the landlord's social responsibility did little to retard agricultural change in our period. But it did retain some force, serving to modulate landlord-tenant relations and preventing them from becoming exclusively dictated by the market.[19]

Professor Everitt, noting that two-thirds of the Kentish gentry married within the shire, argued that endogamy also enhanced introversion and localism. Sixty per cent of the Lincolnshire gentry married endogamously, but, amongst the élite, exogamy was more common: just over half the men named to the commission of the peace between 1602 and 1636 married outside Lincolnshire. And exogamous marriage might entail considerable social interaction and thus a broadening of horizons. It certainly did for the Pelhams of Brocklesby. The Pelham family, originally from Sussex, had settled in Lincolnshire in the sixteenth century. There they were often visited by their southern relatives, whose legal adviser was

---

[19] W. H. Hosford, 'An eye-witness account of a seventeenth-century enclosure', *EcHR*, 2nd ser. 4 (1951–52), p. 216 (Hussey); STAC 8 10/4; 17/4; 279/8; LAO, CRAGG 2/8 (Carr).

Henry Pelham, a Brocklesby cadet.[20] The latter's elder brother, Sir William, married a daughter of Lord Conway. It is not surprising, perhaps, to find Sir William Pelham engaging in a friendly correspondence with his father-in-law, the secretary of state: such court ties had obvious utility if one sought, as did Sir William, to secure the punishment of a particularly scandalous local cleric or to avoid the shrievalty.[21] More surprising are the close ties that developed, as a function of the Conway match, between the Lincolnshire family and the Herefordshire Harleys, for Lady Pelham and Lady Brilliana Harley were sisters. Social visits and a regular correspondence were maintained: Edward Harley, an undergraduate at Oxford, was enjoined by his mother to watch over his freshman Pelham cousin, to 'be. . . kinde to him'. The ties survived the death of Lady Pelham, and were more than purely social. Lady Brilliana recommended a favoured godly minister upon learning that a Lincolnshire living in Pelham's gift was vacant; she maintained a constant, and ultimately critical, concern for Sir William's political affiliations.[22]

So the horizons of Lincolnshire families could be broadened by exogamous marriage and the resultant ties of kinship. But, as has been shown in a meticulous analysis of the Sussex gentry, the bulk of the most intimate social relations, the patterns of friendship, were usually formed within a county.[23] The inner circle with whom a Lincolnshire gentleman hunted, dined or went horse-racing, the men who became trustees in his estate settlements and who were remembered in his will, were his neighbours. Yet the existence of a cohesive community formed by the gentry of a county cannot be distilled from the simple fact of the narrow geographical range of the patterns of friendship. Most of a man's friends lived in the same shire, certainly: so, too, did most of his enemies. The clash of economic interests, differences concerning the exercise of office, an imagined slight or calculated insult amongst men whose code insisted upon a touchy concern for personal and family honour ('coward and schoolboy', Richard Bolles sneered at John Ledgard: he died in the ensuing duel): all could provoke bitter feuds. The usual pattern followed by such feuds is neatly exemplified in Gervase Holles's account of a quarrel

[20] A. Fletcher, *A County Community in Peace and War: Sussex 1600–60*, London, 1975, p. 53.
[21] SP 14/162/58; 16/514/29.
[22] *The Letters of Lady Brilliana Harley*, ed. T. T. Lewis, Camden Soc., 58, 1854, pp. 9, 27, 30, 32, 59, 68, 81, 107, 130, 161.
[23] Fletcher, *County Community*, pp. 44–53.

between his father and Francis Guevara of Stenigot: first, the exchange of personal insults, stemming from Guevara's mockery of one of Holles's friends, then the exchange of blows; thereafter, in the arraying of family relations and friends by the principals to the quarrel, the division of the gentry into competing factions.[24] The Holles-Guevara feud ultimately involved most of the gentry in the Grimsby area, twice in the seventeenth century such feuds fissured the entire county. During the reign of Charles II Lincolnshire politics were dominated by the conflict between the earl of Lindsey and Sir Robert Carr; in the first decade of James I's reign few of the gentry were not involved in the prolonged dispute between Henry, earl of Lincoln, and Sir Edward Dymock.

Analysis of ties of marriage and friendship, of sources of income, of antiquity of settlement, among the Lincolnshire gentry suggests that they were less an introverted, clannish group than were their Kentish contemporaries as described by Professor Everitt. Two other elements in their social experience reinforce this impression: their education and the attraction of London to them.

The antiquary and historian, Gervase Holles, was educated at Grimsby grammar school, then in the household of his noble relative, the earl of Clare. This experience was atypical. The 'logicke and philosophy' which the earl personally taught Gervase was more usually inculcated, in the early seventeenth century, in the formal routines of the university, supplemented or replaced by a spell at the inns of court. In 1636 two-thirds of the county magistracy had attended a university, or one of the inns, or both. After 1660, while the inns fell from favour, the grand tour of Europe, an experience previously reserved for the scions of the aristocracy, was increasingly being undertaken by the heirs of affluent gentry families. In 1676 Pury Cust was appreciating the Titians at Turin ('all incomparably well done') while his father impatiently totted up the bills at Stamford.[25]

The significance of the gentry's educational experience is debatable, however. Certainly we should not imagine that a stint at Cambridge or Gray's Inn automatically transmuted the country gentleman into a philosopher or constitutional lawyer. Justice Shallow's fictional career at the inns of court was paralleled in reality by that of William Welby of Gedney who, as a student at

[24] *LNQ*, 2 (1891), pp. 57–59, 82; Wood, ed., *Memorials of the Holles Family*, pp. 196–97.
[25] Ibid., pp. 227–28; E. Cust, *Records of the Cust Family . . . 1479–1700*, London, 1898, pp. 226–27, 339–53. The 1636 figure is calculated from the 1636 commission of the peace, SP 16/405, ff. 37v–41v.

Gray's Inn, was prosecuted in the Star Chamber for an assault upon a Lambeth brothel with a gang of drunken rowdies. Yet a common educational experience, besides bringing men into contact with their peers from other regions — none of Welby's fellow hell-raisers was from Lincolnshire — did produce a common language of intellectual discourse and, thus, a common gentry culture. The Lincolnshire gentry were perfectly capable of appreciating the arguments of divines, philosophers and lawyers who wrote for a national audience. In 1631, having read the manuscript two or three times, Thomas Hatcher of Careby forwarded his comments on *The Monarchy of Man* to its author, Sir John Eliot. The treatise, on moral and political philosophy, marshals serried ranks of authorities: classical poets, philosophers, rhetoricians, and historians; the church fathers; commentators on the civil law; modern political theorists and casuists like Bodin, Cardano and Ames. Yet Hatcher, who, while the bulk of his political experience had been as a local administrator, had been educated at Emmanuel College and Lincoln's Inn, revelled in Eliot's dense and learned work: he lauded 'the excellency of the matter; the exquisitenesse and beauty of the forme, the contrivall and disposition of each part, the elegancy of the phrase and expression, and the riches and majesty of the whole'.[26]

Debate about the influence of a formal education upon the gentry's attitudes is founded upon analysis of the fluctuating pattern of enrolments at the universities or the inns. Discussion of the influence of London lacks even this basic statistical ground. The evidence suggests that the local gentry increasingly resorted to London in the course of the seventeenth century but does not enable us to determine how general the process had become. Professor Everitt has argued both that a journey to London was still exceptional for the gentry, and that the majority of those who visited the capital did so in circumstances — the pursuit of 'some wearisome lawsuit' — hardly likely to endear the place to them.[27] Yet a visit to London could be a broadening experience. During the last fifteen years of the seventeenth century, when it would seem that most of the wealthier Lincolnshire gentry were in regular communication with London, William Massingberd of Gunby failed to visit the metropolis only in 1691. On average he spent nine weeks each year in the city; fighting his lawsuits, certainly, but also

---

[26] *Les Reportes del Cases in Camera Stellata*, ed. W. P. Baildon, London, 1894, pp. 315–16; *The Monarchie of Man, by Sir John Eliot*, I, ed. A. B. Grosart, London, 1879, p. 114; II, passim.
[27] Everitt, *Community of Kent*, p. 44.

seeing the sights, shopping for luxury items, and drinking and gambling in taverns and coffee houses. Those who could not visit the city were kept informed of events in London by their legal agents, factors or relatives.[28]

I have argued that aspects of the social experience of the major gentry families, far from breeding introversion, involved them in relationships and attitudes which were not enclosed by their county boundaries. Exogamous marriage, their common educational experience, the lure of London, their exploitation of their estates with an eye to the market, all ensured that their horizons were not narrowly local. What of the second element in the local élite's experience which, it has been suggested,[29] was a foundation of the county community sentiment? Did the gentry's participation in local government in a period marked by 'the growth of county administration, the development of county institutions', reinforce their local particularism?

THE GENTRY AND LOCAL GOVERNMENT

The increasing burden upon local magistrates was a theme of many contemporary commentators. In addition to their traditional police functions — supervising investigations, handling preliminary hearings, and trying those accused of misdemeanours and minor felonies at quarter sessions — the justices were responsible for a host of administrative duties, the product, for the most part, of Tudor social legislation. They regulated wage rates, conditions of apprenticeship and master-servant relations; they controlled alehouses; they were responsible for the condition of roads and bridges. The administration of the poor law, particularly settlement cases, probably represented the heaviest commitment of time.

Increasing responsibilities partly explain the growing numbers of gentlemen commissioned as justices of the peace. But the expansion of the commission also reflected gentry demand: as Robert Sanderson noted, men coveted office because they were 'ambitious of honour and reputation'.[30] The exercise of local office joined ancient lineage, wealth and 'port' as a confirmation of the status of a gentleman.

Not that all magistracy was honourable. Frescheville Holles's acceptance of a post as alderman of Grimsby infuriated his father, Sir Gervase, 'because the most of them were mean and mechanicke

[28] LAO, MG 5/2/9, ff. 58–94; LAO, MON 7/14/123–26, 131–32, 136, 138–39.
[29] A. Everitt, *The Local Community and the Great Rebellion*, London, 1969, p. 6.
[30] Jacobson, ed., *Works of Sanderson*, II, pp. 290–91.

fellowes'.[31] Nor were all honourable offices enthusiastically pursued. The shrievalty was considered 'troublesome': the sheriff was unable to leave the county during his year of office and was obliged to employ and supervise a staff who performed, often corruptly, the basic legal and administrative routines of the office, and for whose deficiencies he was unaswerable. The post also involved 'much charge'. The fees of the exchequer officials who audited the sheriff's account were heavy; so were the costs of entertaining the judges of assize on their half-yearly visits to Lincoln — at least until 1676, when these spiralling expenses, as each sheriff sought to outdo his predecessor in lavish ostentation, led the Lincolnshire gentry to conclude an agreement limiting the sheriff's outlay. The office was so unpopular that those who learned that there was a prospect of their selection rushed to mobilize any court influence they might possess to avoid being chosen.[32] Only between 1681 and 1684 is there any evidence that the position was sought after. Then, in the aftermath of the Exclusion Crisis, the earl of Lindsey nominated 'a Church of England sheriff' who could be guaranteed to empanel a grand jury eager to subscribe loyal addresses to the king, and petty juries which, in cases commenced by informers against nonconformists, 'may not be influenced to the advantage of the contrary party'.[33]

The scramble to avoid the shrievalty was reversed in the case of the other major magisterial positions. The plum was a deputy lieutenancy, a post held by a very select group of the county élite: formally responsible for the organization of the militia, their general primacy in the county establishment was officially recognized by such acts as Charles I's instructing them to audit the accounts of the corrupt sheriff, Sir Walter Norton, in 1636. The commission of the peace was a more accessible goal: the commissions usually contained the names of about one hundred local gentlemen. Appointment was actively solicited and failure to attain the desired prize was a matter for bitter recrimination.[34] As honour accrued to such offices, so dismissal from them was a signal

---

[31] Wood, ed., *Memorials of the Holles Family*, p. 197.
[32] For a description of the sheriff's functions, see Peyton, ed., *Minutes of Quarter Sessions for Kesteven*, pp. xv–xxi: for attacks on the sheriff's staff, and his supervisory role, see STAC 8 140/18; E 134 24 Charles I Easter 6: for attempts to avoid the office, and complaints about its cost and inconvenience, see *CSPD 1635–36*, pp. 189, 192, 241, 304; *1675–76*, p. 361; SP 29/386/215; E. Cust, *Records of the Cust Family . . . the Brownlows of Belton*, London, 1909, p. 65.
[33] *CSPD 1680–81*, pp. 376, 529–30, 581; *1682*, pp. 137–38, 514; *1683–84*, p. 82.
[34] HMC *Cecil*, XIX, p. 152; SP 29/386/215.

I and *II Farmhouses of substantial yeomen:* above, *Kirkby Laythorpe;* below, *The Old Grange, Revesby.*

III Noble patronage: the great mace and punchbowl of the corporation of Stamford. The mace was
presented in 1678 by Charles Bertie after his election as M.P. for Stamford, which broke the
Cecil family's stranglehold on the representation of the borough. He presented the punchbowl in
1685 on his re-election. Its Latin inscription is a clear statement of an aristocratic patron's
perception of his relationship with the client borough. 'Charles Bertie, brother of Robert, son of
Montagu, grandson of Robert, earls of Lindsey and hereditary great chamberlains of England,
who was twice, in 1678 and 1685, the representative of this borough of Stamford in parliament
. . . gives and appoints this cup freely and with good will to the . . . now mayor and to his
successors for ever, in which the citizens of Stamford may celebrate first their fidelity towards the
most serene kings of Great Britain, then their friendship to the house of Bertie.'

IV and *V* *Market towns:* above, *late seventeenth-century inn signs from Sleaford;* below, *from the same period, the butter cross at Burwell.*

VI and VII Early seventeenth-century pulpits with testers to improve the acoustics: left, Boston (1612); right, Croft (1615 — the benches are from the same period). Both were occupied by eminent 'preachers of God's word' — John Cotton at Boston; William Worship at Croft.

IX Robert Bertie (1582–1642), twelfth Lord Willoughby of Eresby, created first earl of Lindsey in 1626. Lord lieutenant of Lincolnshire from 1629, and the chief participant in the Lindsey Level drainage scheme. General of the king's forces in 1642, killed at Edgehill.

VIII Robert Sanderson (1587–1663): the great Anglican preacher and casuist was rector of Boothby Pagnell (1619–46) and bishop of Lincoln (1660–63).

X Great Humby chapel (photographed in 1980 during restoration by the Lincolnshire Old Churches Trust). The only surviving Anglican place of worship built in the seventeenth century, it was erected by Sir William Brownlow in 1682 adjacent to his mansion.

XI Dissent. The interior of the Friends' Meeting House at Brant Broughton: the building and furnishings date from c.1701.

XII and XIII Changing taste in funerary monuments. Above, the tomb of Sir George St Paul (1613) at Snarford church: below, the tomb of John, fifth earl of Exeter (1703) in the church of St Martin, Stamford.

H. S. E.

JOHANNES CECIL, Baro de Burghley, Exoniæ Comes Magni Burleij Abnepos haudquaquam degener. Egregi indolem optimis Moribus optimix Artibus excoluit. Humanioribus literis bene instructus peregre pius vice Si profectus est et ab excultis Europæ regionibus multam Antiquitatum Linguarum: nec non et rerum scientiam reportavit Cui Nemo forte melius vel Aulam ornare vel curare Res Publicas potuit

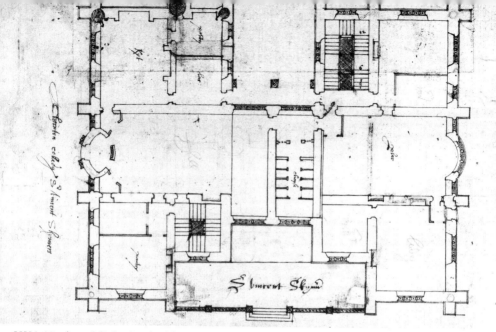

XIV 'Such as delighted to build, undid themselves without the help of any enemy'. John Thorpe's plan of Sir Vincent Skinner's house at Thornton Abbey (c.1610), which collapsed and had to be rebuilt. Skinner died in a debtor's prison in 1616. (See Walpole Society, 40 (1966), pp 65–66)

XV 'Gentlemen of bloud'. From the family lineage compiled by Sir George Heneage of Hainton in 1622. Each of Sir George's ancestors, back to 1100, is provided with an heraldic achievement and a short encomium. (LAO, HEN 14/2)

William Heneage of Haynton Esquire third some of John Heneage of Towes Esquire, after the death of his elder brother Sr George that had no issue, and John that had no issue maste, succeeded at Haynton, where he lived in great estimation, both for his hospitallitie, for which he is worthily celebrated, and his good gouerment in that County, continewing a Comissioner and Justice of the peace and quorum 50 yeares togeather, being twice high Sheriffe of that Shire, and many waies employed in publique seruices for the gouerment of that Country, and benefit of the comon wealth. All which nothing at all impaired, or declyned his estate, for he added vnto the inheritance his disgrace. William Blythe of Stroxton attended the midsummer sessions at Bourne in 1660 only to learn that he might not participate with his fellow justices as his name had been omitted from the commission of the peace, probably through the efforts of a rival who had bribed the chancery clerks. ' 'Tis not the employment I value in the least', he informed John Newton, M.P., but the public affront of attending the sessions and there being denied his place on the bench: he begged Newton to get him back into the commission 'for I am asshamed to appeare any where with such a disgrace on me'.[35]

The honour that attended the office and the disgrace associated with exclusion gave the government a measure of control over the conduct of the justices. The incompetent or corrupt risked dismissal.[36] This could also be used to punish those who opposed government policies. In 1635 Sir John Wray and Thomas Ogle, reported by the sheriff for refusing to pay ship money, were struck from the commission of the peace. Between 1680 and 1685 Charles II and his brother purged the commission even more drastically, with unhappy consequences at least in Holland where the sessions were not held in the latter half of 1680 because a number of 'active and useful' magistrates had been dismissed.[37]

Magistracy was honourable. For some gentlemen it was more: it was a religious duty. One such man was the zealous Puritan Sir George St Paul, the 'bell-wether in the flocke' of the Lincolnshire commission: he never refused any public service, 'any paines or endeavours, though to the spending of his estate . . . to the wearying of his body and the empayringe of his health'.[38] The belief that magistracy was a Christian duty incumbent upon the gentry was expressed by divines of all theological persuasions. It is a theme of Robert Sanderson's series of assize sermons. A gentleman could not, because of 'birth, or breeding, or estate' suppose that 'labour in any vocation' was beneath his dignity. Public office was his proper 'calling', that 'settled course of life, wherein mainly to employ a man's gifts and his time for his own and the common good'. And the administration of justice should be his 'greatest glory and delight'. Yet, despite the rhetoric of the preachers and the

---

[35] LAO, MON 7/12/3.
[36] See the case of John Hobson, SP 18/101/82; 124/81; 128/67; *CSPD 1655–56*, p. 194.
[37] For Wray and Ogle's dismissal, see SP 16/315/121; C 193/13/2: for the 1680s, see S.N., *A catalogue of the names of all His Majesties Justices of the Peace*, London, 1680, pp. 10–11, 30; PC 2/71, p. 369; SP 29/415/15.
[38] Chadwick, *Sermon*, pp. 19–20, 31.

G

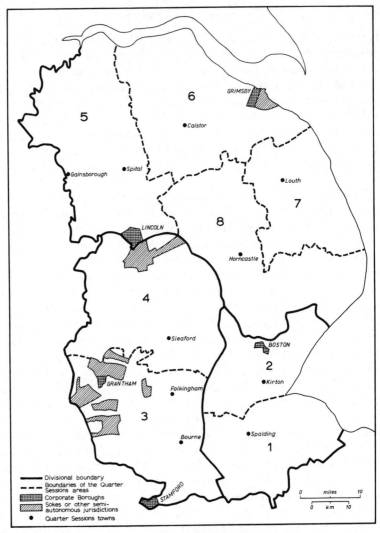

Figure 3   *Administrative divisions*

1. HOLLAND: hundred or wapentake of Elloe; 2. HOLLAND:
hundreds of Skirbeck and Kirton; 3. KESTEVEN: hundreds of Ness,
Aveland, Beltisloe, Winnibriggs and Threo; 4. KESTEVEN: hundreds
of Aswardhurn, Flaxwell, Langoe, Loveden, Boothby Graffoe; 5.
LINDSEY: hundreds of Lawress, Well, Aslacoe, Corringham, Manley;
6. LINDSEY: hundreds of Yarborough, Walshcroft, Bradley Haverstoe;
7. LINDSEY: hundreds of Louthesk, Hill, Calceworth; 8. LINDSEY:
hundreds of Wraggoe, Gartree, Candleshoe: sokes of Horncastle,
Bolingbroke

Lincolnshire was also divided for the purposes of ecclesiastical administration. The area marked 5 formed the archdeaconry of Stow; the
remainder of the county formed the archdeaconry of Lincoln

example of men like Sir George St Paul, some men were less concerned with the exercise of their authority than with the empty title of magistracy. Sanderson rebuked those who sought to get themselves 'put into the place of magistracy . . . having neither head nor heart for it', but merely 'ambitious of the honour and reputation'. In 1623 he presented a bleak picture of the diligence of the justices:

peradvanture here and there one or two in a whole side of a country can be found, that makes a conscience of their duty more than the rest, and are forward to do the best good they can . . . But what cometh of it? The rest, glad of their forwardness . . . leave all the burden upon them, . . . making common packhorses of them.[39]

Analysis of the Kesteven quarter sessions for 1680–85 gives force to Sanderson's jeremiad. Thirty-six residents were in the commission of the peace throughout these years: nineteen were totally inactive as magistrates while only five attended more than half of the sessions and these men were also, to judge by recognizances, most vigorous in out-of-session activity. The 'packhorses' were Christopher Beresford, who was present at seventeen of the twenty Sleaford sessional meetings, and Lister Tigh, the backbone of the Bourne/Folkingham division with a score of twenty out of twenty-three attendances. A similar core of assiduous gentlemen dominated proceedings at Horncastle sessions 1665–73, and the activities of the Lindsey coast commissioners of sewers in the decade before the civil war.[40]

That many of the Lincolnshire gentry were more diligent in their pursuit of office than in its exercise must qualify any sense of 'the development of county institutions' in the seventeenth century. So, too, must the administrative fragmentation of the shire (see figure 3). Quarter sessions were not a county event — certainly not a kind of local parliament. A separate commission of the peace was issued, with only a limited overlap of personnel, for the three ancient divisions of the county. Decentralization was enhanced by the further subdivision of Lindsey into four administrative districts, and Holland and Kesteven each into two: every one of these eight areas had its own series of quarter sessions, served, if the experience

---

[39] Jacobson, ed., *Works of Sanderson*, II, pp. 173–74, 176, 180, 197, 203, 256–57, 260, 274, 315–16; III, pp. 95–108.
[40] For attendances at Kesteven 1680–85, I have compared the relevant commissions of the peace (S.N., *Justices of the Peace*, pp. 10–11; C 193/12/4, 5) with the quarter sessions minute book (Peyton, ed., *Minutes of Quarter Sessions for Kesteven*, pp. 107–257): LAO, LQS Minute Book 1665–73; LAO, Alford Sewers 1630–40.

of Kesteven 1680–85 is typical, by a distinct cadre of justices.[41] So most of the Lincolnshire gentry's administrative experience was forged in units smaller than the county, and it may be argued that their loyalties focused upon these sub-divisions as much as upon the county itself. Justices frequently challenged their colleagues on the county bench over demands, chiefly the apportionment of taxation, which were thought to be inequitable or otherwise contrary to the interests of their immediate locality. And they might refer to the latter as their 'country': in 1638 Sir Edward Hussey of Honington was praised by a colleague for his concern for 'the good of . . . the country'; but the country in this case was Kesteven, unfairly rated by a Holland sheriff.[42]

Some gatherings were attended by the magistracy of the entire county, but these were both comparatively infrequent and Janus-faced. The assizes, general meetings for the execution of special royal commissions, county elections: each affirmed the corporate identity of the county élite, and yet at each the gentry were reminded of their involvement in a national polity, with a centralized system of government and law.

The half-yearly assizes were an important social occasion, and general attendance ensured both that local matters of common concern to the gentry would be discussed and that those who wished to affront or asperse their rivals could do so with maximum publicity: it was at the assizes, 'in the face of the countrie', that Sir Walter Norton 'did . . . scandalouslie traduce' the earl of Lindsey 'endeavouring thereby to drawe him into disesteeme with . . . the gentlemen and others of the . . . county'. Moreover, in the 1620s in some counties the magistrates sought to realize Bacon's ideal, that the assizes should be a place where 'the distastes and griefs of the people' could be represented to the government, by developing formal mechanisms — petitions from the bench or grand jury presentments — to bring the latter to the judges' attention. Lincolnshire seems to have been slow to employ these mechanisms; not until 1682 did a tory grand jury (carefully packed by the earl of Lindsey's tame sheriff), declare itself to be 'the representative body' of the county and then express its abhorrence of the whig association. Thus the assizes provided the fullest expression of the corporate existence of the county community and a forum where its collective concerns could be articulated: it is in these respects that

[41] Peyton, ed., *Minutes of Quarter Sessions for Kesteven*, pp. xxxv, lxix–lxx.
[42] SP 16/380/60.

Professor Everitt argues that the assizes 'resemble a kind of informal county "parliament"'.[43]

The assizes *were* an important county gathering, but they also emphasized the local magistracy's responsibility to and dependence upon a national system of government and law. Some of the aura of royal majesty inhered in the assize judges; it was symbolically represented by the ceremonial panoply of their visitations and the respect upon which they insisted so pertinaciously. It was not only Quakers seeking to 'flourish before the country' who felt their ire, but members of the magistracy: in 1695 Sir John Bolles, though a justice of long standing and member of parliament for Lincoln city, was fined £100 and ejected from the assize court when he had the temerity both to challenge a ruling by the judges and to inform them that 'he knew the laws as well as they'.[44]

The judges' prestige was a function, in part, of their reputation as the oracles of the law; as such they played a vital role in articulating the local magistracy into a national system of government. The judges' legal expertise provided a vital resource and valued instruction to the justices. Technicalities beyond the capacities of the local bench might be resolved by the judges in answer to a question propounded formally by the county magistrates or informally by an individual justice, or in their decision in a specific case. If a case or inquiry raised legal issues of any magnitude the judges could debate it with their colleagues at Westminster and then issue a general ruling which would be promulgated at the assizes. So in 1633, when Sir Anthony Irby challenged the rate demanded from him by Boston's overseers of the poor, on the grounds that it improperly took into account his property held in other parishes and his revenues from rents, the judges overthrew the contentious assessment: 'this hath been so resolved by all the judges of England, upon a reference made to them, and upon conferency by them had together'.[45]

The system whereby the local magistracy was controlled and informed by professional jurists did ensure, to quote Professor Barnes, 'that the expanse of the common law . . . would remain

---

[43] H of LMP (Parchment box) 4 March 1640/1 — petition of the earl of Lindsey; STAC 8 168/31; *London Gazette*, no. 1706: Everitt, *Community of Kent*, p. 95 n. 2.
[44] John Whitehead, *The Written Gospel-Labours*, London, 1704, p. 278; Hill, *Tudor and Stuart Lincoln*, p. 173.
[45] *The English Reports*, London, 1907, 80 (2 Bulstrode), pp. 354–55: other Lincolnshire examples are LAO, LQS File 1634, no. 167; Peyton, ed., *Minutes of Quarter Sessions for Kesteven*, p. 338. In general, see J. S. Cockburn, *A history of the English Assizes, 1558–1714*, Cambridge, 1972, pp. 168–72.

common'. It is worth insisting upon this. The institutional arrangements of local administration varied from shire to shire; conventions and customs to meet local needs might develop with respect to matters where the relevant legislation gave the justices discretionary powers. But in fundamentals the English counties were governed by a common law. Failure to observe the substantive or procedural rules of the latter could involve a heavy fine upon the delinquent justice or, as the Caistor bench discovered in 1662, a public rebuke from the judges.[46]

The other element in the status and respect accorded the judges by the local gentry was a product of their intimate contacts with the central administration. Reports of local administrative inefficiency or corruption could be made to them and subsequent investigation would be attended with all the publicity of the assizes. They were the overseers of the various government programmes for the more efficient execution of criminal justice and of administrative law, notably the Book of Orders.[47] In their formal charges the judges apprised the local gentry not only of the current administrative and law enforcement goals of the government, but of its political and religious policy priorities. In 1627 chief justice Richardson blasted those Lincolnshire ministers who, in their prayers, had criticized 'his majestie's religious and most just proceedings', while in 1635 and again two years later the judges were instructed to dilate upon the legality of ship money. The judges' comments on individual cases could perform a similar propagandist function: in 1683 Judge Gregory prefaced his sentencing of the Lincolnshire Quaker leaders with a defence of the necessity of oath-taking as the cement of a civilized society.[48] If an assize judge publicly opposed central policy, as did Windham at Lincoln in 1658 when he argued that ministers might not exclude their tithe-paying parishioners from the communion service, it sent shock waves through the locality and the central government.[49]

The assizes, then, were a county-wide forum, but a forum in which the local élite were reminded of their involvement in a national polity. There they were educated in the common law, received administrative direction and were informed of the government's religious and political priorities — priorities which, as

[46] Somerset Assize Orders, 1629–40, ed. T. G. Barnes, Frome, 1959, p. xxvii; Whitehead, Gospel-Labours, pp. 112–17, 121.
[47] STAC 8 217/4; 279/27; PC 2/48, p. 28.
[48] SP 16/85/99; John Rushworth, Historical Collections, II, London, 1680, pp. 294–98, 352–56; Whitehead, Gospel-Labours, p. 283.
[49] CSPD 1658–59, pp. 194–95.

during the levy of ship money, might directly raise national constitutional issues. We could analyse the other, irregular, county-wide meetings of the gentry — to execute special royal commissions, to elect knights of the shire to parliament — in the same way. Amphibious occasions, affirming the county's corporate existence, yet forcing the élite to contemplate national concerns.

We have argued that the Lincolnshire gentry were not as deeply rooted in their county as were their Kentish counterparts. The manner in which their class was recruited, the frequency of exogamous marriage among them, their involvement in market production; all necessarily eroded local isolation. Perhaps more indicative of the influence of national cultural norms and values upon the Lincolnshire gentry is their movement into the universities and the inns of court, and the attraction which London exercised upon them. And their role in local government, which introduced them to the administrative hierarchy and to the common law, enhanced their awareness of national identity. The gentry, then, like the lawyers or the clergy, were brokers, channelling the products and the commands of the national system into the localities and representing the latter to the central authorities.

This is not to suggest that the Lincolnshire gentry were merely functionaries, tame hacks of the government. Of course they would interpret, or avoid, or resist the latter's instructions. But I would argue that they did not do so by evoking the ideal of the county community or by a narrow assertion of local autonomy in the face of central interference. However much their opposition might be inspired by their class interests or by a shrewd assessment of the viability of the policies which the government required them to administer in the localities, it was expressed in terms of national legal and political priorities and proprieties. The narrative sections which follow should demonstrate this contention.

PART II:
NARRATIVE

CHAPTER 7

LINCOLNSHIRE AND WESTMINSTER, 1603–28

O N 22 April 1603 Sir William Pelham, the high sheriff of Lincolnshire 'being gallantly appointed with both horse and men', and accompanied by 'divers worshipfull men of the same countrey', greeted King James at the county boundary on the Newark road and convoyed him to Belvoir Castle. Next morning, in an incongruous assembly-line procedure, the king knighted forty-eight men, half from Lincolnshire, before breakfast, and then rode on towards Burghley House, hunting across the heath as he went. He entered Stamford in great state, 'having the sword borne before him, the people joyfull on all parts to see him'. Going out of the town southwards he was met at the Welland bridge by the high sheriff of Northamptonshire and a deputation of the leading gentlemen of that county. And so King James's solemn progress from Scotland to the capital of his new kingdom continued.[1]

The Lincolnshire gentry, some basking in the warm glow of enhanced status, must have felt a certain relief that the transition from the house of Tudor to that of Stuart had been accomplished so painlessly. Fears that the great queen's death would spark a bitter succession dispute, insurrection, foreign invasion, had proved groundless. Only a few fenmen, voicing the ancient popular belief that 'there was noe lawe' until the new monarch's coronation, had rioted in early April against the drainage works at Deeping.[2] Otherwise all was tranquil. But did any of those 'worshipfull men of the . . . countrey', as they dispersed from Stamford, speculate about the character and quality of the government that the new, foreign king's reign would represent in Lincolnshire? Would the

---

[1] *The progresses, processions and magnificent festivities of King James I*, I, ed. J. Nichols, London, 1828, p. 88.
[2] STAC 8 7/3.

régime provide vigorous leadership for the local governors, or would the latter be left to their own devices?

The king's initial actions with respect to religious policy argued that the new government was determined to exercise firm control in the localities.

JAMES AND THE PURITANS

In the last decade of Elizabeth's reign the Puritans, under fierce pressure from the establishment, had abandoned their efforts to establish, *sub rosa*, a Presbyterian system in the localities and to persuade parliament to legislate a reorganization of the church. Yet many ministers remained dissatisfied with the Anglican liturgy and ritual and the accession of a king from Presbyterian Scotland aroused their hopes for a further reformation of the church. In the millenary petition, presented to James soon after his arrival in London, the ministers expressed their concerns over clerical incompetence, pluralism and ecclesiastical courts, and their objections to wearing the surplice and to certain 'popish' rituals retained by the church. They requested a hearing on these issues, and, in response, James summoned a conference attended by the bishops and Puritan spokesmen which met at Hampton Court in January 1604. The Puritans' hopes were dashed: some very minor concessions were made but the ceremonies and vestments to which they had objected were retained, and the king insisted on absolute conformity. On 16 July 1604 James issued a proclamation warning the refractory clergy that they had until 30 November to conform or risk the consequences.

The bishop of Lincoln, William Chaderton, prepared to execute the royal policy. In the summer of 1604 his agents conducted a visitation in which the diocese was subjected to a scrutiny of unparalleled intensity. In Lincolnshire sixty-one ministers were reported for their failure to wear the surplice or their omission of ceremonies enjoined by the Book of Common Prayer, and proceedings were begun against them: the Church, declared Chaderton, 'might well be without them'. Yet the bishop, 'old and weak', was reluctant to use the ultimate sanction, deprivation, against nonconformists. This 'fearfulness' angered James and Chaderton received firm instructions to proceed to displace the recalcitrant from their livings; in response, he agreed that 'it is full time some strict course be used against them'.

The hard line upon which the government insisted provoked a powerful negative reaction in the county. The vicar of Boston, when offered a surplice 'in scorne thereof. . . maketh it his cushion to sitt on'; Cooke of Louth counterattacked with a sermon denouncing 'the lawes and ceremonies of the church'; Richard Bernard, vicar of Worksop, a divine whose influence was considerable in west Lindsey, preached in a number of different parishes, taking Daniel 3: 16–18 for his text — 'O king, we will not serve thy gods, nor worship the golden image which thou hast set up'. Protests were not merely individual. In December Puritan ministers in the diocese presented a book to the king in which they not only attacked all ceremonies lacking scriptural warrant as unlawful, but argued for a strict limitation of the royal prerogative in ecclesiastical matters: the king 'may not appoint to the Church what rites and orders he thinks good', for 'absolute authority in matters ecclesiastical' appertains to 'the Lord alone'. In January the Lincolnshire gentry were reported to be organizing a petition to the king on behalf of the nonconforming ministers.

In the winter of 1604–5 the battle lines were straightly drawn. Yet ultimately only two Lincolnshire ministers, Cooke of Louth and Pike of Donington, were deprived and the latter was readmitted to his living upon submission. Many of the nonconformists reported in the course of the summer visitation conceded swiftly when proceedings were begun against them, fearful of the loss of their livelihoods or considering that the performance of their callings as ministers of the word was too important to sacrifice on the issue of ceremonies. Even the zealous Richard Bernard, whose oft-repeated sermon had dwelt upon Nebuchadnezzar's fiery furnace, conformed upon consideration of 2 Kings 5: 18 — Elisha's allowance of Naaman's worship in the house of Rimmon. Not only did the Puritans back off from the confrontation that had threatened in the winter of 1604–5, so too did Chaderton. In January at the urging of the government the bishop proceeded to deprive three ministers in his diocese; in the following year a further five incumbents lost their livings. All were not merely contumacious but had expressed vocally their opposition to the ceremonies. But in many more cases, by virtue of what the king thought of as Chaderton's 'fearfulness' — his reluctance to deprive 'men of great learning, pains and fruit', his concern for their wives and children, and his desire to win converts 'by conference and brotherly exhortation, with mildness and discretion' — the nonconformists escaped censure. Proceedings against some were dropped upon receipt of a bare certificate from their parishioners of their conformity and others were given endless opportunities for 'further deliberation'; at least five eminent Lincolnshire Puritans were dismissed without any final guarantee of their conformity. Chaderton was moved by consideration of their 'labours for God's Church and its dignity' and their 'peaceable and honest behaviour'; also, perhaps, by representations from their lay patrons, influential country gentlemen like Sir William Wray, Sir John Hatcher and Sir William Rigdon.[3]

In the months following the proclamation of 16 July 1604 it became apparent that the government possessed the machinery to recognize and to weed out the Puritan ministers if it chose to exercise it. But in 1605, when central government pressure was removed, Chaderton, giving way to his own moderate and charitable inclinations and to pressure from the local gentry, chose to tolerate a measure of nonconformity in his diocese rather than deprive 'men of great learning, pains and fruit'. Such official connivance became the norm for the next two decades, although it stemmed more from episcopal indolence than from Chaderton's conscientious scruples. Bancroft's successor, Abbott, provided little leadership as archbishop of Canterbury, and the bishops of Lincoln from 1608 to 1625, when Williams was dismissed from his court posts, were not vitally involved in the administration of the diocese. The machinery for the detection and discipline of clerical nonconformity still functioned, but without strong central direction it lacked the cutting edge it had displayed in 1604. Subsequent visitation returns are far more sketchy, though, ironically, they do record the continued nonconformity of many of those who had benefited from Chaderton's leniency in 1605: in 1611 it was noted of Simon Bradstreet of Horbling, as of Robert Atkinson of Glentworth, that he was of good behaviour 'saving he is unconformable'.

Those who were presented for nonconformity had little difficulty in escaping serious consequences. Hugh Tuke of Silk Willoughby was the doyen of Lincolnshire Puritanism, having refused Whitgift's three articles in 1584. Yet although he was presented at the episcopal visitations of 1607 and 1611 for not wearing the surplice or using the sign of the cross in baptism, he avoided censure by virtue of the readiness of his patron, Sir William Armyne of Osgodby, and other local gentlemen to approach the bishop and secure a favourable hearing of his case.[4]

[3] This account is based upon Foster, ed., *State of the Church*, pp. xlviii–cxvi, 366–71, and S. B. Babbage, *Puritanism and Richard Bancroft*, London, 1962, pp. 43–219, particularly pp. 162–91. Additional details from *An abridgment of that booke which the ministers of Lincoln diocess delivered to his Maiestie*, London, 1605, pp. 43–44, 46, 53; *The Works of John Smythe*, ed. W. T. Whitley, Cambridge, 1915, pp. 331–33.

[4] Foster, ed., *State of the Church*, pp. civ–cv, cxv; Hill, *Tudor and Stuart Lincoln*, pp. 113–14.

The lethargic pliancy of the establishment could be secured without the intercession of potent members of the county élite, however, as appears in a couple of incidents in the career of John Cotton. In 1612, when the corporation presented Cotton to the Boston incumbency, Bishop Barlow considered refusing institution on the grounds that Cotton was too young 'to be over such a numerous and such a factious people'. However, Cotton's supporters in the town 'understanding that one Simon Biby was to be spoken with, who was neer to the bishop, they presently charmed him so the business proceeded without further trouble'. The charm that proved so effective is indicated by Biby's nickname, 'Simony and Bribery'. In 1616 Cotton was presented for his failure to employ the ceremonies: he escaped censure through the efforts of one of his parishioners, Thomas Leverett, 'a plain man . . . yet piously subtile to get such a spiritual blessing' who 'so far insinuated himself into one of the proctors of that high court, that Mr Cotton was treated by them as if he were a conformable man'.

So between his institution in 1612 and 1621, with the exception of the one incident deflected by the 'piously subtile' Leverett, John Cotton 'enjoyed rest' at Boston, and his experience provided an illustration of the degree to which a Puritan minister in the county enjoyed effective autonomy in James's reign. At Boston the ceremonies were abandoned or performed by another cleric; Cotton experimented with the order of the service and employed a catechism of his own making rather than that set out in the Book of Common Prayer; the minister and the godly members of his congregation 'entered into a covenant with the Lord, and with one another, to follow after the Lord in the purity of his worship'. Some of Cotton's most zealous followers engaged in unauthorized iconoclasm in St Botolph's: raiding parties were organized on 'darke winter nights' to demolish the medieval statuary; the stained glass windows, which depicted biblical stories, were replaced with plain glass, and the carved stone font cover with a piece of black wood 'in the likeness of a pott lid'. According to Sanderson these doings in Boston were the talk of 'all the country far and near'. Yet Cotton 'enjoyed rest' until 1621, when the iconoclastic zeal of some of his congregation went too far and the crosses were cut from the royal arms upon the mayorial mace. Although Cotton was absolved from personal involvement in the incident, it necessarily focused government attention upon his ministry. He was suspended 'upon speciall complaint . . . to the king', and informed by Bishop Mountain that unless he conformed, at least to the degree of receiving the sacrament on his knees with the bishop the following

Sunday, he might abandon 'all hope of restitution'. Cotton rejected Mountain's offer, responding to it with a syllogism in defence of his failure to kneel during the communion service, but the bishop did not execute his threat: Cotton was restored to Boston without any promise of conformity.[5]

At the beginning of the reign the government had displayed a powerful determination to ferret out and to destroy those ministers who refused to observe the injunctions of the Book of Common Prayer. Yet, after little more than a year, central pressure relaxed and after 1606 Puritans like John Cotton enjoyed unofficial toleration. The lethargy which came to characterize Westminster's attitude to the enforcement of its stated religious policy typified the general quality of the leadership it provided for local governors.

THE JACOBEAN RÉGIME AND LOCAL GOVERNMENT

The government was not entirely moribund: an emergency — war, insurrection — could galvanize it into action. In the first decade of James's reign the central authorities totally neglected the county militias. Responsibility for efficiency rested with the individual lords lieutenant, and it does not appear that, in general, they gave more than the most perfunctory attention to their duties. However, after 1613, and particularly after 1618 with the outbreak of war on the continent, the Privy Council displayed renewed concern, insisting that the annual musters be held to ensure that the trained bands were at full strength and adequately equipped. These orders appear to have enjoyed some success in Lincolnshire.[6]

The outbreak of war and the threat of invasion moved the central government to action; so, too, did popular insurrection. On May eve 1607 riots against enclosure broke out in Northamptonshire, which throughout remained the centre of the disturbance, and then spread into the neighbouring counties. Lincolnshire was mildly affected. In late June a mob of poor Lincoln artisans with the probable connivance of the civic authorities marched to Burton

---

[5] In general for this period of Cotton's career, see L. Ziff, *The career of John Cotton: Puritanism and the American Experience*, Princeton, 1972, pp. 36–55. Other details are from Cotton Mather, *Magnalia Christi Americana*, ed. T. Robbins, Hartford, 1855, p. 259; *Chronicles of the First Planters*, ed. A. Young, Boston Mass., 1846, pp. 423–24; *Memoir of John Cotton by John Norton*, ed. E. Pond, Boston Mass., 1834, pp. 34, 37; Jacobson, ed., *Works of Sanderson*, II, p. 74; STAC 8 259/25; Pishey Thompson, *The History and Antiquities of Boston*, Boston, 1856, p. 418.

[6] For the Jacobean militia, see L. Boynton, *The Elizabethan Militia, 1558–1638*, London, 1967, chapter 7: for the Lincolnshire force, see p. 229, and LAO, 10 ANC 355/1.

where they demolished Sir Thomas Dallison's enclosure. There was a disturbance at Canwick at the same time, while in July written attacks upon the gentry were being disseminated in the county and some Kirton men sought the aid of the neighbouring parish of Waddingham for a proposed assault on enclosures. The government reacted to the revolt with a carrot-and-stick policy. The riots were forcibly suppressed but an enquiry was also promised into the abuses of enclosure and depopulation. In August a commission was appointed to determine the extent since 1578 of enclosure, engrossing and the conversion of arable to pasture in seven midland counties. From January 1608 the commissioners' returns were the foundation of a series of suits commenced by the attorney general in Star Chamber against enclosing landlords, including the earl of Lincoln and a number of major gentry families — the Wrays, Ayscoughs, Carrs, Husseys, Thorolds, Hatchers and Sandersons.[7]

The government's interest in the quality of the militia, once revived, and their readiness to press local governors to secure the execution of their orders were sustained to the end of James's reign. Not so its concern for enclosure and depopulation. A number of offenders were fined and ordered to rebuild farmhouses upon their estates and to attach thirty to forty acres of land to each: in 1609 the attorney general was still prosecuting enclosing landlords, accusing them of provoking 'mutinous seditions and rebellions . . . which of late were raised in many of your highnes counties' by their anti-social behaviour. But as the spectre of popular revolt faded the government's interest waned. Enclosure continued apace, and when, in the mid 1630s Archbishop Laud revived the commission of depopulation his agents found plenty to investigate in Lincolnshire.[8]

The campaigns against nonconformity in 1604 and against enclosure in 1607–8 demonstrated that the Jacobean government was capable of effective intervention in the localities: the machinery of local government *could* be spurred into activity designed to

---

[7] For the midland revolt, see E. F. Gay, 'The Midland Revolt and the Inquisition of Depopulation of 1607', *Trans. Royal Hist. Soc.*, n.s. 18 (1904), pp. 195–244: for the revolt in Lincolnshire, see STAC 8 61/9; 219/20; HMC *Cecil*, XIX, p. 196. J. D. Gould, 'The Inquisition of Depopulation of 1607 in Lincolnshire', *EHR*, 67 (1952), pp. 392—96 analyses the commissioners' returns. For the resultant Star Chamber prosecutions, see STAC 8 10/4; 14/2; 17/17, 23, 24.

[8] SP 16/206/71; STAC 8 15/3. For Archbishop Laud's commission, see H. R. Trevor-Roper, *Archbishop Laud, 1573–1645*, London, 1940, pp. 167–70; SP 16/514/29; LAO, MON 7/12/1; 19/7/1 nos 8, 9; NEL 7/17/25.

H

promote central policy. But such Privy Council activism was exceptional and, excluding the renewed interest in the militia from 1613, ephemeral.

The basic routines of local government continued even though the Council eschewed a vigorous directive role. It was in the interests of the local gentry that drains be scoured, vagabonds whipped and felons hung. Yet in the absence of central direction the efficiency of local administration and law enforcement depended to a pre-eminent degree upon the enthusiasm of individual justices of the peace, deputy lieutenants and commissioners of sewers. For some, like the godly Sir George St Paul, thorough and zealous performance of their administrative responsibilities was a 'calling', a religious duty.[9] Others were less public-spirited and exhibited their energies chiefly when their own or their friends' interests, whether economic or those of status and prestige, were involved.

Almost every position in local government could be abused for personal or sectional benefit. As sheriff in 1616 Sir John Thorold revised the freeholders' book to secure a jury that would favour his nephew, Sir Edward Tirwhitt, in his dispute with Lady Rich over the St Paul estate; Sir Nicholas Sanderson, sheriff in 1614, embezzled fines that should have gone to the crown. Lord Clinton was also accused of embezzlement of money he had received as a commissioner of musters, while, as a commissioner for the subsidy, Sanderson took it on himself to lower his own assessment.[10]

The powers of a justice were susceptible to infinite abuse. The authority to command to keep the peace, to arrest and imprison suspects, to give bail, were the weapons (besides riot and assault) by which Sir Richard Williamson and Sir William Hickman fought out their quarrel which racked Gainsborough between 1605 and 1610; each man used his magisterial position to prosecute his opponent's supporters upon trumped-up charges and to protect members of his own party. In feuds of this kind the private sessions was a favourite device: magistrates of one faction would secretly summon a court, impanel a packed or intimidated jury, and enter judgement against their rivals. So in the summer of 1604 two intimate confidants of Henry, earl of Lincoln, summoned a private sessions ostensibly to hear an unimportant case, in fact to indict the servants of the earl's deadly enemy, Sir Edward Dymock of Scrivelsby, for riotous

[9] John Chadwick, *A sermon preached at Snarford . . . at the funerals of Sir George Sanct-Paule*, London, 1614, pp. 20–21, 28.
[10] STAC 8 245/18; 145/25; 279/27.

assault. The under-sheriff compliantly gave Lincoln the warrant ordering the impanelling of a special jury, and the earl instructed the hundred bailiffs whom to return: a man engaged in a suit with Dymock was chosen foreman of the jury. In fact the earl's complex machinations miscarried, as Dymock got wind of the attempt. Sir Edward thereupon attended the special sessions with two justices of *his* faction, who insisted on sitting with Lincoln's friends who had summoned the court. Dymock was also accompanied by his legal advisers, by his witnesses, and by all his tenants summoned for the occasion. Predictably the sessions ended in a major riot, with the justices of the rival factions hurling abuse and challenges at each other. Even the more public quarter sessions were not free from the abuse of authority by magistrates. Sir Nicholas Sanderson, whose deficiencies as sheriff and a commissioner for the subsidy have already been remarked, having ordered his servants to expel a poor widow of Tetney from her property, then sat upon the bench at Caistor sessions when she sued her assailants and 'did discountenance, check, disgrace, and threaten' her witnesses, and publicly levelled a charge of witchcraft against the woman herself.[11]

Not only the machinery of law enforcement, but even the apparently innocuous meetings of the commission of sewers could become the plaything of gentry rivalry and faction, as appears in the long dispute concerning Boston sluice. In August 1609 a group of commissioners of sewers, many with Boston connections and headed by the earl of Exeter, the recorder of the borough, upon receipt of a petition setting out the decay of the town's sluice, passed a law of sewers that its repair should be at the charge of the whole level which benefited from the sluice. In September the commissioners met again and laid the necessary taxes, £125 each upon Kesteven and Lindsey, £187 10s. 0d. upon Boston, and £562 10s. 0d. upon Holland. This procedure did not go unchallenged. In October another meeting of the commission was held, attended by a majority of the pro-Boston commissioners who had participated in the earlier meetings, but also by Henry, earl of Lincoln, and some of his Fiennes relatives. After considerable debate the earlier proceedings were confirmed, except that it was ordered upon Lincoln's request that a jury should be summoned to declare which Lindsey towns benefited from the sluice and upon which the £125 should be laid. This modest concession frustrated the entire scheme. No

[11] STAC 8 167/4, 13; 222/13; 293/30; 303/24 (Gainsborough): 91/16, 18; 126/19 (Lincoln *v.* Dymock) — for a similar manipulation of a private sessions, see 145/25; 217/4.

Lindsey jury was ever impanelled; so the money was never levied, and the other areas refused payment until Lindsey produced its share.

In 1622, with the sluice in a ruinous condition, Exeter made another attempt on behalf of the borough. In the intervening years the arguments of those opposed to the country's funding the repair had sharpened: it was claimed, first, that the ancient records by which the borough had sustained its contention that the sluice had been built and repaired at the charge of the level were forgeries; second, that the sluice did more harm than good, and that the corporation only wanted it renovated because it supported their bridge over the Witham. Accordingly at a commission of sewers meeting at Stamford in August 1622 Exeter proposed a compromise: £900 would be raised as a voluntary contribution from the level for the immediate repair of the sluice on condition that no future demand would ever be made. Fierce debate among the commissioners ensued, a majority favouring the earl's proposal. However, a month later, Theophilus, fourth earl of Lincoln, taking up the cause championed by his grandfather, and twenty-two commissioners of sewers, absolutely refused to accept the August compromise. Lincoln was prepared to offer Boston only a £400 *ex gratia* payment, and also worked, with a group of commissioners of sewers almost entirely distinct from that which had backed Exeter's compromise, to destroy the borough's legal claim to assistance. In October 1622 a jury was impanelled to determine what benefits were received by the level from the sluice: it dutifully reported that, far from providing any advantage, 'the piles or stakes . . . called a sluice' were a common nuisance. In August 1623, after Boston had finally rejected the proposed £400 payment, the earl and his allies on the commission of sewers 'utterly anulled, repealed, anihilated and made frustrate, voyde and of none effect in law' all the earlier decrees that supported the borough's claims.[12]

The Boston sluice affair, besides displaying how the organs of local administration could be manipulated by gentry factions, also illustrates a theme already discussed: the absence of determined Privy Council leadership in the Jacobean period.

In the summer of 1618, the Council, mobilized by a petition from Boston, ordered the commissioners of sewers to determine why the 1609 decrees had not been put in execution, to take 'speciall and effectuall order for the reparacion' of the sluice, and to inform the

---

[12] The basic narrative of this dispute is in LAO, SS 503/34–50: for additional details, see ibid. 460/5/56, 134; 503/5–8, 15, 20, 57, 58.

Privy Council of those who opposed the project. In reply the commissioners offered the unhelpful information that previous laws had not been executed, that the sluice was indeed in decay and that 'who properly ought to repayre the same remaines yet to us doubtful'. Despite the vigorous tone of the initial letter the Council were apparently satisfied by this ambiguous and unsatisfactory answer, and there the matter rested until the earl of Exeter sought to assist Boston again in 1622.

In 1623, after the rejection of its legal arguments by Lincoln and his faction, Boston invoked the aid of the Privy Council a second time. The latter, considering 'that (besides the safetie and maynten-ance of havens . . . hath in it Reason of State) the preservacion of this haven in particular doth . . . much concerne the welfare and support of that towne in matter of trade and . . . consequently his majestie's revenewes in matter of customes', displayed an immedi-ate interest in the borough's plight. Yet its initial sympathy and its belief that the borough had presented the stronger case in hearings at Westminster in January and October 1624 did not lead the Privy Council to issue any final determination of the dispute. The earl of Lincoln fought on in 'the defence of the contry against the . . . towne', and in 1627 Boston was still complaining that nothing had been done to repair the sluice, that its harbour was silting up and its trade decaying.[13]

COURT *VERSUS* COUNTRY IN THE 1620S

Attempts by the Jacobean government to give direction to its local agents were spasmodic. The Privy Council's role *vis-à-vis* the localities was passive; it acted at best as an umpire, not a leader. Yet, despite his abandonment of the counties to the effective control of the gentry, James's rule was hardly popular in the localities. Distrust and resentment festered, until they received public expres-sion in the parliaments of the 1620s.

In part the antipathy was because the surrender of local control was not complete; the government's infrequent interventions, usually occasioned by the chronic shortage of money in the royal coffers, had considerable nuisance value. So, in the first decade of the reign, the inhabitants of the coastal marshlands were subjected to the attentions of Robert and William Tipper. The Tippers were authorized to compound with those who occupied lands recovered from the sea. The crown argued that, despite long prescription, the

13 For 1618, see *APC 1618-19*, p. 180; LAO, SS 503/59a: for 1623–24, see *APC 1623-25*, pp. 112, 181—83, 345; LAO, SS 503/51; 460/5/10, 36; SP 14/173/9; SP 16/52/31.

locals had no legitimate rights of ownership or common in such lands, which properly vested in the crown by virtue of the royal prerogative. But the king through his agents the Tippers who undertook the preliminary surveys of the marshes, was graciously prepared to sell his rights to the current occupiers and so remedy their defective titles. The legal basis of this claim was dubious — it was challenged by the eminent local lawyer, Anthony Irby — but many owners and commoners purchased the Tippers' grants rather than risk the costs of a tedious lawsuit. Buying off the king's novel claim was not, however, the only nuisance associated with the Tippers' commission. Some villagers, like those of Surfleet, found that unscrupulous local landowners had bought the title to lands which had previously been common pasture and sought to exclude them. Some landowners, having purchased a patent for their lands from the Tippers, then found their title challenged by others, usually courtiers, who had contrived to beg or purchase an alternative grant from the king.[14] The activities of the Tippers were highly localized: more general were the financial depredations of the local agents employed by the monopolist, Sir Giles Mompesson, to supervise his patent for the licensing of ale-houses.[15]

If the government's fiscal forays into the localities aroused resentment, so too did its partial exercise of its role as referee — at least among those without access to the well-springs of favour. In the first decade of the reign Lincolnshire was racked by the feud between Henry, earl of Lincoln, and Sir Edward Dymock. The feud was marked by riot and assault, by the perversion of magisterial authority and by the exchange of spectacular insults. The earl characterized his enemy as a 'mongrill, a curre, a rebell, a pesant of the order of clownes, ale knight'. Sir Edward's riposte was to stage an elaborate charade, before a large invited audience, in which an actor impersonating the earl in 'apparell, speeche, and gesture' was carried off by the devil while a chorus of notorious whores sang his dirge.[16] An appalled government expressed its

---

[14] For a general survey of the legal situation, see S. A. Moore, *A history of the foreshore*, London, 1888, pp. 180–317: for Irby's legal opposition, BL Lansdown MS 166, f. 9: for the Tippers' projects and surveys, see ibid., ff. 1–8, 10–27; HMC *Cecil*, XIX, p. 40; E 178 4036, 4063, 4086: for the Surfleet case, see STAC 8 195/11; E 134 1 Charles I Trin. 13: for duplicate grants, see LAO, TYR 2/1/6.
[15] *Commons Debates 1621*, III, eds W. Notestein, F. H. Relf and H. Simpson, New Haven, 1935, p. 226: see also BL Lansdown MS 166, f. 263.
[16] See STAC 8 91/16, 18, 19, 22, 23, 24, 28; 126/19, 20, 21; L. Stone, *The Crisis of the Aristocracy*, Oxford, 1965, p. 224.

abhorrence by a series of swingeing fines and prison sentences upon both the irascible principals. Yet in 1611 the earl, languishing in prison, contrasted the ease with which his rival achieved the mitigation of his punishment through the mediation of his courtier relatives, the Monsons, with his own vain efforts to secure his freedom — despite his substantial donations to certain 'skottysh gentlemen'.[17]

Lincoln's reference to the 'skottysh gentlemen' suggests a dimension of the government's unpopularity which cannot be appreciated solely by examining its direct interventions in the localities. The general reputation of the Jacobean court was tainted. Early in the reign, royal patronage was controlled by 'a crew of necessitous and hungry Scotts'. Their dominance waned after the lurid fall of the earl of Somerset in a scandal that must have been common knowledge in Lincolnshire, since one of the local gentry who had sought his fortunes at court, Sir Gervase Elwes, was executed for his role in Overbury's sordid murder and died accusing another, Sir Thomas Monson, of equal complicity. Yet the duke of Buckingham, who replaced the earlier 'trotting companions' in the king's affections, was no great improvement. Buckingham monopolized royal patronage and presided over the sale of honours and titles — 'temporall simony' — practised by the régime. Buckingham dominated a policy which appeared over-tolerant of domestic popery and left England a pusillanimous spectator, as, from 1618, the Hapsburgs devoured the territories of the Elector Palatine, who was both a Protestant and James's son-in-law.[18]

Local suspicion of a corrupt and frivolous court emerges in the defeat of the government-backed Sir Thomas Monson in the shire election of 1614, and in Lincolnshire's return of one knight of the shire clearly identified with opposition to aspects of the policies of the régime in each of the four parliaments of 1621 to 1626 — Sir Thomas Grantham in 1621 and 1624; Sir John Wray and Sir William Armyne, Puritan patrons, in 1625 and 1626.[19] Local suspicion also emerges in the actions of the county's representatives in parliament;

[17] Huntington Lib., MS EL 2723, 2735–37.
[18] For a critical account of the Jacobean court by a contemporary, see Wood, ed., *Memorials of the Holles Family*, pp. 94, 95, 99: for Elwes and Monson, see *Progresses of James I*, II, p. 417, n.; III, p. 121.
[19] *The Court and Times of James I*, I, ed. R. F. Williams, London, 1849, p. 236. There is an excellent account of Lincolnshire's electoral history in Dr K. Sommers's 'Court, Country, and Parliament: Electoral Influence in Five English Counties, 1586–1640', unpublished Ph.D. thesis, Yale, 1978, pp. 177–91.

in Sir George Manners's attack on monopolies in 1621; in Armyne and Grantham's political alliance with the opposition leader, Sir John Eliot, in 1626.[20] The Lincolnshire members, with the exception of Sanderson in 1625, were also reluctant to vote away their constitutents' money. They claimed local poverty, but one senses an underlying distrust of the government's policies.[21] Neither England's involvement in the continental war, nor the death of James, eroded the suspicion in which the court was held, for Buckingham's continued dominance represented an element of malign continuity. 'If we could send posts into all parts', said Sir John Wray in 1628, 'they would tell us the duke were cause of all our miseries'.[22]

In fact, 'all parts' — the localities — had more to complain of by 1628. The declaration of war, followed by the accession of Charles, a man of far sterner mettle than his pliant and indolent father, resulted in considerably enhanced demands by the central government. Subsidies had to be raised, men impressed for military service, deserters rounded up.[23] The outbreak of the Thirty Years War in 1618 had occasioned enhanced governmental concern for the quality of the trained bands, but with England's actual involvement in hostilities from 1624 Charles launched an ambitious programme — 'the perfect militia' — to secure an effective force for domestic defence, adequately drilled and equipped in 'the best modern forme'. In 1626 veterans were seconded from the Low Countries to drill the trained bands. Sir William Pelham reported that the 'wonderful paines' which the two sergeants sent into Lincolnshire had taken at weekly trainings had produced a rapid and substantial improvement in the militia's standards. The increased intensity of military preparation which occurred during the war years (1624–29) is apparent not only in Pelham's laudatory comments but in the emergence of opposition to certain practices of the county's deputy lieutenants which, though sanctioned by tradition, lacked strict legal warrant. The soldiers had been obliged to contribute sixpence apiece at each training to meet their officers' out-of-pocket expenses, while the general cost of the musters was met by levying a penny an acre rate upon landowners backed by the threat of imprisonment. Such levies appear to have been tolerated in

---

[20] *Commons Debates 1621*, III, p. 226; V, p. 285; Trinity College Dublin, MS E. 5. 17, pp. 106, 131; Cambridge Univ. Lib., MS Dd 12 22, f. 15.
[21] HMC *House of Lords*, n.s. XI, p. 42; House of Lords RO, Diary of Sir Nathaniel Rich 1626, f. 72v; Trinity College Dublin, MS E. 5. 17, p. 28.
[22] Trinity College Dublin, MS E. 5. 36, p. 41.
[23] *CSPD 1623–25*, pp. 408, 409; *APC 1627*, pp. 98, 101, 161; *1627–28*, p. 156.

the Jacobean period when they were infrequent, but in the mid 1620s with weekly musters the rule they came to represent a considerable charge. Complaint was made to parliament in 1626 and again in 1628, when the matter received a full hearing and the traditional practice was denounced as an oppression by those members 'tender of the liberty of the subject'.[24]

Royal military projects were less troubling than Charles's fiscal experiments to the local governors and to those 'tender of the liberty of the subject'. The king, at war and confronted by obstreperous, critical parliaments that would vote only insufficient taxation, when they would vote any at all, sought to acquire both military supplies and revenue independent of parliamentary sanction. In 1626, relying on Elizabethan precedents, Charles ordered the coastal towns and counties to provide ships for his fleet: The demand that Lincolnshire equip a vessel at a cost of £2,000, when repeated in 1627, was considered 'unusuall and unexpected' by the local magistrates.[25] Even more unusual were the king's fiscal demands. In 1625 and early 1626 he invited his subjects to lend money: only negligible sums were raised as little pressure was applied to the local authorities and opposition went unpunished. In the autumn of 1626, however, the government commenced an altogether more formidable undertaking: the forced loan. The mulct, for there is no indication that the government ever intended repayment, was a flagrantly illegal attempt to raise an amount equal to five parliamentary subsidies. The king's justification for the levy emphasized the development of an international situation in which the 'honor, the reputation of this nation, the true religion, and common safety of us and our people' were all jeopardized. In consequence, 'necessity (which makes laws to itself) puts him upon this course', a course 'to which noe ordinary rules of law can be prescribed'.[26]

The king's novel constitutional doctrine found few adherents among the Lincolnshire subsidymen at the first meeting for the collection of the loan in January 1627. There was an immediate and

---

[24] For the 'perfect militia' programme, see Boynton, *Elizabethan Militia*, ch. 8: for Lincolnshire's response, see p. 247; LAO, 3 ANC 8/1/9b, d; *APC 1627*, pp. 131-33; *CSPD 1625-26*, p. 291; *1625-49*, p. 67; SP 16/6/55; 7/23; *Commons Debates 1628*, III, eds R. C. Johnson, M. F. Keeler, M. J. Cole, W. B. Bidwell, New Haven, 1977, pp. 355, 356, 359, 360.
[25] *APC 1627*, p. 161; SP 16/60/31: for the 1627 ship money in general, see T. G. Barnes, *Somerset, 1625-40*, Cambridge Mass., 1961, pp. 203—5.
[26] *Instructions which his Majesty's commissioners for the loan of the money . . . are exactly and effectually to follow*, London, 1626; for the loan and its predecessors, see Barnes, *Somerset*, pp. 161-67.

general refusal to pay, led by the county élite. Many of the local
commissioners assigned to collect the loan refused to subscribe to
the levy themselves, while the earl of Lincoln's servants dispersed
letters among the freeholders encouraging resistance, addressed 'to
all true hearted Englishmen'. The next meeting for the loan was
delayed until early March when a deputation of privy councillors
could attend, but even their threatening presence did not cow
the more determined opponents of the loan. Eight of the commissioners, headed by Sir William Armyne and Sir Thomas
Grantham who had sat in the parliament of 1626, still refused
to lend, and their lead was followed by a number of lesser gentry
and by a large group from Boston including the mayor and from
the neighbouring Holland towns. In a solemn ritual the privy
councillors warned refusers that they risked 'his majesty's highe
displeasure', then their names were enrolled to be forwarded to
Westminster, where Charles's 'highe displeasure' was realized in
the imprisonment of those of the county élite, headed by the earl of
Lincoln, who had opposed him. One freeholder experienced regal
wrath more immediately: upon his refusal to pay, Robert Roe of
Algarkirk was 'dismissed of the trayned band, and pressed by the
earle of Rutland to serve in the warres with the kinge of
Denmark'.[27]

Such unprecedented conciliar vigour brought Lincolnshire to
heel. The city of Lincoln had paid the full assessment by early July,
when only small amounts were still owed from Kesteven and
Lindsey. The Holland men proved more recalcitrant but on 20 July
the local commissioners could report 'noe great sommes' outstanding, and that if a Privy Council officer were sent down to threaten
the refusers with arrest the opposition would quickly collapse.[28]

But the opposition did not collapse, largely because the Council
failed to act with the vigour that had marked its efforts earlier in
1627, when its single-minded dedication entailed the neglect of all
other business, as the Venetian ambassador complained. By the
summer of 1627 other matters, particularly the preparations for the
Rhé expedition, demanded attention, and conciliar supervision of
the loan necessarily waned. Central muddle and want of direction
became apparent: the Lincoln civic authorities did 'much marvaile'
to receive conciliar missives blasting them for their slackness when

[27] *The Court and Times of Charles I*, ed. T. Birch, London, 1848, pp. 190, 201–2,
222; SP 16/56/39; *APC 1627*, pp. 74, 128, 142, 240–41, 252, 395; *1627–28*, p. 217;
CSPD 1627–28, pp. 294, 302.
[28] SP 16/58/110; 71/19, 50; 73/45; 78/8, 11, 32.

they had two months previously forwarded the full sum due; defaulters were no longer hounded and their immunity encouraged others who had previously submitted to refuse payment. Significantly, many gentlemen who had been coerced into acting as loan commissioners by the formidable demonstration of central authority at Lincoln in March slipped away as the government's grasp wavered. In July only two gentlemen were acting as commissioners in Holland: the others, they noted sardonically, 'perchance have justifiable excuse'.[29]

The king's novel constitutional doctrine, that in cases of 'necessity' he was not obliged by the 'ordinary rules of law', split the Lincolnshire gentry. Some, like Sir Thomas Grantham, resisted it to the point of imprisonment; most were reluctant to act but equally reluctant to risk 'his majesty's highe displeasure'; some, like Sir Edward Heron and Sir Nicholas Sanderson accepted the doctrine enthusiastically. In the 1625 parliament Sanderson had spoken in favour of the provision of a substantial subsidy for the king; in 1627 he was active in the levy both of ship money and the forced loan: in 1630 he was the government's zealous agent in the collection of fines for distraint of knighthood. His perception of the constitutional situation emerges in a letter concerning the 1627 ship money: the royal demand was 'unusuall and unexpected', but 'we must obey necessity'.[30]

Sanderson's ready acceptance of Charles's theory of government had few popular echoes in Lincolnshire. At the elections in 1628 five of the defaulting loan commissioners were returned to parliament: two, Sir William Armyne and Sir John Wray, for the shire; two, Sir Edward Ayscough and Sir Thomas Grantham, for Lincoln city. Sir Anthony Irby was elected for Boston in interesting circumstances. In the three preceding elections the corporation had return a nominee of Bishop Williams. The town was perfectly capable of resisting aristocratic importunity, for in 1621 it had rejected attempts by the earls of Lincoln and Exeter to secure parliamentary seats for their friends. The Boston oligarchy must have calculated that the benefits of gratifying a man who, as bishop, was prepared to wink at their nonconformity, and as a politician could aid them in their dispute with the county over their bridge and sluice, outweighed those which would result from the return of 'two of

---

[29] SP 16/71/50; 79/45.
[30] HMC *House of Lords*, n.s. XI, p. 42; SP 16/60/31; 78/8, 11; E 178 5414; J. Foster, *Sir John Eliot*, II, London, 1864, p. 652: for Heron, see SP 16/71/50; 72/36.

their owne free men now dwellinge amongst them'.[31] In 1628, however, the wisdom of this policy split the corporation. After the recorder, the zealous Puritan Richard Bellingham, had been unanimously selected, fifteen of the town oligarchs voted for Richard Okely, Williams's secretary, fourteen for the loan refuser, Sir Anthony Irby. Then the populace took a hand: sixty-seven freemen sought to cast votes for Irby. The Commons' committee of privileges ultimately approved Irby's return, arguing that the right of election 'in all boroughs did of common right belong to the commoners'; unless the corporation could show, as Boston could not, the 'constant usage, beyond all memory' of a limited franchise.[32]

[31] Boston Common Council Minutes 2, ff. 146v, 149v: for the connections between William Boswell and Richard Okely, the Boston M.P.s, and Williams, see The 'Liber Famelicus' of Sir James Whitelocke, ed. J. Bruce, Camden Soc., 70, 1858, pp. 89–90; John Hacket, Scrinia Reserata, 1, London, 1693, p. 86. I am grateful to Dr K. Sommers for these references.

[32] Commons Debates 1628, II, pp. 324-26, 331.

CHAPTER 8

THE PERSONAL RULE OF CHARLES I, 1628–40

I N 1628 parliament compelled the king in the Petition of Right to acknowledge the impropriety of his actions with respect to the forced loan and of the theory that legitimized it. Despite this achievement the parliament ended in a total breakdown: the Speaker pinned weeping in his chair, Black Rod hammering at the locked door, and the Commons passing the three resolutions savaging royal policy. Furious, Charles resolved to govern without the dubious assistance of so turbulent and factious a body.

Despite the volcanic termination of the 1628–29 parliament, however, the assassination of Buckingham and the end of England's involvement in the war gave the king the opportunity to place his relationship with the localities on a new footing. The 'honest sonnes of Lincolnshire' — Armyne, Ayscough and Hatcher; a group who had served in parliament together, and fallen under the spell of Eliot's charisma — could hardly be expected to forget or forgive the events of 1627 and 1628.[1] But other members of the county élite were prepared to co-operate with an activist central government once the threat of fiscal exploitation was removed.

That central direction *per se* was not resented, and may even have been welcomed by the gentry after the torpid leadership of the Jacobean government, although it required of them a far more energetic performance, appears from consideration of the local response to the Caroline Book of Orders.

THE BOOK OF ORDERS

The magistracy was responsible for the execution of a host of Tudor enactments concerned with social regulation — statutes concerning, *inter alia*, the relief of the poor, the licensing of

---

[1] J. Foster, *Sir John Eliot*, II, London, 1864, pp. 566, 631, 653, 656, 658–59, 692.

alehouses, the establishment of wage rates, enclosure, the repair of highways and bridges, the binding of apprentices. Despite its formidable bulk, this legislative structure, developed piecemeal, was ramshackle and many of its provisions remained a dead letter or the source of minor income for informers, until a particular crisis — plague, dearth or riot — spurred the local governors or, more occasionally, as during the midland revolt of 1607, the central authorities, into action.

In 1631, however, Charles's government made a determined effort to secure the universal enforcement, by the promulgation of the Book of Orders, of the policies embodied in the neglected social legislation; to 'make the statute book an effectual reality'.[2] The immediate cause of this conciliar initiative was a major subsistence crisis. The harvests of 1629 and 1630 were bad: corn prices rocketed and rioting broke out in some parts of England; in Lincolnshire the seriousness of the situation was exacerbated by the outbreak of plague. In 1630 the Council responded with a series of instructions to the justices designed to ensure that the dwindling stocks of grain were not hoarded by speculators or diverted by brewers and maltsters but were made available to the poor at reasonable prices. In January 1631 the government moved to establish a more permanent system of social regulation. Copies of the Book of Orders were distributed to all local authorities, listing the statutes which fell within their cognizance and insisting upon their thorough enforcement. To secure the latter the Book also decreed a system of close central supervision. The justices were to meet monthly in each division and after consultation with their subordinate hundred and parish officers were to report to the sheriff on their activities with respect to the requirements outlined in the Book. The sheriff was to forward each quarter a composite report to the judges of assize, who relayed the information to the Council.

None of the specific injunctions of the Book of Orders was original. No new legislative regulations were promulgated; no new institutional forms were devised. The novelty lay, in the words of Professor Barnes, in 'the inclusiveness and intensity of the programme . . . elements lacking in every previous attempt to spur the local government'.

In May Lincolnshire justices made their first reports in accordance with the Book of Orders. They are extremely detailed, and demonstrate the degree to which the magistracy had been energized

---

[2] T. G. Barnes, *Somerset, 1625–40,* Cambridge Mass., 1961, p. 178: see, in general, chap. 7.

by the Council's directives. So William Coney and George Ashton, justices within the division for the wapentakes of Gartree and Wraggoe and the soke of Horncastle, reported that they had surveyed the stocks of grain and, having made allowance for seed corn, had organized the farmers to ensure that forty-one quarters of grain would be available at the local market towns each week. They had halted speculation in oatmeal, the 'greatest reliefe' of the poor, and forced down its price. They had forbidden all malting within the division until the following February. They had reacted sharply to any breach of their injunctions, imprisoning the recalcitrant and taking bonds for their future compliance. In addition numerous alehouses had been suppressed, and three hundred poor children bound apprentices. Such assiduity was matched in all the administrative divisions of the county.[3]

Subsequent reports from Lincolnshire were less detailed than those forwarded in 1631; some provide little more than a bare assertion of the division's conformity to the Book of Orders. We may suspect that the fervour which had marked the justices' proceedings initially, in the face of a serious subsistence crisis and the Privy Council's initiative, had cooled. Yet the monthly meetings established by the Book of Orders, at which the justices interrogated the local officers and exhorted them to renewed diligence, continued to be held at least to 1637. A series of better harvests after 1631 ensured that the grain supply was no longer a prime concern. Attention was given to the condition of the highways; weights and measures were scrutinized; unlicensed alehouses were closed down and 'many disorders of alehouse haunters' — swearing, drunkenness and carousing on the sabbath — were punished. The major focus of attention became the enforcement of the multifarious provisions of the poor law: parochial rates and accounts were examined, stocks of raw materials for the employment of the destitute were provided, pauper children were bound apprentices, and vagabonds, rooted out by 'privy searches', were punished and returned to their place of legal settlement. Some justices noted enthusiastically that the campaign against 'idle and wandringe people' had brought about a reduction in petty crime.[4]

The Book of Orders was one of the most successful products of the activism that marked the operations of the Caroline Privy

[3] The 1631 reports are SP 16/189/50, 58; 190/14, 43; 192/30, 40, 53; 193/1.
[4] Post-1631 reports: (1632), SP 16/220/58; 221/16; 223/54: (1633), 224/29: (1634), 260/115; 271/54, 64, 99, 100; 272/23, 99; 281/82; 294/12: (1635), 293/121, 122; 294/14, 31–35: (1636), 315/23, 99; 342/105–9: (1637), 349/105, 113, 123.

Council in the 1630s. It guided the energies of the magistracy, which had been aroused by the spectre of famine and riot in 1630–31, into channels that led to the efficient execution of legislation previously moribund. The Book of Orders was not just a temporary response to a particular crisis, as the Council made clear when it enjoined the continuance of the programme in 1632. By 1635 when the Council withdrew from a direct supervisory role, leaving responsibility with the judges of assize, monthly meetings of the justices and local officers for the purposes of stock-taking, exhortation and the punishment of petty offences had become an established part of the routine of local government — a routine that ensured the unprecedentedly rigorous administration of the law.

But if the Book of Orders programme was respected it is clear that other aspects of Charles's policy were far less popular. In his assize sermons in 1632 and 1634 Sanderson expressed surprise that many 'men otherwise discreet and . . . in some reputation for virtue and godliness' were so ready to attack the régime. The same theme was addressed by Thomas Hurst, D.D., at the assizes in March 1637: he rebuked those who 'are disrespective to them that are in authority, not speaking of them or to them, publickly or privately, as to God's viceregents, but with quips and girds, to please themselves and to stroke the people'.[5] The swelling under-current of resentment and criticism noted by these commentators grew not because of the activism which characterized Charles's government but because its energies were increasingly directed to ends which offended the religious prejudices of the bulk of the populace, and which, as in 1627, jeopardized their property rights.

ARCHBISHOP LAUD AND ARMINIANISM

The unofficial toleration which the Puritans had enjoyed in James's reign ceased with his successor's promotion of Arminian ecclesiastics, notably William Laud, bishop of London in 1628 then raised to Canterbury in 1633, to positions of authority in the Church. The Arminians followed the Dutch theologian Arminius, from whom they derived their name, in a revolt against the uncompromising rigidity of Calvin's predestinarian theology and by emphasizing human free will. As Thomas Gibson preached to his Horncastle parishioners, 'a man sinninge is reprobate and repenting is elect,

---

[5] Jacobson, ed., *Works of Sanderson*, IV, p. 317; see also pp. 318–19, 341; Thomas Hurste, *The Descent of Authorite*, London, 1637, p. 23.

and sinninge again the same elect is reprobate . . . neither eleccion nor reprobacion are from eternity'. Gibson was also accused of saying 'that if the pope weere received into England . . . hee would not be against itt'.[6] This was probably a canard, but the Arminians did move closer to Catholicism not only in their ideas on justification but also in their sacramental and eucharistic doctrine. They believed that in the sacraments, dispensed by the priest, the believer could acquire divine grace, the means of salvation. Nor was the communion merely a commemorative service: the elements became the mystical body and blood of Christ. This belief had important consequences for ecclesiastical ritual. For the defenders of the Elizabethan Church and their successors like Robert Sanderson, the ceremonies and vestments were *adiaphora*, doctrinally indifferent, 'being neither expressly commanded nor expressly forbidden in the word of God'. They were to be employed, however, because of the religious duty of obedience to the magistrate, who had required them for 'order, comeliness and uniformity sake'.[7] But for the Arminians the vestments were a sign of the especial status of the priest by virtue of his mystical intercessory role; the reverent performance of the ceremonies was the essential adjunct of the mystery of the eucharist. Surplice and ritual were doctrinal, not merely obedential, necessities.

Laud, a man of single-minded conviction and tireless energy, employed his authority to promote those who subscribed to his principles and to persecute his Puritan opponents. The press was muzzled, the universities were purged and vacant professorships and headships of houses given to Arminian divines. Men who mirrored both Laud's ideals and his zeal were promoted to bishoprics and conducted vigorous campaigns of repression against those ministers who refused to conform to the newly enhanced ceremonial demands. The Court of Ecclesiastical High Commission, which had languished during Abbott's primacy, was revived and again acted as a supreme tribunal, exercising a formidable and nationwide competence in ecclesiastical matters.

Laud's programme entailed ideally the renovation of the entire Church of England. In practice the degree to which Arminian ceremonial was enforced and Puritan clerics harried for nonconformity depended upon the dedication and enthusiasm of the local bishop. Wren at Norwich was relentlessly efficient: the huge diocese of Lincoln under Bishop Williams remained, at least until

---

[6] 'The Royalist Clergy of Lincolnshire', ed. J. W. F. Hill, *LAAS*, 2 (1940), p. 59.
[7] Jacobson, ed., *Works of Sanderson*, II, pp. 20, 158.

1637, in Professor Trevor-Roper's words 'a great loophole in the Laudian system'.[8]

It is often argued that the resistance which Williams offered to Laud's ideals was a function of frustrated ambition and personal pique. Laud and Williams had been rivals for court patronage: Williams's rise had been the swifter initially but in 1624 he fell from favour and in the next decade watched from exile at the episcopal palace of Buckden the triumph of his opponent at Westminster. So he found some release for his injured pride and his resentments by seeking to hamstring the Laudian programme in his own diocese. Certainly Williams resented Laud's success and this may have sharpened his response to the demands of his metropolitan; but the bishop was more than the 'ecclesiastical careerist whose calculated self-interest was obscured by no destructive idealism' described by Trevor-Roper. His ideals were those embodied in the Elizabethan settlement, those defended by Hooker and Sanderson.

Even before the period of Laud's dominance, Williams had displayed scant sympathy for the enthusiasm of those clerics who sought to institute Arminian practices at the parish level. In 1626 Peter Titley had become one of the vicars of Grantham, and had immediately commenced a local campaign that was a microcosm of the programme which Laud sought to develop at the national level in the following years. Titley fought to improve his income from tithe. He refused the lecturers, who were funded by the town to secure more frequent preaching, the use of the church. He revelled in ritualism: his genuflexions at the mention of the name of Jesus in the service were so extreme that his book frequently dropped from his hands, and on one occasion he toppled over 'to the derision of those that were not well affected to that religious ceremony'. Titley was cordially detested by his parishioners, but the specific incident which threatened violence and secured Williams's intervention arose over the placement of the communion table.

Before the Reformation most English churches contained a stone altar at the east end of the chancel, railed in and appropriately decorated, lit, and perfumed to symbolize its especial sanctity. Within the sanctuary, upon the altar, the priest offered the euchar-istic sacrifice, the essential mystery of the mass. For Protestants, rejecting transubstantiation, the communion was a commemora-tive service and the communion table was a *table*. In a wave of

---

[8] H. R. Trevor-Roper, *Archbishop Laud 1573–1645*, London, 1940, p. 184: in this study Trevor-Roper provides a brilliant, if malicious, characterization of Williams, pp. 52–56, 58–62, 179–84, 325–32.

officially sanctioned iconoclasm under Edward stone altars were demolished and replaced by simple tables, usually situated in the nave. Under Catholic Mary, efforts were made to re-establish the altars. In 1559 Elizabeth enjoined a compromise which, typically, combined theological ambiguity with a pragmatic conern for practicality: the table should stand at the east end of the chancel but be moved into the most convenient position for access and audibility during the communion rites.

In 1627, without consultation, Titley removed the table to the chancel, perhaps as much from concern that the youth of the town would frequently lean against it, play around and under it, and even sleep upon it during the service, as for Arminian ritualism. The civic authorities inquired by what authority Titley had overthrown the traditional custom of the town and placed the table in a position where he would be completely invisible and inaudible to the bulk of the congregation, and, receiving only insults in reply, ordered their officers to replace the table in the body of the church. An unseemly tug-of-war developed which was lost by the vicar. Titley retired with ill grace, informing his opponents that what they did 'with their old tresle' was of no concern to him since he intended to build a stone altar at his own cost, and would officiate there and nowhere else. In return, the 'rude people' threatened to demolish both the projected altar and the vicar himself.

With tempers at boiling point, both sides appealed to Williams, who replied in a formal letter to the vicar. The bishop began by asserting that the position of the table 'was unto me a thing so indifferent that . . . I should never move it'. Then, with copious citation of the sixteenth-century royal injunctions and articles, he rejected the vicar's arguments for the canonical necessity of situating the table in the chancel and demonstrated the legal validity of the 1559 compromise. Williams concluded with a pointed rebuke to his over-zealous subordinate:

whether side soever (you or your parish) shall yeeld to th'other in this needless controversie shall remaine in my poore judgement the more discreet, grave and learned of the two. And by that time you have gained some more experience in the cure of soules, you shall finde no such ceremonie as Christian charities; which I recommend unto you.

Williams's letter to Titley not only exemplifies the bishop's attitude to Arminian practice prior to Laud's supremacy; it also became an important propaganda statement after Laud was elevated to Canterbury. When in 1633 the Privy Council enjoined the placing of the communion table as an altar in all churches, Williams's letter was widely circulated in manuscript by the opponents of the policy, and sparked a heated polemical exchange.[9]

In 1627 Williams recommended the obstreperous vicar of Grantham to practice Christian charity. It was a virtue which he displayed in his dealings with the Puritan leaders in Lincolnshire. Like Bishop Chaderton in 1605, Williams respected their learning and their dedication and sought to persuade them to conformity by argument, not to compel it by threats. In January 1625 Williams received a letter from John Cotton thanking him for recognizing that Cotton's 'forbearance of the ceremonies was not from wilful refusal of conformity, but for some . . . scruple in conscience', and for allowing him time to consider his stance. The letter then detailed the progress of Cotton's studies, which had led him to see 'the weakness of some of those grounds against kneeling', and gave an account of the degree to which the ceremonies were practised in Boston; it concluded with a plea for 'yet further time for better consideration' of his remaining doubts. Further time was forthcoming. In May 1633, as Cotton prepared to leave for New England, he wrote to Williams again with his final, negative determination with respect to the ceremonies: he had studied the arguments favouring ceremonial practices but though he revered 'other men's judgment and learning and wisdom and piety, yet in things pertaining to God and his worship, still I must, as I ought, live by mine own faith, not theirs'. Nevertheless, he felt obliged to thank the bishop for the concern, respect, and patience which he had displayed throughout their extended discussion of the issues. Hanserd Knollys also experienced his diocesan's charity. In 1631 Williams had presented Knollys to the miserably poor living of Humberstone, where the new vicar was assiduous in the performance of his ministerial duties, particularly the preaching of the gospel. In 1634, however, Knollys became convinced that the ceremonies enjoined by the Church were sinful and determined to resign his living. Williams was reluctant to lose so dedicated a pastor and offered him a more profitable benefice if he would continue in his ministry. Knollys was adamant, and the bishop

[9] The altar controversy is reviewed by E. Venables, 'The altar controversy at Grantham in the seventeenth century', *AASR*, 13 (1875–76), pp. 46–60. Other details are from the tracts generated by the controversy: Peter Heylyn, *A coale from the altar*, London, 1636, pp. 4, 58, 67–78; Heylyn, *Antidotum Lincolniense*, London, 1637, pp. 1–27; (John Williams), *The Holy Table — name and thing*, London, 1636, pp. 5–12.

reluctantly accepted his resignation, but allowed him unofficially to undertake a career of itinerant preaching in the county.[10]

Clearly Laud's ambitious programme for the regeneration of the national church could make little headway in the diocese of Lincoln, given Williams's rejection of the doctrinal necessity of Arminian ritual and his reluctance to harass able and conscientious divines for their rejection of practices which he admitted were 'so indifferent to me'. Accordingly the archbishop sought to bypass Williams and to assert his own authority directly in the diocese. Laud encouraged those who challenged the bishop's presentations to benefices in his gift, but more important, since Williams refused to employ the disciplinary machinery at his disposal against nonconformity, were his attempts to establish an alternative system for the discovery and prosecution of Puritanism.[11]

Early in 1634 Laud announced his intention of conducting a metropolitan visitation of his entire province, a task not undertaken by an archbishop of Canterbury for nearly a century. He chose pointedly to begin the investigation in the diocese of Lincoln, and, inhibiting Williams and his subordinates from the exercise of their jurisdiction, he instructed the ministers and churchwardens of the diocese to attend his commissioners and answer his articles concerning the condition of the church. Williams, his bitterness at the intrusion certainly enhanced by Laud's employment of a personal enemy, Sir John Lambe, as one of the commissioners, and by the fact that 1634 was the year of his own visitation and that he and his officers would lose a substantial sum in fees, fought vigorously against the proposed descent of Laud's agents into his diocese. His legal arguments were unavailing. The attorney general ruled for the archbishop's right to conduct the visitation and in August 1634 Laud's agents visited Lincolnshire. They reported back to the archbishop on the decaying fabric of the cathedral and other churches, on expropriations of ecclesiastical property, on ministerial improprieties and flagrant examples of lay immorality, and on nonconformity.

The metropolitan visitation was symbolic of Laud's determination to assert his overriding authority, but it was not an efficient vehicle for detailed investigation: the information which Laud secured from his agents was far inferior to that which Chaderton

[10] Pishey Thompson, *The history and antiquities of Boston*, Boston, 1856, pp. 418–20; *Chronicles of the First Planters*, ed. A. Young, Boston Mass., 1834, pp. 434–37; *The Life and Death of that old disciple of Jesus Christ . . . Mr Hanserd Knollys*, London, 1692, pp. 17–18, 25–26, 42.

[11] John Hacket, *Scrinia Reserata*, II, London, 1693, p. 88.

had extracted in 1604. The visitors had little opportunity to check the reliability of the information provided then or to determine whether facts had been suppressed by compliant churchwardens; nor could they ensure that their injunctions were subsequently observed.[12] An altogether more formidable weapon against the Lincolnshire nonconformists was the Court of Ecclesiastical High Commission.

With Charles's support Laud sought to reinstill the vigour that had marked the Court's proceedings under Whitgift, when it had been the main arm of the establishment in the assault upon the Puritans. One of the advantages the High Commission enjoyed, from Laud's perspective, was that it possessed a universal jurisdiction and could take cognizance of cases originating in any diocese. Thus it could be employed against those nonconformists protected by Williams. The attack began in 1631 with the condemnation of the obstreperous John Vicars whose fiery zeal had split Stamford into factions. Some years before Vicars's behaviour had been brought to the attention of Williams, who had required him to make a public apology in the church, having first read the service in his surplice: the High Commission fined Vicars £100, deprived him of his living and suspended him from the ministry for seven years. In 1632 the Court received an information accusing some of the leading citizens of Boston of refusing to receive the communion kneeling. The informant was pressed into implicating John Cotton, who was summoned before the High Commission. Efforts were made to divert the impending prosecution, but Cotton's friends were no longer dealing with Simon Biby — 'Simony and Bribery' — or the pliant proctor with whom the 'piously subtile' Leverett had 'insinuated himself', but with the implacable archbishop. The earl of Dorset, who had been so moved by Cotton's preaching that he had promised to abandon 'certain pastimes on the Lord's day', interceded at court, but could make no headway against Laud's determination to maintain the case: if Cotton had been a drunkard or an adulterer, the earl wrote in chagrin, a pardon could have been obtained, but not for a nonconformist. Rather than face prosecution Cotton sailed for New England, and his example was followed in 1636 by two other ministers, Whiting of Skirbeck and Knollys, when the High Commission began prosecutions against them. Another emigré, John Wheelright, was also investigated by the Court for preaching that God intended the destruction of England,

---

[12] For Laud and Williams's conflict over the metropolitan visitation, and for an assessment of its efficiency, see Trevor-Roper, *Laud*, pp. 189–95. For the report by the visitors on Lincolnshire, see SP 16/274/12.

though his deprivation from Bilsby was ostensibly for a procedural irregularity in his presentation.[13]

The exodus of Lincolnshire ministers who preferred flight to prosecution is a good indication of the reputation that the High Commission enjoyed in Puritan circles. Yet while the Court could effectively silence prominent nonconformists, it was not an adequate replacement for an active diocesan administration. The Court was overburdened and, unless strong direction was exercised by Laud or another interested party, cases could drag on interminably or be forgotten. Edmund Lynold of Healing benefited from this: he was condemned in 1634 yet a definitive sentence of deprivation was delayed for three years.[14]

By the 1634 metropolitan visitation and by the employment of the over-arching Court of Ecclesiastical High Commission, Laud sought to circumvent the diocesan machinery which Williams refused to activate. However, as we have seen, these extra-ordinary measures were not an entirely satisfactory replacement for a zealous bishop like Wren of Norwich. Accordingy Laud worked not only to bypass the able yet recalcitrant Williams but to displace him absolutely.

In 1629 a Star Chamber prosecution was begun against Williams. Some years before in a private conversation he had advised his aides to deal leniently with the Puritans, claiming that this was the policy determined upon by King James for reasons of state: this remark, it was argued, could be construed as revealing the secrets of the Privy Council. It was a tenuous accusation, but with Laud's backing the tortuous case dragged on, undergoing protean transmutations as new charges were brought by those eager for the archbishop's favour and the prosecution probed for weaknesses in Williams's skilfully handled defence. In 1634 the hunters found a new scent and their quarry made a fatal error. It was claimed, probably correctly, that Williams's star witness, John Pregion, the registrar of the diocese, had fathered a bastard child. Williams, to prevent any challenge to the credit of his witness, bribed and threatened Prigeon's accusers to forswear the testimony. The sordid and complex manoeuvres were revealed and Williams found himself before Star Chamber charged with subornation of perjury. His final efforts to extricate himself were dashed on the rock of Laud's

[13] For Vicars, see above, p. 43, n. 7; for Cotton and Whiting, see Cotton Mather, *Magnalia Christi Americana*, ed. T. Robbins, Hartford, 1855, pp. 262–63, 501–11; for Knollys, *Life and death*, pp. 25–27.
[14] J. Martin, 'Edmund Lynold and the Court of High Commission', *LAAS*, 5 (1953–54), pp. 70–74.

unswerving determination to destroy his rival; in July 1637 the bishop was convicted. He was fined £10,000, suspended from the exercise and enjoyment of the profits of his ecclesiastical pre-

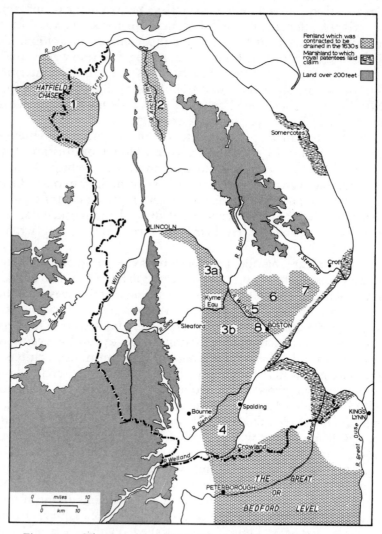

Figure 4   *The 'Levels' established for the purposes of fen drainage*

1. The Isle of Axholme
2. The Ancholme Level
3. The Lindsey Level
   (a) North: from Kyme Eau to Lincoln
   (b) South: from the R. Glen to Kyme Eau

4. Deeping Fen
5. Wildmore Fen
6. The West Fen
7. The East Fen
8. The Eight Hundred Fen

ferments and imprisoned during the king's pleasure: Williams was to remain in the Tower until 1640.[15]

Before 1637 Lincolnshire had been insulated from the full force of the demands of an aggressive régime by the recalcitrance of the bishop. Yet even in this period Laud, particularly through the High Commission, could circumvent diocesan authority: godly ministers, like Cotton, were silenced or forced into flight by the threat of prosecution; the Boston magistrates were compelled to observe the ceremonial injunctions. The bishop's fall, a process in which the moral reputation of the Church was hardly enhanced by the accusations of fornication and perjury levelled against a number of ecclesiastical dignitaries, left the diocese under Laud's direct control. In the metropolitan visitation of 1638 particular care was taken to ensure that communion tables had been placed as altars, while unauthorized lectures were suppressed.[16] Resentment seethed. It appears in the generally negative, occasionally abusive, response to requests for subscriptions to Laud's favourite project, the rebuilding of St Paul's Cathedral, or in old Lady Pakenham's insistence that she not be buried 'neare, no not in the sight of that place they call the altar'.[17]

FEN DRAINAGE

Lincolnshire, unlike Norfolk, never felt the full weight of the Laudian ecclesiastical programme. By contrast, the challenge which Charles's fiscal policies in the 1630s posed to established property rights was driven home particularly forcefully. The county experienced not only those demands which were common throughout England — levies of ship money from 1634, the efforts to raise an army against the Scots in 1639 — but a series of drainage projects initiated or approved by the king involving the expropriation of fenmen from their traditional commons. As the legal counsel for the fenmen said in 1650, 'the judges for ship money were accused for treason, by reason it was destructive to propriety, yet that was not three in the pound: but the fenne-project cuts our estates asunder at a blow'.[18]

In 1621, in a typical flourish of rodomontade, King James proclaimed that 'for the honour of his kingdom, he would not any

---

[15] Trevor-Roper, *Laud*, pp. 183–84, 326–32.
[16] LAO, Vj 30, passim, esp. f. 230.
[17] A. R. Maddison, 'Preambles and bequests of wills in the seventeenth century', *LNQ*, 7 (1902–3), p. 216; *CSPD 1633–34*, p. 270; *1637*, p. 512; PC 2/43, p. 447; SP 16/271/82.
[18] *The picklock of the old fenne project*, London, 1650, p. 5.

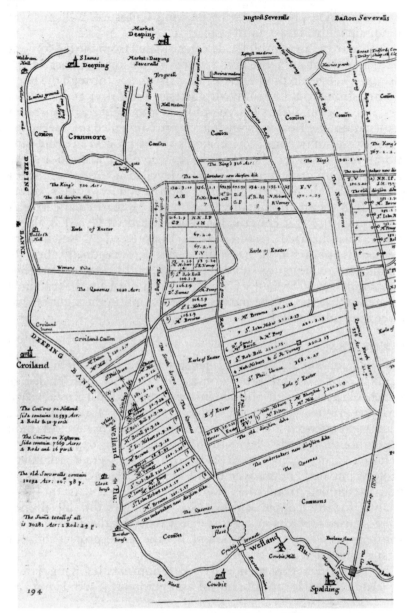

Figure 5   *Part of a map of Deeping Fen, after the drainage operations of the late 1630s. The map shows the enclosed tracts allocated to those who had invested in the drainage scheme and the limited amount of common left for the villagers.* (William Dugdale, History of Imbanking and Drayning, London, 1662, p. 194)

longer suffer these countries to be abandoned to the will of the waters, nor to let them lie waste and unprofitable'.[19] As typical was the fact that the bombast had absolutely no practical consequence. Indeed, the one major drainage project in Lincolnshire established under his predecessor failed in James's reign. Local opposition from the populace and the gentry, and inadequate technology, ensured that Deeping Fen returned to its original condition despite the efforts of the engineer, Thomas Lovell, and his powerful Cecil patrons. In 1619 another project to drain Deeping was entertained with enthusiasm by the Privy Council, but, in the face of the procrastination of the local commissioners of sewers, nothing came of it. Not until 1632 was the fen drained, as a by-product of the earl of Bedford's project for the Great Level.[20]

The accession of Charles I, in fen drainage as in so many other areas of governmental activity, dissipated the lethargy which had characterized his father's reign. North-western Lincolnshire was first to experience the heightened current of royal energy.

In 1626 the king and the Dutch entrepreneur, Sir Cornelius Vermuyden, concluded an agreement whereby in return for a third of the drained land Sir Cornelius would raise the capital and provide the technical expertise necessary to drain the fens of Hatfield Chase and the Isle of Axholme, some sixty thousand acres in all. Charles's interest as lord of the manors of Hatfield and Epworth was to enhance his profits from lands which in their undrained state produced little for the royal coffers. The crown claimed a proportion, half in the case of Hatfield Chase, of the drained land after Vermuyden had received his allotment, leaving the residue to the fenmen who had previously employed the entire fen as common pasture. And, despite a smokescreen of pious sentiment about 'the good and welfare of his subjects inhabiting near or about the places', it is clear that the crown neither knew of nor cared about the 'perfectly satisfactory and profitable farming routine' based on pasturage in the rich common fen which the local peasants had evolved and which would be shattered by the drainage.[21]

---

[19] W. H. Wheeler, *A history of the fens of south Lincolnshire*, 2nd edn, Boston, no date, p. 204.
[20] Ibid., pp. 316–21; *APC 1619–21*, pp. 15, 27, 85, 250–51, 257.
[21] J. Thirsk, 'The Isle of Axholme before Vermuyden', *AHR*, 1 (1953), pp. 16–28 provides an excellent account of the pre-drainage system of husbandry. For a fuller account of events in the 1630s, see J. D. Hughes, 'Drainage disputes in the Isle of Axholme and their connection with the Leveller movement: a re-examination', *LH*, 2 (1954), pp. 14–22.

The men of the Isle of Axholme were faced with the loss of some two-thirds of their common and with it the dislocation of their traditional pattern of husbandry. Their complaints were not only concerned with the practical consequences of drainage, however. They argued that the expropriation was wholly illegal, for, kept in a 'chest bound with iron' at Haxey church was a deed dating from 1360 in which the then lord of the manor, John de Mowbray, bound himself and his heirs to make no further 'approvement' within the Isle. The fenmen claimed and eminent lawyers concurred that the Mowbray deed barred the right which the king claimed under the statute of Merton to make an improvement on the commons of his manor.

The fenmen were fortified by a sense of their legal right to defend their common and their life-style. Sir Cornelius Vermuyden was compelled by the demands of his unpaid workmen, of his Dutch partners who had put up the capital and expected a swift return on their investment, of predatory courtiers for bribes and douceurs, to secure the successful fulfilment of his project without regard to the protests of the locals. So he pressed ahead with his operations before attempting to secure the agreement of the commoners to the future division of the drained lands, although such an agreement was a prerequisite according to his contract with the crown. Popular anger exploded in riot and assaults when, in the summer of 1628, Vermuyden's men began work in Haxey Carr. Materials were destroyed; the workmen were abused, stoned, beaten and thrown into the rivers. Vermuyden reacted vigorously. A number of his Dutch overseers were instructed to carry weapons and when the workmen were again attacked, these guards opened fire, killing a man.[22] The murder was viewed complacently by the royal authorities in the area — it might 'procure conformitie in the people to permitt him to goe on with his worke' — while the government put its full resources at Vermuyden's disposal to quell the riots. The justices were instructed to act forcefully. The ringleaders were sent to London and suits commenced against them in Star Chamber; lesser men were imprisoned and only released upon giving bond not to offend again. A royal proclamation was read in every village by a sergeant-at-arms accompanied by the sheriff and fifty horsemen. Such 'exhortation mingled with threats of fire and vengeance' had the desired salutary effect: the works progressed without major interruption. Similar governmental assistance was forthcoming in 1629 and the 1630s when the drainers reported

[22] SP 16/113/38 and attached deposition.

further riots on the Isle.[23] Indeed, Vermuyden and his agents were accused of inventing riots or inflating their violence in order to secure the continued assistance of the central government in keeping the local populace in awe, and of abusing the royal authority placed at their disposal to intimidate 'poore men' into compounding with them with threats that they would 'carry them from Lincolnshire to London'.[24]

The vigour and absence of scruples which marked Vermuyden's attempts to keep order on the Isle of Axholme were duplicated in his manipulation of legal proceedings in the 1630s. In 1629 the fenmen, with the exception of a small minority, 'absolutely refused' to accede to any division of their common. Nevertheless the commissioners surveyed the drained lands, set out Vermuyden's third and tentatively suggested a division of the remaining lands which would have given the king 2,620 acres, and leave the commoners with six thousand acres. Sir Cornelius, who had purchased the crown's share, thereafter bent all his energies to securing a legally binding agreement to this. In 1631 a number of the leaders of the Axholme men had been fined £1,000 apiece in Star Chamber for their part in the 1628 riots. Vermuyden approached them, offering to free them from their crushing fines if they would participate, ostensibly as the representatives of their fellow fenmen, in a collusive action in the Court of Exchequer ratifying the 1629 award. The men, cowed by their fines, went along with the nefarious scheme but the objections of the other freeholders were powerfully represented to the Exchequer and nothing came of the ploy. In 1636, however, a similar exercise in quasi-blackmail succeeded. Vermuyden made preparations to levy a substantial sum awarded in damages by the King's Bench and then offered to release those commoners who would agree to conclude a settlement. Many, at the advice of their solicitor, who had been bribed by the drainers, succumbed: 370 individuals, a number inflated by including those who had no right of common, but only a minority of all the freeholders, agreed to accept an award to be made by the attorney general. The latter's decision basically followed the 1629 division, though a few sops were thrown to the fenmen — for instance a £400 dole from the drainers to buy materials upon which those of the poor might work who could no longer find employ-

[23] For 1628, see *APC 1628–29*, pp. 114, 125, 160, 162, 164, 166, 171; *CSPD 1627–28*, p. 366. For events after 1628, see *APC 1629–30*, pp. 73, 129; PC 2/43, pp. 159, 187; *CSPD 1633–34*, p. 145.
[24] *CSPD 1629–31*, p. 35; W. B. Stonehouse, *The history and topography of the Isle of Axholme*, London, 1839, p. 88; Harvard Law Lib., MS 1128 case no. 396.

ment in fishing and fowling. The award was then ratified by the Exchequer as though it had received the general consent of all parties. Vermuyden had secured a legal title and the Axholme men were silenced — at least until 1642.[25]

In his unscrupulous employment of force and chicanery, Sir Cornelius is the archetypical 'projector', that unsavoury figure who prowls the Jacobean stage. Yet throughout his questionable proceedings he had received the aid and protection of the government. The Privy Council had placed its resources at his disposal to suppress riots; it had instructed the local commissioners of sewers who might have been sympathetic to the fenmen not to meddle with his plans. The Court of Exchequer leaned in his favour, showing little interest in the fenmen's legal claims, condoning his exercises in blackmail and blandly approving the final award although only a minority of the fenmen had agreed to it. The drainage of the Isle of Axholme was a formidable example of the deployment of royal authority to crush a peasantry who were forced to watch the dismemberment of their traditional economy.

In Hatfield Chase and the Isle of Axholme the king as lord of the manors had negotiated directly with Vermuyden to secure the improvement of the waste. This process could not be employed successfully where a number of landlords claimed rights in the common fen and thus had interests to be considered and balanced in any large-scale drainage operation. To meet this situation the crown's lawyers devised an ingenious procedure whereby the statutory authority of the commission of sewers was employed to legitimize drainage operations and to compel the participation of recalcitrant local landowners.[26]

The phrasing of the statute, 23 Henry VIII c. 5 upon which the authority of the commissioners of sewers rested, was 'dark and intricate'. Late in Elizabeth's reign chief justice Popham had argued cautiously that the commissioners might order the construction of new works. Despite the formidable dissent of the great Coke, who believed that the Act empowered the commissioners to do no more than renovate old works, Popham's view became the accepted opinion in the 1620s and the vital legal underpinning for

[25] For the legal machinations, see Hughes, 'Drainage disputes', pp. 14–22; LAO, MON 7/15/51.
[26] The discussion that follows relies considerably upon the article by M. Albright, 'Entrepreneurs of fen drainage in England under James I and Charles I: an illustration of the use of influence', *Explorations in Entrepreneurial History*, 8 (1955), pp. 50–65.

the drainage schemes.[27] Let us examine the process by which the commissioners' authority was employed as it emerges in the history of one of the smaller drainage operations: the Ancholme Level.

On 31 March 1635 the local commissioners of sewers met, and having judged certain lands in the villages alongside the river Ancholme 'hurtfully surrounded' they taxed those lands at the deliberately high rate of 13s. 4d. an acre for the provision of new works. The tax should have been paid by 19 May but, as was intended, nothing was received. On 24 August the commissioners met again, and invoking their statutory power to condemn the lands of those who neglected to pay a rate they sold 5,827 acres to Sir John Monson, a local landowner who had outbid a group of London-based entrepreneurs for the contract, on the condition that he drained the level. Monson then formed a consortium, chiefly of other local gentlemen, who purchased shares in the 5,827-acre grant by putting up the capital to build the necessary works. In February 1639 the commissioners of sewers viewed the level and declared it drained sufficiently to meet the terms of the contract and in March the lands were surveyed and the drainers' 5,827 acres were set out.[28]

The Ancholme project was essentially a local venture, employing the newly devised legal machinery to expedite the drainage. Monson stressed his role as 'a servant to . . . the country'; his fellow participants were local men and he was careful to invite all the major landlords in the area to buy into the consortium if they wished. Yet even the Ancholme Level project depended upon royal favour. The law of sale, and the verdict upon the completion of the drainage had to be exemplified into Chancery under the Great Seal to acquire full legal validity. Monson also got an expression of approval by the Privy Council entered in its register, to emphasize the public character of the operation and of the benefits that would ensue. And such favour had to be bought — although the price was not high.[29]

In southern Lincolnshire, however, where the same basic legal device was employed, the crown played a far more active role in the operation. Charles did so in part because the potential profits were higher, but royal intervention was necessitated because, given the size of the operation and the number of interested parties, the

---

[27] For the legal debate, see *The reading of the famous and learned Robert Callis Esq., upon the Statute of Sewers*, ed. W. J. Broderip, London, 1824, pp. 114–28; 10 Co. Rep. 141–43, see *The English Reports*, 77, Edinburgh, 1907, pp. 1139–43.
[28] LAO, MON 3/9/132; 7/18/1.
[29] Ibid., 3/9/130; 7/17/4; PC 2/46, pp. 128–29.

project would have languished without strong central direction. Even Monson, who had carefully sought to placate all landowners with an interest in the fens, was harassed in the courts by some disgruntled local gentlemen who also encouraged the commoners, the real losers by the drainage, to riot.[30] In the Lindsey Level an earlier attempt to establish a drainage operation broke down in the wrangling among landowners.[31]

So the crown gave considerable direction to the drainage operations in southern Lincolnshire. The king recommended the undertakers — himself, in the case of the Eight Hundred Fen — and suggested an adequate recompense for their services, to the local commissioners of sewers. The latter were then barraged with peremptory royal missives insisting that they expedite those proceedings necessary for the legal establishment of the drainage operations. When in 1630 the commissioners forwarded a sewers jury's verdict that the Lindsey Level area was not 'hurtfully surrounded' Charles angrily ordered them to reject the 'partial and unsafe' verdict of 'ignorant and froward men who had rather live a poor and lazy life than a rich and industrious one', and to proceed in future without the assistance of a jury by their own view or knowledge: the letter concluded, 'we expect that you will comply with our pleasure herein, that we be not constrained to interpose our regal power and prerogative'.[32]

The crown could also deal with those commissioners not terrified into compliance by such high language through its power to nominate to the commission. It was alleged that the contract with Sir Anthony Thomas, who received 16,300 acres for draining 45,000 in the East, West and Wildmore Fens, was only concluded after a·packed commission of sewers had been issued, which included those who 'were sharers with him and favourers of his design'. Similarly in the Lindsey Level 'worthy patriots' were 'put out of commission' and replaced by 'courtiers, sharers, sharks and strangers', before the earl of Lindsey's contract, whereby he received 24,000 acres for draining 72,000, was approved.[33]

---

[30] PC 2/48, pp. 398, 531; 50, p. 391; 51, p. 271; CSPD 1637–38, p. 157; 1639, p. 232; LAO, MON 3/9/133; 7/17/23.
[31] Sir William Killigrew, Answer to the fenne men's objections, London, 1649, p. 15.
[32] Quoted in Albright, 'Entrepreneurs', pp. 56–57; see also HMC 12th Report, App. 2, p. 69; A breviate of the cause depending, London, 1651, pp. 3, 4, for similar letters.
[33] For Thomas's project, see the pamphlet quoted in Thompson, Boston, pp. 629–32; for the Lindsey Level, see The picklock, pp. 2, 9; Killigrew, Answer, pp. 5–6. See also CSPD 1635–36, p. 27 for the manipulation of the commission of sewers for the Eight Hundred Fen.

After the commissioners of sewers, packed or browbeaten, had provided the legal footing for the drainage operations, the crown continued to perform many services for the undertakers: securing them from importunate creditors, for instance, or arbitrating disputes that arose among them.[34] Its major activity, however, was in the defence of the drainage operations from the assaults of the peasantry who had lost a considerable proportion of their ancient common. As in the Isle of Axholme, the justices were exhorted to move swiftly against rioters, imprisoning the small fry and sending the ringleaders up to Westminster to answer before the Privy Council or for prosecution in Star Chamber.[35] The Privy Council also sought to prevent local gentlemen from harassing the drainers with barrages of lawsuits. Nehemiah Rawson of Birkwood who led the opposition to Sir Anthony Thomas's operations was compelled to enter a bond of £500, which was ultimately forfeited, not to disturb the drainers; he was twice imprisoned by the Council, his release being conditional upon his abandoning all his suite against Thomas; when the common law courts heard his case and awarded him damages the Council instructed the attorney general to speak with the lord chief justice to get final judgement in Rawson's favour stayed.[36]

The crown justified the powerful assistance it had provided in establishing and protecting the drainage operations in southern Lincolnshire by emphasizing the great benefit which would accrue to the nation by the conversion of unproductive, waterlogged morass to valuable arable, where the inhabitants, previously sunk in indolence and depravity, might pursue 'rich and industrious' lives. Yet the king had a far more direct material interest in the success of the schemes, from which he benefited substantially. From his 16,000 acres Sir Anthony Thomas gave Charles an 'honourable acknowledgement for his grace and favour'; moreover, once Thomas's drainage was complete the king's agents were able to improve the Duchy of Lancaster lands in the West Fen, enclosing 4,798 acres and raising royal income from the area from £18 to £600 p.a. The earl of Lindsey, besides giving fen land to the queen, the secretaries of state, the chancellor of the Exchequer, and the lord keeper, presented the king with one-eighth of the 24,000 acres he had been offered in his contract. In the Eight Hundred Fen,

---

[34] For protections, see PC 2/41, p. 381: for arbitration, 44, p. 192; *CSPD 1635–36*, p. 457; LAO, 3 ANC 8/1/11.
[35] PC 2/44, p. 606; 46, pp. 297, 340, 424, 425, 457; 50, pp. 400, 693; *CSPD 1636–37*, p. 98.
[36] PC 2/46, p. 289; 47, p. 210; 48, pp. 429–40; 50, p. 700; E 134 15 Charles I Mich. 24.

K

where Charles himself was declared undertaker, the king received by contract 8,000 out of the 21,500 acres, although he was obliged to give 1,500 acres to the earl of Lindsey who subcontracted to build the actual works for the drainage.[37]

After the undertakers' portion had been set out and the manorial lord had then taken a portion of the residue for his improvement in accordance with the statute of Merton, the fenland peasants lost from a half to two-thirds of their ancient common. The loss entailed to a major dislocation of their traditional pastoral economy.[38] Popular protests were frequently backed by local gentlemen. The economic motives of the latter were more various: some had kept large stocks on the old commons; some found that the drainers had little respect for the enclosures and severals which they claimed in the fen; some argued that the condition of their estates had been worsened by the drainers' operations.[39]

This disruptive expropriation had been conducted by foreigners — Sir Cornelius Vermuyden (most obviously, with his Dutch capital and Walloon settlers), Sir Anthony Thomas, Sir William Killigrew — well connected at Court. For their benefit and his own Charles had packed and harried the commissioners of sewers, approved legal chicanery, and mobilized repressive force against the commoners.

SHIP MONEY

In the Petition of Right, Charles acknowledged that his endeavours to raise a forced loan and its justification by a naked appeal to 'necessity' had been illegal. The fenmen of Axholme in 1630 might have questioned his *bona fides*, but the drainage operation was localized and had some legal warrant in statute. Not until 1635 with the annual levy of ship money did Charles once again attempt a scheme of national scope which combined conciliar activism with dubious constitutional propriety. Charles's claim, upheld by the judges in Hamden's case, was akin to that of 1626–27: that the king might levy extra-parliamentary taxation by virtue of his prerogative when he considered that a present danger called for extra-

[37] Albright, 'Entrepreneurs', pp. 59, 60–61; SP 16/487/37 II.
[38] For the Isle of Axholme, see Thirsk, 'Axholme before Vermuyden'; for the East and West Fens, see DL 44 1166.
[39] The drainers frequently charged that the opposition was led by 'rich men' with 'great stocks'; see, *A paper delivered and dispersed by Sir William Killigrew*, London, 1651: for arguments about boundaries, see PC 2/48, pp. 342–43, 593; 50, p. 32: for the claim that the drainers had damaged adjoining lands, see H of LMP 19 November 1640, the petition of the earl of Lincoln.

ordinary measures. Ship money thus represented the high point of Stuart absolutist claims. As Sir John Wray complained in the Short Parliament, 'wee have not propertie' in our goods and lands 'if they may bee converted to any other use as by demaund of shipp money'.[40] Yet the history of the ship money levy is the measure of the failure of the king's attempts to revamp constitutional norms. For the levy, despite conciliar pressure, faced ever-growing resistance which culminated in 1639–40 in a strike by taxpayers and by the officers responsible for collection. In Lincolnshire the first general writ for ship money, issued in August 1635, imposed £8,000 upon the county: the same sum was demanded in 1636, 1637 and 1639; in 1638 a lesser amount, £2,900, was required. The sheriffs for 1635 and 1636, Sir Walter Norton and Sir Edward Hussey, paid the full sum to the treasurer of the navy, although they faced considerable complaint and resistance. A substantial sum remained in arrear upon all subsequent writs:[41]

writ	sheriff	arrear	as of
Oct. 1637 (£8,000)	Sir Anthony Irby	£2,622 (33.3%)	24 Nov. 1639
Nov. 1638 (£2,900)	Thomas Grantham	£797 (27.5%)	24 Nov. 1639
Nov. 1639 (£8,000)	John Brownlow	£6,560 13s. 0d. (82%)	Nov. 1640

Why did this deterioration occur? Basically because Charles, in part from the want of any alternative, in part because he sought to insist upon the absolute legality of the tax, employed the existing machinery of local government to secure its collection. The sheriff, answerable to the Privy Council for the full sum imposed on the county, was to organize the assessment and collection by parish constables and assessors and by high constables. This machinery proved ultimately quite inadequate.

First, the Privy Council's leadership was deficient. Its instructions to the sheriffs were often confusing, sometimes contradictory. Early in 1638 Irby's re-assessment of the shire provoked a vigorous complaint from Kesteven that the new rates discriminated against them in favour of Holland. The sheriff replied sharply that his predecessor, Hussey, 'a Kesteven man', had for the benefit of his division broken with the traditional rates, to which Irby was returning. In fact Hussey had received a specific sanction from the Privy Council for the basis upon which he imposed his rate, while Irby was following correctly the practice outlined in the Council's general instructions. The incident not only highlights the confusion

---

[40] BL Add. 6411, f. 34b.
[41] From PC 2/51, pp. 102–3 and M. D. Gordon, 'The collection of ship money in the reign of Charles I', Trans. Royal Hist. Soc., 3rd ser. 4 (1910), p. 159.

of the Privy Council but also its failure to provide firm and determined leadership. Upon receipt of the petition from Kesteven the Council ordered Irby not to break 'any ancient use of assessing'. Their reply was published at Sleaford sessions, and the Kesteven men thus encouraged gleefully refused to pay the new rates. Belatedly realizing that any change after the sheriff had completed the entire rating process 'cannot bee without manifest impeachment and disturbance to the service', the Council then backed Irby, but the favourable reception they initially accorded the Kesteven claim emboldened recalcitrants and the dispute dragged on for a further four months.[42] Sir Anthony Irby's difficulties were enhanced by another example of misguided conciliar interference, in this case in the assessment of newly drained lands. These presented an acute problem in Lincolnshire: the fen towns that had lost their common claimed that their assessments should be reduced proportionately; the undertakers argued that their new lands were not realizing sufficient profit to be taxed. Irby, having solicited the advice of the Privy Council, determined upon an equitable assessment, but then the Council entertained a petition from the drainers and ordered the sheriff to present a full account in justification of his proceedings. The Privy Council finally upheld Irby's rate, but their intervention had compelled the sheriff to undertake a good deal of additional work and delayed collection by at least six weeks.[43]

Not only does deficient conciliar direction appear in these incidents; so, too, does the folly of making the sheriff, a local gentleman holding an already unpopular office for a single year, responsible for the levy. There was .a complete absence of administrative continuity. Each sheriff from 1635 to 1637 felt obliged to rate the county afresh; some of Hussey's inquiries concerning drained lands were subsequently repeated by Irby; the Council failed to inform Irby that they had permitted Hussey to rate the county in a manner contrary to that established in their general instructions, thus provoking the fracas concerning the assessment of Kesteven. Nor was any additional care taken in the choice of the sheriff to ensure the promotion of an able and conscientious officer. Sir Walter Norton was a newcomer to the shire, 'a stranger in that country', who was distrusted by the local élite, and who in return displayed only contempt for both the 'ancient customes' governing

[42] *CSPD 1636–37*, p. 186; *1637–38*, p. 211; PC 2/48, pp. 260, 559–60; 49, pp. 7, 241; SP 16/380/60; 382/47, 48; 391/101.
[43] *CSPD 1636–37*, p. 403; *1637*, pp. 57, 92, 526; *1637–38*, p. 126; PC 2/47, pp. 130–31; 48, pp. 362, 466, 547; SP 16/376/122; 378/1.

rating in Lincolnshire, and the opinions of the 'eldest and best experyenced gentlemen in the countrye'. The choice of Irby in 1637 is even more extraordinary: Irby had been a member of the parliamentary opposition in the 1620s and had refused to pay the forced loan in 1627; in 1635 he had been accused of leading the resistance to ship money in the hundred of Elloe. The Privy Council believed that Irby's slowness on paying in the sum due was due to deliberate recalcitrance and ultimately threatened him with Star Chamber prosecution unless he demonstrated more assiduity. Certainly Irby was far more reluctant to proceed against defaulting local officers than was his predecessor, Hussey, whose 'judgment, dilligence and industry' had been applauded at Westminster.[44]

The reliance that had to be placed upon the local officers — parish assessors and constables, hundred bailiffs and high constables — was an equally fundamental weakness in the system. Dissatisfaction and a reluctance to act first appeared among this group in 1636 when Hussey had to raise nearly a quarter of the sum due from the county by 'compulsive means' — distraint of the goods of recalcitrants. This could be a hazardous procedure for the local officers. The animals taken in distress might be forcibly rescued by their owners; worse, persons of 'great quality' might be antagonized. Sir Gervase Scrope informed the high constable of Louthesk when the latter distrained his goods that his temerity 'would . . . cost him a thowsand pounds' — 'I will teach you to knowe the difference there is betwixt you and mee'.[45] Understandably many local officers were reluctant to involve themselves in the process. Neither of the Elloe high constables would make distraints, nor would they receive or sell those taken by the sheriff's bailiffs. 'He had rather', declared one, 'answere afore the Lords of the Counsell then distreine his neighbors'.[46]

Reluctance of local officers to perform their assigned functions increased in the ensuing years. Irby was obliged to report more high constables to the Privy Council than had Hussey. Although the shire was only required to raise £2,900 during his year of office,

---

[44] For Norton, see SP 16/315/121; H of LMP Parchment box 7A, 22 April 1641, deposition of Edward Skipwith: for Irby, PC 2/49, pp. 354, 390; 50, pp. 67, 134, 192–93, 242, 386; 51, pp. 184, 218, 224, 312; *CSPD 1639–40*, p. 420: for Hussey, PC 2/48, pp. 185–86. Hussey reported defaulters to the Council before the expiration of his year of office; Irby waited a full year before reporting recalcitrants.

[45] PC 2/50, pp. 242, 348, 349, 351; SP 16/417/52; *CSPD 1638–39*, pp. 249, 566; *1639*, p. 25. For a similar case, see *CSPD 1637*, p. 171; PC 2/48, p. 610.

[46] *CSPD 1636–37*, p. 566; *1637*, pp. 104, 123, 163; SP 16/357/96; 376/121.

Thomas Grantham was confronted by the refusal of local officers to make assessments; they claimed that they were completely tied up in levying troops and money to be employed against the Scots.[47] With the 1639 writ again requiring £8,000 from the county, the sheriff, John Brownlow, reported that many officers were delaying to make the necessary assessments and a few were refusing outright: where the assessments had been made little money had been collected, some excusing their failure to pay by reason of poverty, others absolutely denying the tax. Local officers were reluctant to distrain, claiming that law suits and violence had been threatened against them, and where distraints were made, no one would buy them. In June 1640 Brownlow could forward only £1,284 0s. 0d. and the names of fifteen high and twenty-eight petty constables who had refused to provide any assistance, and the names of twenty towns where assessments had not been made.[48]

The high-flown theory of royal prerogative with which Charles justified extra-parliamentary taxation lacked any foundation in hard administrative reality. The Privy Council could not bully or cajole the hierarchy of local officers, all unpaid amateurs, into levying an unpopular tax, particularly after 1638 when both the Council itself and the local authorities wrestled with the enforcement of additional heavy burdens upon the localities. This analysis of the failure of ship money is broadly applicable to the experience of all the English counties in the late 1630s. Yet there are specific dimensions of Lincolnshire's response to the levy which require explanation, notably, as emerges from the following table comparing Lincolnshire with its immediate neighbours, the early breakdown of the collection in the county.

| | % collected by Nov. 1639 | | | % collected by Nov. 1640 |
	1636 writ	1637 writ	1638 writ	1639 writ
Yorks.	100	89	88	0
Notts.	100	100	80	20.4
Leics.	100	91	95.3	38.5
N'hants.	89	70	61	0.5
Cambs.	100	96	88	35.4
Norfolk	100	99	94	21.3
Lincoln	100	72.5	72.5	18

[47] For Irby, see *CSPD 1639*, pp. 466, 493, 510, 517: for Grantham, ibid., p. 28; PC 2/50, pp. 139–40, 318.
[48] SP 16/457/92; PC 2/51, p. 591.

The explanation of the county's unusual recalcitrance in 1637–38 may lie in part in matters already examined. The Council believed that Irby's performance as sheriff was unusually lethargic. Fen drainage may have affected adversely the response to the writ for ship money. Most directly, the drained lands were a fertile source of rating disputes between the villages that had once held common in the fen and the undertakers. Further, the resentment aroused by the undertaker's operations in the Holland fen and the Lindsey Level may have been transmuted into a general opposition to the policies, particularly those involving taxation, of a government that was vigorously supporting the drainers' expropriations: it certainly led to the diversion of the energies of many local officers to the maintenance of order.

Irby's half-hearted shrievalty; the unique problems of the fens: these contributed to the early development of opposition to the levy. But equally important was the immediate association of the tax with illegality and corruption, and the fact that the sordid history of events in 1635 was kept in the forefront of the county's attention in the following years.

The sheriff in 1635, Sir Walter Norton, a newcomer to the shire, rejected the 'ancient customes' governing assessment which he claimed were inequitable, and proceeded to rate the county according to a novel scheme of his own devising. Having abandoned the traditional practice, and spurned the advice of the justices who protested against his arbitrary procedures, Norton then proved to be extremely pliant with respect to his new assessments. Complaints were entertained and the sums imposed upon a number of villages were reduced substantially — though a gratuity to the sheriff's agent was required to lubricate the appeal procedure. So Croft, for a douceur of £2, had its assessment lowered from £45 to £35; it cost the less favoured constables of Rowston £3 for a £7 rebate.

The result of this piecemeal tampering was to leave the sum assessed upon the county short of the required £8,000. In order to make up this deficiency and the arrears which had developed, Norton then proceeded to demand a further £1,756 15s. 0d. in personal assessments upon supposedly able individuals, most of whom had already paid their proportion to their village's charge. This gave Norton and his accomplices the maximum opportunities for partiality, bribery, crude bullying, and embezzlement, which they employed to the full.

In January 1636 Norton's term as sheriff expired, and the Privy Council were soon receiving bitter complaint s from his successor,

Sir William Pelham, about his predecessor's reluctance to provide adequate accounts and related documentation. Their suspicions of Norton's probity were aroused, and in August they instructed the earl of Lindsey with any two deputy lieutenants to examine the accounts and report back. Lindsey, who had already received many complaints about Norton's exactions and had begun a private investigation, responded with alacrity to the Privy Council's instructions. In order 'to trace out . . . [the sheriff's] . . . intricate and unimitable ways in that service' and his 'many windings and turnings', warrants were issued to high constables instructing them to consult with village constables and to present an exhaustive account, backed by warrants, receipts and acquittances, of all sums levied by Norton. A series of meetings was arranged for the presentation of this information.

Norton protested vehemently that 'the cuntry should be sumoned by troopes against me or be thus pressed to complaine by speciall warrants at every sessions', and claimed that the deputy lieutenants conducting the investigation under Lindsey's auspices had been those most backward in paying their own assessments of ship money. The king took Norton's part; Lindsey had vastly exceeded his commission in conducting such an 'inquisition . . . contrarie to our lawes', and the earl was ordered to halt his investigation, and, with the deputy lieutenants, to attend the Privy Council to explain his proceedings. Norton's triumph, which he savoured to the full by scornfully presenting the Council's letter superseding Lindsey's commission to the earl at a public meeting at Lincoln, proved temporary. In the winter of 1636 the auditors of the Exchequer found the sheriff's account wholly unsatisfactory, and the Privy Council ordered the judges of assize to investigate the complaints against Norton. At the assizes in March 1637, 'in the face of the countrie', they heard the accusations against Norton and his defence, and reported back to the Council. The latter was 'noe way satisfyed' with the sheriff's answer, and instructed the attorney general to commence proceedings against him in Star Chamber; during 1639 depositions against Norton were taken at a series of hearings in the county.[49]

Not only did ship money start badly in Lincolnshire through Sir

[49] *CSPD 1635–36*, pp. 312. 348; SP 16/315/121; 318/51, 52; 330/11; 331/26; 332/20, 68; 333/23; 336/78; 338/37; PC 2/46, pp. 82, 226–27; 47, p. 10; 48, p. 28; HMC *12th Report*, App. 2, pp. 138, 142–44; H of LMP Parchment box, 30 June 1640, attorney general's interrogatories; 4 March 1640/41, petition of the earl of Lindsey; H of LMP Parchment box 7A, charge against Norton, plus interrogatories and depositions.

Walter Norton's unprincipled exercise of his office, but the memory of the peculation and bribery which he had sanctioned was kept fresh by the continuing investigations into his proceedings by the earl of Lindsey, the Privy Council, and the Star Chamber. Norton's catastrophic term as sheriff in 1635 does much to explain the comparatively swift development of outright opposition to the levy of ship money in the county.

THE BISHOPS' WAR

The problems which beset Grantham and Brownlow were exacerbated by the fact that they did not command during their shrievalties the undivided services of the assessors and constables. The local officers were also acting at the behest of the deputy lieutenants, raising men, supplies, and money, as Charles sought to put an army into the field against his rebellious Scottish subjects. Not only did the king's military requirements place new responsibilities upon already overburdened officers, they also aroused considerable resentment among all classes. Charles's insensitive and ill-considered policies offended in a number of respects, and, ultimately, like the drainage projects and ship money, they raised the constitutional issue of royal intrusions upon property rights.

Local resentment was intially aroused when the king replaced the local officers by professional soldiers. The change was 'much disliked': the local gentlemen who officered the companies were insulted by the slight to their military competence; their men were reluctant to march under the command of 'strangers'.[50] Then the government, which had required the service of only a portion of the county's trained bands in the north, permitted the employment of untrained substitutes by the militiamen, and, to the anger of the deputy lieutenants — 'they holly cansell our authorities' — empowered the new captains to pick and choose which members of the trained band should go on active service and which substitutes were acceptable. Given that few men were enthusiastic to fight in the north (a Boston woman presented the earl of Lindsey with her husband's toe, deliberately cut off in order to ensure that he would not be able to march), these orders provided opportunities for graft and blackmail which Sir John Falstaff would have appreciated hugely. His real counterparts in 1639, the professional officers, were quick to capitalize upon them: they were accused of raising 'great somes of money uppon the countrye in sparinge some'. The new captains were not alone in cashing in upon the popular

[50] HMC *12th Report*, App. 3, p. 149; App. 4, p. 503.

reluctance to serve: some local officials responsible for raising substitutes impressed men only to allow them to buy themselves off from service.[51]

Charles's instruction had insulted the local élite, and created a situation in which graft and corruption flourished. His final demand, to borrow the arms of those of the county's trained bands who were not on active duty to supplement his magazine, raised a constitutional issue. A vocal group among the gentry protested, emphasizing the county's defencelessness 'to the Romish invasion if any such should arise' and questioning the king's legal authority to make such a demand. This opposition infected the militiamen and it cost Lindsey considerable effort, 'daily visiting the companies', before 'these mists were cleared' and the owners were prepared to surrender their arms.[52]

The forces which Charles could raise were no match for the Scots, and in April 1640 the king summoned parliament, hoping to tap a nationalist sentiment which he believed should have been aroused by the invasion of the northern counties, to secure sufficient funds to crush the rebels. In the country, however, the session was seen very differently: as an opportunity to vent grievances against the king's government. The concerns that exercised the Lincolnshire voters appear in the rhyme that circulated before the election:

> Choose noe shipp sheriffe, nor Court Athyst
> Noe fen drayner, nor Church papist.

'No fen drayner': the fenmen were particularly active in preparation for parliament's meeting, concerting strategy and securing signatures to a petition to the Commons and Lords claiming that the drainage operations represented an assault on fundamental property rights.[53]

Faced with a parliament that mirrored popular concern and insisted upon the discussion of grievances before taxation, Charles dissolved it and made a last-ditch attempt to defeat the Scots by mobilizing every extra-parliamentary resource. Throughout the summer his efforts were met by a sullen passive resistance that in some areas sparked into riot. Lincolnshire was no exception. Laud's new canons, particularly the 'etcetera oath', provoked a current of

---

[51] LAO, MON 19/7/2 nos 1, 2; *CSPD 1639*, pp. 334, 416, 453; PC 2/50, pp. 473, 474, 569, 605, 609; Bodleian Lib., MS Top. Lincs. c3, ff. 69–229.
[52] *CSPD 1639*, p. 19; LAO, MON 7/11/71; BL Add. 6411, f. 34b.
[53] M. F. Keeler, *The Long Parliament*, Philadelphia, 1954, p. 54; *CSPD 1640*, pp. 34, 111.

hostile discussion in the county; 'papers . . . pass secretly from hand to hand containing large collections of sundry reasons against the . . . oath', and 'multitudes' of clergymen had determined to refuse it.[54] In June the sheriff's excuses for the tiny proportion of the ship money levy which had been collected were dismissed as frivolous by the Privy Council and he was threatened with 'a quick and examplary reparation . . . proportionable to the ill effects and dangerous consequence of your neglect'. This thunderbolt procured a derisory £154 17s. 0d. from Lincolnshire in the ensuing four months. Sheriff Brownlow could make no headway against the refusal of the local officers to make or levy assessments.[55] The few deputy lieutenants who struggled to meet the king's demand for men and coat-and-conduct money faced similar opposition. Many constables, claiming that they had been threatened and assaulted, refused to execute their warrants to levy money, to impress men, or to pursue deserters. The men who were raised, many of whom were physically unserviceable, were 'mutenous and rebellious' and desertion was endemic despite the proclamation of martial law.[56] Rioting again broke out in the fens and the Privy Council, overwhelmed with the problems of rebellious Scots and resentful English, received a series of plaintive wails from the undertakers throughout Lincolnshire: rioters had driven cattle into their enclosures, had cut their banks, had carted off their hay; a new series of vexatious law suits had been commenced against them.[57] Far from raising forces to crush the Scots, the king's policies had provoked a domestic situation of virtual insurrection.

In November Charles caved in to the pressure, and parliament was again summoned. None of the twelve Lincolnshire members returned showed much inclination to defend the government's record in the initial months of parliament's sitting, but eight of them, allied by family and by their previous political records, were active opponents of the policies the court had pursued since the late 1620s. Sir John Wray, the premier knight of the shire, virtually embodied the county's opposition. Sir John was a patron of Puritan divines and a friend of Bishop Williams; he had refused the forced loan in 1627, and in 1636 had both failed to pay his own ship money assessment and been one of the deputy lieutenants who had hounded the sheriff for peculation; in 1630 he had taken the part of

---

[54] Jacobson, ed., *Works of Sanderson*, VI, pp. 360–62.
[55] SP 16/457/92; PC 2/51, p. 591.
[56] SP 16/454/49; *CSPD 1640*, p. 247.
[57] *CSPD 1640*, pp. 157, 158, 535; PC 2/51, pp. 485, 486, 548, 595, 663; LAO, MON 7/17/18; 7/18/3.

the commoners of the Isle of Axholme, expressing doubts concerning the crown's legal right to improve in the face of the Mowbray deed.[58] In this last action, and in the prosecution of sheriff Norton, he was joined by his half-brother, Sir Christopher, the member for Grimsby. Sir John's fellow knight of the shire and Sir Christopher's brother-in-law, Sir Edward Ayscough, was a forced loan refuser in 1627: from 1629 he was one of the 'honest sonnes of Lincolnshire' who had fallen under the spell of the opposition leader, Sir John Eliot, in the 1628–29 parliament. Others in this group included Ayscough's brother-in-law, Thomas Hatcher (Stamford) and Sir William Armyne (Grantham), who had refused to pay the forced loan and was a patron of Puritan ministers and an opponent of the Lindsey Level scheme. Sir Anthony Irby (Boston) joined his brother-in-law, Sir John Wray, in refusing the forced loan and hounding sheriff Norton; his own poor performance as sheriff in the collection of ship money aroused suspicions of deliberate neglect in the Privy Council. Finally we may tentatively add the two Lincoln members to the list of court opponents: John Broxholme had refused the forced loan in 1627; Thomas Grantham's father, Sir Thomas, had been a member of all the 1620s parliaments, a forced loan refuser, a close friend of Eliot's, and a sympathizer with the Axholme men.[59]

At the county elections the knights of the shire were specifically charged to represent the electors' grievances against royal policies that offended both their religious sensibilities and their conceptions of property rights. Sir John Wray wasted no time in doing so. On 9 November he protested at the undertakers' 'taking their lands from them'; on 12 November and again on 20 November he attacked idolatry in the church, and demanded 'a thorough reformation'; on 7 December Wray joined the assault on the judges who had upheld ship money, 'let the common law destroy them, that would have destroied it'.[60] The personal government of Charles I was over: a parliament promising to end 'all exorbitencies of state, innovations in the church, and invasion of our liberties' was in session.[61]

[58] Keeler, *Long Parliament*, pp. 400–1. See also LAO, Court Papers 68/1/22; Hacket, *Scrinia Reserata*, II, p. 124 for Wray's friendship with Williams: SP 16/336/78 for his refusal to pay ship money and actions against the sheriff: E 178 4512 for his opposition to the crown's improvement on Axholme.

[59] Keeler, *Long Parliament*, pp. 87, 93–94, 120, 208, 230–31, 400. Additional information on Armyne from Hill, *Tudor and Stuart Lincoln*, p. 114; *A breviate*, p. 4.

[60] *A breviate*, p. 7; *The Journal of Sir Simonds D'Ewes from the beginning of the Long Parliament to the opening of the trial of the Earl of Strafford*, ed. W. Notestein, New Haven, 1923, pp. 19, 118; Sir John Wray, *Eight occasionall speeches made in the House of Commons this Parliament*, London, 1641, pp. 1–5.

[61] *The copy of a letter from a Lincolneshire Gentleman*, London, 1660, p. 4.

CHAPTER 9

THE OUTBREAK OF THE CIVIL WAR

LINCOLNSHIRE's twelve members joined a house of commons resolved to strike down both the institutions and the instruments of the eleven years of personal government. Ship money and the other fiscal expedients employed by the king were declared illegal; Star Chamber and the Court of Ecclesiastical High Commission were abolished; legal proceedings were begun against Strafford, against Laud and the most obnoxious of the Arminian bishops, against those counsellors and judges who had advised or sanctioned objectionable royal actions.

These proceedings during the first session of the Long Parliament met with negligible opposition in the Commons. In the autumn of 1641, however, members began to divide. John Pym and his friends, who had orchestrated parliament's policies during the period of virtual unanimity, were still distrustful of Charles and led the majority in the Commons in demanding even greater concessions from the crown. During the first session Pym had sought to play down the contentious issue of ecclesiastical government, for on the occasions upon which it had arisen the fragility of the consensus in the House had been revealed. In the winter of 1641–42, though, Pym and his party were adamant in demanding the expulsion of the bishops from the house of lords, a demand that shaded into unqualified insistence by many of his supporters upon the outright abolition of the episcopal hierarchy. Charles's recognition of parliament's right to nominate royal counsellors was also required, and with the need to raise a substantial army upon the outbreak of the Irish revolt, was extended to the choice of military commanders. While Pym and the majority sought further limitations upon the royal prerogative, other members, a minority but increasingly vocal and well-organized, argued that the enactments of the first half of 1641 provided sufficient guarantees against future royal excesses; any further radical demands upon the king, any further assaults upon the traditional system, could only provoke an absolute breach between the crown and parliament and encourage lower-class agitation against the social hierarchy — a conjunction of the most dangerous consequence for the political and social establishment.

How did the Lincolnshire members respond to Pym's increasingly radical leadership, and to the fissure that was developing within the Commons? Gervase Holles of Grimsby was one of the few men who openly took exception to the policies associated with Pym's leadership even before the end of the first session. A crucial element in Pym's programme was to maintain the most friendly relations with the Scots while retarding the final settlement of their demands for reparations stemming from the bishops' wars and thus the Scottish army's removal from England. A powerful force still occupying the northern counties was an iron-clad guarantee that Charles could not dissolve parliament. This policy eventually proved too much for Holles and on 26 April 1641, during a debate on the Scots' demands for reparations, he made a vigorous appeal to the xenophobia of his colleagues. Holles proposed that if the Scots insisted upon their intolerable conditions, demands that were 'dishonourable for . . . [this] . . . nation to suffer', then parliament should threaten war. Holles's diatribe was barely heard out by the horrified Commons who, at its conclusion, expelled him from the House.[1]

More typical of the growth of opposition in the Commons was the career of Geoffrey Palmer, the able, well-regarded lawyer who sat for Stamford. During the first session Palmer had attacked the temporal ambitions of the clergy and the 'legislative and iuditiall powere' of bishops in the house of lords. He was also one of the managers of Strafford's impeachment; his arguments were considered particularly persuasive, although his refusal to engage in stock vituperation, treating the accused with 'decency and modesty', made him unpopular with some more radical members.

Palmer's conflict with Pym's group over a matter of rhetorical style was followed after the recess by a breach over substance. Palmer joined with those — Hyde, Falkland, Colepepper — who sought to restrain Pym's enhanced demands, and during the fierce debate on the Grand Remonstrance he was one of the leaders of the

---

[1] Yale University, Beinecke Lib., Osbourn collection Box 45 no. 19; *CJ*, II, p. 128.

minority. His demand to record his protest against the motion that the Remonstrance be printed nearly provoked an affray in the overcharged House — members 'tooke their swords in their scabbards out of their beltes and held them by the pumells in their hands' — and for this offence he was sent to the Tower.[2]

While Holles and Palmer identified with the growing royalist group in the Commons, the other Lincolnshire members stuck with Pym's majority. In the cases of William Ellis (Boston), Henry Pelham (Grantham), Sir Christopher Wray (Grimsby), Thomas Grantham, John Broxholme (Lincoln), and Thomas Hatcher (Stamford), this can be argued only from their readiness to act as parliament's agents or to contribute liberally to its war chest in the spring and summer of 1642: they were not frequent speakers or otherwise active in the deliberations of the Commons. Additional evidence of the affiliation of the other county members with Pym's party is available: Sir Edward Ayscough (Lincolnshire), whom a contemporary associated with 'the religious and sound men of the House', and Sir Anthony Irby (Boston) were the tellers in favour of measures backed by Pym. Sir William Armyne, elected for Grantham upon the death of Hussey in March 1641, was on the committee responsible for the formulation of parliament's Scottish policy, and in December 1641 was a teller for the most radical version of the Militia Bill by which parliament sought to assert its control over the armed forces in defiance of the traditional royal prerogative.[3]

The most interesting example is that of Sir John Wray, by far the most vocal of the Lincolnshire representatives, who from his speeches emerges as a committed adherent of Pym's policies. He supported the terms of the Scottish treaty which had driven Holles to his intemperate outburst, piously desiring 'brotherly love' between the two countries. Wray sought to expedite the conviction of Strafford and expressed resentment at the drawn-out impeachment proceedings in the house of lords. He supported the Protestation proposed by Pym, by which the members bound

---

[2] *The journal of Sir Simonds D'Ewes from the beginning of the Long Parliament to the opening of the trial of the Earl of Strafford*, ed. W. Notestein, New Haven, 1923, pp. 160, 469–70, n. 13; *The history of the rebellion and great civil wars in England . . . by Edward, Earl of Clarendon*, I, ed. W. D. Macray, Oxford, 1888, pp. 290, 420–24; *The journal of Sir Simonds D'Ewes from the first recess of the Long Parliament to the withdrawal of King Charles from London*, ed. W. H. Coates, New Haven, 1942, pp. 186, 187, 192–96.

[3] *D'Ewes's journal*, ed. Coates, pp. 105, 244–48; *D'Ewes's journal*, ed. Notestein, p. 432.

themselves to defend liberty, religion, the law and the king against conspiracy and violence.[4]

Yet Wray's speeches in echoing the party line also indicate its radical shift. This appears in Wray's comments on religion. His early speeches are filled with the rhetoric of reform — of 'pulling Dagon from the altar', of levelling 'the groves and high places of idolatry'. But the episcopal system as such was not, apparently, included among Dagon's adjuncts. In a speech of 15 December 1640 Wray disclaimed any intention to 'overthrow their [the bishops'] government': the office had been filled by evil men who had abused their positions to claim temporal dominion or to persecute the godly, but the episcopal order had been graced by divines of the quality of Cranmer, Ridley and Latimer; such men 'I would esteeme and prise them as rich jewels fit to be set in the king's owne cabinet'. In 1641, whether swayed by the pamphlet campaign conducted by the clerical opponents of episcopacy or influenced by a recognition of political realities, Wray's views swung to the left. In February, in response to the London 'root and branch' petition against bishops, Wray argued that the continuance of the established ecclesiastical order was an appropriate subject for parliamentary debate. In May his presentation of a petition from his own constituents against episcopal government was the prelude to the introduction of a bill for the abolition of episcopacy. In a speech on 8 November 1641 Wray pronounced categorically that unless the bishops 'be able to justifie by the holy scriptures that such rights . . . as they pretend for their spirituall primacy over the ministers of Christ be in deed and truth inferred unto them by the holy law of God' then they should be abolished. This is a far cry from the praise of the good bishops of Foxe's martyrology, delivered a year earlier.[5]

In late 1641 the majority party in the Commons had assailed the existing ecclesiastical establishment and demanded that Charles surrender his prerogative to choose his advisers and his generals. Early in 1642 after the king's flight from the capital they began to insist upon these constitutional innovations in increasingly extravagant terms, and then in the spring to make preparations to coerce Charles by force. The Lincolnshire members, with the exception of Holles and Palmer, approved of these extreme measures. What of the constituents whom they represented?

[4] Sir John Wray, *Eight occasionall speeches, made in the House of Commons this Parliament*, London, 1641, pp. 7, 9–12.
[5] Ibid., pp. 5–7; *D'Ewes's journal*, ed. Notestein, p. 336; BL Harl. 163, f. 237; Sir John Wray, *An Occasionall Speech*, London, 1641, p. 5.

THE COUNTY

Certain incidents suggested the Lincolnshire men's wholehearted approval of the increasingly radical thrust of the Commons. In May 1641 the county petitioned the House for the abolition of episcopacy. In early March 1642 the Protestation had been generally subscribed in Lincolnshire; only the Roman Catholics and a couple of intransigent Laudian clergymen had refused it.[6] Later in the same month, as the king moved north to establish his court-in-exile at York, he received a petition presented by a deputation of Lincolnshire gentlemen expressing the county's fearful loathing of the 'malicious and insolent designs of the popish party', and their hope that he would return to Westminster and 'listen to the faithful counsels of. . . parliament'. The county's delegation was jeered by the courtiers and was informed acidly by Charles that his withdrawal from Whitehall had not been voluntary; he had been hounded from his capital.[7]

Yet there were other voices in the shire. The anti-episcopacy petition of May 1641 had encouraged the defenders of the ecclesiastical *status quo* to set a counter-petition on foot. Although no document was ever presented to parliament, it is clear that there was a considerable sentiment in the county for the retention of the Book of Common Prayer and 'for the holdinge upp of bishopps in theire former glory'.[8] That elements in the county were unsympathetic to the direction of parliament's policies became increasingly apparent after the king settled at York and failed to gain control of the magazine at Hull. In April 1642 it was expected that forces would be raised in the county to be employed against Hull, while the earl of Lindsey and a number of the leading gentry attended the royal court. In late May it was said in the Commons that the Lincolnshire gentlemen 'were most of them ill affected to the parliament'.[9]

The county's proximity to Hull, the focal point of the conflict in the summer of 1642, ensured that the belligerents would soon be compelled to test the real strength of support in Lincolnshire.

[6] BL Harl. 163, f. 237: the discussion of the Protestation is based on the returns in H of LMP collection; see, especially, the returns for Bracebridge and Deeping St James, and *CJ*, II, p. 577.
[7] *The memoirs of the life of Colonel Hutchinson . . . by his widow Lucy*, ed. C. H. Firth, London, 1906, pp. 389–90; J. G. Williams, 'Lincoln Civic Insignia — the Charles I or third sword, *LNQ*, 8 (1904), pp. 98–99.
[8] 'The Royalist clergy in Lincolnshire', ed. J. W. F. Hill, *LAAS*, 2 (1940), pp. 45, 49, 53, 54, 78–79, 81, 85, 106, 108, 109.
[9] *LJ*, v, pp. 87–88; *Letters of Lady Brilliana Harley*, ed. T. T. Lewis, Camden Soc., 58, 1854, p. 161; BL Harl. 163, f. 130.

L

Parliament acted first, in response to the rumours of disaffection among the gentry. On 28 May Lord Willoughby of Parham, newly appointed lord lieutenant of the county by parliament, and a committee of Lincolnshire members were instructed to execute the Militia Ordinance in the shire, thus securing control of the trained bands and their arms and munitions for parliament, and to employ the reorganized county forces to defend Hull should the need arise.

Willoughby and his colleagues moved swiftly. On 31 May the high constables were summoned to Lincoln to report on military supplies in their jurisdictions and to receive instructions for the local musters, 'which service', the committee wrote exultantly, 'they performed with all readiness and alacrity, even beyond our expectations'. In the following two weeks Willoughby and his colleagues reviewed the trained bands and purged those officers whose enthusiasm for the parliamentary cause they doubted. By the end of the month the Militia Ordinance had been executed successfully; 'very few or none of the trained bands had failed to appear at the musters', despite the dissemination in the county of the royal proclamation against the Militia Ordinance and copies of a letter from the king to Lord Willoughby interdicting his operations. On 4 July 1642 Willoughby was able to offer parliament a declaration, whose signatories, several thousand strong, announced their 'resolutions to spend our lives and estates in the defence of his majesty's person, the true Protestant religion, the peace of the realm, the maintenance of the rights and privileges of parliament, the laws of the land, and the lawful liberties of the subjects'.[10]

The self-congratulatory tone adopted by Willoughby and his colleagues in their June correspondence with Westminster is understandable. Apparently, despite the doubts of the county's reliability expressed in May, Lincolnshire in its acceptance of the Militia Ordinance had convincingly declared itself for parliament. Yet a deeper consideration of the events in the county might have given them some pause in their jubilation. The attitude displayed by the gentry, in particular, should have troubled them.

There had been little overt opposition. Some members of the lesser gentry — 'some gallants' sneered Willoughby — during the musters at Caistor and Louth, had sought to provoke the trained bands to mutiny by deriding parliament and its local representatives and by reading the royal proclamation, and had then engaged the

[10] LJ, v, pp. 87–88, 104, 115, 127, 131–32, 155; CJ, II, pp. 593, 615, 621, 637; LAO, Holywell 93/18.

parliamentary committee in an ill-tempered argument on the legitimacy of the Militia Ordinance. Two members of major county families, Sir Philip Tirwhitt and Sir William Pelham, refused to surrender the munitions in their custody to Willoughby, claiming that express orders from the king forbad their doing so.[11] The bulk of the county gentry accepted Willoughby's authority — but without any enthusiasm. Willoughby's puff of the county's pro-parliamentary declaration, that some of its signatories 'are persons of the greatest estate and quality in this country', was a manifest exaggeration: twenty-three gentlemen signed, and only nine of these were of sufficient eminence to have been involved in county government in the late 1630s.[12]

Events in July were to demonstrate the limitatons of the county's commitment to parliament and to blast the confidence that Willoughby and his colleagues had displayed. Since April the king had considered visiting Lincoln in person, and in early July, 'invited thereunto by a great number of the best gentlemen of that county', Charles decided to conduct a progress into Lincolnshire and its western neighbour, Nottinghamshire. After visiting Newark on 12 July the king and his entourage rode to Lincoln the next day; Willoughby and the parliamentary committee had prudently retired from the city and the king was accorded an extraordinary reception. While royalist and parliamentarian commentators differed in their assessment of the number and intentions of the populace at Lincoln, it is clear that despite the short notice a vast crowd, including a considerable number of gentry and clergymen, acclaimed Charles enthusiastically and that the civic dignatories and trained bands were present to greet the king. Next day two aldermen who had been active in their support for Willoughby were arrested and a group of seventy-five gentlemen and high-ranking ecclesiastics personally subscribed a body of 172 cavalry, promising eventually to make the number up to four hundred. A number of leading gentlemen also drew up a petition to parliament, in which they urged that it abandon Hull to the king, that all forces be disbanded and the Militia Ordinance abrogated, that the established church government be 'put in execution for the suppressing of those unparalleled prophanesses, schismes and disorders that are broken in amongst us', and that parliament

---

[11] *LJ*, v, pp. 127, 128, 131–32; William Booth, *The humble petition of*, York, 1642; England: Parliament, House of Commons, *A declaration . . . in vindication of divers members . . . Julii 21, 1642*, London, 1642.
[12] *LJ*, v, p. 155; H of LMP 4 July 1642, 'the declaration and protestation of divers of the knights, gentry, freeholders and others of the foresaid countyes'.

adjourn to some place where the king would be able to meet with them to discuss 'further lawes, as may justly tend to the peace and stability of the Church, . . . crowne, and state'. Upon its presentation to the Commons the petition was voted 'false, scandalous, and seditious . . . tending to set division between the king and his people'.[13]

The appearance of the bulk of the trained bands at the summons of the parliamentary committee, yet their subsequent readiness to welcome Charles; the gentry's acquiescence in June, yet their mid-July subscription of cavalry: the paradox was not lost on contemporaries. While royalist commentators enthused that the reception accorded Charles at Lincoln 'was the funerall of the new militia', parliamentarians consoled themselves by playing down the significance of the event, viewing it as an atavistic response to the physical presence of royalty that did not qualify the county's fundamental loyalty to parliament. And the problem with which they wrestled still demands an explanation: how could the county which had accepted the Militia Ordinance with such readiness and alacrity proceed, little more than ten days later, to show itself 'beyond all expectation affectionate and ready to serve the king'?[14]

Popular motivation in this period is most difficult to comprehend, in part because we cannot determine whether the *volte-face* which contemporary commentators believed to have occurred was a general phenomenon: how many villagers who mustered with Willoughby then cheered the king? Certainly Boston, whose 'great chearfulness and readiness' to support the parliamentary cause had been remarked by Lord Willoughby, remained aloof from the mid-July festivities and politely but firmly rejected a royal command to cease mustering and drilling the town's trained bands and volunteers.[15] The corporation's institutional commitment to the parliamentary cause may have been mirrored in the behaviour of a host of nameless individuals. If we accept the contemporary belief that there were many 'turncoats', the motives that underlie their collective behaviour are in the absence of personal statements still largely inscrutable. Yet we may offer a hypothesis. The tergiver-

---

[13] In addition to the contemporary accounts printed by Williams, 'Lincoln insignia', pp. 130–47, see I. P., *A diurnall and particula of the last weekes daily occurents*, London, 1642; *CSPVen. 1642–43*, pp. 105, 112; *CSPD 1641–43*, p. 359; *LJ*, v, pp. 216, 227, 265; *CJ*, II, pp. 677–78, 685; BL Harl. 163, f. 275; *Some Speciall Passages*, 8, *sub* 18 July 1642.
[14] Williams, 'Lincoln insignia', pp. 131, 154; *CSPD 1641–43*, p. 359; *LJ*, v, p. 104.
[15] *LJ*, v, pp. 132, 228, 231; Charles I, *A message sent from the Kings Majesty with certain propositions*, London, 1642.

sations of this group demonstrate that in Lincolnshire, as in other counties, enthusiastic commitment to either of the competing sides was anything but universal. Many would have given the same answer as the Grantham man, who, when asked by his radical neighbour whether he would be for king or parliament, replied 'for king *and* parliament'. Such men sought to avoid offending either of the contestants by obeying the immediate orders of both: so they observed Willoughby's instructions in June, and in mid July, impressed by the king's presence as they had not been by his remote manifestos, they applauded Charles. Thus they believed they could demonstrate that they were not 'malignants either against the king or parliament'.[16]

This sentiment was not foreign to the gentry. Sir Philip Tirwhitt informed Lord Willoughby that he would have obeyed his order to deliver the local magazine had he not received an express command from the king to the contrary; he concluded with the wish that 'a little time may produce so good effects betweixt his majesty and his parliament that I may be enabled with the liking of them both, and my owne safety, to give you a clear resolve'.[17] But the attitudes of the bulk of the Lincolnshire gentry in the summer of 1642 involved more than a desire to avoid commitment to either party. Analysis of the July events in Lincoln suggests a richer interpretation of the gentry's ambiguous reaction.

Courtiers waxed lyrical in describing the reception accorded Charles at Lincoln. The plaudits of the crowd, the heady rhetoric of the formal speeches — Lincoln's recorder proffered 'all that we have to be disposed of by your majesty, for the maintenance . . . of your just rights' — the subscription of the petition that gave such offence to parliament; all gave substance to their euphoria. Yet despite a broad hint from Charles no action was taken to execute the Commission of Array, while the levy of four hundred cavalry was *not* raised, as secretary Nicholas reported, 'to be commanded as the king shall direct'. The undertaking to provide horse repays examination: the raising of forces was justified by reference to parliament's vote that there was a necessity of 'putting the kingdom into a posture of war'; the force, which was to be 'disposed of within the county', was intended, a commentator asserted, to secure the 'peace of the countie' against overseas invasion, against

---

[16] BL Harl. 163, f. 235; I.P., *Diurnall*; *CSPVen. 1642–43*, p. 105; *Exceeding joyfull newes from Lincoln-shire*, London, 1642; P.M., *True intelligence from Lincolnshire*, London, 1642.
[17] *LJ*, v, p. 128.

the soldiers in adjacent counties, specifically those in Hull who were terrorizing the Humber coast, and against internal insurrection by 'men of desperate fortunes'.[18]

No doubt some of those who contributed horse, like Heron, Monson and Scrope — the men who drafted the petition to parliament — were enthusiastic royalists, whose subscription to a levy purportedly designed to guarantee 'the peace of the countie' was disingenuous; they would have been happy that the force should be 'commanded as the king shall direct'. But for many of the subscribers there was no pretence. Some were later to become agents of parliament. Others eventually drifted into royalism and were sequestered, but they were hardly enthusiastic supporters of the king's cause. Sir Daniel Deligne of Harlaxton, who promised three cavalrymen, had been one of those insulted by the courtiers in March when he presented the county's petition requesting the king to return to Westminster. By the spring of 1643 he had fled his house and was living privately to avoid positive involvement with either party; finally when the royalists threatened to plunder his estate he felt compelled to settle in the Newark garrison. His neighbour, Sir Robert Markham of Sedgebrook who offered four horses, was another who 'was unwilling to declare himselfe on either side' and, in consequence, was plundered by both.[19]

In the elections in the autumn of 1640 the county had been unanimous in its support for reform through parliament: in June 1642 Willoughby believed, after the 'successful' execution of the Militia Ordinance, that the pro-parliamentary sympathies of the county had survived intact. Yet, while some of the county's gentry and some of the populace, notably the inhabitants of Boston, did not waver in their commitment, events in July demonstrated that there were a number of active royalists among the leading gentry, and a considerable body of neutralist sentiment among all elements. The latter appeared both as a reluctance to give offence either to the king or to parliament and thus a readiness to obey the commands of either side, and, among the gentry, a positive policy which sought to protect the county from the ravages of belligerent forces or internal riots — essentially to isolate Lincolnshire from the conflict.

Before continuing the study of Lincolnshire's experience during the war, the development within the county of royalist and neutralist sentiment must be explained in its social context.

---

[18] CSPD 1641–43, p. 359; Williams, 'Lincoln insignia', pp. 133–47; P.M., True intelligence.

[19] SP 23/184, pp. 687, 689, 695; 175, p. 393.

THE SOCIAL BACKGROUND:
POPULAR REVOLT IN LINCOLNSHIRE 1641-42[20]

The erosion of the pro-parliamentary enthusiasm of England in 1640 is attributable to a number of distinct yet interlocking developments. First was an intellectual revulsion from the increasingly radical turn taken by Pym's policies. Certainly in Lincolnshire the episcopal system of church government had received considerable support, while parliament's innovatory constitutional demands may have aroused antagonism: Charles thought it worthwhile to inform his auditors at Lincoln that parliament's acts were 'against the known law, and an invasion of my unquestionable right, and of your liberty and property'. Others turned against parliament from self-interest: the earl of Lindsey and Sir John Monson who had benefited substantially from close connections with the court in the 1630s swiftly aligned with the king after his flight from Westminster. Others were motivated by basic loyalty to the crown: Sir William Pelham felt bound by the oath he had taken when he had accepted a minor court post to join the king at York; Gervase Holles of Grimsby's young cousin, William, enlisted for 'the honour to serve his souveraigne as his duty obliged him'.[21]

Yet these sentiments did not develop without reference to their proponents' perceptions of the contemporary social situation. In the parliamentary debates on the Grand Remonstrance and on the abolition of episcopacy it is clear that members who opposed Pym's leadership were as concerned with the social consequences of those policies as with their intrinsic religious or constitutional merits. They argued that the abolition or emasculation of agencies by which the Stuart government had muzzled the press and checked religious radicals and Pym's encouragement of popular petitions and demonstrations, had already produced popular unrest, particularly in London. They feared that any further official assaults upon the principle of hierarchy embodied in episcopacy or upon the existing constitutional and legal framework would only encourage the lower classes in a dangerous radicalism and might result in popular insurrections.[22]

[20] Lincolnshire's response in this period parallels that of other counties; for a general discussion, see J. S. Morrill, The Revolt of the Provinces, London, 1976, pp. 31-51.
[21] J. G. Marston, 'Gentry Honor and Royalism in Early Stuart England', J. British Studies, 13 (1973), pp. 21-43 examines this topic; for Pelham, see p. 39 note 67; for Holles, see Wood, ed., Memorials of the Holles Family, p. 186.
[22] See B. Manning, The English People and the English Revolution, London, 1976, pp. 19, 46-70.

The sense expressed at Westminster that Pym's policies threatened the bonds of society was shared by elements in the localities. County petitions favouring the retention of episcopacy invariably emphasized the pernicious social consequences that had followed the relaxation of ecclesiastical discipline and argued that worse would ensue if further innovations were undertaken. Although no copy of the Lincolnshire pro-episcopacy petition has survived, such sentiments certainly existed in the county. In a visitation sermon preached in October 1641 Robert Sanderson bewailed these times of 'connivance and licentiousness', in which, encouraged by 'a world of base and unworthy pamphlets that, like the frogs of Egypt, croak in every corner of the land, . . . covies of new doctrines spring up'. He concluded:

we find, by late experience, what wildness in some of the lay-people, what petulancy in some of the inferior clergy, what insolency in some both of the laity and the clergy, our land is grown into, since the reins of ecclesiastical government have lain a little slack.[23]

In parliamentary speeches, as in petitions from the counties, the spectres of popular insurrection and anarchy which are invoked are frequently hypothetical; they emanate from an interpretation of the very real restlessness and dissatisfaction among the lower orders in 1641 in the light of the gentry's old prejudices and fears of the potential for subversive violence inherent in 'the many-headed monster, the giddy multitude'.[24] In Lincolnshire, however, such fears were well grounded. Popular agitation had flared into overt violence in the fens, where the dispossessed commoners began to assail the works and the enclosures made by the drainers in the 1630s.

The proceedings of the fen drainers were brought to parliament's attention at the very outset of the session. On 9 November 1640 Sir John Wray presented a petition from the county to the Commons against the 'taking of their lands from them' by the machinations of the undertakers. The earl of Lincoln's petition to the Lords, received ten days later, stating his objections to the earl of Lindsey's operations, was followed by a series of complaints from the Lindsey Level and Holland attacking the manner in which the draining had been conducted and the drainers' perversion of legal

[23] Jacobson, ed., *Works of Sanderson*, II, pp. 155, 161, 167. For the Cheshire petition favouring episcopacy, see J. S. Morrill, *Cheshire 1630–60: County Government and Society during the English Revolution*, Oxford, 1973, pp. 46–51.
[24] For the gentry's fears of popular insurrection, see C. Hill, *Change and Continuity in Seventeenth-Century England*, London, 1974, pp. 181–204; the quotation is from p. 185.

procedure to defend their expropriations. The Lords gave some minor redress to victims of the latter but the central question, of the legality of the undertakers' operations, was reserved by the Commons for themselves, and a committee was appointed to hear testimony and to review the issues.[25]

The Commons were sympathetic to the fenmen, refusing to countenance interference by the Lords in their investigation and throwing out a bill giving Lindsey secure possession of his 14,000 acres, but their committee moved with ponderous deliberation. In the Grand Remonstrance parliament excoriated the 'abuse of commissions of sewers', but by this date the committee had reached a determination in only one minor case and had completed hearing testimony only in the case of the Lindsey Level.[26]

While the Commons' committee undertook their leisurely investigation, tempers were fraying in the Lincolnshire fens. In April 1641 enclosures were broken down at Pinchbeck and there were apprehensions of similar tumults in the Lindsey Level and the Holland fen: these fears provoked the house of lords to issue an order granting quiet possession of the drained lands to their occupants pending the settlement of the question of title. The order was unavailing. 'Contemned and rudely despised' by the populace, it received little better reception from some of the local gentry, who claimed that its wording was ambiguous; they encouraged and protected the rioters and even arrested the drainers' tenants when they sought to protect their property. Through the early summer minor attacks were launched upon the drainage works; ditches were dammed, banks breached, sluices torn down, and cattle driven into the arable enclosures.[27] At harvest time the riots increased in intensity as the fenmen endeavoured to carry off the newly reaped crops. In mid August a party of over sixty men and women from Donington entered the grounds of the earl of

[25] D'Ewes's journal, ed. Notestein, p. 19: H of LMP 19 November 1640, petition of the earl of Lincoln; 14 December 1640, petition of Thomas Kirke; 16 December 1640, petition of the inhabitants of Surfleet; 17 January 1640/1, petition of Peregrine Cony et al.
[26] Manning, English People, pp. 128–29; A breviate of the cause depending, London, 1651, pp. 7–8; Sir William Killigrew, Answer to the fenne mens objections, London, 1649, pp. 2, 12.
[27] For riots, see LJ, IV, pp. 204, 208, 220, 269; CJ, II, pp. 205, 254, 263; H of LMP 4 June 1641, petition of Dame Mary Thomas; 8 July 1641, petition of Sir William Killigrew et al. For the local reaction provoked by the Lords' order, see LJ, IV, pp. 221, 247, 248, 264, 297, 299, 375, 390; H of LMP 4 June 1641, petition of Matthew Cooke; 22 June 1641, petition of the earl of Lindsey; 25 August 1641, affidavit of John Smith.

Lindsey's tenants and reaped and carted the corn, hemp and flax growing there. Later that month the house of commons received a report from two Lincolnshire justices of a major riot, extending over three days, in the fens north of Boston. 'Great multitudes' had assembled, and 'committed greate wast and destruction theire of wheate and other graine and behaved themselves furiously and outragiously'. The mob scorned the justices' order to disperse and threatened violence against anyone who endeavoured to stop them. The justices warned the Commons that some effort must be made to halt the riots, 'there is just cause to feare further and greater mischiefe and a more evill consequence will ensure hereupon . . . the indangeringe of a rebellion'.[28]

The winter brought some measure of peace to the fens, though rioters pulled down some of the houses built by the drainers, but in the spring the violence of the previous summer was renewed. In March 1642 the new sheriff of the county, Sir Edward Heron, himself deeply involved in drainage operations, and a number of justices made a determined effort to execute the order of the house of lords that the occupants of disputed lands should retain possession pending final judgement. But while the sheriff might drive off the commoners' cattle and temporarily restore the lands to the drainers, he could not guarantee their possession. No sooner had the sheriff and his men left than the fenmen would again forcibly expel the undertakers' servants and tenants. Not only were the sheriff's efforts unavailing, they appear to have infuriated the commoners who renewed their attacks on the enclosed land throughout the Lindsey Level and the Holland fen. On 1 April there was a great riot in the West Fen near Bolingbroke; houses were demolished, dikes filled in and the enclosures, with coleseed and rape worth £1,000, were destroyed. The authorities were powerless: the rioters consisted of 'all or the most parte of the inhabitants thereabouts and the . . . outrages comitted by a generall combination or approbation of that parte of the cuntrey'; the justices' attempts to disperse the mob by formally proclaiming the order of the house of lords were greeted only with derisive insults. Next day the sheriff and justices met at Boston to commence legal proceedings. Some rioters attended the session 'in a bravinge and daringe manner' and sheriff Heron was able to arrest two of the ringleaders. It was a rash move. The house in which Heron and the justices were lodged was immediately besieged by a huge crowd,

---

[28] Manning, *English People*, pp. 131–33 describes the August riots: the justices' report is SP 16/484/8.

more than a thousand strong, who beat up the sheriff's servants, smashed the windows and threatened to pull down the house unless the prisoners were released. The Boston magistrates refused to assist the sheriff, who for his own safety was obliged to allow the prisoners to escape; as he and his colleagues rode from the town the mob 'followed them allonge the streetes with shouts and outcryes, throwinge durte and stones at them'. This humiliation of the authorities further encouraged the fenmen, who attacked the drainage works and the drainers' enclosures and houses throughout the Level. They affirmed their right of common in a ritual game: the fenmen 'throwing out a foot-ball, and playing at it drove it against a new house set up in the drained fennes, and because it stood in theyr way pulled it downe . . . and so have they pulled down many'. Local juries refused to indict the participants in these riots, and by the end of May the fenmen had regained possession of all their ancient common in the Lindsey Level and the fens of Holland: the works had been 'layd waste by a rude multitude'.[29] Other dispossessed commoners soon followed this lead. In the saltmarsh, at Gedney, Surfleet and Sutton in Holland, and at Somercotes on the Lindsey coast there was a series of affrays between commoners and tenants; the latter only retained possession 'by stronge hand'. In June 1642 the drainage works and enclosures on the Isle of Axholme were first attacked; the assaults were to continue through the war years.[30]

The gentry, with the possible exception of those from the fens who had encouraged the rioters in 1641, viewed with real apprehension this humiliation of authority. To whom should they turn for assistance to restore order? The sympathies of the commoners were not clearly for parliament for they had expected swifter results from the investigation begun by the committee of the Commons, and by 1642 were stating that 'if the parliament would not helpe them, they would helpe themselves'. But parliament was not prepared to authorize strong measures. The Lords wavered in their attitude. They had issued orders giving the drainers quiet possession in 1641 and in late May 1642 they instructed Lord Willoughby to use force to protect the undertakers' lands. Two weeks later they modified this and required that

[29] These events are described by Manning, *English People*, pp. 133–34; for additional details, see H of LMP 23 May 1642, the certificate of Sir Edward Heron; Bodleian Lib., Tanner MS 63, f. 16; LR 2/287, ff. 2–3, 139–40.
[30] SP 23/208, p. 531; 218, pp. 779–88; H of LMP 7 March 1642/3, letter to Lord Willoughby, plus affidavits; 9 August 1643, petition of Edmund Nicholson; 12 August 1644, affidavit of William Hodson; *CSPD 1652–53*, p. 373.

Willoughby merely inform them of the situation in the fens. The Commons were divided, but the majority favoured the fenmen. On 6 April 1642, after a report of the 'insolencies' committed in Lincolnshire, some members favoured sending for the principal rioters as delinquents; others wished to leave the dispute to trial before the courts, arguing that the enclosures had been illegal. The matter was finally laid aside. Parliament's attitude was mirrored by its local representative; when in June Lord Willoughby was requested to employ the militia to suppress the rioters he refused to act, for 'the times were dangerous'.[31]

Parliament was supine in the face of the formidable insurrection in the fens. Some of the gentry turned to the king to guarantee order: this was the course taken by the men most actively involved in the various drainage operations — Lindsey and his Bertie relatives, Sir John Monson, Sir Edward Heron — though they may have been won to the royal cause as much by virtue of their connections with the court as by consideration of the risk to their investments through parliament's refusal to put down the riots. Other gentlemen, perhaps still suspicious of Charles, certainly fearful that the county would become the 'seat of war' if hostilities broke out, would not commit themselves so far. It was their sensibilities that were embodied in the formal rationale justifying the agreement to raise cavalry to which the gentry subscribed during the royal visit to Lincoln. The troops were to be employed within Lincolnshire, to defend 'the peace of this countrie' not only against the threats of invasion by foreigners or incursions by troops based outside the county but also against 'strange insolencies by men of dispicable condition'.

As the spokesmen of the neutral gentry wrote,

The reine of government hath beene so slackned as now is cutt in peeces amongst us, many men of desperate fortunes . . . live togeather without the acknowledgement of any law . . . They resist it in a warlike manner, accumulating all manner of insolencies, by adding to their rebelion violences upon mens houses, goods and lands, burning, stealing and devestating of them, so as men of fortune had need to serve them against such spirits.[32]

'Men of fortune had need to serve them against such spirits'. The gentry who favoured a neutrality between king and parliament and the isolation of the county from the war that seemed about to kindle

---

[31] BL Harl. 163, f. 65; *LJ*, v, pp. 55, 79, 115, 128, 137.
[32] P.M., *True intelligence*; Williams, 'Lincoln insignia', pp. 145–46; *Two petitions presented to the King's most excellent Majestie at Yorke*, London, 1642, pp. 6–8.

were profoundly affected by consideration of the popular turmoil in the fens that threatened social hierarchy and property.

By the summer of 1642, while some of the Lincolnshire gentry and the populace were prepared to accept the leadership of Lord Willoughby and the parliamentary deputation with enthusiasm, the broad consensus that had characterized the county in November 1640 shattered into a kaleidoscopic array of political attitudes. Some gentlemen, either antagonized by the radicalism of Pym's religious and constitutional projects and their destructive social consequences, or tied by loyalty or by self-interest to the crown, followed Charles. A substantial group, perhaps confused by the propaganda barrage of both parties or suspicious of their professed motives, avoided commitment to either side. They raised forces to secure 'the peace of this countrie' from the incursions of the troops of the belligerents and against the insurgent fenmen. Neutralism at the popular level was an equally common though more passive sentiment: it took the form of a desire to avoid being labelled 'malignants either against the king or parliament', and, in consequence, formal obedience to the commands of both.

Dr Morrill has suggested that the neutralist movement, whereby men 'closed ranks behind county barriers' in a number of shires in 1642 and 1643, represents the 'triumph' of 'provincialism'.[33] If Lincolnshire's experience is typical, it emphasizes rather the inchoate and nebulous character of local sentiment. The gentry were confronted by a fissure within the traditional institutions of central government, and with the spectre of popular insurrection: strong motives for their coalescence about an ideal of county autonomy. Yet the number of those who agreed to take an independent line and neutralize the shire were few, and their uneasiness emerges in the apologetic tone of their manifestos, and their hopes that their actions would meet with the approval of both the belligerents. Not surprisingly, their efforts were futile. Lincolnshire could not be insulated from the national conflict.

[33] Morrill, *Revolt*, pp. 36, 37.

CHAPTER 10

THE PROGRESS OF THE WAR, AUGUST 1642–46

I N the early summer of 1642 the adherents of, first, parliament, and then King Charles had boasted of Lincolnshire's unqualified devotion to their respective causes. In late July and August, aware of the strength of neutralist feeling in the shire, both parties quietly dropped such claims and contented themselves with limited operations. Active royalists led by the earl of Lindsey raised forces for the royal army, but made no attempt to implement the commission of array throughout the county and restricted their operations to areas where their estates lay and where their personal influence was greatest. Their opponents meanwhile consolidated their hold over Boston and its hinterland, where support for the parliamentary cause had always been most in evidence: at the end of August a London journalist claimed that Boston and its neighbouring towns could raise four thousand volunteers at six hours' notice if threatened by the cavaliers.[1]

Not only did the activists of the two parties, aware of the strength of moderate and neutralist sentiment, make no attempt to insist upon the general involvement of the county in their military preparations; each appears to have studiously disregarded the activities of the other. The king rebuked the corporation of Boston but made no attempt to suppress their mustering and drilling of volunteers: the parliamentarians did little to hinder the Berties and their allies, who 'beate up drummes publiquely in the county and raised forces'.

With the troops raised by local royalists marching with the king's field army into the west midlands, and with Willoughby and most

---

[1] LAO, ANC XII/A nos 5–7; SP 23/204, p. 649; England: Parliament, *The Parliament's resolution to raise forces to suppresse*, London, 1642, sig. A 3 v; (A. Mason), *Sad and fearfull newes from Beverley*, London, 1642, unpag.; Wood, ed., *Memorials of the Holles Family*, p. 186; *Speciall Passages*, 4, p. 28.

of his committee returning to Westminster to participate in the central deliberations and administrative duties occasioned by the mobilization of the earl of Essex's force, the fragile situation in Lincolnshire was sustained from late July until the end of September, disturbed only by two isolated incidents. The first occurred shortly after the raising of the royal standard of Nottingham on 22 August, when the king ordered the arrest of Captain Thomas Lister and two other Lincolnshire parliamentarians. The sheriff, Sir Edward Heron, accompanied by sixty troopers sent from the royal headquarters broke into Coleby Hall and carried Lister prisoner before the king's council. The parliamentarians were soon provided with an opportunity to reply in kind: in late August a number of officers with continental experience landed near Skegness from the Netherlands, intending to join the royal army; they were seized by local volunteers and sent up to London by the mayor of Boston.[2]

Yet even these two incidents did not herald a sustained attempt by either party to secure control of Lincolnshire or provoke a general outbreak of hostilities. Not until the final days of September, when Westminster began to evince a renewed interest in Lincolnshire, was the uneasy, snarling *modus vivendi* between the two parties broken. On 27 September parliament, hoping to employ the county as a staging point for assistance to be sent to Lord Fairfax in Yorkshire, issued a new set of instructions for Willoughby and his colleagues: with the troops they had raised in London they were to occupy the county, where they were to raise new forces and to invite subscriptions to the cause upon the propositions, to co-operate with the parliamentarians in neighbouring shires, and to arrest seventeen leading loyalist gentlemen and disarm all other 'malignants'.[3] Apparently apprised of this, those royalists who had not marched with the king's army endeavoured to strike first, ordering sheriff Heron to raid the houses and confiscate the arms of a number of parliamentary supporters. On 4 October 1642 the sheriff's agents, having searched the residence of Sir Edward Ayscough, M.P., at South Kelsey, were bringing their booty to the sheriff's house, Cressey Hall in Surfleet, which he had garrisoned and fortified. Close to Surfleet they were halted by a force led by Sir Anthony Irby who had recently arrived from London with a group of officers preparatory to raising a troop of dragoons in the county. Heron and his followers rode from Cressey Hall to try to recapture the arms, but they were repulsed after a sharp skirmish and the sheriff was captured.[4]

The arrest of Heron and the arrival of yet more parliamentary forces in the county disheartened the local royalists. Those compromised by their involvement in raising of money and men for the king fled the county; others, with the moderates, passively accepted parliamentary authority. Although their hold was weak on western Kesteven, the region where the earl of Lindsey had most influence, by early December 1642 the parliamentary committee apparently exercised unchallenged control of the greater part of the county. New forces were raised and the reorganization of the trained bands, begun in June, was completed; horses and equipment were sent to Essex's army; money for the parliamentary war chest had been raised by gifts, more or less voluntary, upon the propositions.[5] Parliament was impressed and anticipated that the Lincolnshire forces would soon be available for service in Yorkshire.[6]

Their hopes were soon dashed. In mid December the earl of Newcastle, the royalist commander in the north, sent a detachment of his army under Sir John Henderson to occupy Newark. The creation of a friendly garrison so near revived the Lincolnshire royalists: the committee found it increasingly difficult to raise money on the propositions, and supplies were secretly conveyed from the county to the enemy. Worse, a number of gentlemen who had tacitly accepted parliamentary supremacy fled to Newark, as did Thomas Harrington of Boothby Pagnell, who, 'being an ancient justice of peace . . . and much in the eye of the country did . . . drawe many after him and alien the affections of very many others'. In early January, with Newark as their base and supported by some of Henderson's troops, the royalists began to levy men and money in Kesteven. Parliamentary control of Lincolnshire, apparently so secure at the beginning of the month, suddenly seemed fragile, and Lord Fairfax received the assistance of only a couple of troops, as the committee insisted on retaining the bulk of its forces in Lincolnshire to meet the threat from Newark.[7]

In January 1643 the two parties skirmished on the western

---

[4] SP 28/31, f. 575; *CJ*, II, pp. 801, 812; E. Sandys, *A vindication from*, London, 1642, sig. A 4–A 4v.

[5] SP 28/4, f. 56; 31, f. 575; HMC *15th Report*, App. 5, p. 141; LAO, MM 6/1/5, f. 4v; SP 19/113, f. 118; Nalson MS II, no. 113; SP 23/188, pp. 7–23.

[6] *LJ*, v, pp. 473, 495; *CJ*, II, pp. 873, 893.

[7] *LJ*, v, p. 527; Nalson MS II, no. 113; SP 23/181, p. 295; 197, p. 755; H of LMP January 1644/5 (*sic* — an error), Sir John Henderson to Mr Slingsby.

borders of Lincolnshire with mixed fortunes. On 12 January royalist cavalry occupied Grantham, where they were publicly welcomed by the authorities. The latter's royalism proved premature, however; the approach of a superior parliamentary force sent the cavaliers scuttling from the town and the mayor of Grantham was carried to Lincoln to explain his and his colleagues' ill-timed enthusiasm to the parliamentary committee. About the same time the Boston volunteers crushed a putative royalist rising in the south Holland fens led by Captain Welby of Spalding.[8] But these royalist disappointments were balanced by two major successes in January, with important consequences for the future development of the war in Lincolnshire. Gainsborough had erected fortifications and raised a small force 'but declared neither for king or parliament, intending only to stand upon their guard against rovers'; however, despite this neutral posture, when the Newarkers appeared before the town it was surrendered without resistance and garrisoned for the king. Also in late January a small raiding party from Newark daringly surprised and captured Belvoir Castle.[9]

Although the parliamentarians were able to contain royalist attempts to secure bases other than on the western margins of Lincolnshire, it is clear that the Newarkers' presence was generally weakening the committee's control, particularly in Kesteven. During the royalists' short occupation of Grantham the committee summoned the trained bands to assist their troops retake the town: the response was negligible.[10] Many countrymen, fearing retaliation, must have thought passivity the safest posture until one or other side had secured more than a temporary control. Clearly the establishment of complete parliamentarian dominance in the shire and the provision of the promised, but long-delayed, support for Lord Fairfax, depended upon the capture of Newark; in February the committee launched a major effort to secure the prize. A substantial detachment of the main parliamentary field army, commanded by Lord Willoughby of Parham and the professional soldier, Colonel Ballard, marched into Lincolnshire with instructions from the earl of Essex to take Newark and then move into Yorkshire. Willoughby and Ballard joined up with the forces raised by the local committee, and on 27 February the army marched from

---

[8] *Certaine Informations*, 1, pp. 2–3; 2, p. 11; *Mercurius Aulicus*, 2, p. 18; 3, p. 23; *Speciall Passages*, 23, p. 191; Grantham Hall Book 1, f. 108v.
[9] *The works of Symon Patrick D.D.*, ix, ed. A. Taylor, Oxford, 1858, pp. 411–13; LAO, BRACE 17/1, p. 24; A. C. Wood, *Nottinghamshire in the Civil War*, Oxford, 1937, p. 31.
[10] *Mercurius Aulicus*, 3, p. 28; *Certaine Informations*, 1, p. 2.

M

its bases at Lincoln and Grantham against Newark, where it was joined by the detachments from Nottingham, Leicester and Derby: a combined force of six thousand men, with a small train of light artillery. Despite the impressive preparations, the assault on 28 February was a failure, in part through the skilful defensive strategy of governor Henderson, and in part through Ballard's lukewarm leadership and pusillanimity, treachery even, in ordering a prema-

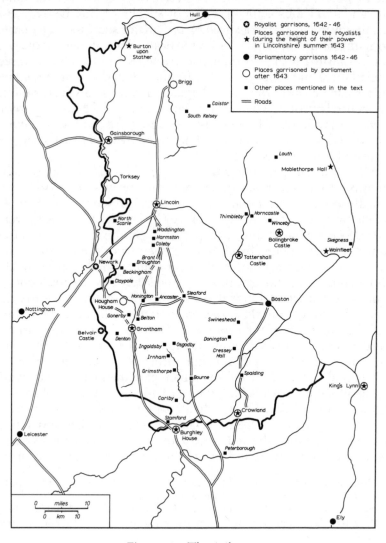

Figure 6   *The civil war*

ture retreat which turned into a rout. Next day Ballard refused to renew the assault and the combined forces broke up and returned to their respective bases.[11]

Even before the failure of the attack on Newark there is evidence that, through royalist successes and uninspired leadership, enthusiasm amongst some parliamentary supporters in the county was waning: in early February many previously active were 'thinking how to sit downe and save themselves'.[12] The Newark debacle and the suspicion of treachery that attended it both enhanced such demoralization, and encouraged the Newarkers. The latter redoubled their efforts to raise men and money in the areas within their reach. The parliamentarians appear to have done little other than savagely plunder suspected royalist sympathizers, the barbarities of which they were accused perhaps being a frustrated reaction to their failure.[13] By mid March there was wholesale desertion from some parliamentary troops, and when on 24 March the cavaliers surprised Grantham, the loss of the town was in part attributed to a feud between two of the parliamentary officers in the garrison.[14] Immediately after the fall of the town the two members of parliament then in the county wrote bitterly to Westminster: they complained of the 'burthen daylie increasing', of parliament's failure to send supplies, and demanded that the other county members should return to Lincolnshire to assist in local administration — a service which had become 'a punishment' to them.[15]

But worse was to follow the loss of Grantham. On the following day the men of Crowland led by their martial vicar, who had already demonstrated royalist sympathies during Captain Welby's abortive January rising in the fens, declared for the king and raided Spalding, carrying off the Puritan minister and a number of parliamentary supporters. By early April the Newarkers had taken Grantham, Stamford and Peterborough; Kesteven had been brought under contribution; their cavalry had appeared before the walls of Lincoln and in Sleaford, and had raided into the Holland

---

[11] Wood, *Nottinghamshire*, pp. 39–42; *Speciall Passages*, 23, p. 190; 27, p. 225; HMC *Hastings*, II, p. 189.
[12] *Speciall Passages*, 28, p. 229. See also *Mercurius Aulicus*, 2, p. 28.
[13] *CJ*, III, pp. 1–2; *The Kingdomes Weekly Intelligencer*, 12, p. 92; *Mercurius Aulicus*, 10, p. 121; *LNQ*, I (1889), p. 75; H of LMP 14 March 1642/3, petition of Henry Noel.
[14] *Speciall Passages*, 33, pp. 273–74; *Mercurius Aulicus*, 13, p. 155; *The Kingdomes Weekly Intelligencer*, 13, p. 104; John Lilburne, *The iust mans iustification*, London, 1646, p. 20.
[15] Nalson MS II, no. 182.

fen, threatening Boston.[16] On 11 April 1643 the cavaliers emphasized their superiority at the battle of Ancaster Heath. The royalist
commissioners at Newark summoned the country to a sessions at
Grantham on that day, where they proposed to indict the leading
parliamentary supporters in Lincolnshire of high treason — a
fairly pointless undertaking except as an exercise in public relations designed to demonstrate their control in Kesteven. Lord
Willoughby, reinforced by troops from Yorkshire, approached
Grantham seeking to surprise the assembly, but he was outman-
œuvred by the royalist commander, Cavendish, and forced to retire
towards Lincoln. Cavendish pursued the parliamentarians, and his
cavalry finally caught and routed Willoughby's retreating forces on
Ancaster Heath.[17]

The presence of a contingent from Yorkshire in Willoughby's
army of Ancaster requires explanation. In December it had been
intended that the forces being raised in Lincolnshire should assist
Lord Fairfax, but with the threat posed by the royalist occupation
of Newark only a couple of troops of dragoons were sent. To
Fairfax's annoyance these had deserted him and returned to
Lincolnshire in mid March to defend their own county as the
military situation there worsened. Early next month a further
detachment commanded by John Hotham abandoned Yorkshire to
assist in Lincolnshire. Hotham was brother-in-law to the two
Lincolnshire members of parliament, Sir John and Sir Christopher
Wray, but his arrival in Lincolnshire was less a function of his and
his force's local connections than of his pique that Lord Fairfax had
been preferred for supreme command in Yorkshire. He chafed
under his rival's authority and, on 10 April, without consideration
of Fairfax's untenable military position at Leeds, brought his troops
across the Humber to serve with Willoughby.[18] Shortly after his
arrival Hotham was appointed commander-in-chief of all forces in
the county, but his presence scarcely revived the parliamentary
cause in Lincolnshire. His men were poorly disciplined, and guilty
of 'plundering . . . divers persons of great affection to the
parliament'; in this they were probably encouraged by officers like
Hotham's lieutenant, Matthias Frome, 'a desparate rude man . . . a
great plunderer'. Soon it was being suggested in the London press

---

[16] *Speciall Passages*, 35, p. 285; *Mercurius Aulicus*, 15, pp. 185–86.
[17] Ibid., 16, pp. 193–95; *A relation of a fight in the county of Lincolne . . . neere Ancaster*, Oxford, 1643, passim.
[18] BL Add. 31116, f. 35; *Mercurius Aulicus*, 16, pp. 204–5.

that some of Hotham's officers were of questionable loyalty.[19] The rumours were correct although it was Hotham himself rather than his subordinates who posed the real threat. Since late 1642 Hotham had been in communications with the earl of Newcastle, with whose moderate royalism he sympathized, offering to secure the pacification of Yorkshire under the earl, and limiting his own military operations to avoid a direct confrontation with the cavaliers. Once in Lincolnshire Hotham played the same game. Boasting that he could ensure that the county would 'be wholly at . . . [the king's] . . . devotion', he again promised to restrict his military operations and emphasized the readiness of the two members of parliament then in the county, Sir Christopher Wray and Sir Edward Ayscough, to abandon the struggle if they were guaranteed a free pardon.[20] That the committee was prepared to sell out to the royalists is doubtful but some official correspondence does suggest that the picture Hotham presented to Newcastle, of the parliamentary administration in Lincolnshire demoralized and frustrated by the succession of disappointments in March and April, was not imaginary. On 2 May Ayscough and Wray wrote to the Commons detailing the royalists' successes and bewailing the negligible assistance they had received from parliament; they inveighed with particular bitterness against those 'gentlemen of great estates' who had retired 'to take their ease at London', leaving the whole burden of county administration to them. In another letter of 5 May they sarcastically referred to those members and committee-men who had abandoned Lincolnshire for the safety of Hull or London, 'so they may with great ease sit safe and talk . . . of those actions and particulars they take up at second hand'.[21]

Two weeks after the arrival of the perfidious Hotham and his unruly troops from Yorkshire, the parliamentary cause in Lincoln-shire was provided with a further, less dubious, source of assist-ance. In late April Cromwell, commanding a detachment of the army of the Eastern Association, having advanced from Hunt-ingdon to Peterborough moved against Crowland, where he was joined by a regiment of infantry from Norfolk and local troops from Boston. The Crowlanders, protected by their marshes and

[19] *CJ*, III, pp. 86, 138; *Mercurius Civicus*, 4, p. 31; SP 23/20, p. 318; SP 28/265, unfol., the case of Capt. Frome.
[20] Bodleian Lib., Tanner MS 62, ff. 71, 90; HMC *13th Report*, App. 1, pp. 80, 87, 89-90, 99, 105, 109, 699, 701-2, 702-3, 704, 707.
[21] Nalson MS XI, nos 243, 253. For Lincolnshire worthies who were 'sitting safe' in London, see *CJ*, III, p. 232; *LJ*, VI, p. 299.

assisted by foul weather, had beaten off an assault by the Lincolnshire parliamentarians in mid April, but, disheartened by the
strength of Cromwell's force and three days' bombardment, they
surrendered the town on 29 April.[22]

Following Cromwell's success at Crowland the Lincolnshire
parliamentarians sought his further assistance, and their appeals
were reinforced by orders from the central authorities instructing
the commanders in the east midlands to join forces and intercept a
convoy of munitions which had been sent from the north to supply
Oxford. The execution of this order was tardy. Hotham informed
Newcastle that he would endeavour to prevent or delay the
conjunction of forces; Lord Grey of Groby refused to march from
Leicester, which was threatened by the royalists; even Cromwell
was more concerned to secure his lines of communication and raise
money, by rounding up potential royalists in Huntingdonshire and
the Soke of Peterborough. When Cromwell finally joined the
Lincolnshire forces at Sleaford on 9 May it was too late to intercept
the crucial convoy, although the conjoined forces were employed
in a raid into western Kesteven, carrying off supplies which would
otherwise have been employed by the royalists.[23] On 13 April the
raiders, having scoured the countryside, marched up to Newark
and 'faced' the town, displaying their strength and confidence, and
challenging the cavaliers. This exercise may have boosted morale
but it nearly ended in disaster. Hotham and Cromwell, having
bearded the Newarkers in their den, retired to Grantham and the
adjacent villages to take up their quarters; late in the evening a
strong body of royalist cavalry, marching by back roads, surprised
the Lincolnshire troops that manned the outposts, taking many
prisoners. The cavaliers pressed on, hoping to catch the main
parliamentary force quartered in Grantham unawares, but the latter
had been warned, marched out of the town and met the Newarkers
at Belton. A confused action followed in the gathering darkness:
Cromwell's troopers routed the cavalry drawn up against them but
Hotham's force made no impression on the enemy's left wing.
Nightfall terminated the action, and, despite Cromwell's euphoric

[22] Speciall Passages, 37, p. 303; Divers remarkeable passages of Gods good providence,
London, 1643.
[23] SP 23/184, p. 445; SP 19/149/109, 110. For the proposed combined action
against the royalist convoy see my The Eastern Association, Cambridge, 1974, pp.
72–74.

claims of a great victory (echoed by his hagiographers) the combined force prudently continued its withdrawal to Lincoln.[24]

After a week's rest at Lincoln, Cromwell and Hotham's forces marched to Nottingham to participate in another combined action with the troops of the other east midland counties. The operation, initially designed to provide assistance to Fairfax so that he might capitalize on his victory at Wakefield, then, failing that, to prevent another convoy of munitions getting through to Oxford from the north, was wholly abortive. Fairfax received no assistance; the munitions reached Charles. A single benefit resulted from the month-long period of inaction: the unmasking of John Hotham. Disturbed by Hotham's insufferable temper and by the appalling lack of discipline among his troops, the other commanders of the joint force became increasingly suspicious that he was playing a double game. They secretly informed the earl of Essex, the parliamentary commander-in-chief, of their doubts, and Essex sent Sir John Meldrum, a Scottish professional soldier, to Nottingham, where he arrested Hotham on 18 June. A few days later the prisoner escaped, going first to Lincoln and then to Hull, where he was recaptured, but not before he had offered to surrender both those towns to the royalists.[25]

The removal of Cromwell and Hotham's forces to Nottingham in late May, leaving only a small garrison at Lincoln, provided the cavaliers with an excellent opportunity to raid Lincolnshire. In the south the garrison of Belvoir ranged over the Stamford area in early June. The Newarkers, having plundered Sir William Armyne's property at Osgodby marched to Donington, where on 13 June they routed a force being sent from Boston to join the Nottingham army, and then seized a great number of horses grazing in the fens.[26] To the north the garrison of Gainsborough was equally active in late May, marching up to Lincoln, where they skirmished successfully with the city's garrison, and raiding north-western Lincolnshire. One such raid begun on 1 June ended inauspiciously when the cavaliers were surprised at Louth by a party from the

[24] For a narrative, see A. C. E. Welby 'Belton Fight', *LNQ*, 13 (1915), pp. 38–47. Welby, and other historians of the battle, are so intent on Cromwell's victory, that they fail to notice the failure of Hotham's force — for this see J. Rushworth, *Historical Collections*, v, London, 1721, pp. 745–46.

[25] Wood, *Nottinghamshire*, pp. 44–49.

[26] Essex Archaeological Society, Colchester, Morant MS 46, f. 27; H of LMP 1 January 1647/8, note concerning Lord Camden's composition; *A perfect diurnall of the passages in Parliament*, 53, *sub* 17 June; *Mercurius Aulicus*, 24, p. 321.

Lincoln garrison reinforced by troops from other parts of the county. Despite this setback the Gainsborough men were still able in mid June to 'range over the county, to assess towns, to take prisoners and to drive men's horses'. With the cavaliers raiding into the county as deep as Donington and Louth the earl of Lincoln decided that it would be prudent to garrison Tattershall Castle.[27]

July brought some respite to the beleaguered parliamentarians. After Hotham's arrest his forces returned to Lincoln, strengthening the city's garrison, which on 1 July, beat off an assault by royalists from Gainsborough and Newark. The cavaliers expected help from the military governor of Lincoln appointed by Hotham, who had agreed to betray the city; but his intentions were discovered and the garrison, forewarned, was able both to prevent a group of royalists who had entered the town in disguise with the governor's connivance from seizing the magazine, and to beat off the forces which arrived to second the efforts of the conspirators within the town. This success, and the fact that the bulk of the cavalier forces were engaged in escorting the munitions convoy, encouraged Lord Willoughby to take the offensive, and on 20 July his forces, assisted by treachery within the town, surprised Gainsborough.[28] Paradoxically his coup was the prelude to a period in which the fortunes of the Lincolnshire parliamentarians reached their lowest ebb.

Gainsborough, 'the most considerable passage over the river Trent except Newarke', was a vital link in the lines of communication between the northern royalists and the Newarkers, and a force under Sir Charles Cavendish immediately besieged Willoughby, who appealed for reinforcements and supplies. The remaining contingents of the combined army assembled at Nottingham under Cromwell and Sir John Meldrum were deputed to relieve Willoughby, but first Cromwell's troops rode to the Stamford area where the cavaliers from Belvoir had been active, threatening Peterborough and the Nene frontier of the Association. Cromwell's swift approach surprised the royalist forces, who took refuge in Burghley House, which they surrendered on 24 July as Cromwell, reinforced by two infantry regiments, prepared to storm the great mansion.[29] From Stamford, Cromwell pressed on to

---

[27] I. Beckwith, *Gainsborough during the Great Civil War*, Gainsborough, 1969, p. 9; *Mercurius Aulicus*, 24, p. 312.

[28] John Vicars, *Jehovah-Jireh*, London, 1644, pp. 372–73; Beckwith, *Gainsborough*, p. 11; *Mercurius Aulicus*, 30, p. 402.

[29] BL Egerton 2647, f. 51; *The writings and speeches of Oliver Cromwell*, I, ed. W. C. Abbott, Cambridge Mass., 1937, p. 239; *A true relation of Colonell Cromwels proceedings*, London, 1643.

the appointed rendezvous at North Scarle, linking up with the Nottingham forces under Meldrum and the cavalry from Lincoln. On 27 July the combined force advanced to Gainsborough and, having defeated the royalist cavalry outside the town in a sharp action in which the opposing commander, Cavendish, was killed, resupplied Willoughby with munitions. While the commanders were conferring in the town the advance of a small royalist force was reported, and the parliamentary troops confidently sallied out to complete their victory. A shock awaited them. Coming to the brow of a hill above the town they saw 'a whole regiment of foot, after that another and another, and, as some counted, about fifty colours of foot, with a great body of horse'. Newcastle's entire army had marched against Gainsborough. Meldrum and Cromwell hurriedly retired to Lincoln, leaving Willoughby again besieged by Newcastle's formidable force.

Both Meldrum and Cromwell hoped to organize another, more powerful, expedition to relieve the town, but for once Newcastle's generalship, so often lethargic, was enterprising and determined. A continuous bombardment brought the townsmen and the garrison to the verge of mutiny, and, after three days, Willoughby surrendered.[30] The defeated parliamentarians were permitted to retire to Lincoln, but Newcastle gave his opponents no time to organize the defence of the city. The royalists advanced and the demoralized garrison deserted in shoals; Willoughby was obliged to abandon both the city and his heavy artillery, and retired to Boston with only a remnant of his original force. Cromwell too fell back, withdrawing his forces to Peterborough and Spalding as the cavaliers poured into the county, capturing Tattershall Castle, exacting contributions of men and money in eastern Kesteven and on the Lindsey coast. Even Holland was not immune; on 8 August 'twelve flying colours of horse and foot' were reported within a mile of Swineshead. In Boston the disheartened garrison and townsmen waited in trepidation for the tide that had inundated the county to smash against their puny bulwarks.[31]

Yet the expected attack, a prelude to a further advance by the northern royalists, never came. Newcastle withdrew the bulk of his forces to his interminable siege of Hull, leaving Sir William Widdrington with a small force in command of Lincolnshire. Newcastle thus missed the opportunity for a potentially decisive

[30] Beckwith, *Gainsborough*, pp. 11–16.
[31] Bodleian Lib., Tanner MS 62, ff. 208, 232; BL Egerton 2647, f. 120; *The Parliament Scout*, 7, p. 54; 8, p. 61; 9, p. 69; *Cromwell's writings*, I, ed. Abbott, pp. 251–53; *Mercurius Aulicus*, 33, p. 447.

military operation, and the error was compounded when the royalists sent no assistance to King's Lynn, which declared for the king on 23 August. Widdrington preferred to secure his hold on Kesteven and Lindsey, where garrisons were established at Bolingbroke and Mablethorpe Hall, rather than undertake an aggressive strategy.

The royalists' failure to pursue their advantage in August 1643 was ultimately to prove fatal to their cause in Lincolnshire. Parliament responded to the threat of Newcastle's advancing into East Anglia, and perhaps on London, by reorganizing the Eastern Association: its new commander-in-chief, Edward, earl of Manchester, was empowered to raise a new and vastly enlarged army in the eastern counties. If parliament gave Manchester the authority, Newcastle, by failing to assail Boston or relieve Lynn, gave the earl a more precious commodity: time. Steadily the parliamentary legislation was transmuted into troops, companies and regiments before the walls of King's Lynn, which, with no prospect of relief, surrendered on 15 September.[32]

Whilst Manchester commanded the forces besieging Lynn Cromwell organized a screening force of cavalry based on Spalding and Boston. A week after the surrender of the town Cromwell's troops undertook a more dangerous operation. In Yorkshire the earl of Newcastle had pinned the parliamentarian forces in Hull, where the cavalry under Sir Thomas Fairfax were virtually useless. Accordingly it was decided to ferry Fairfax's troops across the Humber; their landing was covered by Cromwell's cavalry, which had ridden up from Holland. Despite harassment from a large force of royalist cavalry the operation was concluded successfully, and Fairfax's twenty-two troops joined those from Lincolnshire and the Eastern Association at their base in Boston, which was also the rendezvous for the infantry which had participated in the siege of Lynn.

Early in October, Manchester felt strong enough to challenge the royalist dominance in Lindsey. On 9 October the earl marched from Boston, forcing the royalists to quit the fortifications they had begun at Wainfleet, and laid siege to Bolingbroke Castle with his infantry: the cavalry were quartered in villages to the north and west as a screen for the besiegers. Manchester believed that the threat to Bolingbroke would provoke the royalists into mounting a relieving force and thus lead to a more general engagement, and he was not disappointed. On the evening of 10 October a large body of

[32] See Holmes, *Eastern Association*, pp. 91–96.

royalist horse and dragoons, culled from the garrisons of Newark, Gainsborough and Lincoln, surprised Manchester's cavalry at Horncastle and Thimbleby, and then had the best of some confused fighting as the rest of the parliamentary horse struggled to pull back from their advanced positions to a general rendezvous appointed by Manchester on the hill overlooking Old Bolingbroke. Next morning, encouraged by this success, the royalists marched from Horncastle towards Bolingbroke, but were met and totally shattered by Fairfax and Cromwell's cavalry at the battle of Winceby. On the same day Lord Fairfax sallied from Hull, overrunning the besiegers' emplacements: this was as important a success as Winceby for the parliamentary cause in Lincolnshire, for Newcastle could spare no assistance to redeem the loss suffered by his lieutenants in the county.[33]

After their victory at Winceby the parliamentarians spent the remainder of the year mopping up. The city of Lincoln surrendered to Manchester on 20 October, and was garrisoned by a regiment from the army of the Eastern Association. While the bulk of the earl's army then retired to winter quarters the cavalry under Cromwell and Fairfax moved into Kesteven, skirmishing with the garrisons of Newark and Belvoir and preventing any royalist incursions. Lord Willoughby of Parham's troops cleared the petty garrisons on the Lindsey coast, then in early November occupied and fortified Brigg, presumably as a precaution against the raids of the Gainsborough royalists. On 20 December Gainsborough itself was taken by a force commanded by Sir John Meldrum from Hull, which first captured the royalist fort covering the Trent at Burton Stather.[34] With the exception of the forces in the Isle of Axholme, no royalist garrison was left within the county: 'good riddance for poore Lincolnshire', smirked one London diurnal; another waxed poetic — Lord Willoughby and the local members of parliament were 'by an orbicular providence, by an admirable revolution, re-estated, re-entred, re-possessed, re-Lincolnshired again'.[35]

The counterpart to the delight of the parliamentary press was the

---

[33] For the battle, see A. H. Burne and P. Young, *The Great Civil War*, London, 1959, pp. 111–18. For additional details, see *Memorials of the Civil War*, ed. R. Bell, London, 1849, pp. 62–65; *A true relation of the late fight betweene the Right Honourable the Earle of Manchesters forces*, London, 1643.

[34] *The Parliament Scout*, 19, pp. 165, 168, 170; 21, p. 180; 24, p. 208; *Mercurius Civicus*, 22, p. 174; 25, p. 194; 28, p. 222; SP 28/161, the account of Edward Rossiter; SP 23/239, ff. 159, 162; LAO, Addlethorpe-cum-Ingoldmells constables' account 1643; Beckwith, *Gainsborough*, p. 17.

[35] *The Parliament Scout*, 27, p. 228; *Mercurius Britanicus*, 18, p. 143.

deep gloom which overshadowed the royalists. On 31 January 1644 the commissioners at Newark informed the king in the most dejected terms of the situation of their garrison. The Newarkers had not done badly in their winter skirmishing: their cavalry could still raid Grantham and Sleaford and on 12 January they scored a minor triumph by taking three of Cromwell's crack troops unawares in their quarters at Harmston and Waddington.[36] But such successes could not compensate the royalists for their lost footholds. The parliamentarians, wrote the Newark commissioners, now 'enjoy Lincolnshire in quiet possession'. As 'absolute masters of that county', they had seized and sold the goods of all royalist sympathizers, levied a succession of heavy taxes, and with the revenue thus raised were equipping new forces — forces which, the commissioners stated ominously, soon 'will be poured down . . . upon us'.[37]

The Newark commissioners proved good prophets. The withdrawal of Newcastle's army into the northern counties to face the invading Scots further weakened Newark's position and made it a tempting prey to the parliamentarians. In early February the town was blockaded, but the wretched weather restricted operations and it was not until 29 February that a parliamentary army of some five thousand men closed in and commenced a formal siege of the town. The besieging force was an extraordinarily heterogeneous body. The overall commander was Sir John Meldrum who, having cleared the Isle of Axholme, marched from his base at Gainsborough. He was joined by two Eastern Association regiments that had been garrisoning Lincoln; by the forces newly raised by Colonel King, the earl of Manchester's appointee as governor of Holland and Boston; by Lord Willoughby of Parham's Lincolnshire troops; and by detachments from Leicester, Nottingham and Derby. The diverse origins of the parliamentary force proved to be the salvation of the Newarkers. 'Dissentions and jealousies' among the various local commanders and their incompetence gave Prince Rupert time to organize a relief column. On 21 March, to the dismay of the besiegers, Rupert appeared before the beleaguered town and in a fierce action scattered the parliamentary horse. Lacking cavalry support, caught in a vice between Rupert and the town's garrison, short of provisions and with some regiments on the verge of mutiny, Sir John Meldrum was forced to seek terms of

[36] *The Weekly Post*, 9, p. 62; *The Parliament Scout*, 30, p. 253; *Mercurius Aulicus*, 2, p. 779.
[37] Rushworth, *Historical Collections*, v, pp. 305–6.

surrender: it was agreed that his infantry should abandon their arms and ammunition and be allowed to return to their bases.[38]

But, disarmed and demoralized, the parliamentary forces were in no mood to make a stand against the victorious cavaliers. While Meldrum was able to destroy some of the fortifications of Gainsborough before retiring to Hull with his mutinous troops, Hobart's men refused to attempt to hold Lincoln against Rupert and the city with its artillery was hastily abandoned to the royalists on 23 March. In the south Crowland was seized, and there were fears for the safety of Boston until its depleted and ill-supplied garrison was reinforced by troops from King's Lynn.[39] Crowland was soon recovered, but Rupert's victory heralded another phase of royalist dominance over a considerable portion of the county. Lincoln was garrisoned and the royalist commissioners began seizing the estates of their opponents and levying men and money in the county; their cavalry raided deep into Holland, gathering horses and cattle from the fens.[40]

The rescue of the beleaguered Lincolnshire parliamentarians was again accomplished by the earl of Manchester. After some delay occasioned by uncertainty at Westminster as to the strategy to be pursued by the army of the Eastern Association, Manchester was ordered to clear the cavaliers from Lincolnshire and then to link up with Fairfax and the Scots besieging York. On 25 April the army of the Association marched into Stamford and parties of its cavalry drove the royalists from Grimsthorpe and Sleaford which they were attempting to fortify. Having secured adequate supplies for his army Manchester pushed forward to Lincoln, occupying the lower city on 3 May; three days later the Bail was stormed, and the earl captured the royalist commissioners for the county, besides many common soldiers and much equipment. In the next two weeks Cromwell and the Association's cavalry drove the Newark horse from Lincolnshire and from the west bank of the Trent.[41]

Manchester's second capture of Lincoln finally terminated royalist dominance in the county, but it could not secure Lincolnshire from the attentions of its neighbours, the garrisons of Newark and

[38] Wood, *Nottinghamshire*, pp. 67–82, provides an excellent account of the siege; see also BL Harl. 166, f. 99v.
[39] *The Scottish Dove*, 25, p. 196; *The Military Scribe*, 6, p. 46; Beckwith, *Gainsborough*, p. 17; A. A. Garner, *Boston and the Great Civil War, 1642–51*, Boston, 1972, pp. 19–20; HMC *9th Report*, App. 2, p. 435.
[40] BL Add. 18981, ff. 120, 132; *CSPD 1644*, pp. 116–17, 120, 123; *The Parliament Scout*, 43, pp. 358, 360.
[41] BL Add. 18981, ff. 160, 161, 168, 169; W. Goode, *A particular relation of the severall removes*, London, 1644; Hill, *Tudor and Stuart Lincoln*, pp. 157–58.

Belvoir. When on 25 May Manchester marched his army over the bridge of boats at Gainsborough to join the siege of York, he left a regiment to garrison Lincoln, and ordered new forces of cavalry under Rossiter and infantry under Rainsborow to be raised for the defence of the county. But this did not deter the Newarkers, who regrouped and recommenced their career of plunder. In early June the royalists were active in southern Kesteven, occupying Stamford and preparing to fortify Irnham House. Their raiding parties operated further afield: two Norfolk merchants were seized and robbed on the road between Swineshead and Sleaford. In July Rossiter was involved in a series of skirmishes on the western fringes of the county.[42]

The return of the army of the Association in early August following its victory at Marston Moor and the fall of York gave the county some relief from the raiders. Manchester made Lincoln his headquarters and infantry detachments were quartered at Claypole, Beckingham and Brant Broughton, while the cavalry occupied the villages between Newark and Belvoir. Despite these precautions the Belvoir garrison were able to organize a raiding party that captured some of the Association's supplies at Ingoldsby.[43]

Throughout August the London press anticipated Manchester's besieging Newark, yet this proposal, frequently discussed at headquarters, came to nothing: Manchester was increasingly disillusioned with the war and reluctant to undertake any decisive action. And so the earl dithered at Lincoln, until, in early September he received categorical instructions from Westminster to march into the Thames valley. On 3 September the army of the Association abandoned its quarters in the vicinity of the royalists' garrisons, and marched through Sleaford and Bourne: the defence of the shire was left to Rainsborow and Rossiter's regiments. The Newarkers, no longer bottled-up and reinforced by the remnants of the royalist cavalry scattered at Marston Moor, were not slow to capitalize on the situation. In mid September a substantial royalist force approached Sleaford where Rossiter was building fortifications and, having forced him to retire to Lincoln, plundered and levied assessments in the surrounding villages. In the next fortnight the parliamentary committee's treasurer was seized within five miles of Lincoln, another committee-man was captured at Caistor, and a small garrison at Torksey ferry was overrun. In early October a detachment from Belvoir, having plundered the Stamford area,

---

[42] *CSPD 1644*, pp. 200, 208, 217; Norfolk RO, Q/S box 35, the information of John Titshall; *The Weekly Account*, 49, p. 237; *The Parliament Scout*, 56, p. 449.
[43] *A continuation of true intelligence*, 7, pp. 2–4; *Mercurius Aulicus*, 35, pp. 1139–40.

surprised the parliamentary garrison of Crowland. The island stronghold, for the third time in royalist hands, had considerable nuisance value. Forces had to be diverted to besiege it and the cavaliers took advantage of their absence to make further raids deep into Lindsey: Sir Charles Bolles surprised a number of Yorkshire parliamentarian worthies at Louth en route for London and took substantial booty.[44]

But the royalist star was not long in the ascendant. Rossiter was reinforced by some troops of horse from Yorkshire and by Fleetwood's cavalry regiment which Manchester had sent to assist in the defence of the county. Rossiter scored a number of successes in skirmishes and then, on 29 October emphasized his superiority in a clash near Denton, where he intercepted a force of infantry and cavalry, two thousand strong, which was to have relieved Crowland. The victory enabled the parliamentarians to occupy Grantham for their winter quarters, and, without hope of relief, the royalists in Crowland were forced to surrender in early December.[45]

Lincolnshire was still not freed from its tormentors, the garrisons of Newark and Belvoir. Their most extensive inroad was made in March 1645. On 22 February Sir Marmaduke Langdale was dispatched from Oxford with instructions to link up with the Newarkers and then relieve Pontefract Castle. Rossiter moved to prevent the royalist conjunction, but on 25 February his smaller force was beaten and pushed aside by Langdale at Melton Mowbray. Having regrouped his force, Rossiter was ordered to shadow the royalists into Yorkshire and then back into the west midlands: he did not return to Lincolnshire until late March. In Rossiter's absence the Newarkers enjoyed a field-day: their attack on Grantham was beaten off but the royalist cavalry poured into Kesteven and Holland, levying assessments and driving off horses and cattle.[46] Besides this major incursion, the military history of Lincolnshire in late 1644 and 1645 consists of a series of skirmishes: the surprise of the parliamentary infantry quartered at Gonerby in early December 1644; the royalist seizure of Hougham House on 10

[44] The Parliament Scout, 66, p. 525; 68, p. 542; The London Post, 14, p. 4; CSPD 1644, pp. 537, 545; LAO, South Kyme constables' account 1644; BL Add. 5508, f. 9; The Letter Books of Sir Samuel Luke, ed. H. G. Tibbutt, London, 1963, pp. 339, 344, 349–50, 359.

[45] Ibid., pp. 361, 370–71; The Parliament Scout, 72, pp. 574, 576; The True Informer, 57, p. 430.

[46] Wood, Nottinghamshire, p. 89; The Moderate Intelligencer, 5, pp. 35, 36; LAO, South Kyme constables' accounts 1645; Luke Letter Book, ed. Tibbutt, pp. 493, 502; E 113 Box 4 part 2, the answer of Samuel Thompson.

June 1645 and its swift recapture by Rossiter; the Newarkers' destruction of the fortifications at Torksey on 1 August; the rout of a party of Newarkers which had been raiding the Stamford area at Carlby a week later. But more important than this series of skirmishes to the country people was the continued ability of small Newark raiding parties to elude Rossiter's patrols and to plunder the countryside. In December 1644 and again in the summer and autumn of 1645 the Newarkers were in Lindsey; in September 1645 it was reported that estates in the vicinity of Sleaford were still subject to contributions to both sides.[47]

The winter of 1645–46 brought increasing relief to Lincolnshire. As the king's cause faded, further parliamentary troops could be brought to bear against Newark, a process which culminated in late November with the arrival of the Scottish army before the town. It was not until March 1646 that Newark was closely invested, but the previous three months were employed in mopping up the petty garrisons in the vicinity, including Belvoir, which capitulated on 3 February. Lincolnshire was still subject to intermittent incursions from Newark in this period, although these operations were increasingly undisciplined, disorganized and concerned more with the acquisition of plunder than with tactical advantage.[48] Finally on 8 May, Newark surrendered and Lincolnshire was finally freed of the threatening presence of its royalist neighbours: the first civil war was over.

[47] *Luke Letter Book*, ed. Tibbutt, p. 408; Wood, *Nottinghamshire*, pp. 92, 94, 95; HMC *13th Report*, App. I, pp. 237–38; R. E. G. Cole, 'The Royal Burgh of Torksey', *AASR*, 28 (1905–6), pp. 520–22; SP 20/1, f. 415; SP 23/181, p. 295; 183, p. 418; 202, p. 318.
[48] Wood, *Nottinghamshire*, p. 109; *The Moderate Intelligencer*, 45, p. 262; 46, p. 264; 52, p. 316; Cambridge Univ. Lib., Buxton MSS Box 34, Anna Watson to John Buxton; Correspondence Box (i), Robert Fitchell to John Buxton.

CHAPTER 11

THE EFFECTS OF THE
CIVIL WAR

FOR four years Lincolnshire was a major theatre of the civil war. What effects did it have upon the economy, the social and political structure, the religious experience and the texture of life in general in the county?

Regrettably, many of the questions germane to this theme cannot be answered without further detailed local study. We know that the war occasioned considerable material damage in certain areas: at Grantham; at Gainsborough, twice besieged, where 'the shopps and warehouses belongeinge to the . . . marts . . . are soe ruined and decaied that the summe of £300 will nott sett them in soe good repaire as formerly they were before these sad wars'; at Lincoln, where Manchester's men sacked the upper town after storming the Bail in May 1644, and the earl felt obliged to distribute a small dole among 'the poore plundered people'; in the Torksey area, where flooding, deliberately undertaken to prevent Newarker incursions, did damage worth over £500.[1] But how typical were such incidents and, more important, to what extent did these losses result in permanent economic dislocation?

Similar problems confront us with respect to the effect of the war upon the fortunes of individuals. The burden of taxes and free quarter was heavy, particularly in the disputed lands in the western margins of the shire, where contributions were exacted by both sides — though even the inhabitants of the hundred of Elloe and of Boston, more remote from the fighting, could claim that they

---

[1] SP 23/198, p. 119; C. Holmes, *The Eastern Association*, Cambridge, 1974, p. 197; *LJ*, VIII, p. 179; SP 23/175, p. 287. A. Everitt, *The Local Community and the Great Rebellion*, London, 1969, pp. 25–26, has argued that the economic consequences of the civil war have been over-emphasized by historians who have failed to place them in the context of the peacetime catastrophes to which seventeenth-century England was prone — plague, dearth, fire. The subject requires more detailed local investigation.

N

were 'very much impoverished' by assessments, free quarter and the charges of building fortifications.[2] In some areas farms lay untenanted while rents might not be paid for many years, for, as a farmer explained to his landlord, his lands 'were not worth anything to mee in regard the garrison of Newarke was so nigh and did fetch away catell from us'.[3] Plundering parties could wreak havoc. In May 1643 the parliamentarians seized Sir Edward Hussey's store of wool from his Honington estate, the clip of thirteen thousand sheep, valued at £2,500; in June the Newarkers raided Sir William Armyne's Osgodby estate, and drove off beasts worth £2,000; in October the parliamentary forces were back at Honington from which they removed cattle and sheep worth £1,794.[4] Sir William Armyne later complained that for three years he had received nothing from his estate, since the cavaliers 'have used it as if it had bin theire owne'. Yet his experience was happier than that of the bulk of the royalist gentry: their goods were seized; some of them mortgaged their credit to raise money for the king; as soon as parliament achieved military dominance, the revenues from their estates were sequestered and employed by the county committee; to redeem their lands from sequestration they were compelled, after dilatory and expensive hearings in London, to pay heavy compositions.[5]

We know that the burden pushed some royalist families — the Locktons of Swineshead, the Welbys of Gedney, the Quadrings of Burgh — already tottering on the edge of financial collapse, over the brink. Others barely survived, after a period of very considerable hardship: Sir Gervase Scrope of Cockerington spent a good deal of time in debtors' prison and his son was 'in worse condition'. Yet others managed to recover financial stability with only temporary inconvenience, selling off some small outlying part of their estate to pay the composition fine.[6] From these isolated

[2] SP 23/183, p. 418; 184, p. 441; 202, p. 318 (contributions to both sides): *LJ*, IX, p. 118; Nalson MS V, no. 106 (complaints from Elloe and Boston).

[3] Cambridge Univ. Lib., Buxton MSS correspondence box I, Robert Fitchell to John Buxton: see also, for arrears of rent, Buxton MSS box 34, Anna Watson to Buxton, and SP 23/198, p. 125. For untenanted lands, see SP 23/194, p. 116; LAO, LIND DEP 15/6 L 87, 88.

[4] SP 23/184, p. 445; H of LMP I January 1647/8, draft order concerning Lord Camden's delinquency.

[5] See Bodleian Lib., Clarendon MS 73, no. 401, for royalists raising money upon their personal security for the royal forces: SP 23/210, p. 396; 213, p. 745; 224, p. 316 for the expense and delay of proceedings at London.

[6] SP 23/186, pp. 852–64 (Lockton); 208, p. 531 (Welby); 112, p. 902 (Quadring); SP 19/117/77, 79 (Scrope); SP 23/123, p. 404; 210, pp. 190–96 (Tirwhitt). For small sales of land to pay the composition fine, see SP 19/110/94, 118; 130/97.

examples, however, it is scarcely possible to generalize about the ultimate effects of the war upon the economic condition of the cavaliers, and we have even less sense of the experience of the non-royalist gentry, or of tenant farmers, or tradesmen, who, if they seldom became the victims of sequestration, were likely to be swept up by those charged with impressing recruits for both armies.

More detailed work on family papers and on probate records may fill these gaps in our understanding, but greater difficulties confront any attempt to determine the consequences of the war for the texture of life in village or family. We have records of families bitterly divided; of unscrupulous attempts to work off old scores or to reverse earlier legal decisions during the civil war years; of factionalized parishes in which the officers during periods of royalist dominance gleefully hounded their fellow-villagers whose sympathies were with the parliamentarians — getting them impressed into the royal army, for instance, as at Caythorpe.[7] Yet old friendships and mutual respect could survive the clash of arms and ideological differences, while some men scrupulously sought to protect the property of their countrymen: so, though Symon Patrick had 'the name of a Puritan' and was expelled from Gainsborough when it became a royalist garrison, Sir William Pelham invited him to live at Brocklesby and to store his goods there. And in many parishes the constables executed the warrants of both sides, impartially impressing men and levying money for king and for parliament with the general agreement of their fellow-villagers — a throwback to the popular neutralist sentiment of the summer of 1642.[8] The anecdotal record, then, presents us with a series of disparate cameos, it does not enable us to conclude which is more typical: factionalization or the survival of corporate family and village sentiment despite the war. Nor can we easily determine why Caythorpe was riven by internal strife while at South Kyme

[7] For inter-family dissention, see SP 23/118, p. 691; 195, pp. 468–77 (both cases involve disinheritance); Wood, ed., *Memorials of the Holles Family*, p. 233: for working off old scores and re-opening of legal disputes under cover of the war, see SP 23/85, p. 895; 119, p. 411; 239, pp. 159–63; LAO, LIND DEP 15/6 L 21; HMC *12th Report*, App. 4, p. 226: for village faction, see SP 19/22, p. 54; 149/109, 110.

[8] *The works of Symon Patrick D.D.*, IX, ed. A. Taylor, Oxford, 1858, pp. 411–13. See also Wood, ed., *Memorials of the Holles Family*, p. 189; SP 19/113, pp. 278–81, for the survival of pre-war friendships. For villages raising men and money for both parties, see T. Allen, *The History of the County of Lincoln*, II, London, 1833, pp. 133–36; LAO, constables' accounts of Addlethorpe-cum-Ingoldmells, 1643; Claypole, 1642; South Kyme, 1643–45.

local officers serviced both royal and parliamentary forces without arousing fierce animosities within the village.

Many important questions with respect to the effects of the war on life in Lincolnshire remain unanswered: some are unanswerable. Yet, upon two subjects which are central to the theme of this work we can speak with more confidence: the consequences of war upon the structure of local government, and upon religious experience and the development of new religious groupings. These must be examined in more detail.

LOCAL ADMINISTRATION

Throughout England the novel pressures generated by civil war enforced a reorganization of local administration. The county governors had, of course, prior experience of raising conscripts and levying taxation, but the difference in degree entailed by the continuous, heavy demand for men and money of the war years transmuted such traditional functions beyond recognition. And in a divided county over which the war raged the fighting was an additional corrosive, dissolving traditional forms of local government, its personnel and its ideals, and necessitating the creation of new structures.

Initially both king and parliament endeavoured to establish administrations in Lincolnshire which closely paralleled pre-war local government. In 1642 the parliamentary committee charged with securing the county militia consisted of the local members of parliament, all of whom, with the exception of Broxholme, had considerable administrative experience: at least half of the men nominated as commissioners of array by the king in the summer of 1642 had been justices in the 1630s. The earliest parliamentary ordinances stressed that taxation should be based on the traditional rates and established due process for appeals against assessments. Royalist fiscal policy was informed by similar considerations: the decision of Thomas Harrington of Boothby, 'an ancient justice of peace', to join the king's party was particularly welcome to the royalists because of his being 'soe fully acquainted with the rates of the country'.[9] But such intentions, shared by both parties, to establish administrations modelled upon, and thus invested with the prestige and authority of, the traditional forms of local government, were frustrated by the burgeoning demands for supplies and by the circumstances of war.

---

[9] LAO, ANC XII/A/4; SP 23/197, p. 755.

The divergence between the tradition-oriented ideal and wartime reality is most apparent with respect to the royalist administration. With the exception of two periods, the two months following Newcastle's advance in July 1643 and the month after the second royalist capture of Lincoln in March 1644, when the commissioners of array raised men and money at Bourne, Lincoln, Louth and Bolingbroke, the royalist administration was based outside the county at Newark. There the king's commissioners formally approved and issued warrants enjoining the levying of assessments, the conscription of troops, and the sequestration of the goods and rents of parliamentary supporters. However, the enforcement of these orders was contingent upon the ebb and flow of the tides of war. So at the end of February 1644 the town council of Grantham received a warrant to raise £125; they were sent reminders, backed by threats, of the sums outstanding upon this assessment on 29 March, shortly after Rupert's relief of Newark, and on 19 July when Manchester's army had left the county to participate in the siege of York. A similar situation appertained at Stamford in 1645, and clearly from 1643 to 1645, given the fluctuations of the war, any village constable in Kesteven might find himself imprisoned in Newark for failing to collect assessments levied months earlier, during a previous period of temporary royalist dominance. Steadily the formal process of taxation was obscured by the fact of the forcible military execution of assessments; cavalier parties began to raise money and supplies with little regard for such punctilios. The reliance on opportunistic plundering increased as the parliamentary net closed about Newark and the garrison became more desperate: there was more than black humour in the attempt by the sheriff of Lincolnshire to indict a Newark foraging party as highwaymen in early 1646.[10]

The royalist administration in Lincolnshire underwent a steady degeneration from the ideals invoked at its establishment. Despite the ultimate victory of the parliamentarians their administrative organ, the county committee, underwent a very similar though more convoluted transformation.

The Lincolnshire committee itself developed from the caucus of local members of parliament who had been instructed to secure control of the county for parliament in the summer of 1642. Each

[10] Grantham Hall Book I, ff. 114–16; *The Parliament Scout*, 84, p. 671; *CSPD 1645–47*, pp. 79, 234, 236, 314; H of LMP 1 January 1647/8 — materials on Lord Camden's delinquency; 11 June 1660, the petition of Thomas Booth and others; LAO, South Kyme constables' accounts for 1644, 1645; SP 23/184, p. 443; 188, p. 21; 198, pp. 510, 516; 200, p. 277; 203, p. 75.

legislative enactment passed from March 1643 onwards and designed to improve parliament's war effort — the ordinances establishing new tax demands, for the impressment of soldiers, for the sequestration of the estates of royalist partisans — not only enhanced the responsibilities of local administrators but added further assistants to the original core group. The sequestration ordinance of March 1643 afforced the nine members of parliament with fifteen local gentlemen and four urban worthies: the mid-1647 assessment listed 119 potential committee-men.[11]

Yet to concentrate solely upon the burgeoning lists of personnel in parliament's legislative enactments would be to miss much of the fascination of the history of the Lincolnshire committee, a history that was to render it by 1646–47 an institution as alien to the traditions of early Stuart local government as the plundering parties sent out by the garrison of Newark.[12]

In November and December 1642 Lord Willoughby's control of Lincolnshire had been virtually unchallenged: eight months later the shattered remnants of his force cowered at Boston while the cavaliers scoured the countryside. The succession of defeats, accompanied by the proven treachery of Hotham and some of his officers, had sapped not only the morale of the troops but the ardour of those gentlemen nominated by parliament to assist Willoughby in administration. The members of parliament seconding Willoughby in Lincolnshire, who themselves described their function as a 'punishment', excoriated their colleagues in the house of commons and the bulk of the local gentry who had left the county, preferring to 'sit safe' at London and merely 'talk of . . . those actions . . . they take up at second hand'. Continuous competition with the royalists for the resources of the county and the lack of adequate assistance forced Willoughby to rely upon a highly informal, even chaotic, administration: the procedures required by parliament's fiscal ordinances were forgotten; any device was legitimate that enabled Willoughby 'to make some monyes . . . to keepe the solgiers togeather'. The result was disastrous for the reputation of the parliamentary administration. Willoughby's agents, virtually unsupervised, were accused of gross

---

[11] See G. M. Hipkin, 'Social and economic conditions in the Holland Division', *AASR*, 40 (1930–31), pp. 160–61.

[12] I have examined the incidents discussed in this and the following two sections in far more detail in my article 'Colonel King and Lincolnshire Politics, 1642–46', *Hist. J.*, 16 (1973), pp. 451–84. Full references to the sources are provided in that article and have been omitted from these sections.

malfeasance and his unpaid, demoralized troops, encouraged by the pernicious example of Hotham's men, plundered the countryside.[13]

The crushing defeat of the royalists at Winceby raised Willoughby's hopes of establishing a more viable administration; he reorganized the county committee, began to levy assessments on the areas previously under royalist control and appointed agents to seize the property of malignants.[14] But, while no longer in competition with the royalists for the control of the shire's resources, Willoughby soon found that his authority in Lincolnshire was challenged. His new rival was the earl of Manchester, his co-victor at Winceby. On 20 September, recognizing that Manchester's was the only force capable of clearing Newcastle's army from the county, parliament joined Lincolnshire to the six East Anglian counties which formed the Eastern Association: thus Manchester could operate in Lincolnshire without raising the vexed question of the constitutional propriety of the army of the Association serving beyond the borders of the constituent counties. This piece of legislative legerdemain had anomalous consequences soon apparent once the dust of battle had cleared. After Winceby there were two putative supremos in Lincolnshire, both empowered to exercise sole command over the parliamentary forces in the county and claiming to monopolize the men and money raised there. Though informed of this ridiculous situation in October, parliament dithered; for the next three months Willoughby and Manchester, the latter through his nominee as governor of Holland and Boston, Colonel Edward King, sparred for the control of the county. King, a local man who had served under Lord Willoughby until captured at the fall of Grantham, was a vigorous and unscrupulous champion of the claims of the Association. He refused to supply Willoughby with munitions from the Boston magazine and sought to inveigle Willoughby's troops to desert their commander and enlist in his newly raised regiment; he appointed sequestrators and collectors who competed with Willoughby's agents for the fiscal resources of the county. His major

---

[13] SP 28/256 unfol., letter (15 May 1646) from Willoughby to the central committee of accounts; 161 unfol., account of Thomas Welby; 253B unfol., depositions against Welby; H of LMP 19 June 1646, the petition of Capt. Kingerby; 27 October 1646, the petition of George Sibsey; Edward King, *A discovery of the arbitrary, tyrannicall and illegall actions*, London, 1646, p. 2.

[14] E 113 box 4 part 2, the answer of Francis Langley; SP 28/11, ff. 9–10; 161 unfol., the account of Edward Rossiter.

coup was to intercept a large quantity of wool which Willoughby's agents had already seized from royalists and which was to be sold to pay the arrears of Willoughby's troops; he re-negotiated its sale for the benefit of the Association's treasury. Besides harassing Willoughby's administrators, King and other officers of Manchester's collected signatures to a petition pressing parliament to invest Manchester with absolute control of the county. This demand was backed by a scathing indictment of Willoughby's dismal military record and denunciation of the continued indiscipline of his troops, from whom 'wee have had as little favor, mercy and justice and expect as little from them whilst they abide amongst us as from the cavaleers'.

In late January parliament finally took action to terminate the 'disorders and distractions by reason of the variety of commands' which plagued Lincolnshire. After an ill-tempered debate, in which Cromwell lashed Willoughby's military incompetence and the 'loose and prophane' behaviour of his subordinates — evidenced by a warrant from one of them to a village constable 'to bring him in some wenches for his turne' — the Commons voted that Manchester should exercise uncontested authority in the county. Willoughby was furious. He sought to provoke Manchester to a duel and then, thwarted in this and presumably seeking to redeem his battered reputation by a signal victory, hurried back to Lincolnshire and led his forces to participate in Meldrum's siege of Newark. Yet defeat still dogged him: quarrels between his men and those of Colonel King were partly responsible for the failure of the siege. When the parliamentarians' abject surrender to Rupert irreparably shattered the Lincolnshire troops which had served with him since early 1643, Willoughby returned to London; he sought some consolation for his discomfiture by prosecuting Colonel King before the Lords for authorizing the defamatory petition and other abuses committed in the autumn of 1643 which were construed as breaches of the privilege of a member of the upper house. His fellow-peers were sympathetic but the Commons vigorously defended King, much to Willoughby's chagrin, and in June 1644 his bitterness and frustration burst out in a letter to the earl of Denbigh: 'heare wee are all hasting to a erlei ruine . . . Nobillity and gentry are going downe apace . . . I thought it a crime to be a nobleman'. From that point Willoughby devoted himself to opposing the policies of the radicals in parliament until in early 1648 he joined the royalist court in exile; he played no further role in Lincolnshire affairs. Willoughby's reluctance to participate in county administration was shared by the local members of parliament who had worked with him in 1643 and who must have considered themselves equally slighted by parliament's elevation of Manchester to supreme command in *their* county.[15]

After January 1644 Lincolnshire was administered as a member of the Eastern Association. Its committee of local men and the county treasurers lost their independence and were answerable to the earl of Manchester's administration based at Cambridge; the county's conscripts and revenues were at the disposal of the army of the Association. The controversy which had surrounded the supersession of Lord Willoughby and the enforced subordination of the local committee to an external authority could have resulted in a tension between Manchester and the Lincolnshire administrators. Yet, despite the potential for conflict an amicable relationship developed, disturbed only by a single incident — the struggle between the committee and Willoughby's old assailant, the irrepressible Colonel King, Manchester's nominee as governor, first of Holland and Boston, then of Lincoln.

Rivalry between military and civilian authorities was frequent throughout England during the civil wars; it was enhanced in Lincolnshire by the fact that, during the struggle with Lord Willoughby, Manchester had delegated considerable administrative authority to King, who had nominated assessors and sequestrators and collected revenue. After January 1644 the committee sought to exercise these functions and when King resisted their pretensions a sharp conflict developed. In August the matter came to a head when the committee petitioned Manchester, demanding King's removal. Besides trespassing in matters reserved for them by parliamentary ordinance, levying money and refusing to account for it, and independently determining the guilt or innocence and appropriate punishment of accused royalists, the committee complained that King

did quarrell with and slight the committee at Lincoln, which was setled by ordinance of parliament, who were the men of the best estates, quallity and integrity, and such as were especially commanded to serve the country, and publickly vilifying them and their actions, and assuming their power without any authority.[16]

King had served Manchester well during the conflict with Willoughby and the committee's charges were in part informed by a desire for revenge for the colonel's role in savaging the previous

---

[15] Holmes, 'Colonel King', pp. 452–62. For Willoughby's outburst to Denbigh, see HMC *4th Report*, App. 1, p. 268.

[16] John Lilburne, *The iust mans iustification*, London, 1646, pp. 8–9, 19–20.

administration of Lincolnshire and in the consequent termination of the county's autonomy, but Manchester did not defend his nominee. The earl rejected demands for King's trial, but replaced him as governor by the local member of parliament, Colonel Thomas Hatcher. Manchester's decision probably hinged on a number of considerations, such as the committee's demonstration that King's military judgement was clouded by his inordinate self-esteem and the obvious need for compatible civil and military authorities in the county; but it was also determined by the pressure exerted by powerful allies that the committee had won among Manchester's immediate subordinates. King was a zealous Presbyterian and his employment of his authority as governor of Boston to break up sectarian meetings in the town and to persecute those officers and soldiers involved had earned him the implacable hatred of the Independents; Cromwell, once his most vigorous supporter, backed the demand for the colonel's dismissal in August. The committee reinforced its summer's triumph over King in the winter of 1644–45. After Manchester's decision both the colonel and his opponents appealed to Westminster, where new charges and counter-charges were introduced. The county committee had the better of this exchange: in February the committee was fulsomely thanked for its services, while all King's commissions were revoked and he and his supporters were purged from the county administration.[17]

But, with the exception of the King affair, the potential conflict implicit in both the circumstances of Manchester's appointment and the inferior role to which the committee was relegated was not realized. Two reasons may be suggested for the development of harmonious relationships between Manchester and the local committee. First, despite the technical subordination of the county authorities to the Cambridge-based administrators of the Association, the effective independence of Lincolnshire was retained; Manchester did not sacrifice the county's interests to those of the larger entity. Although John Weaver, the central treasurer of the Fifth and Twentieth tax, accounted for the money raised in Lincolnshire, the entire sum was used to equip forces like Rossiter's cavalry regiment which were employed for local defence. The Cambridge treasurers did not even account for the Lincolnshire returns on the monthly assessment, from which the county forces were paid. So, to a considerable degree, Lincolnshire's autonomy,

[17] Holmes, 'Colonel King', pp. 462–71.

in fact if not in theory, survived the county's incorporation in the Association.[18]

Another more compelling reason may be suggested for the committee's placid acceptance of Manchester's authority: the changed social profile of the committee itself after Willoughby's dismissal. In 1643 the county had been governed by its natural rulers — by Lord Willoughby, by the Wrays, Ayscough and Irby, whose status and prestige commanded obedience. Collectively, the men upon whom the county government devolved in 1644 were of lesser rank, relative newcomers to the shire, with negligible administrative experience. John Archer of Panton, the chairman of the county committee, was typical — a local lawyer, originally from Essex, enjoying only a remote connection by marriage to the county establishment, uninvolved in county government prior to the war. Similarly, while the presence of five knights might appear to lend a measure of respectability to the committee's proceedings, only one of them, Sir Hamond Whichcote of Harpswell, combined ancient lineage and pre-war administrative experience. The brothers Sir John and Sir William Brownlow, justices in 1636, were the sons of a wealthy law officer whose buying his way into Lincolnshire society in the 1610s had occasioned some resentment among the local élite. Neither Sir Richard Earle nor Sir Thomas Trollope had served on the bench in the 1630s: the former was the son of an attorney, the latter of a wealthy yeoman from Bourne.[19] Such men could not hope to play the traditional role of local governors, to mediate the needs of the locality and the requirements of the centre: they could not effectively resist the latter. Lacking the natural authority of the established élite, the committee-men could be little more than the functionaries of that power whose commissions alone legitimized their role.

The committee's subordination was thrown into clearer relief after the termination of Manchester's command in 1645 with the passage of the Self-Denying Ordinance, when the Lincolnshire authorities became directly answerable to Westminster.

Large areas of the county had suffered directly from the conflict as the war washed back and forth across Lincolnshire between 1642 and 1644: Kesteven and western Lindsey were still subject to the raids of the Newarkers until early 1646, and then to the depreda-

---

[18] Holmes, *Eastern Association*, pp. 133, 135.
[19] For biographies of the Lincolnshire committee-men, see A. A. Garner, *Colonel Edward King*, Grimsby, 1970, pp. 43–49. For Richard Brownlow, see STAC 8 257/27; for Trollope, see *LAOR*, 9, p. 62.

tions of the unpaid Scottish forces blockading the garrison.[20] Places even more remote from the conflict had not emerged unscathed. The townsmen of Boston staggered under the burden of billeting their mutinous garrison, the inhabitants of Elloe wapentake were 'very much impoverished by . . . free quarter'.[21] Understandably there was a considerable sentiment in the county that parliamentary taxes should be waived in areas under contribution to the royalist garrisons, and until the expenses of billeting troops had been repaid.

The committee may have sympathized but did little in the face of parliament's insistence upon the collection of revenues for the maintenance of the army.[22] So the committee made every effort to collect outstanding taxes without respect to the equitable claims of those subject to free quarter or plunder. The chief sufferers by their policy were the inhabitants of Kesteven. When the Newarkers were finally blockaded in 1646, the areas previously subject to their attentions were immediately required to pay their outstanding assessments from 1645.

Called upon to execute unpopular policies the committee-men compounded the antipathy that their hard line on the payment of assessments understandably engendered, and enhanced their isolation from the populace by governing with little respect for traditional concepts of due process or individual rights. Local officers in arrears with their tax collections, however compelling their excuses, and those who protested at the committee's assessments, were given short shrift: a contemptuous 'take them provost marshall' and arbitrary imprisonment.[23] The committee's involvement in civil suits, determining the ownership of property and interfering in the relationship between debtor and creditor, was also resented. While their intrusion in such matters was unavoidable — the normal legal machinery had been dislocated by the war, and, if taxes were to be paid such questions demanded settlement — it emphasized the exceptional, the alien character of the committee's role and its powers.

Popular disgust at the committee's activities finally exploded in the summer of 1646: the trigger was, once again, Edward King. In the winter of 1644–45 King had endeavoured to indict the Lincolnshire committee before parliament: he excoriated them for their severity in levying taxes, for their harsh treatment of

[20] *The Moderate Intelligencer*, 61, p. 422.
[21] Nalson MS V, no. 106; *LJ*, IX, p. 118.
[22] *CSPD 1645–47*, pp. 376, 436. For the committee's attitude, see *LJ*, VIII, p. 179.
[23] King, *A discovery*, p. 8.

individuals, for their shameless feathering of their own nests. His complaints were dismissed after the most perfunctory hearing and his opponents exonerated. Parliament had no interest in seriously investigating the activities of the local administrative machine in a strategically vital area at a critical juncture of the war, however plausible the accusations.

Though vindicated by parliament, the committee was in no mood to display magnanimity to its detractor. They hounded King, refusing to pay his arrears for his military services, sequestering his goods on a specious charge, persecuting his tenants for taxes. In May 1645, when the wapentake of Elloe voted that King should command the militia to be raised there in accordance with a new parliamentary ordinance, the committee vetoed the choice, and, in the face of the Elloe men's persistence, refused to execute the legislation. In October, the committee, in conjunction with the county members who had not forgiven King for his role as Manchester's agent in 1643–44, thwarted his attempt to gain a seat in parliament at the Grimsby bye-election by the most devious machinations.

King responded vigorously to the committee's harassment. He sought to employ the local sub-committee of accounts to investigate the charges of peculation levelled against the county committee. Encouraged by King, the sub-committee delved into the papers of the county committee, arrested its agents, and forwarded a series of denunciations to the central accounts committee in London concerning abuses in the shire. Not only did King refuse to wilt before the committee's persecution but it was clear that he had a considerable following in the county, popular support that he and his allies organized skilfully.[24] During the attack on the committee in the winter of 1644–45 parliament was bombarded by representations from the colonel's sympathizers; he had been elected to a military post by the Elloe men despite the strenuous objections of the committee; in the course of the Grimsby election the voters had received a petition, purportedly from the inhabitants of Lincolnshire, pressing them to return the colonel to parliament.

In the summer of 1646, harassed and thwarted by the committee and frustrated in his endeavours to bring them to book before parliament, King determined upon a public confrontation. The issue he chose was the popular grievance of assessments.

[24] For examples of King's organizational skills, see Lilburne, *Iustification*, p. 20, art. 20; Nalson MS XXII, no. 148; Hunts. RO, D/DM 8A 5, the petition of 'many of the inhabitants of the county of Lincoln'.

Since late 1645 King had questioned the legality of the committee's levies of taxes upon the county. He argued that the committee had failed to observe the legal procedures for the assessment, collection and accounting of the levies. But his objections were based less upon technicalities than on broader, equitable considerations. One of the major taxes upon Lincolnshire had been granted by parliament to enable forces to be raised for the protection of the county. King insisted that no new troops had been raised, nor had the county been adequately defended. King's contentions were partly true and their credibility must have been enhanced by the byzantine complexity of the legislation in question, confusion concerning military arrangements in the shire, and the committee's habit of holding fiscal legislation in abeyance to be executed when the military situation rendered royalist interference less likely.[25]

In September 1646, after some skirmishes on the issue in May, battle was joined in earnest when King instructed his tenants in Flaxwell wapentake to refuse to pay the committee's most recent demand. The latter had no legal warrant, and was unfair, given recent royalist incursions into the area and the sums owed for free quarter. King's àrguments found a receptive audience. On the day that the first instalment of the assessment was due, the committee's treasurer received a derisory £65 17s. 0d. of the anticipated £5,000.

The Lincolnshire committee reacted swiftly. They endeavoured to demonstrate the legality of their demands; they prosecuted refusers; they sequestered King's estate. In reply King made a public appeal for popular support. On 5 October at the Folkingham quarter sessions for Kesteven King gave the charge to the grand jury and used the opportunity to launch a full-scale assault upon his opponents, repeated next day at Sleaford sessions.[26]

King began a long preamble to the formal charge with an encomium of the 'wisdome, piety, and justice' of parliament. The latter's good intentions were being subverted by the committee, whose dealings with the county were compared to Pharoah's demands upon the Israelites and Hanun's abuse of David's servants — 'whose beard is not shaven, whose clothes are not cutt off by the buttock?' King then launched into a catalogue of the specific abuses perpetrated by the committee. Blasphemy, heresy and profanation of the sabbath were being tolerated; assessments levied illegally or upon legislation that had expired were being enforced by arbitrary

[25] I have sought to unravel this extremely complicated situation in 'Colonel King', pp. 475–76.
[26] For the charge, see ibid., pp. 477–79. King published a copy of his speech in A discovery, pp. 11–18.

punishment; taxes had been grossly mismanaged and the excise, in particular, was a crying scandal; the county had not been adequately defended by virtue of the failure to execute the ordinance for the reorganization of the militia. The committee, King continued, had attained its status as 'our Egyptian taskmasters' only through the timidity of the county. If the Lincolnshiremen would band together in a firm appeal to parliament, then their liberties and properties would be secured and the arbitrary government of the committee overthrown.

King then addressed the specifics of the charge to the grand jury, but these only reinforced the themes developed in his prologue. The jurymen should present not only popish recusants but sectaries and those who 'speake irreverently of the person of the king our undoubted soveraigne'. The instructions to present those guilty of perjury, bribery, false imprisonment and extortion were glossed to comprehend the operations of the committee and its agents.

The charge made a powerful and immediate impression. The grand jury indicted a number of the excise officers whose activities touched the widest spectrum of society and who were universally hated: thereafter the collectors faced stiff resistance to their demands. Those towns in Kesteven which had not collected the September assessment absolutely refused to do so; those that had paid the tax demanded refunds.

The committee was incensed and determined to crush the gadfly colonel. Evidence concerning King's opposition to assessments and a copy of his Folkingham charge were forwarded to Westminster. The committee, insisting that parliament exonerate them, then adjourned for a month, 'all expressing a great offence at this charge, and that untill they were vindicated therein they should be ashamed to appear in the face of their county'. Their remonstrance was reviewed in parliament on 4 December 1646, and referred to the central committees of the army and for the regulation of the excise. This manifestation of official interest revived the Lincolnshire committee, and they began to collect further evidence against King. Men were compelled to appear before them and interrogated as to whether the charge had obstructed the collection of taxes; witnesses were pressed into answering in the affirmative, testimony favourable to King was suppressed and he was given no opportunity to cross-examine. King, who believed that these proceedings overthrew 'the ancient fundamentall laws of the kingdome', was no better satisfied with the hearings at Westminster, and resolved upon another public stand. On 21 December he published a tract which consisted of his speech at Folkingham reinforced by materials designed to emphasize the committee's malfeasance. The tract was soon circulating in Lincolnshire, and, on 11 January, King made another polemical charge to the grand jury at the Sleaford sessions.[27]

His speech there, in which he was primarily concerned to answer the accusations levelled against him at Westminster, was far less trenchant than its predecessor, but was sufficient to sustain the taxpayers' strike which he had inaugurated. This popular response, in addition to some of King's less restrained language in the charge — the committee's behaviour was compared to that of Jezebel and the earl of Strafford — and the publication of his tract 'stuffed with not lesse falshood then malice, which rendered us instead of patriotts, oppressors of our country',[28] made the committee even more determined to secure his punishment by parliament. Their demand was backed by a further refusal to continue in session, 'till . . . that they be vindicated not any gentlemen in the countrey thinketh them selves in a capacity to acte'.

The Commons refused to gratify the committee.[29] The parliamentary committees instructed to investigate the incident favoured prosecuting King, as did an incongruous alliance in the Commons of radical members and the Lincolnshire representatives who, though they normally aligned with the moderates, had still not forgiven King for his condemnation of their leadership in the county in 1643. But the bulk of the Commons sympathized with the colonel's stand. The majority, led by Denzil Holles sought, once the war was won, to achieve an immediate return to normality in the country, and were intensely suspicious of the county committees, a wartime excrescence which threatened the traditional pattern of local administration and the social order. King's attack on the committee, on its arbitrary actions, on its sympathy for religious sectaries, on the low-born men who staffed it, struck a chord with them. Accordingly they refused to hear the report from their committee in March: in September, reminded of its existence by the army, they finally agreed to debate the report, but then postponed a hearing five times in the next four months. Eventually the issue was quietly forgotten. The Lincolnshire committee in late March and again in July sulkily reminded parliament of their determination not to meet until they were cleared, claiming that they could do no service as they had lost all credit with a populace

[27] Bodleian Lib., Tanner MS 59, ff. 668–69.
[28] SP 23/247/30.
[29] For a full analysis relating parliament's response to the committee's charge to the nature of party affiliation in 1646–47, see Holmes, 'Colonel King', pp. 480–85.

who abused their agents and slighted their warrants; in September they were still not meeting. Finally they resigned themselves to the fact that the Commons would not act in the matter and, initially with some reluctance, recommenced their sessions.

The aftermath of King's public stand is, on the face of it, anti-climactic: the colonel escaped punishment; the committee abandoned its intransigent refusal to meet. The *status quo* was restored. Yet the incident itself is of considerable interest. It demonstrates the degree to which the country's administration, manned by men of lesser status after the withdrawal of the traditional governing élite in 1644 and necessarily less responsive to local sentiment than to the dictates of Westminster because it was from the latter's commission that their authority alone derived, had become isolated from the governed. King had given a focus to the smouldering resentment engendered by an increasingly alien institution.

RELIGIOUS PLURALISM

'I feare that God is angry with our nationall lukewarme temper', warned Sir John Wray on 12 November 1640; 'the zeale of his house hath not kindled that flame in our hearts . . . I hope our constant resolutions will be to settell religion in his splendor and purity, by pulling Dagon from the altar; and whipping the buyers and sellers out of the temple'. Sir John went on to insist that parliament was duty bound to secure 'true reformation of all disorders and innovations in church or religion'. Echoing the millenarian expectations advanced in the sermons of the Puritan ministry, such exhortations to zeal, such insistence upon godly reformation, were the staple of the rhetoric of Wray and his colleagues in the early days of the Long Parliament.[30]

Yet by the late summer of 1641, despite the initial euphoric sense of the potential for the realization of a new age of religious truth, little had been done. The Court of Ecclesiastical High Commission had been abolished, the lesser church courts shorn of secular coercive sanctions, and the obnoxious canons recently passed in convocation declared illegal. Laud and his firmest adherents upon the episcopal bench were in prison awaiting prosecution. A committee of the Commons had spent much time reviewing a multitude of petitions from parishes denouncing their incumbents,

[30] Sir John Wray, *Eight occasionall speeches, made in the House of Commons this parliament*, London, 1641, pp. 2, 3. For the general background of millenarian enthusiasm, see L. Stone, *The Causes of the English Revolution, 1529–1642*, New York, 1972, pp. 51–53.

though no policy had been agreed upon as to whether those found deficient might be displaced by parliament. Indeed, despite much debate, the only positive measures to improve the quality of the parochial ministry were the Commons' order of 8 September encouraging parishioners to establish lecturers to be maintained by voluntary contribution, and the House's subsequent readiness to support such lecturers in the face of the hostility of the incumbent.[31]

These limited achievements were hardly an adequate realization of parliament's duty 'to settell religion in his splendor and purity'. Puritans chose to attribute the poor performance to deliberate sabotage — 'the malicious and insolent designs of the popish party' — and continued to place their hopes for godly reformation in Westminster. But moderate opinion became impressed with the fact that the negative policies parliament had pursued in 1641, striking down the existing mechanisms of ecclesiastical control without replacing them, were creating a situation from which only confusion could result and in which no settlement of religion would be possible. The emasculation of the church courts, the prosecution of certain bishops, and the encouragement of popular attacks upon parochial ministers had rendered ecclesiastical discipline powerless. In the resultant vacuum the most subversive and radical ideas, expressed in a press freed from censorship and by preachers (some laymen) independent of the authority of the hierarchy, could be proselytized. Thus argued Robert Sanderson in a sermon preached at Grantham in October 1641: with printing and preaching uncontrolled, 'covies of new doctrines spring up'; more superstitious and heretical opinions had been canvassed in England in the last year than in the previous eighty.[32]

The erosion of orthodox doctrine and practice which Sanderson bewailed in 1641 was enhanced by a number of circumstances during the civil war years: by the disruptions occasioned by the war at the parish level, by parliament's policy with respect to scandalous ministers, and by its failure to institute an alternative system of ecclesiastical government with sufficient expedition.

Upon the outbreak of hostilities a number of clergymen abandoned their livings, either because they had made themselves obnoxious to the party controlling the area within which their parish lay or to demonstrate their active commitment to one or the other cause by military service. For two years Edward Reyner took

[31] For the attempts to improve the standards of the parochial clergy, see W. A. Shaw, *A History of the English Church during the Civil Wars and under the Commonwealth 1640–60*, II, London, 1900, pp. 175–84.
[32] Jacobson, ed., *Works of Sanderson*, II, pp. 161–63, 167.

refuge at Norwich before returning to his lectureship at Lincoln; Thomas Coleman, rector of Blyton since 1623 'being thence driven by the cavaliers', fled to London and accepted a post at St Peter's, Cornhill. Conversely, Dr Hurst took up residence in Newark, encouraging the garrison in anti-parliamentary sermons; John Williamson of Saltfleetby left the parish in November 1642 and 'road upp and down the country with the cavaleers with his sword and pistols'.

Such desertions created confusion in the parishes. When the minister of Keelby, 'a godlie and able divine', fled to the protection of the parliamentary army, the patron instituted a committed royalist, Henry Pight; since Pight was a substantial pluralist, he then hired for £5 a year an illiterate whose previous employment had been as a gentleman's kennel-boy. More frequently the responsibility for the maintenance of the services and other duties fell upon the shoulders of the villagers: at Saltfleetby, after the martial rector had joined the royal army 'there was noe body to officiate the cure but such as the parish provided'. A bad situation was worsened by Lincolnshire's experience as a centre of military operations. When the king's forces were in the ascendant the villagers of Frodingham and Welbourn received the ministrations, and the tithe demands, of their incumbents; the latter sheltered inthe royalist garrisons when parliament secured a temporary military superiority.[33]

Party division at the onset of war and then the progress of military operations corroded the institutional framework of religious experience at the parochial level; so too did parliament's policy of ejecting objectionable clergymen from their livings. From December 1642 a committee of the Commons, for 'plundered ministers', purged incumbents who had fled to the royal army; in the course of the next six months the committee broadened its operations to include displacing those clerics who had expressed malignancy against parliament, who had been exponents of Arminian doctrine or ritualism in the 1630s, or who were noted for ignorance or immorality. Distance ensured that the committee's operations scarcely touched Lincolnshire, but the situation changed dramatically in January 1644, when Manchester was deputed to exercise a cognate authority within the counties of the Eastern Association. He established local committees, with instructions to entertain charges against 'idle, ill-affected, scandalous and insolent clergy', to

[33] Hill, *Tudor and Stuart Lincoln*, p. 166; Thomas Coleman, *The heart's engagement*, London, 1643, dedication; 'The Royalist clergy in Lincolnshire', ed. J. W. F. Hill, *LAAS*, 2 (1940), pp. 6, 9, 72–73, 103, 105; E 134 1650–51 Hilary 8.

take testimony in support of the charge and to hear any defence the accused minister might offer. The committee was to forward the record of the case to Manchester and his two chaplains who, upon review of the evidence, could eject the accused from his living. The parish might then nominate a replacement, whom Manchester would appoint to the vacant living if he were persuaded of the nominee's 'guiffts and abillities for the ministry'. At least twenty-three Lincolnshire ministers were ejected before the expiration of Manchester's commission in the spring of 1645: thereafter the local committees forwarded the records of the cases they heard to the committee for plundered ministers at Westminster for final determination — perhaps another fifty ministers were purged in this manner.[34]

Manchester believed that the purge he supervised would forward 'that blessed reformacion soe much by the parliament desired', and he exhorted local committees to unrelenting diligence:

By the providence of God it now lyes in your power to reforme . . . abuses, and to remove . . . offenders; your power is greate and soe is the trust reposed in you . . . If a general reformacion follow not within your county, assuredly the blame will be laid upon you; and you must expect to be called to accompt for it, both here and hereafter.

While we may believe that the religious situation at Frodingham or Hareby could only be improved by the dismissal of, respectively, the lecherous John Leake and the incompetent William Underwood, the overall prospects for the 'general reformacion' were almost certainly not enhanced by ejections.

First, it was not easy to find replacements to serve poorly endowed sequestered livings. For thirty years the inhabitants of Morton 'groaned under the heavy burthen of one Humfrey Boston', their vicar, a drunkard, swearer and gamester: in 1646 Boston was sequestered, but the parish found it impossible to retain any 'powerfull preacher of God's worde here' for any period as the living was worth only £25 a year.[35] Parliament was aware of the problem and sought to increase the values of poorer livings by granting augmentations from episcopal or capitular revenues and by encouraging royalists to meet a percentage of their composition fines by surrendering their impropriations. The intention was admirable, but the augmentation often proved difficult for the

---

[34] For the history of ejection within the Association, see *The Suffolk Committees for Scandalous Ministers*, ed. C. Holmes, Ipswich, 1970, pp. 9–18; 'Royalist Clergy', ed. Hill, pp. 37–41. The number of ministers displaced is calculated from A. G. Matthews, *Walker Revised*, Oxford, 1948, pp. 247–59.

[35] SP 23/193, pp. 204–5.

incumbent to realize; the problem of poor livings, often after the wave of ejections lacking adequate supervision, remained.[36]

Second, the ejection of a minister, usually achieved by the activism of a committed minority, whether motivated by godly zeal or by self-interest, could divide a village and arouse bitter animosities. Many intruding ministers found that their ejected predecessors retained considerable support among their old parishioners. Paul Presland, ejected from Market Deeping, was accused of combining with 'several disaffected persons' to 'raise parties and factions to the discouragement and hindrance of any minister to accept of' his old living. Other intruders became locked in struggles with their predecessors, who often enjoyed popular support, for the control of the parsonage, of the glebe and of the tithes of the parish.[37]

The impossibility of finding adequate replacements in sequestered livings, the feuds between the intruder and the minister he displaced, and their respective adherents in the village could only add to the instability which the war itself had visited upon the corporate religious life of the parish. But the erosion of orthodoxy cannot be explained by these circumstances alone. Equally important was parliament's failure to establish a system of ecclesiastical government.

In the autumn of 1641 Sanderson argued that by dismantling the traditional system of ecclesiastical government without making any provision for its replacement, parliament was encouraging the growth of heresy. The same point was made more forcefully by the royalist petitioners in July 1642 when they pressed parliament to join with the king in extirpating 'those unparalleled prophanesses, schismes and disorders that are broken in amongst us, and will prove destructive to all piety'.[38] Yet for four years thereafter the Commons and the ministers in the Assembly of Divines argued, in unceasing, ill-tempered and futile debate, the merits of *jure divino* Presbyterianism as against Erastianism as against Independency. No adequate system of ecclesiastical discipline was ever established. In the absence of a clear directive from the centre, those parliamentary administrators in the localities who feared religious

---

[36] For augmentations in Lincolnshire, see Shaw, *English Church*, II, pp. 479, 484, 486, 487, 488, 491; W. E. Foster, *The plundered ministers of Lincolnshire*, Guildford, 1900, passim; for difficulties in collecting augmentation revenues, see BL Add. 15671, f. 132v.; SP 23/140, p. 189; Cambridge Univ. Lib., MS Dd 9 43, p. 23.

[37] Foster, *Plundered ministers*, pp. 30, 32–39, 59, 99–103, 131.

[38] *The humble petition of divers barronets, knights, esquires . . . of Lincoln*, London, 1642.

pluralism could do little more than harass the burgeoning sectarian congregations.

In Lincolnshire, the challenge to religious orthodoxy was enhanced by the presence of the parliamentary army, which had become a fertile breeding ground for radical religious opinions. In 1644 Colonel King, governor of Holland and Boston, aroused a storm of protest in his own regiment when he arrested those who refused to attend public services and met privately 'for exercising the very power of godliness' — or, as King thought, 'to vent theirown novelties'. This conventicle was attended by some inhabitants of Boston; one of the preachers arrested by King was Thomas Moore, a Lynn weaver and leader of the Manifestarian sect, whose followers professed to 'have seene Christ visibly, and seene the Devill also', and who permitted women to preach. By 1646 the Manifestarians' following in Holland was very strong and Moore preached frequently in the county.[39] In the same year the Baptists were gaining adherents: Henry Denne of the Eltisley church proselytized in the Spalding area, where he was arrested for baptizing two women in a river. In 1647 his co-religionist Samuel Oates was preaching in the vicinity of Stamford and also distributing copies of the Leveller *Agreement of the People*. The most extreme opinions, however, were still associated with the military. In 1647 the preacher to one of the companies of the Lincolnshire regiment was Lawrence Clarkson, like Oates a Leveller apologist and theologically an Antinomian, who argued that the elect were incapable of sinning and that 'none can be free from sin till in purity it be acted as no sin'.[40]

The breakdown of the parochial system during the civil war and the proliferation of novel doctrines provided an unprecedented opportunity for individual religious experiment in the 1640s. Some quickly discovered a congenial society among the sects, whose truths they continued to affirm with absolute conviction. Thus Thomas Grantham, the leading Lincolnshire Baptist, in 1691 reviewed a spiritual pilgrimage that had begun in Boston in the late

---

[39] For King and the Independents, see my 'Colonel King', pp. 464–67; also Lilburne, *Iustification*, p. 20, art. 16; John Bastwick, *A just defence of*, London, 1646, p. 4. For Moore, see Thomas Edwards, *The first part of Gangraena*, London, 1646, p. 38; *The second part of Gangraena*, London, 1646, p. 86; *The third part of Gangraena*, London, 1646, pp. 9, 80–81.

[40] For Denne, see ibid., pp. 85–86; *CJ*, IV, p. 593: for Oates, *LJ*, IX, pp. 571–73: for Clarkson, A. L. Morton, *The World of the Ranters*, London, 1970, pp. 132–34; Lawrence Clarkson, *The lost sheep found*, London, 1660, pp. 24–26.

1640s, without regret and with a proud yet peaceful sense of accomplishment; his faith was confirmed by

great labours and painfullness; by many perrils, and tenn imprisonments; by the loss of friends and substance; by evil report and good report; by being poor, and yet I hope in some measure enriching others . . . by honour and dishonour; and above all by the blessing of God upon my poor labours. These are the things which chiefly satisfie my soul, that our gracious God hath counted me faithfull.[41]

Others, in initial heady enthusiasm, sampled a variety of the competing faiths, ultimately to surface in black disillusionment or cynicism: this was the military chaplain, Clarkson's, experience, and that of a number of the Manifestarians, who fell ultimately 'into a loose spirit and corrupt notions'.[42]

The opportunity was there, and some seized upon it avidly. It is impossible to determine just how many were touched by religious ferment, but the opportunity itself must have been profoundly disquieting to the social élite. The dangerous social consequences of sectarianism would have been self-evident, even had Oates and Clarkson not been active Leveller propagandists: the attack on the legitimacy of tithes and of oaths, and on the need for an educated, professional ministry; the allowing of women preachers; the emphasis on the individual conscience as the touchstone of religious truth — all involved an assault upon the norms, not merely of traditional official religious belief, but of the established social hierarchy.

In 1646 Edward King gave expression to the resentment engendered by the activities of an alien institution, the county committee: he also played upon the fears aroused by the breakdown of religious order in the county: he instructed the grand jury,

present all Papists, Anabaptists, Brownists, Separatists, Antinomians and Hereticks, who take upon them boldness to creep into houses, and lead captive silly women laden with sinnes . . . If false teachers be among you, who privily bring in damnable heresies . . . shall it be said in a time of reformation that my people delight to have it so?

[41] American Baptist Hist. Society, Rochester, Champlain Burrage's notebook, no. 37.
[42] *The Christian progress of . . . George Whitehead*, London, 1725, p. 170.

CHAPTER 12

THE INTERREGNUM

THE SECOND CIVIL WAR

THE disturbed situation in Lincolnshire in the wake of Edward King's public stand, with popular resentment at the activities of the parliamentary committee given a focus and the committee itself disgruntled and ineffective, made the county an obvious target for royalist plotters as England drifted into renewed war in 1648. An insurrection, involving the seizure of a number of key strongpoints in the county, was contemplated. In May rumours of royalist designs on Belvoir frightened the local parliamentarians into garrisoning the castle; in early June the Lincolnshire committee, warned of a plot to seize Bolingbroke and Tattershall castles, placed strong guards in both. At the same time Michael Hudson D.D., the king's scoutmaster-general and erstwhile rector of Uffington, who had escaped from a London prison, and another parson with martial aspirations, Thomas Styles, who had twice defended his parish, Crowland, for the king in the first civil war, sought to surprise the garrison of that town. This was the only royalist scheme to proceed beyond talk: the parsons gathered a small force at Stamford and engaged in a little casual plundering; but, before their plot could mature, the royalists were surprised and dispersed by troops from Rutland. These incidents persuaded parliament that more vigorous and experienced military leadership was required in Lincolnshire and Edward Rossiter was sent down to take command. Rossiter acted with energy, raising new troops, keeping a close watch on suspects and co-operating with the parliamentarians in the other east midland counties; yet, despite his indefatigable leadership the county was again to experience the bitter taste of war.

Rossiter's strategy was conditioned by information that the royalists would attempt to occupy their old stronghold, Newark; accordingly, to prevent this and to facilitate communications with the Leicester and Nottingham forces, the bulk of his troops were stationed at Belvoir. But this deployment left Lindsey open to attack and, in late June, the royalists sought to capitalize on the situation. On 3 June Pontefract Castle had been seized, and quickly became a rallying-point for the Yorkshire royalists. In mid June a party of cavalry from Pontefract led by Sir Philip Monckton moved into the Doncaster area and then swept into the Isle of Axholme, where Rossiter's attempts to establish a volunteer force had been vitiated by local intransigence. On 29 June the royalists, having plundered the inhabitants of the Isle without interruption, commenced a more significant operation. Monckton, encouraged by promises that Boston would be surrendered and that a substantial group of Lincolnshire royalists would join his force, ferried his men across the Trent and moved swiftly on Lincoln. Having routed out a pathetically small parliamentary force from the bishop's palace, the cavaliers seized the county treasury and plundered the city, displaying special animosity to the Puritan lecturer, Edward Reyner, and to other active parliamentary supporters and to functionaries of the county committee.

The senseless violence displayed in the plundering of the city suggests the frustration of desperate men seeking to sustain their courage by a show of bravado. For Monckton's position was tenuous: Boston stood firm; the promised reinforcements from Lincolnshire royalists did not materialize; worse, Rossiter was preparing to march in superior strength from Belvoir upon the city. On 1 July, after more plundering, the royalists thought it prudent to retire and moved back towards Gainsborough, only to find the passage over the Trent guarded by parliamentarian forces from Yorkshire. After some indecision Monckton doubled back, moving south up the Trent valley, slipping by Rossiter who had advanced from Belvoir through Lincoln and on towards Gainsborough. But Rossiter was not eluded so easily, and his forces were soon pursuing the cavaliers as they fled south and along the Fosse Way. The exhausting chase concluded on 5 July, when Monckton's men turned at bay at Willoughby-on-the-Wolds (Notts.), where, after a sharp encounter, Rossiter routed them.[1]

So the royalists were cleared from Lincolnshire, but this was achieved not by any great upsurge of popular pro-parliamentary sentiment in the county. By 20 June the Leicestershire committee had organized 1,800 volunteers, serving 'upon their own charge',

[1] The narrative is based upon the accounts in A. C. Wood, *Nottinghamshire in the Civil War*, Oxford, 1937, pp. 146–51; Hill, *Tudor and Stuart Lincoln*, pp. 161–62; E. W. Hensman, 'The East Midlands in the Second Civil War', *Trans. Royal Hist. Soc.*, 4th series, 6 (1923), pp. 126–59. Additional details from *The Moderate Intelligencer*, 169, p. 1385.

into operational units; Lincolnshire could boast only of a single troop of horse raised by this date, while Rossiter's efforts to form an infantry company to defend the Isle of Axholme had been thwarted by the 'aversnes' of the inhabitants. The Lincolnshire men remained indifferent to the appeals of the committee, the unpopularity and ineffectiveness of which had been revealed in 1646–47.

In the light of the tepid pro-parliamentary sentiment displayed in Lincolnshire during the second civil war, the limited involvement of the county's ex-royalists in the struggle is very remarkable. Much was expected of them. Monckton deluded himself with hopes of considerable reinforcement from the county, while Rossiter awaited a major insurrection. Rumours of plots abounded in early June and numerous royalist meetings were reported at the latter end of the month; in mid July a thousand men were said to be ready to rise for the king. Yet virtually nothing came of this: only a handful of minor gentlemen ultimately joined the cavaliers at Stamford and Lincoln. The 'very frequent meetings in divers parts' noted by Rossiter appear to have been a substitute for action, not a prelude to it. Drained psychologically and financially, the old royalist leaders were reluctant to involve themselves in renewed military adventures. After watching the king's cause perish in the first war, for the next two years they had exhausted themselves in the toils of the central committee for compounding or the clutches of moneylenders as they sought to negotiate, and then scrape together, the fines that would allow them to redeem their sequestered estates — estates ruined by plunder and heavy contributions during the first war. The spirits of the leading royalist gentry were crushed by defeat and by debt; the preservation of what remained of their estates was their prime concern. Towards the end of the first civil war Sir John Monson, while acknowledging the claims of loyalty and allegiance, argued that in certain circumstances these had to be subordinated to prudential considerations: he could not be expected 'by a rash boldness [to] provoke danger, splitting my vessel upon a roke wheare I may recover a harbow though torne and weatherbeaten; which would rather prove self murther than martirdom'. This attitude informs his and his fellow ex-royalists' passivity in 1648.[2]

But the second civil war was not initiated solely by ex-royalists. In some parts of England the insurrection was led by men who had initially supported parliament but who were now disillusioned by

[2] Hensman, 'East Midlands in the Second Civil War', pp. 139–40; HMC 13th Report, App. 1, pp. 466–67, 482–83; SP 19/22, p. 61; LAO, MON 19/7/2 (4).

the radical policies, religious and constitutional, of Westminster or were disgusted by the pretensions of the New Model and the local committees. Men of this stamp certainly existed in Lincolnshire but only a couple committed themselves to the revolt. Lord Willoughby of Parham, whose vocal opposition to radical policies and his support for the City Presbyterian coup in July 1647 had resulted in his impeachment, finally abandoned the parliamentary cause and fled in February 1648 to the exiled royal court; but his appointment as vice-admiral of the royalist fleet in May prevented him from employing his influence in Lincolnshire on the king's behalf. Willoughby was sequestered for his actions, a fate shared by Molineux Disney who had raised a troop of horse for parliament in 1642 and had been an active member of the local administration in 1645–46: yet Disney's commitment to the insurrection was very limited — he had merely corresponded with the enemy.[3] Others who might have been expected to act did nothing. The earl of Lincoln, whose growing distaste for the radical's policies after 1643 parallels that of Lord Willoughby, was also impeached in 1647; yet in 1648 he contented himself with bickering with the county committee over their garrisoning his house at Tattershall.[4] More remarkable is Edward King's silence in 1648. In Kent and Essex popular grievances similar to those which King led, focused and exploited in 1646–47 were a crucial factor in the outbreak of the local insurrections. Yet King, despite his fervid Presbyterianism, his constitutional conservatism, and his hatred for the county committee, made no attempt to provoke into revolt those who had backed him in the previous years.

In 1648 Rossiter found the county sullen, but passive. Despite an abundance of plots and meetings, no prestigious local leader emerged to activate potential royalist sentiment. Lincolnshire provided a stage for two military incidents in the second civil war but very few actors in that tragedy.

THE RUMP

Upon the conclusion of the second civil war the majority in parliament tried yet again to negotiate a settlement with the king. In response the army, infuriated by Charles's demonstrated perfidy and insistent upon his personal responsibility for 'all the blood shed in these intestine wars', purged parliament and brought the king to

---

[3] For Disney, see SP 23/218, p. 71; for Lord Willoughby, see DNB article.
[4] *LJ*, x, pp. 541–42. For Lincoln's clashes with the radicals in 1643 and 1644, see *LJ*, vi, pp. 567, 574, 610, 641, 667; *Mercurius Aulicus*, 39, p. 543; 25, p. 1641.

trial and execution. England was proclaimed a commonwealth; its government devolved upon the 'Rump' of members who had survived the purge and who ruled until their dismissal by the army in April 1653.

Four Lincolnshire members — Ayscough, Irby, Pelham and John Wray — were secluded, while Grantham, Hatcher, Rossiter and Sir John Wray refused to attend the House after the army's coup. The county was represented by but two of its original twelve members: the lawyer, William Ellis, first secluded by Colonel Pride then allowed to take his seat, played a negligible role, but Sir William Armyne, though he kept clear of Westminster during the proceedings against the king, became extremely active in the Rump. Equally committed were two members elected from the county after the war. Thomas Lister, Armyne's son-in-law, who had been a leading figure in the parliamentary administration of the shire in the 1640s, was from the traditional ruling élite. John Weaver was a *parvenu* from Stamford who had risen to prominence as an administrator and Cromwell's ally in the army of the Association: prior to Pride's purge he had been associated with the most radical groups in the Commons. In 1651 Lincolnshire gained another representative, also a leading radical, when Sir Henry Vane the younger purchased the earl of Lindsey's Belleau estate. Vane who had Lincolnshire contacts through his Wray relatives, settled in the county and became intimate with a few local gentlemen who shared his predilection for cloudy theological speculation and his messianic hopes.[5]

In mid December two very different statements from Boston were received in London. The garrison, in an address to Fairfax, expressed their full concurrence with the army's demands for impartial justice and for constitutional reform as expressed in the *Remonstrance* of 18 November and applauded the coup — a 'just course, though extraordinary' — undertaken to secure those ends. At the same time Sir Anthony Irby, imprisoned during the army's purge, received a glowing testimonial from his leading constituents. They reviewed his role in the parliaments of the 1620s, his opposition to the crown during the eleven years' tyranny, his diligence in the Commons and in the county during the war though to the detriment of his own estate, and concluded: 'Sir, we write not thus to flatter you . . . but in a way of testifying our hearty

---

[5] Information on the Lincolnshire M.P.s at Pride's purge and during the Rump is from D. Underdown, *Pride's Purge*, Oxford, 1971 and B. Worden, *The Rump Parliament*, Cambridge, 1974. For Vane's correspondence, see E. Cust, *Records of the Cust family . . . 1479–1700*, London, 1898, pp. 217–20.

thankfulnesse unto you, and to encourage you in that further public service which your place and trust calls for from you'.[6]

It is doubtful that any group in the country would have expressed such fulsome sentiments to their representatives after 1649. Like the revolutionary acts which had brought it to power, the rule of the Rump was accepted with sullen resentment in the localities. In Lincolnshire the grievances upon which Colonel King had dilated in his speeches in 1646–47 were if anything enhanced. Taxes remained high yet the county was still subjected to free quarter and other depredations by the soldiery.[7] The challenge posed by the rise of the sects to orthodox religious doctrine and ecclesiastical forms was sustained. The Baptists organized a number of congregations in Lincolnshire and proselytized actively, though their energies were increasingly diverted into bitter internecine squabbles and from 1653 in feuding with the Quakers.[8] This radical sect rapidly rose to prominence in the county. George Fox toured Lincolnshire in 1652 and in that year and in 1653 his disciple, the visionary enthusiast Richard Farnsworth, was leading meetings in the Isle of Axholme, where 'much fier kindled'; local authorities accused him of disturbing the peace. The Quakers, with their insistence that the promptings of the light within must take precedence over the letter, posed a threat not only to orthodox theological values and norms but to the social order. Their rhetoric was fierce and uninhibited. Farnsworth began a letter to Fox exulting in the success of his missionery efforts at Haxey:

In the eternall power of God which bindeth kings in chaines and princes in fetters of iron, which power shaketh kingdomes and turns the world upside down.

Their acts of witness, interrupting church services for instance, or publicly lecturing the authorities on the proper performance of their duties, were intensely disruptive. Equally resented was their refusal to pay formal respect, 'to moufe the hat or bow the bodey', to social position or magisterial authority: so Martin Mason, the Lincoln scrivener, denounced the city's lecturer Edward Reyner for addressing the mayor and aldermen as 'right worshipful'; such 'hollow, deceitfull, unwarrantable titles' were 'Babylonian', the 'inventions of the beast'. And the early Quakers were alert to the miseries of the poor and the oppressed. The concern for social

[6] *The Moderate*, 24, pp. 214–15; Pishey Thompson, *The History and Antiquities of Boston*, Boston, 1856, pp. 394–95.
[7] *CSPD 1649–50*, pp. 150, 209; *1651–52*, pp. 40, 53; *The Moderate Intelligencer*, 149, p. 1126.
[8] A. Taylor, *The history of the English general baptists*, London, 1818, pp. 131–38.

justice also appears in Mason's attack on Reyner's sermons to the populace:

Thou bids them be content with such things as they have, though they have but from hand to mouth; with food and rayment, though they have no more. The poor, it seems, must be preached into patience and contentedness . . . but the priests and the proud ones, who live in pomp and plenty, may purchase lands and possessions without any check.

The local authorities, seeking to uphold the social order in a period of turmoil and dislocation, were understandably troubled by men prepared to invoke a power which 'shaketh kingdomes and turns the world upside downe'.[9]

Taxes remained high; radical sectaries multiplied. Nor did the third of Colonel King's targets, the government of the county by an administration which was unresponsive to local needs, disappear during the commonwealth régime.

The structure of local government developed during the war underwent a number of changes in the Rump period, but their ultimate effect was to enhance the centralizing tendencies which had aroused such resentment earlier. This was most obviously the case with the reorganization of the sequestration system. From 1649 revenues raised by sequestration, employed by county committees to meet their expenses, were to be returned directly to Westminster; in 1650 local responsibility for sequestration was transferred to functionaries appointed by the central authorities and answerable directly to them. This erosion of the power of the county committee was paralleled in other areas: the assessment and militia committees appointed in 1649–50 lacked many of the powers that their war-time predecessors had enjoyed. Indeed, in many areas of local government authority was reinvested in the justices of the peace. This might be considered a return to the pre-war system of local government, to the normality which Colonel King had hymned. In fact, the social status of the men who staffed both the commission of the peace and the Rump's local committees ensured their dependence on the central government.[10]

[9] For Farnsworth in Lincolnshire, see Swarthmore Hall MS 3/52, 53, 58 (I am extremely grateful to the librarian of Haverford College for allowing me to consult the microfilm of this collection deposited there). For the attack on traditional forms of honour, see Martin Mason, *The proud pharisee reproved*, London, 1655, p. 4; also Swarthmore Hall MS 4/213: for the concern for social justice, see Mason, *Proud pharisee*, p. 39.

[10] For an extended discussion of the character of local government, both county and urban, under the Rump, see Underdown, *Pride's Purge*, pp. 297–335; for sequestration arrangements in Lincolnshire, see *Calendar of the Proceedings of the Committee for Compounding*, I, ed. M. A. E. Green, London, 1889–92, pp. 172, 672; SP 23/122, pp. 127–41; 249, p. 44; 251, pp. 51, 133.

In 1649 the Rump left the personnel of local government basically intact: the régime's origin was tainted, its authority insecure, and there was little point in further antagonizing local sentiment. However, in the summer of 1650 the Rump began an extensive purge of those justices and committee-men who had refused to act under commissions from the commonwealth (apparently a significant number in Lincolnshire), or who failed to sign the Engagement, a loyalty oath 'to be true and faithful to the commonwealth, as it is now established without king and lords'. In Lincolnshire half of the men who had been involved in the administration of the county prior to the army's coup were dismissed from office.[11] Their places, in a group which had already been sneered at for the predominance of 'mean men' in its ranks, were taken almost exclusively by *parvenus* — minor gentry for the most part, leavened with a sprinkling of military officials and rising lawyers.[12] And it was the 'mean men' rather than the few surviving members of the old county élite who became the backbone of local administration.[13]

The rule of the Rump had less effect upon the procedures and personnel of the governing bodies of the Lincolnshire towns. At Boston, despite the corporation's public support for Irby after Pride's purge, and at Grimsby, despite rumours of the royalist sympathies of the authorities, the urban magistracy went virtually undisturbed during the entire civil war period. In 1647–48 the corporation of Lincoln was purged of those who had actively supported the king: in the same period fourteen of the thirty-seven

[11] Fifty-three men were regularly named to the Lincolnshire committee between 1645 and 1648 (lists in *Acts and Ordinances of the Interregnum*, I and II, eds C. H. Firth and R. S. Rait, London, 1911): twenty-seven of these were dismissed in 1650. Of the fifty-three, sixteen were demonstrably active participants in the committee in the winter of 1645–46 and the following summer (committee correspondence in SP 23); nine of these were dismissed. Remarks on the dismissal of justices are based on comparison of the pre-March 1650 list (C 193/13/3) with the lists for late 1650, 1652 and 1653 (*The names of the Justices of the Peace . . . this Michaelmas term 1650*, London, 1650, pp. 31–33; BL Stowe MS 577, p. 30; C 193/13/4; Cambridge Univ. Lib., Dd viii 1). For reluctance to serve under the Rump in the autumn of 1649, see SP 23/248/81.

[12] Nineteen men joined the local administration in this period; three had risen through service in the army or in military administration; three were local lawyers; two were younger sons from families of the traditional élite; the remainder were parochial gentry whose families were new to the shire or who had only recently risen from yeoman status.

[13] Based on an analysis of the names of justices who were active in taking recognizances in Lindsey in 1649 and 1652: of these nine men, seven became involved in local government after 1648 (LAO, LQS File for 1649, 1652).

members of Stamford's common hall were displaced; ten of twenty-five at Grantham. Yet after 1648 there were no further upheavals; only a single resignation at Stamford may be attributable to reluctance to serve the Rump or to take the Engagement. A major revision of borough charters was contemplated in 1652 and Boston dutifully forwarded its charter for review, but as with so many of the Rump's schemes nothing came from this initiative. [14]

The commonwealth régime aroused little enthusiasm in the country in general. Lincolnshire, poorly represented in the Rump, shared the general weary resentment of high taxes, of the enhanced centralization of local government and its control by mean men, and of the government's policy of toleration which encouraged radical sectarian religious experiment. But for one group in the county — the fenmen — the Rump posed a more direct challenge to their interests.

In 1640–42 the Long Parliament had first encouraged those petitioners from the fens and saltmarsh who denounced the chicanery and illegalities of the undertakers and had then passively condoned the riots, beginning in mid 1641 and rising in intensity as the country slid into war, in which the drainers had been forcibly divested of their acquisitions. Yet the ultimate legal right of the contending parties had never been determined. With the conclusion of the war the drainers reopened the question, seeking to recover their property through legal proceedings and to validate their title by parliamentary enactment. The Rump was sympathetic. On 29 May 1649 the Bedford Level Act was passed: on the grounds that their operations were 'of great advantage to the commonwealth' and would 'redownd to the . . . strengthening of this nation' the undertakers were given statutory authority to complete the drainage works begun in the Great Level in the 1630s, in return for an allotment of 95,000 acres. [15]

The precedent encouraged the undertakers in the Lindsey Level, where the drainage works had been almost entirely destroyed in 1642, to secure a similar parliamentary title. They petitioned for a hearing, the inhabitants counter-petitioned, and the Rump referred the matter to its committee, chaired by John Goodwin, which had brought in the Bedford Level Act. The committee conducted extensive hearings. The spokesmen for the fenmen argued that the

---

[14] Boston Common Council Minute Book 3, ff. 348–401; Grantham Hall Book I, ff. 108v–264; E. Gillett, *A history of Grimsby*, London, 1970, pp. 164–65; SP 24/77, petition of the inhabitants of Stamford; Stamford Hall Book I, ff. 402–50.
[15] *Acts and Ordinances*, II, eds Firth and Rait, p. 130.

actions of Lindsey and his fellow participants in the 1630s were subversive of the fundamental law and 'destructive to propriety'. They also emphasized that the public benefits of draining had been vastly overestimated and reminded parliament that all the drainers had fought for the king in the civil war, seeking 'to maintaine those oppressions and arbitrary proceedings'. For the undertakers Sir William Killigrew sought to answer these specific objections but the recurrent theme of his arguments was the Bedford Level Act: 'the commonwealth will receive all the benefit by the earle of Lindsey's draining that it receives by the earle of Bedford's drayning, and doth merit an Act to settle it equall with Bedford Levell, and we desire it on the same terms'.[16] Goodwin finally reported in the spring of 1652. In the subsequent debate the fenmen's arguments that the benefits of draining were illusory went unsupported. Some members moved for the appointment of a commission empowered to investigate the technical problems of draining the area and to develop a scheme which would balance 'the advantage of the commonwealth' and 'the right and benefit of the owners and commoners'; they were also to consider how best to reimburse the earlier undertakers for their expenses. The majority rejected this compromise and voted simply that a bill be prepared 'for the settling of the fens already undertaken to be drained'. The fenmen were outraged. It was suggested that Goodwin and a number of members were in collusion with Sir William Killigrew, and the petitioning campaign against the projected draining was vigorously renewed. Yet despite the Commons' vote no bill was introduced before the forcible dissolution of the Rump a year later. Killigrew offered some explanations for his failure: whereas many members had a vested interest in the Bedford Level and thus the Act had been 'carryed smoothly on without any delaye, . . . in Lindessey Levell none are conserned enough to looke after that'. Killigrew also believed that the Rump was fearful of the conse-quences of the bill for public order in the region; 'terrours of the peoples' discontents' led them to shelve the project. Yet the threat that the Commons' vote represented to the fenmen hung over them until Cromwell's coup: on the penultimate day of the Rump's

---

[16] H of LMP 8 May 1649, petition of the undertakers in the Lindsey Level; CJ, VI, p. 242: For the arguments before the committee, see Sir John Maynard, The picklock of the old fenne project, London, 1650; A breviate of the cause depending, London, 1651; Sir William Killigrew, Answer to the fenne mens objections, London, 1649.

existence Killigrew was still soliciting sympathetic members to get the bill brought before the House.[17]

The fenmen in the Lindsey Level were not the only group whose interests were directly challenged by Westminster from 1649 to 1653: their fellows in the Isle of Axholme had little reason to regret the expulsion of that 'parliament of clouts', as they derisively characterized the Rump. In 1642 the drainers' works and enclosures on the Isle were first attacked and by 1643 the commoners had seized possession of about half of the 7,400 acres originally granted to Vermuyden and the participants. At the conclusion of the war both parties sought to make good their claims to the land in contention. The fenmen began proceedings at common law; the drainers successfully employed injunctions from the equity courts to delay those suits. They also secured an order from the house of lords in an effort to regain immediate possession, if not title, to the full 7,400 acres. The endeavour proved futile. The fenmen were prepared to resist any attempt by the participants' agents to re-enter those 'grounds . . . which they had thrown down', and the local authorities proved sympathetic to the commoners when participants sought to prosecute them for riot.[18]

In 1650 the dispute entered a new phase.[19] First, the Court of Exchequer after four years' delay began hearing the case. Simultaneously the 'poorer sort' of inhabitants, 'conceiving themselves highly injured by such insufferable delays', began to·attack those enclosures which had remained in the participants' possession in 1643. These assaults were the prelude to a sustained attempt to expropriate the drainers, rather than seeking a compromise settlement with them, a change of policy associated with the new leadership of the commoners' cause. For in 1650 Daniel Noddell, the local attorney who represented the interests of the fenmen, believing that 'Lilborne was a powerfull man and hee having freinds would give a sooner end to the business', invited the Leveller

[17] CJ, VII, pp. 67, 106, 107, 111, 117, 118; Sir William Killigrew, A paper delivered and dispersed by, London, 1651; BL Add. 21422, f. 40.
[18] LJ, VIII, p. 36; IX, pp. 428–29, 451; H of LMP 6 February 1645/46, petition of the inhabitants of the manor of Epworth; 21 March 1645/46, petition of Arthur Samwell and John Gibbon; 11 August 1646, petition of the participants; 8 September 1647, copy of the Court of Exchequer order of 10 July.
[19] The best account of events in the Isle of Axholme in 1650–53 is provided by J. D. Hughes, 'Drainage disputes in the Isle of Axholme and their connection with the Leveller Movement: a re-examination', LH, 2 (1954), pp. 22–31, which also provides a very full bibliography of the contemporary sources. For additional details, see SP 18/37/11, no. III.

leaders, John Lilburne and John Wildman, to assist him. The latter
entered an agreement with the commoners whereby, for 2,000 of
the 7,400 acres in dispute, they would both successfully resist the
participants' claims and maintain the necessary drains on the Isle. In
June the fenmen seized the village of Sandtoft where the bulk of the
participants' French and Dutch tenants lived; in October Lilburne
led a party that ejected the foreign congregation from their ruined
church in the village during the service. 'This is our common', he
informed the wretched settlers, 'you shall come here noe more
unles you bee stronger than wee'.

The legal suits in which they were engaged went well for the
commoners in 1651. In February the Exchequer ruled that possession should be settled as it had been in 1646, that is, with the fenmen
in control of half of the 7,400 acres in dispute. The court also ruled
that the commoners might proceed to trial of their title to the
residue of the lands, and the participants allowed the first case
brought after this ruling to be lost by default in Michaelmas term.

Yet, despite the favourable verdicts, the commoners' destructive
attacks upon Sandtoft and, worse, their association with the
Leveller leaders, were politically suicidal. The Rump was determined to crush Lilburne, one of the most articulate and popular
radical opponents of its régime, and on 15 January 1652, after
hearings stemming from an accusation that he had slandered a
leading member, Sir Arthur Haselrig, they voted fines of £7,000
against him and banishment upon pain of death. With meticulous
timing the participants presented a petition next day, detailing the
riots committed in the Isle of Axholme and dwelling upon
Lilburne's leadership and the 'high, reproachful, and seditious
language' he had employed against the 'present government'. The
Commons voted to refer this petition to the committee that had just
reported unfavourably against Lilburne in his dispute with Haselrig: a month later they excluded the persons involved in the riots
from the benefits of the general pardon granted in the Act of
Oblivion.

The hostility of the Commons in general was reflected in the
investigating committee, which proceeded with extreme partiality.
The committee chairman, William Say, himself involved in
drainage operations and a business associate of John Gibbon the
spokesman for the participants, refused to permit the tenants to
establish their legal title; in his final report he misrepresented the
Exchequer decree of February 1651, suppressed or explained away
the evidence presented by the fenmen of the viability of their
pre-drainage economy and of their parliamentary sympathies

during the civil wars, and dwelt almost exclusively upon the destruction wrought by the rioters and their Leveller affiliations.

The committee's proceedings were dilatory and expensive for the fenmen as well as partial, but the delays did ensure that the report was not completed before the Rump's demise. Yet Cromwell's coup benefited the Axholme fenmen less than their fellows in Holland and Kesteven, for Say's 'wicked contrived' report, finally presented to the Council of State in June 1653, appears to have been the foundation of the attitudes and policy of all the succeeding régimes at Westminster until 1660. Certainly the participants' successful attempt to recover the full 7,400 acres was viewed sympathetically by the Cromwellian régime, whose information on the case derived from Say's report, and Major–General Whalley employed his troops to suppress the riots that greeted the participants' efforts. By resorting to direct action and by their association with radical subversives, the men of the Isle of Axholme lost the advantage that might have occurred from the legal decisions in their favour of 1651.[20]

THE PROTECTORATE[21]

Few tears were shed for the demise of the commonwealth in April 1653. Paradoxically, the successor to the Long Parliament had come to embody centralizing tendencies and a lack of sympathy with the interests and aspirations of the local gentry akin to those which the country had rejected so forcefully in 1640. The manner of the Rump's dissolution, however, and the ensuing political developments — the radical experiment of the Parliament of Saints, then the elevation of Cromwell as lord protector by the Instrument of Government — gave serious cause for concern. They emphasized the impermanence and instability of government and its dependence on military force, and they renewed fears for the dislocation of a fragile social order.

Not only were the Protectorate's beginnings inauspicious, it shared the Rump's authoritarian zeal and in many respects continued and even enhanced the centralizing tendencies of the commonwealth period.

The policy of toleration was retained. When John Hobson, J.P., arrested and imprisoned a number of Baptists travelling to a

---

[20] *CSPD 1653–54*, pp. 57, 118; SP 18/126/57; 129/144; *The diary of Thomas Burton*, I, ed. J. T. Rutt, London, 1828, pp. 199–200.
[21] The best introduction to local government under the Protectorate is provided by D. Underdown, 'Settlement in the Counties, 1653–58', in *The Interregnum*, ed. G. E. Aylmer, London, 1972, chap. 7.

meeting at Gedney, the Council of State ordered Hobson to appear before them, dismissed him from office and encouraged complaints against his other abuses of authority.[22] Local justices were swift to punish those Quakers who were moved to disturb church services, while some encouraged the mob violence to which Friends were occasionally subject, but in the government-inspired atmosphere of toleration the movement flourished. Itinerant Quaker zealots travelled through the county, speaking 'the word of the Lord, as I was moved, to the priests, people and rulers' in steeplehouse or alehouse, while public disputations and pamphlet exchanges were conducted with the ministers of the established church and with other sectarian groups. Numbers grew, particularly in Lincoln, where 'mane . . . seeth the emteynes of the priestes' and some of the corporation were won over.[23]

The government was associated with earlier régimes not only in its policy of toleration but in its determination to secure godly reformation without reference to local sentiment. In October 1654 committees were appointed in each county, instructed to purge those scandalous ministers who had escaped the ejections of the 1640s. When the Lincolnshire committee proved reluctant to execute its charge the Council of State pressed for action and eventually added new members to the committee, mostly *parvenus* who had only become associated with local government under the Rump: the bulk of the committee's work appears to have been undertaken by such men. The operation was hardly a signal success in Lincolnshire, where the committee was accused of gross partiality and procedural irregularities, but it does demonstrate the régime's determination to secure the execution of its policies of reformation in the localities.[24]

The rule of the major-generals in 1655–56 represents even more dramatically the authoritarian, centralizing tendencies that can be

---

[22] *CSPD 1654*, p. 395; *1655*, pp. 46, 157, 262, 385; *1655–56*, p. 194.
[23] For persecution of the Quakers, see LAO, SOC F I 3, pp. 37, 38, 39, 41: for missionary work, see *The Christian Progress of . . . George Whitehead*, London, 1725, pp. 22–23; Miles Halhead, *A book of some of the sufferings and passages of*, London, 1690, p. 16; Swarthmore Hall MS 4/16, 213: for disputations, see ibid., 4/88; Thomas Moore, *An antidote against the spreading infection*, London, 1655; James Nayler, *Satan's design discovered*, London, 1655; Hill, *Tudor and Stuart Lincoln*, pp. 167–68, reviews the pamphlet exchanges in which Martin Mason was involved: for the strength of Quaker support at Lincoln, see Swarthmore Hall MS 4/137, 210.
[24] *CSPD 1655*, p. 144; *1657–58*, p. 186; SP 25/78, pp. 237–38, 240. For complaints of the committee's partiality, see SP 18/181/48; Thomas Grantham, *A complaint to the Lord Protector*, London, 1656.

seen in microcosm in the history of the committee of scandalous ministers of 1654. In 1655 Cromwell, embittered by the failure of his first parliament and fearful of revolt, divided England into military districts, each under a major-general. The latter was assisted in each county by commissioners 'for securing the peace of the commonwealth' who were given extensive police authority and instructed to raise a new militia to be financed by a special tax upon royalists. Whalley, major-general for the midland counties, employed his powers less abrasively than many of his colleagues, yet the alien intervention that his rule represented was only too evident. Whalley sought to get reliable men put into the commission of the peace, and hounded the justices to suppress alehouses in the interests of godly reformation; gentry sports were interdicted; troops were employed to assist the participants against the fenmen of Axholme. At Lincoln Whalley intervened in a dispute within the corporation, enforcing a settlement by assuming, as he wrote delicately, 'a little more power then (I thinke) belonged to mee'. The citizens were more direct in their account: Whalley had acted 'by an usurped, illegall, pretended power'. That may stand as a general comment by the local authorities upon the rule of the major-generals.[25]

The major–generals were the epitome of central interference in local government and their operations aroused very considerable antipathy. The resentment and suspicion generated in Lincolnshire are apparent in the 1656 election. Whalley had hoped that 'there will be a good choice for that country', and asserted that 'not a man from hence would be chosen . . . in whom they conceived a spirit of opposition to the present government'. That was not the Council of State's reading of the election results. Of the ten men returned for the county, according to the Instrument of Government's revised apportionment of seats, the Council felt obliged to exclude six. In response to the exclusion, two of the remaining four members 'refused to take any ticket to go into the House' and abstained from attendance. Only Thomas Hall and Francis Clinton-Fiennes went to the opening of the session and they immediately moved for the admission of the secluded members.[26]

In the 1656 election Lincolnshire voters expressed their unease, their suspicions engendered by the Protectorate, but not their

[25] *A collection of the state papers of John Thurloe*, IV, ed. T. Birch, London, 1742, pp. 185, 197, 273, 495–96, 607; Hill, *Tudor and Stuart Lincoln*, p. 165.
[26] *Thurloe papers*, V, ed. Birch, pp. 299–300; LAO, MM VI/10/5, 6. For the exclusions, see *CJ*, VII, p. 425; A. C. Wood, 'Colonel Sir Edward Rossiter', *AASR*, 41 (1932), p. 232.

outright opposition to Cromwellian government. Those elected had defeated a slate of candidates headed by the radical leader, Sir Henry Vane, and consisting of two of his Wray relatives, his close friend, Richard Cust, with whom he exchanged theological speculations, and William Dowman, a man, like Cust, who had risen to prominence in local affairs during the Rump. The motives that led the electorate to defeat Vane's group are obscure. Vane's slate was less well organized than that formed by the successful candidates. Vane may have been rejected as an outsider: the ten men returned had pursued very different careers in the early 1650s but all were from established gentry families and eight of them had been associated in the government of the shire since the early days of the war. Again, perhaps the moderate oppositionists were preferred because Vane was believed to be too radical, to pose too direct a threat to the stability that Cromwell's government had achieved — a stability upon which a permanent settlement might be constructed.

For the Protectorate should not be characterized solely as the heir to the authoritarianism and centralizing enthusiasm of the Rump. There was a fundamental ambiguity in Cromwell's own character. He was the militant Puritan enthusiast, prepared to ride rough-shod over local interests to secure godly reformation; yet he was also a Huntingdonshire country gentleman, sharing the education, administrative experience and many of the prejudices and aspirations of his class. So in his speeches to his parliaments he constantly returned to the themes dear to them — of settlement, of social stability. 'A nobleman, a gentleman, yeoman: that is a good interest of the nation, and a great one.' Nor was this mere rhetoric. In the localities in 1654 the protector had been ready to work with a broader based group, closer in its social profile to the traditional ruling élite than that which had exercised authority during the commonwealth. The Engagement was rescinded and a number of those purged from local office in 1650 were invited to take up their old positions: in Lincolnshire John Archer, William Bury, William Saville, and Francis Clinton-Fiennes, all leading administrators before Pride's purge, returned.

It was upon this conservative, traditionalist streak in Cromwell that the majority in the parliament of 1656, the protector's civilian counsellors, lawyers, and country gentlemen (including Lincolnshire's Francis Clinton-Fiennes) sought to build. They offered Cromwell the crown, and upon his refusal established a system of government which closely resembled the traditional constitution — a system which proved very attractive to Cromwell himself. The

conservative reaction, marked by the acceptance of the Humble
Petition and Advice at the centre, also penetrated the localities. In
1657 a further twelve of the twenty-seven local administrators
displaced by the Rump, including the ex-members of parliament
secluded by Colonel Pride, Irby and Hatcher, reappeared as
assessment commissioners or were named in the revised commission of the peace. The power of the hated major-general was
terminated.[27]

RESTORATION

In 1657 Cromwell's rule, though still viewed with some uncertainty, had achieved a measure of acceptance not only for the
stability which it had achieved but because it promised a return to a
more traditional form of government, marked by executive
subordination to the common law and by a greater measure of
autonomy for the natural rulers in the localities. Upon Oliver's
death six thousand Lincolnshire men saluted his son with an
encomium on the 'peaceable and prosperous government' to which
he had succeeded, and with an exhortation to restrain those who
sought 'the subversion of magistracy and ministry'.[28] Their hopes
were vain. Richard Cromwell's weakness and the agitation that
developed among the junior army officers swiftly produced a
situation in which, once again, the nation appeared to be teetering
on the brink of anarchy. How did Lincolnshire's political élite react?
Most men lay low, avoiding commitments and hoping that some
acceptable settlement would miraculously dissipate the gathering
confusion. A few sought to control the tide of events.

For the republicans, including John Weaver, member for Stamford in 1658–59, Richard Cromwell's incompetence provided the
opportunity to reassert the priorities of the cause shamefully
betrayed by the apostate Oliver's quasi-monarchical rule. In the
Commons, Weaver assailed the new constitution established by the
Humble Petition and Advice in the name of 'the people's liberties'.
Upon the fall of the Protectorate and the re-establishment of
the Rump in May 1659, Weaver became an active member of
the republican central executive with special responsibility for
Ireland.[29]

[27] The analysis of the personnel of local government during the Protectorate is
based upon *Acts and Ordinances*, II, eds Firth and Rait, pp. 972, 1072–73;
C 193/13/5, 6.
[28] *Mercurius Politicus*, 559, pp. 308–9.
[29] *Burton's diary*, III, ed. Rutt, pp. 29, 76, 142–43, 546; IV, pp. 66, 164, 229, 240; G.
Davies, *The Restoration of Charles II*, San Marino, 1955, pp. 182, 189, 250.

While Weaver denounced the Protectorate, William Ellis, solicitor general and member for Grantham, sought to shore up the tottering régime. His appeal was frankly pragmatic: 'either you have a government now in being, or you have none'. 'If we lose this foundation', he argued, the alternative was 'confusion and anarchy', or, at best, 'we must go to major-generals, and the instrument of government that had no foundation in parliament'. Two other Lincolnshire members, Mussendine (Boston) and Skipwith (Grantham), expressed suspicions of the personnel of the 'other House' — of 'those colonels that sit there' — and of the Scots and Irish representatives — men 'chosen from hence that never saw Scotland, but in a map'. Yet they followed Ellis in regarding the Humble Petition and Advice as a viable basis for a settlement.[30]

In the confused situation following Oliver's death John Weaver sought to advance the republican cause, Ellis to defend the Protectorate: Colonel Edward Rossiter who represented the county in the Parliament of 1658–59 took a third course. He responded to approaches from the agents of Charles II.

Through the 1650s the court in exile, encouraged by Lord Willoughby of Parham, the old parliamentary commander in Lincolnshire who had joined the king in 1648, had high expectations of the strength of active royalist sentiment in the county. Yet the substance belied the hopes: some indiscreet correspondence with the continent, a few secret meetings: little more. Fears of renewed mulcts cowed the bulk of those who had fought for the king in the civil war: some unctuously sought to demonstrate their changed political outlook and 'service to the commonwealth'.[31] But Rossiter's defection in 1659 represented a new and hopeful turn. The colonel was a moderate who had been prepared to serve the various régimes of the interregnum in local government; clearly he and a number of other ex-parliamentarians who were associated with him in 1659 — Anderson, Ayscough, Irby, King, William Wray — had concluded that only the restoration of monarchy could guarantee the political and social stability they sought.

In the summer of 1659 it was planned that Rossiter should seize Lynn and Boston as part of a general royalist rising. The latter

[30] For Ellis, see *Burton's Diary*, III, ed. Rutt, pp. 136–37, 229, 492, 566–67; IV, pp. 52–53, 181–84, 282; for Mussendine, ibid., IV, p. 54; for Skipwith, ibid., III, p. 131; IV, pp. 128–29.

[31] For Royalist hopes, see *CSPD 1649–50*, p. 420; *The Nicholas Papers*, III, ed. G. F. Warner, Camden Soc., n.s. 57, 1897, pp. 32, 220: for conspiracy in the county, see *CSPD 1651*, p. 101; *Thurloe papers*, II, ed. Birch, p. 121: for ex-royalists seeking to demonstrate their loyalty to the Protectorate, see *CSPD 1655–56*, pp. 234, 249.

through poor organization ultimately broke out only in Cheshire and was easily crushed, yet Rossiter was deterred neither by the failure nor by the suspicions that the government entertained concerning his involvement. Once Monk began his preparations to intervene to impose some semblance of order on the chaotic situation in England, Rossiter played an important role in national events: he received the enthusiastic backing of his Lincolnshire countrymen. In December Rossiter was able to raise forces in the county in support of Monk, and in mid February presented a declaration from 'the gentry, ministers, free-holders of the county . . . of Lincolne' to the general. Its signatories complained of their grievances, chiefly 'unheard-of TAXES', which they ascribed to 'the many violences and breaches made upon our known established lawes and fundamentall liberties', and insisted upon the summoning of a 'full and free parliament'; the demand was backed by a refusal to pay taxes or otherwise recognize the authority of any body 'how ever impowered, not having the authority of such a parliament'.[32]

In April 1660 the demand for a 'full and free parliament' was met. Lincolnshire responded by returning Rossiter and four of his fellow ex-parliamentarians — Hatcher, Irby, King and William Wray, men 'who have heretofore disserved His Majesty, and praetend now to be better disposed' — five men who had avoided active commitment to either side during the war and had not been co-opted into local government in the 1650s, one man who had fought for the king, and the son of an eminent royalist. Early in the session, to the delight of royalist agents, it was Colonel King who 'breake the ice' and insisted that the House should 'goe about that which they cheifely meete for, which is the settlement of the kingdome on its old foundation'. Soon Lincolnshire was joining the national rejoicing which greeted the restoration of Charles II.[33]

What were they celebrating? The gentry exulted with Edward King at the 'settlement of the kingdome on its old foundation'. At the centre, guaranteed by antiquity, the ancient constitution, a mixed government acknowledging the pre-eminence of the common law: in the localities the government of the natural rulers,

[32] Wood, 'Rossiter', pp. 232–35; BL Egerton 2541, f. 362; *The declaration of the gentry, ministers, free-holders of the county and citty of Lincolne*, London, 1659; *The copy of a letter from a Lincolne shire Gentleman*, London, 1660.
[33] For King's role in the Convention, see Bodleian Lib., Clarendon MS 67, ff. 63b–63c; 72, ff. 44, 56; Carte MS 30, f. 582. For village celebrations, see R. C. Dudding, *History of the manor and parish of Saleby with Thoresthorpe*, Horncastle, 1922, p. 182.

the gentry. The social order would no longer be challenged overtly by the predominance of mean men in local administration nor insidiously subverted by the radicalism of the sectaries. In the summer of 1660 the natural rulers returned in force to the Lincolnshire commission of the peace. Only about a fifth of the justices who had served in 1658 survived: their places were taken by representatives of eminent royalist families — Fanes, Tirwhitts, Husseys, Monsons, Thorolds, Dallisons, Scropes — and by men who, though they had fought against the king, had withdrawn from participation in local government in revulsion from the radical developments after 1648. The use to which the new rulers of Lincolnshire immediately put their power provides a good indication of their understanding of the meaning of the restoration for local government and society. In July Thomas Grantham and his co-religionists petitioned the king. The magistrates had forbidden their meetings and indicted them at the sessions for failing to attend their parish churches: Baptists had also been the victims of violence and insult by the populace and their complaints to the justices had gained them only abuse as 'knavish, juggling, impudent and fanatic fellows'.[34]

At the village level the restoration had less sophisticated constitutional and social connotations. An incident at Claythorpe in 1657 is revealing as an indicator of popular attitudes to monarchy during the interregnum. Edward Scorr, a fuller of Aby, took a garland with which some little children were playing and placed it on the head of his companion,

and said he therewith crowned him king, and said he would put him into the power of princely government and wayted at his stirrop bareheaded, and desired he would please to take off taxes and excise and other oppressions from the nation.[35]

---

[34] Comments on the justices are based on comparison of C 193/13/5 with BL Egerton 2557, ff. 44–49; Grantham's petition is reprinted in Taylor, *English baptists*, pp. 186–88.
[35] LAO, LQS File Mich. 1657, articles against Edward Storr.

CHAPTER 13

THE RESTORATION
SETTLEMENT AND THE
LOCALITIES

THE restoration of Charles II had been engineered by the
combined efforts of the Presbyterians — those who had
supported parliament in 1642 but whose fundamental conservatism had been alienated by the radical turn of events from 1646
— and the men they had defeated in the first civil war. It was an
uneasy marriage. The royalists had experienced not only defeat, but
the plunder and sequestration of their estates, and, in consequence,
debt: Sir Philip Tirwhitt's goods had been seized, so that 'he hath
scarce bedds left for himself and children . . . to lye on'; to pay his
composition fine of nearly £3,500 he had to sell 'a greate parte of his
lands'. Some royalists were still enmeshed in the web of debt in
1660. They sought the recovery of the lands they had lost, or
reparations — favourable leases of royal estates, honours, jobs.
Failing that — and few were as fortunate as the earl of Lindsey, to
whom the king re-granted the Belleau estate sold to the republican
Sir Henry Vane[1] — they sought revenge: revenge against those
who had supplanted them in local government; revenge against the
canting, Puritan ministers; revenge against the sectaries who
thumbed their noses at religious and social conventions.

The latter group were most vulnerable. Even in the 1650s the
Lincolnshire magistracy had looked askance at the theologically
and socially radical Baptist and Quaker sectaries, and in the spring
of 1660 the conservatism of the local bench was enhanced by the
return of royalist gentlemen, sequestered for their loyalty to crown
and Church in the 1640s. Early in 1660 eighty-six Quakers were
imprisoned for refusing to swear oaths: at the same time the justices

---

[1] For Tirwhitt, see SP 19/123, p. 404; 210, pp. 169–217: for petitions for royal
assistance and favours, see *CSPD 1661–62*, pp. 185, 213; LAO, MON 19/7/1, no.
12: for Lindsey and Belleau, see SP 29/56/62.

sought to prohibit Baptist meetings, claiming that they were hotbeds of sedition, and they encouraged the jeers and stones of the rabble against the persons and meeting houses of the godly. The king, who in April by the Declaration of Breda had promised 'a liberty to tender consciences', was sympathetic. The Quakers were released and a Lincolnshire Baptist deputation was assured by Charles that 'it was not his mind that any of his good subjects who lived peaceably should suffer any trouble upon the account of their judgements or opinions in point of religion'. Yet in the face of the hostility of the local magistracy, the toleration enjoyed by the sectaries was precarious. When early in 1661 in response to the rising of Venner's crazed handful of fanatics in London, the government ordered a crack-down upon seditious conventicles, it appeared that the magistrates needed little such encouragement to take draconian measures. The Lincolnshire Baptists were again obliged to petition the king, emphasizing their loyalty and praying for relief from the over-zealous activities of his local agents.[2]

The cavaliers' opportunity for revenge was much enhanced with the sitting of parliament in May 1661. In Lincolnshire the Presbyterian–royalist alliance which had secured the restoration held up during the elections. Lord Willoughby of Eresby proposed standing as knight of the shire in conjunction with the Presbyterian Sir Edward Rossiter, and, when this plan fell through, took a seat at Boston with another Presbyterian grandee, Sir Anthony Irby, with whom he campaigned.[3] But Irby's return was the lone success achieved by the old parliamentarians in 1661: in a wave of popular resentment against those associated with the Puritans (a wave which nearly swamped Irby) four seats were taken by men sequestered for their loyalty in the 1640s and the remaining seven by men affiliated with royalist families.[4] In this respect the Lincolnshire delegation was a microcosm of the parliament in which they sat — a Cavalier Parliament, *plus royaliste que le roi*.

The cavaliers moved swiftly against their old adversaries, at least those outside the gentry class. Early in 1662 Charles was pressed by parliament into abandoning the promise of toleration embodied in the Declaration of Breda, and the local magistrates gleefully fell

---

[2] LAO, SOC F I 3, p. 45; A. Taylor, *The history of the English general baptists*, London, 1818, pp. 186–88, 191–99.
[3] LAO, ANC XIII/B/1; 10 ANC 342/2; A. Trollope, 'Hatcher Correspondence relating to Parliamentary elections', *AASR*, 23 (1895–96), p. 135.
[4] *CJ*, VIII, p. 484 (Irby was elected by the freemen, Thomas Thory by the inhabitants; the committee of privileges agreed that the right of election lay with the smaller body).

upon the sectaries. Thomas Grantham, the leading Lincolnshire Baptist, was imprisoned for fifteen months; John Whitehead, his Quaker counterpart, was held for ten months while his case was bounced back and forth between quarter sessions and the assizes. The treatment of the sectarian leaders was especially severe, but throughout 1662 and 1663 their followers were hounded by the magistrates. The Quakers of south Holland in particular were subjected to intense pressure: their meetings were broken up by soldiers; those seized were imprisoned in cramped, unhealthy quarters; the neglect of due process at their trials was so flagrant that the judges of assize rebuked the local magistrates; goods valued at considerably more than the legal fines were distrained.[5]

In April 1664 the earl of Lindsey, reporting on the state of his lieutenancy, could note, with grim complacency, that the sectaries were 'more modest and lesse frequent in theire meetings then formerlie' as a consequence of 'the checks that have been given them, and the constant power that is upon them'. Further checks were experienced in 1665 when with the passage of the first Conventicle Act in 1664 and the issue of instructions from the Privy Council for deputy lieutenants to take security for peaceable behaviour from suspected opponents of the régime, magistrates were encouraged to launch a further wave of persecution: the Quaker record of sufferings reports fifty-seven persons imprisoned and a further twenty-one fined and distrained (the largest number for any single year in the period 1660–88) for being present at conventicles, not attending their parish churches or refusing to give bonds for good behaviour.[6]

The sectaries were the chief sufferers but they might have taken some satisfaction in the fact that their sufferings were shared by their old enemies, the Presbyterian ministers. For the Cavalier Parliament obliged Charles to break the other promise embodied in the Declaration of Breda: to establish a latitudinarian, comprehensive settlement of the national church. The parliamentary determination, embodied in the Act of Uniformity of May 1662, was predictably narrow, and in consequence on St Bartholomew's Day 1662 twenty-six Lincolnshire ministers surrendered their livings rather than accept the Book of Common Prayer, which had been revised with an anti-Puritan bent, or promise conformity to the establishment's liturgy and ritual. As a group, the ministers were

[5] A. G. Matthews, *Calamy Revised*, London, 1934, pp. xi–xii; LAO, Vj 32, pp. 108, 113; Thomas Crosby, *A History of the English Baptists*, iii, London, 1740, pp. 80–82; LAO, SOC F I 3, pp. 47–76.
[6] Bodleian Lib., MS Clarendon 92, no. 143; LAO, SOC F I 3, *sub* 1665.

well-educated, dedicated preachers and effective pastors, and upon their dismissal many of their parishioners followed them from the national church. And as nonconformists those ousted parochial ministers who like Robert Durant continued to preach and said he 'would doe soe while any would come to heare him' became victims of the same punitive legislation as their old Quaker and Baptist opponents.[7]

Not only were sectaries hounded and Puritan ministers deprived by the Cavalier Parliament, but those who had offended by their support for the régimes of the interregnum were purged from positions of responsibility. The Act for the Well Governing of Corporations of December 1661 empowered deputations of local gentlemen to administer oaths of loyalty to the governing bodies in the boroughs: they were instructed to oust not only those who refused to swear but at their discretion anyone whose continuance in office was contrary to 'public safety'. In August 1662 six commissioners (four of whom had been sequestered for royalism, the other two from royalist families) met at Grantham where a number of urban officers sequestered for royalism had already been restored and their parliamentarian successors displaced by writs of *mandamus*. The commissioners ordered the removal of three of the second twelve who refused the oaths and two comburgesses, even though they swore. In similar proceedings twelve members of the Stamford corporation and fifteen from Lincoln were displaced. The Act fell hardest upon Puritan Boston where nine of the thirteen aldermen and eight of the eighteen common council members were swept away.[8]

The assault upon their lower-class opponents, nonconformists or parliamentarian sympathizers in the corporations, was conducted rapidly and ruthlessly. The displacement from positions of local authority of the parliamentarian gentry, at least those not closely associated with the commonwealth like Thomas Lister and John Weaver, was a more gradual process. Yet by 1680 the bulk of the Presbyterian families who had participated in the restoration were no longer represented on the commission of the peace. Some individuals were persuaded to resign their positions, as did William Ellis from the recorderships of Boston and Grantham; others were dismissed, as was Edward King. Typically, King went down fighting. In the Convention Parliament, King had been the first to

---

[7] Matthews, *Calamy Revised*, pp. xi–xii; LAO, Vj 32, pp. 108, 113.
[8] Boston Common Council Minute Book 3, f. 476; Grantham Hall Book 1, f. 365v; Stamford Hall Book 2, f. 13v; Hill, *Tudor and Stuart Lincoln*, p. 173.

move the restoration of the Stuart dynasty, but in 1663, disillusioned with the narrow Anglican settlement, he became an active patron of nonconformists and was struck from the commission of the peace. In late August 1665, during one of the frequent 'Presbyterian plot' scares, the deputy lieutenants were ordered to round up suspects and either take bonds for their good behaviour or imprison them.[9] King was the most notable of the fifty-five men, most insignificant dissenters and minor military and civil officers of the interregnum governments, who were jailed. Having sued out a *habeas corpus* and petitioned Charles II, he finally secured his release by bribing his jailer. This, and the fact that he subsequently behaved 'very turbulently', brought further penalties. King was summoned before the Privy Council and upon his refusal to give bond to the authorities imprisoned in the Tower for four months.

King, with the assistance of his friend and political ally from the late 1640s, William Prynne, employed his abundant leisure in antiquarian researches in the records stored in the Tower and in composing a scathing attack on the arbitrary proceedings to which he had been subjected. His *Declaration*, in its rhetoric, its legal citations, its historical examples (Empson and Dudley figure again) and its substance — a powerful affirmation of the protections which should be afforded Englishmen by their fundamental law — is very reminiscent of his civil war attack upon the county committee. And, as had his charges to the sessions in 1646, the *Declaration* enjoyed a considerable reputation among the opponents of the régime in Lincolnshire: six years after King's imprisonment it was reported that the *Declaration* 'hath been and still is spread up and down the county . . . and doth hurt'.[10]

The resurgent gentry sought and took revenge against those who had assailed their social supremacy and challenged their monopoly of local office. What more permanent values did they seek to embody in the restoration settlement?

THE CHURCH

Despite their insistence upon the re-establishment of a narrowly based, ritualistic and intolerant Anglican church, the gentry had no desire to risk subjection to the clericist pretentions of another Laud. The prosecution of nonconformity was placed firmly in their hands, as local magistrates: the hierarchy was permitted few effective

---

[9] For earlier scares in Lincs., see *CSPD 1662–63*, p. 296; G. Lyon Turner, *Original Records of Early Nonconformity*, III, London, 1911–14, pp. 781–82.
[10] SP 29/56/62; 135/123; 314/126 I, IV, V; *CSPD 1665–66*, pp. 247, 296; PC 2/58, pp. 323, 343, 344; *LNQ*, 17 (1922–23), p.149.

weapons of its own with which to combat religious deviation. Attendance at the ecclesiastical courts was time-consuming and their fees were a nuisance but their spiritual penalties held few terrors for those who denied the exclusive pretensions of the established church. Social ostracism supposedly attended excommunication, but the frequent employment of the penalty — in 1664 377 persons were recorded as excommunicate in the archdeaconry of Stow — ensured that this was a dead letter: as William Quipp noted ironically when accused of keeping company with excommunicants, it was something 'he could not possibly avoid . . . one being collector of the assessments for four years past'.[11] The excommunicant ultimately risked imprisonment if the bishop's officers sued out a writ *de excommunicato capiendo*, yet this penalty was seldom invoked: out of over three hundred Quakers imprisoned or fined between the restoration and the Revolution, only seventeen were held upon 'a bishop's writ'. Reluctance to proceed to this final step may have stemmed from the readiness of litigants to appeal to common law, through the writ of prohibition, to interdict proceedings in the ecclesiastical court. In Lincolnshire the battle between the common and canon laws was waged with particular vigour, as the Presbyterian, King, placed his legal learning at the disposal of his fellow nonconformists and launched into the local ecclesiastical courts and the diocesan chancellor, Sir Edward Lake, with all the venom that he had displayed in 1646. King commenced his assault in 1663, advising a number of churchwardens that the oath they were obliged to take at visitations was illegal. By 1672 he had 'counselled or set on or both above ninety actions' against Lake at common law, and Sir Edward's neglect of one prohibition had led to an attachment being issued against him by the judges. In 1665 King abused the chancellor in the face of his own court, and in 1666 complained against him and his officers to the committee of grievances of the house of commons — they had 'committed high offences against his majesty's laws, crown, and dignity, and most grievously vexed, oppressed, and impoverished his majesty's subjects'. A flurry of pamphlets followed, and, from that exchange, cross-suits for libel, in which King had judgement against Lake, while the latter's counter-suit, after four years debate before the courts, failed. A letter from Lake to the countess of Lincoln advising her to dismiss King as her legal counsel set up another successful libel action. In 1672 King was behind an

[11] Crosby, *English Baptists*, III, p. 88; LAO, Vj 33, ff. 117 sqq.; Edmund Calamy, *An abridgement of Mr Baxter's History . . . with an account of the ministers . . . who were ejected*, II, London, 1713, pp. 462–66.

attempt by the nonconformist minister, Theophilus Brittain, to deny the validity of the ecclesiastical jurisdiction on the Cokean grounds that the court's procedures were contrary to fundamental law, [12] as its officers were both prosecutors and judges of the suits that came before them. Lake fought back in a manner befitting a man who, having received sixteen wounds at Edgehill continued in action holding his bridle in his teeth, but King's continuous battery weakened the ecclesiastical courts, and Sir Edward's successors, the first of whom was convicted of simony, lacked his zeal and were content to enjoy the emoluments of their jurisdiction over testamentary matters and moral peccadilloes and to leave the punishment of nonconformity to the civil authorities. [13]

PARLIAMENT

The monarchy was restored in 1660, but a monarchy trammelled by the constitutional restrictions imposed in 1640–41. Conciliar, prerogative government was no longer viable: parliament had a firm control of the purse-strings and its legislative sovereignty was assured. This emerges clearly if we contrast the efforts of the fen drainers of the 1630s with their counterparts after 1660.

In the earlier period the legal basis of the undertakers' operations was a strained interpretation, devised by the crown lawyers, of Henry VIII's Statue of Sewers. The Privy Council packed the local commissions, and employed its authority to block common-law actions against the drainers; rioters were dealt with by the Council in Star Chamber. This entire edifice of conciliar intervention was ultimately founded upon absolutist constitutional doctrine: Charles I warned the local commissioners to observe his instructions 'that we be not constrained to interpose our regal power and prerogative'.

After 1660, with the earlier drainage works ruined by the war-time riots, would-be projectors had to look to parliamentary statute for legal authority for their operations. In 1661 Sir John Monson secured an Act of Parliament for his Ancholme drainage, while legislation benefiting the Deeping Fen adventurers was

---

[12] The ramifications of this convoluted feud can best be followed in Lake's complaint in 1672 to the Privy Council (SP 29/314/126) and in the petitions exchanged in 1666, which are reprinted in the records of the subsequent litigation (A. K. Kiralfy, *Source book of English Law*, London, 1957, pp. 154–63; *The English Reports*, Edinburgh, 1900–19, 85, pp. 128–40). For further details on King and Lake's suits, see ibid., 82, p. 1189; 83, p. 387; 84, pp. 226, 290, 312, 415–16, 417–18, 506, 526; 86, pp. 289, 729; 89, p. 12; 145, pp. 489, 511.

[13] LAO, AND 6/2, f. 29; *CSPD 1689–90*, p. 113.

pushed through in 1665 and 1670. And, with the exception of the decade following the restoration when the house of lords sought to exercise an authority similar to that of the defunct Star Chamber, the drainers had to rely upon the established courts to uphold their rights. The commoners who riotously assailed Monson's workmen were not hauled before Star Chamber and browbeaten and threatened into submission as the Axholme insurgents had been; they were sued in actions of trespass at common law, while other claims were determined by suits in equity in Chancery and the Exchequer.[14]

The new procedures could be frustrating and expensive for Monson and his fellows. Yet legislation gave the post-restoration drainers something Charles I could never guarantee their predecessors: an irrefrangible legal title. The recognition of parliament's sovereignty emerges in a minor incident in the disputes concerning the Ancholme scheme. The villagers of Winterton, claiming that their lands had been spoiled by Monson's works, sued in equity and a special commission was issued for a panel of local gentlemen to investigate their contention. The commissioners split. The minority upheld Winterton: land previously protected by the village's own banks and ditches was now flooded as a consequence of Monson's operations and land values had fallen dramatically. The majority opinion favoured the drainers. The commissioners noted that the 1661 legislation had stated categorically that Winterton's lands were subject to flooding and that Monson's works had successfully drained them; this declaration, they thought, was irrefutable. The authority of the act of parliament itself was sufficient to checkmate any evidence or testimony that countered its pronouncements.[15]

Though the inhabitants of Winterton might dissent, the control exercised by parliament was in general infinitely preferable locally than the arbitrary interventions of the 1620s and 1630s. The murky dealings of Vermuyden and his dubious court associates contrasted with the publicity that necessarily attended the passage of parliamentary legislation. Pamphlets were exchanged designed to impress members of parliament with the public utility of the drainage projects or else with their pernicious social consequences,

---

[14] *Statutes of the Realm*, v, London, 1819, pp. 559–68, 687–89; LAO, MON 7/17/16–18, 31, 39–43; 7/18/5; E 134 17 Charles II Easter 14; E 178 6301: for the intervention of the house of lords, see H of LMP 26 June 1660, petition of the participants in the level of Hatfield Chase; 24 May 1661, petition of the participants.

[15] E 178 6301, the report of Molineux Disney and others.

and eminent lawyers argued the legal merits of the respective cases before committees prior to full-dress debate in the Commons.[16] In the latter the concerns of 'the countrie' were vigorously represented by a number of local members. In the Cavalier Parliament both knights of the shire, Castleton and Carr, opposed drainage bills, while Sir John Newton acted for the Ancholme villagers, and with a series of provisos introduced into Monson's act sought to meet local objections. This opposition, whether motivated by a genuine concern for the rights of the commoners and the sanctity of property, or by the more cynical concern that the improved fens would become so productive that rents in 'the high countrey' would be adversely affected, killed a number of drainage projects. Acts were passed for the smaller ventures but the ambitious schemes of the irrepressible Sir William Killigrew for the re-establishment of the Lindsey Level, and the efforts of the Hatfield Chase participants to secure legislation to unravel the chaotic situation in the Isle of Axholme, were unavailing.[17]

LOCAL GOVERNMENT

The refusal to re-establish an effective independent system of ecclesiastical discipline; the restriction of the crown's power to legislate or to raise funds without reference to a representative assembly: both suggest another concern of resurgent élite at the restoration. That they should exercise the predominant role in local government.

The gentry's concern to establish a monopoly of local power emerges clearly in the history of the persecution of nonconformity. By the Declaration of Indulgence in 1672 Charles II sought to relax the penal laws against nonconformists, but this policy provoked immediate and shrill protests from the hierarchy. 'All these licensed persons grow insolent and increase strangely', wailed Bishop Fuller, 'the orthodox poore clergy are out of heart. Shall nothing be done to support them?' Chancellor Lake, pointing out the unfortunate ambiguities of the Declaration (apparently a Fleet yeoman summoned into the ecclesiastical court for fathering a bastard ingeniously argued that the Declaration barred his prosecution)

[16] For pamphlets, see LAO, MON 7/17/4, 19, 47; 19/7/1, no. 10; 2 ANC 10/1/2; SP 29/403/123; *The case of the manor of Epworth*, London, 169–; Pishey Thompson, *The History and Antiquities of Boston*, Boston, 1856, pp. 629–32: for the legal debate, see HMC *9th Report*, App. 2, p. 99; *11th Report*, App. 2, pp. 310–12; HMC *House of Lords*, n.s. 4, pp. 215–19.

[17] *The Diary of John Milward*, ed. C. Robbins, Cambridge, 1938, pp. 129, 140, 185, 212, 246; LAO, MON 7/12/80; 7/17/30, 47.

resentfully noted the rejoicing among the local dissenters.[18] Ecclesiastical hostility was echoed in parliament, where members questioned the king's right to dispense unilaterally with legislation: Sir Thomas Meres (Lincoln) gave a qualified approval to the policy of toleration, but argued that 'a general suspension of the penal statutes is against law'. Speaking in favour of the Declaration, a knight of the shire, Sir Robert Carr, made a powerful point: 'the thing [i.e. penal code] was dispensed with by justices of the peace, and the people ought not to give that to the justices which should be to the king'.[19] Arguments concerning the propriety of tolerating dissenters, Carr suggested, were irrelevant: nonconformists effectively *enjoyed* toleration by the grace of local magistrates.

Carr's comment certainly reflects the practice of the county. In 1665 the magistrates had fined or imprisoned seventy-eight Quakers; only five were prosecuted in the next four years. The passage of the second Conventicle Act in 1670 spurred the magistrates to renewed action. Seventy-seven Quakers were prosecuted in that year, a further eleven in 1671. But the enthusiasm was only temporary: in the following twelve years, the Quaker account of sufferings records only twenty-two names. The statistics which can be compiled from the Quaker materials may be supplemented by the biographies of the ministers ousted in 1662, which also suggest that the nonconformists enjoyed toleration as a function of local neglect or the half-hearted execution of the laws. John Spademan of Authorpe refused to sign the Oxford Oath appended to the Corporation Act, yet 'his known loyalty and peaceable behaviour induc'd the deputy lieutenants and justices of the peace to permit him to reside unmolested in that place where he had been minister'. The Corporation Act obliged John Birket to remove from Swinderby and John Richardson from Stamford but neither seems to have experienced much difficulty in preaching frequently in their old parishes. Richardson, at Kirton-in-Holland in the 1680s, and George Boheme at Walcot preached in the parish churches and were 'conniv'd at by the authorities'.[20]

New legislation might stir the bulk of the magistracy to action, while some individual magistrates were always ready to ferret out illicit meetings; but the latter were exceptions — like Henry Burrell, who as clerk of the peace took a share for himself from the

[18] SP 29/314/126, 223: see also *CSPD 1672*, pp. 265, 589, 624.
[19] Grey, *Commons Debates 1667–94*, II, pp. 13–14.
[20] LAO, SOC F I 3, pp. 85–116, 475–91; Calamy, *Account*, II, pp. 446, 452–54, 458; Edmund Calamy, *A continuation of the Account*, London, 1717, p. 602.

fines, or the newcomer John Bond whose raid on the Tumby meeting appears to have been designed to display his assiduity in his new position.[21] The typical official attitude of benign neglect was better reflected in the actions of Sir Francis Fane of Fulbeck: Sir Francis was 'an old cavalier, and as high for the hierarchy and ceremonies as any man', yet he became a friend of the nonconformist Michael Drake; in 1670, 'instigated' by the Anglican enthusiast John Stillingfleet, vicar of Beckingham, he arrested the participants of the Beckingham meeting but in 1678 he refused to grant a warrant against Thomas Robinson of Brant Broughton despite the importunities of John Chappel, the local minister, whom the Quaker had denounced in the church 'as a false prophet and a hireling'. Other justices who became involved with Robinson in the late 1670s displayed a similarly tolerant attitude: when no one would buy the Quaker's distrained goods, Sir Christopher Neville restored them; Christopher Beresford of Leadenham showed little inclination to levy a fine upon Robinson at the request of the Nottinghamshire magistrates for his preaching in their jurisdiction.[22]

So the dissenters were 'conniv'd at by the authorities'. Why? Perhaps because the justices were aware of Charles's tolerationist sentiment. Perhaps because the magistracy recognized that the populace was by and large reluctant to participate in harrying their dissenting neighbours, a sentiment which could make the local administration of the Clarendon Code difficult: so the Brant Broughton constable refused to execute a warrant against a village Quaker — he 'knew Thomas Robinson so well that he could not execute the warrant but sin against his own soule', while people would not buy Robinson's goods at Grantham, Sleaford, or Lincoln markets, 'looking on them as the spoile of conscience'.[23]

No such concern for the king's promises, embodied in the Declaration of Breda, or for popular sentiment had retarded the gentry's persecution of dissenters in the five years after the restoration. Basically the élite increasingly connived at dissenters because persecuting them no longer seemed essential to sustaining the gentry's social and political hegemony.

The zeal of the men who had so eagerly fallen upon the sects in 1660–65 waned as they realized that persecution was counterproductive: 'we have seen how little good force will do', said Sir

[21] CSPD 1686–87, p. 387; Joseph Besse, A collection of the sufferings of the people called Quakers, 1, London, 1753, pp. 357–58.

[22] Ibid., p. 354; LAO, SOC F I 3, pp. 475–77.

[23] Ibid.: see also LAO, CH/P 4 September 1671.

Thomas Meres in 1673.[24] Force might pare away some waverers but it strengthened the conviction and dedication of the core. Grantham wrote of the powerful religious experience which flourished among his Baptists in Lincoln gaol in 1662. In the same year and the same prison John Whitehead, a number of whose weaker followers had succumbed, 'let go eternal life and laid hold of this present world', wrestled with his God for an end to the persecution:

shorten these days of trouble . . . that no more may be laid upon thy little ones than they can bear, lest they faint, and their adversaries triumph, and say 'Where is now the God in whom they trusted?'

But this black mood passed. Imprisoned at Spalding in 1665 the Quaker leader could write an impassioned affirmation of 'heavenly love':

When we were little, he carried us in his arms, and in our travels and trials he hath supported us . . . though he doth now, and hath often, suffered us to be distressed, yet have we not been destroyed, because under us hath been the everlasting arm of our God, who every way hath dealt with us as a father with his children in whom he delighteth.[25]

The cynic might also note that not only did persecution appear to strengthen dissent, but that in periods of toleration a good deal of nonconformist energy was expended in acrimonious strife between the sects. Baptist and Quaker relations were particularly bad: Thomas Grantham records the conclusion of one of his many public disputations with John Whitehead in the late 1660s: the latter cursed me in these words, 'Thou whited wall, God shall smite thee; the plagues and curses and vengeance of God is thy portion.' I replied, 'John, I am taught of God not to render railing for railing, cursing for cursing, but continuous blessing; and therfore I desire this folly may not be laid to thy charge.' He replied 'Fainer, fainer, fainer etc.'[26]

In 1672, when the Declaration of Indulgence allowed the sects to come into the open, Baptists and Quakers in Lincolnshire engaged in a vicious pamphlet warfare, begun with the publication of a tract alleging that Richard Anderson of Panton, a Quaker, having cursed the Baptist elder Ralph James with leprosy, was himself with his family afflicted with various mysterious ailments which were only cured by the prayers of James's congregation. The alleged incident

24 Grey, *Commons Debates 1667–94*, II, pp. 13–14.
25 Thomas Grantham, *The prisoner against the prelate*, London, 1662, pp. 10–11; John Whitehead, *The Written Gospel-Labours*, London, 1704, pp. 73–77, 149–60, 214–28.
26 Thomas Grantham, *Christianismus Primitivus*, part 4, London, 1678, pp. 60–61.

was old (c. 1663), and subsequent attempts by both parties to embroider the existing evidence, or manufacture new, were unsavoury. The spectacle of relays of eminent Baptist and Quaker leaders, some from regions as far distant as Oxford, descending upon Panton, where they sought to bully Anderson into reaffirming or denying his testimony, and to jog the memories of his neighbours with the provision of 'much ale', must have afforded a malicious amusement to opponents of the sects. Certainly neither the local Baptists nor their Quaker adversaries appeared in any very good light in the incident.[27]

Persecution may have been seen as counter-productive by the local magistracy; it certainly seemed increasingly irrelevant. By the 1670s it was clear that the dissenters were not movers 'of sedition throughout the world, who turned the world upside down', as a Northampton justice described John Whitehead in 1654: they were neither insurrectionaries nor radical critics of the existing social order who had to be stamped out if the fabric of society was to survive. After the restoration Thomas Grantham continually emphasized his co-religionists' loyalty and peaceableness and their acceptance of the social order: 'all cannot be princes, some must be subjects. Without government all would be in confusion in the republick, and the same may be said as truly of every family.' John Whitehead, too, argued that 'by God's ordinance some have a superiority given them', and that the Quakers 'design to level nothing but sin'.[28] Such avowals would have carried little weight had they not been accompanied by the abandonment of the aggressive proselytizing and the flagrant defiance of the *status quo* associated with the sectaries of the 1650s. The transmutation is most apparent among the Lincolnshire Quakers. Before the restoration the most common cause for official action against the Quakers, other than their refusal to pay tithes and church rates, was their interruption of services, their 'bearing witness in the steeple house': there is only a single recorded instance after 1661. After the restoration the Quakers turned inward. The records of their governmental structure of monthly, quarterly and annual meetings, which was regularized in the two decades after 1660,

---

[27] *A true and impartial narrative*, London, 1672; Thomas Rudyerd, *The Anabaptist's lying wonder*, London, 1672; Thomas Rudyerd, *The Anabaptist preacher unmask'd*, London, 1672; Ralph James, *The Quakers' subterfuge*, London, 1672; Robert Ruckhill, *The Quakers' refuge fixed on the rock of ages*, London, 1673; William Smith, *The Baptists' sophistry discovered*, London, 1673.
[28] Whitehead, *Gospel-Labours*, pp. 35, 142–46; Grantham, *Christianismus*, part 3, pp. 1–10, 61–73.

emphasize the closed corporatism of post-restoration Quakerism. The meetings acted as arbitration tribunals to compose differences and avoid suits at law between Friends. They organized an alternative system of poor relief, supervising the apprenticing to approved Quaker masters of the children of poor Friends, and the distribution of relief to the aged and those who had suffered casual losses. They were concerned to maintain the highest moral standards within the community, and thus avoid any occasion for the jibes of those outside the fold: the perpetrators of any 'disorderly practice which may tend to be the gaining those that are without' — alehouse haunters, those who failed to pay their debts — were censured and ultimately disowned. A similar concern for the reputation of the community led to the strict regulation of marriages: were the parties clear of other commitments? Had they received parental consent? Could they maintain their offspring? The meetings were especially concerned to prevent marriages to outsiders, to a woman 'out of the truth' or, more revealing of their concerns, to 'one of the world'.[29]

In their deliberate isolation from the world within their own closed community, the Quakers lost something of the fierce inspiration, the spiritual violence and heroic quality displayed in the 1650s. John Whitehead, the Yorkshire soldier who had been converted from the Antinomian beliefs of the Ranters in 1652 and who became the first Quaker sufferer in Lincolnshire when he was attacked by the mob for 'bearing testimony' in Lincoln Cathedral in 1654, sensed the change with some regret. He noted in 1682

how that generation which did see the wonders of the Lord, and were upheld by his mighty power, is passing away . . . and another generation that hath heard more, but seen and experienced less, both of the wiles of Satan and operation of God's power . . . are entring.

Yet the change *did* enable Whitehead in 1683 to question the wisdom of the authorities' renewed persecution of his co-religionists: 'you cannot but know that we are a harmless and peaceable people, that do hurt no man, but are willing to live honestly, and to give to every man his own'. If persecuted the Quakers, 'industrious farmers and tradesmen', would emigrate, and thus the nation would be weakened, 'rents brought down and trades decayed'.[30] The force of his argument that Friends, far from

---

[29] Based upon analysis of the records of the Lincoln Quarterly Meeting, and the Gainsborough Monthly Meeting (LAO, SOC F I 3, pp. 535–632; Brace, ed., *Minutes of the Gainsborough Monthly Meeting*, I and II).
[30] Whitehead, *Gospel-Labours*, pp. 231, 287–91.

being those who 'turned the world upside down', were a national asset, a 'laborious and industrious people', appears to have struck the Lincolnshire magistracy with respect to all nonconformist groups in the late 1660s. Mercenary informers still prowled; some Anglican ministers, like Stillingfleet, sought to harass dissenters:[31] but the bulk of the gentry, no longer threatened by their aggressive social radicalism, were prepared to tolerate the sects. The idiosyncratic practices of the latter, like adult baptism or prophesying at the behest of the light within, at which the orthodox had trembled or raged in the 1650s and early 1660s, became merely occasions for the light derision of the sophisticated.[32]

The local élite determined when to activate the Clarendon Code, and their determination depended upon their perception of their best interests: as sectarian dissent lost is radical connotations so their concern relaxed. Local government was firmly in the control of the gentry.

[31] LAO, SOC F I 3, *sub* 1670; John Stillingfleet, *Shecinah*, London, 1664, dedication and preface.
[32] *The diary of Abraham de la Pryme*, ed. C. Jackson, Surtees Soc., 54, 1870, pp. 83, 140.

CHAPTER 14

CRISIS AND REVOLUTION, 1675–89

AFTER the restoration the local élite's mastery of local government was structurally guaranteed: the pretensions of the ecclesiastical hierarchy to independence had been crushed, while the king's freedom of action was apparently circumscribed by the need to consult representatives of the gentry in parliament if he sought funds or legislative action. In consequence, we might anticipate a period of political quiescence after the cataclysmic decades of the civil war. In fact, by the 1670s, despite the earlier persecution of nonconformists and the purge of ex-parliamentarians from positions of local influence, there was a significant opposition to Charles II's government in Lincolnshire. At the end of the decade, during the session of the three parliaments summoned during the Exclusion Crisis, that opposition was vigorously expressed both in the locality and in the Commons. A court *versus* country polarization, similar to that of the 1620s, had again split the local gentry.

Paradoxically, the opposition was not organized and led by the old parliamentarian families eased from local office after the civil war, but by men who had been returned to the Cavalier Parliament on a wave of pro-Stuart sentiment. With the exception of Sir Anthony Irby, the Lincolnshire contingent elected in 1661 were uniformly Anglican and loyalist. Their essential unanimity was sustained through 1665, when upon the death of Sir Charles Hussey they met together and 'pitcht upon Sir Robert Carr' as knight of the shire in opposition to 'the Presbiterian interest'.[1] But thereafter they began to divide.

The restoration settlement left the king dependent upon parliament for taxation and legislation: it also specifically obliged the king to summon a parliament within three years of the dissolution of its predecessor. But it did *not* require him to dissolve a sitting

[1] LAO, MON 7/14/25.

parliament, and the 1661 elections had returned a loyal, Anglican body to Westminster: accordingly Charles kept the Cavalier Parliament in session, with frequent prorogations, for nearly two decades. Its members were obviously not unaffected by their tenure: they necessarily became more aware of the problems confronting the executive, and their comments on international diplomacy, or royal finance, or naval administration became more sophisticated. As the cavaliers became more professional, so the king was obliged to win a majority in support of his policies, not by mere appeals to a naïve loyalty but by the lures of the power of office or the pleasures of the court, or by lucrative pensions and sinecures. It is this development which underlies the division among Lincolnshire's members of parliament.

About 1671 a satirist's list of the court dependents in the Commons included the members for Grimsby and Stamford. Gervase Holles ('a pensioner at court, and two places there'), Peregrine Bertie (a military commission) and William Montague (a legal post) were silent, but reliable in divisions. The frequent, blustering speeches on behalf of the court of the one-armed navy man, Sir Frescheville Holles, who was, in Pepys's opinion, the 'prophane commander' of a crew of 'debauched, damning, swearing rogues', were believed to be the consideration for £3,000 in cash, a pension of £500 p.a., and 'a promise to be rear–admiral'.[2]

Other Lincolnshire members remained untainted by such influence and became increasingly resentful of continued high levels of taxation for the support of a chorus of tame hacks in the Commons, of an unsuccessful foreign policy, and of a court which aped that of Louis XIV in its cultural pretensions, and in its morals and religious sentiments in so far as it had any. In 1676 one of the government's parliamentary managers wrote 'I have little hopes of' Sir Anthony Irby, the old member of the Long Parliament, and his Presbyterian kinsman, returned in a 1666 bye-election at Boston, Sir Philip Harcourt. Others of doubtful reliability from the government's perspective were Sir John Newton (Grantham) and Lord Castleton (Lincolnshire): the latter in 1673 opposed the duke of York's marriage not merely because the prospective bride was Catholic, but, as he believed, the pope's eldest daughter. Newton's

---

[2] E. S. DeBeer, 'Members of the Court Party in the House of Commons, 1670–78', *Bull. IHR*, 11 (1933), pp. 1–2, 5, 11, 14; *Flagellum Parliamentarium*, Edinburgh, 1881, p. 15. For Sir Frescheville, see *The Diary of Samuel Pepys*, VIII, eds R. Latham and W. Matthews, Berkeley, 1974, pp. 116, 129, 131; *The diary of John Milward*, ed. C. Robbins, Cambridge, 1938, pp. 196, 200; Grey, *Commons Debates 1667–94*, I, p. 362.

loyalism had appeared in 1666 in his fears of the 'Presbiterian interest' and in 1669 in his readiness to vote supply for the king, but in the 1670s he shifted into opposition.[3] Since he was a frequent speaker, the waning cavalier sentiments of another Lincolnshire representative, Sir Thomas Meres (Lincoln), can be more exactly detailed. Even in the 1660s Meres's loyalty to the crown was always qualified by his loyalty to the established church and by his concern for the privileges of parliament. The latter went beyond an antiquarian interest in procedure, though he was noted as 'very knowing in the order of the House', to a deeper concern for parliament's legislative role and its independence. Yet in the late 1660s, while displaying a concern at the local impact of taxation and for honest fiscal administration, Meres was diligent in committee and upon the floor of the House to secure a substantial revenue for the crown.[4]

From the twelfth session of the Cavalier Parliament (1673) until its dissolution, with the government directed by, first, the Cabal and then by the earl of Danby, Meres's deep-seated concerns for the welfare of the Anglican church and for the status of parliament led him to play a far more aggressive role in opposition to the régime. In 1673 he expressed grave suspicions concerning the religious principles of those about the king and sought the execution of the penal laws against papists; he challenged Charles's exercise of the dispensing power in the Declaration of Indulgence, less from his old hostility to nonconformity than from a fear that such prerogative actions 'may shake the law and property of the subject'; he questioned the king's requests for money to fund a foreign policy about which parliament had been given no opportunity to express an opinion; he was fearful of the standing army which Charles sought to raise, and with frequent references to the Petition of Right he invoked the old twin spectres of billeting and martial law. Equally reminiscent of the 1620s was his explicit coupling of supply and redress of grievances.[5] The same concerns and suspicions

[3] A. Browning, *Thomas Osbourne, Earl of Danby*, III, Glasgow, 1951, p. 110. For Irby and Harcourt, see D. R. Lacey, *Dissent and Parliamentary Politics in England, 1661-89*, New Brunswick, 1969, p. 101: for Castleton, see Hill, *Tudor and Stuart Lincoln*, p. 185: for Newton, Browning, *Osbourne*, III, p. 41.

[4] *Milward's Diary*, ed. Robbins, pp. 201, 214, 216, 225, 249; *The Parliamentary Diary of Sir Edward Dering*, ed. B. D. Henning, New Haven, 1940, p. 90; Grey, *Commons Debates, 1667-94*, I, pp. 95, 97, 106-7, 121, 123, 125, 126, 129, 130, 142, 150, 151, 158, 166, 178-79, 186, 211, 252, 266, 273, 303, 350, 353, 374, 396, 409; II, pp. 4-5.

[5] Ibid., pp. 9, 27, 56, 81, 145, 208, 215, 235; *Dering's Diary*, ed. Henning, pp. 111, 159-60.

inform his speeches from 1674 to 1679: fears of popery and of 'impiety and corruption of manners' in the court; fears of the growth of France, and that the Caroline régime sought to emulate the absolutism of Louis XIV; suspicions of fiscal mismanagement; angry recriminations at the contemptuous disregard for parliament displayed by the government, for whom the institution apparently existed solely to be milked for money.[6]

Perhaps more interesting than the specifics of Meres's disillu- sioned indictment of Charles's government is the perspective from which they were delivered: Meres spoke for the country. In 1675 he began a speech concerning suspicions of official peculation, 'we men that come out of the country . . . would know . . .', and prefaced a hostile question concerning the king's foreign policy, 'he is glad to inquire, as country gentlemen used to do . . .'. Earlier in 1673 Meres had compared the plain but genuine speeches of 'we poor country-fellowes' with the polished (and, he implied, empty) oratory of the 'fine men about the town', and had been rebuked by secretary Coventry for endeavouring 'to make a distinction in the Houses between the country gentlemen and the courtiers'.[7] The rhetoric of the country which Meres employed, suggested not only the blunt adherence of himself and his 'country-fellowes' to traditional political, religious and moral values as against the francophile, profligate sophistication of the court, but also con- trasted the isolation of the 'fine men about town' from the real concerns of the nation with his and his colleagues' awareness of the needs and fears of their constituents. Sir John Monson (Lincoln), who with Meres expressed fears of French dominance, of popery, of godless and immoral counsellors about the king, of a standing army, expressed the latter point explicitly: '[he] had been lately in the country, and never saw a greater concerne for business — they fear we shall come under the government of France, to be governed by an army'.[8]

The divisions in parliament and the nation in 1661 — loyal cavaliers against 'the Presbiterian interest' — had been supplanted, by the 1670s, by a new polarization: court against country. In parliament Meres and Monson spoke vigorously for the latter, and in doing so claimed to voice the inchoate fears of their constituents and of the kingdom at large. But that in Lincolnshire these

---

[6] Grey, *Commons Debates, 1667–94*, III, pp. 4–6, 136, 341, 357; IV, pp. 113–15, 337, 359; V, pp. 99, 283.
[7] Ibid., II, p. 48; III, pp. 4–5, 64; *Dering's Diary*, ed. Henning, p. 128.
[8] Grey, *Commons Debates, 1667–94*, I, p. 334; II, pp. 198, 226, 258, 311.

grass-roots sentiments, referred to in their speeches and apparent in the popularity enjoyed in the 1670s by Edward King's *Declaration* of 1665, were organized and given focus owed most, paradoxically, to 'a fine gentleman about town' — Sir Robert Carr of Sleaford (see frontispiece).

Shortly before his bye-election return for the county, Carr had married the sister of Henry Bennett, later earl of Arlington, and in the Commons he tacked his political career to the coat-tails of his brother-in-law. He acted with Arlington's other friends in the attack on Clarendon, and, in 1668 worked with the 'undertakers' in their attempt to manage parliament. In 1673 he was a leading spokesman for the Cabal ministry in the Commons, with the incongruous consequence that, though returned as an opponent of 'the Presbiterian interest' and though he was a relentless persecutor of Edward King in 1665-66, he sought to justify the Declaration of Indulgence. His local influence was also put at the disposal of the government: in 1671 he had 'laboured night and day' to expedite the collection of the subsidy in Lincolnshire, and had been abused for his assiduity.[9] He had his reward: £20,000 in cash, it was claimed, and the office of chancellor of the Duchy of Lancaster. Carr, then, was a courtier, and he enjoyed the attendant pleasures: horse-racing at Newmarket; deep drinking in his London house. His personal finances were a shambles.[10]

With the fall of the Cabal, however, and the rise of Danby to prominence in the government, Carr moved into opposition. By 1676 one of Danby's agents wrote of Carr's 'ill influences' in the Commons and wished that he might be dismissed from his offices (impossible, for he had secured a life patent for the Duchy of Lancaster post) or 'imployed abroade'. Carr not only duelled with the ministry in parliament, but began to organize the grass-roots opposition to the régime in Lincolnshire. His ability, given his involvement with the tainted Cabal, to pose as a leader of the country says much for that personal magnetism which contemporaries noted, although his unswerving support for one generally popular cause, the opposition to the attempt to revive the Lindsey Level drainage schemes, and his mobilization of official influence to secure various favours for Boston, may have strengthened his credentials: even when acting as the Cabal administration's local

[9] Ibid., I, p. 32; II, p. 14; D. T. Witcombe, *Charles II and the Cavalier House of Commons*, Manchester, 1966, pp. 81, 94 n. 3, 134; SP 29/290/130; *CSPD 1671*, pp. 260, 337, 547, 577; *1671-2*, p. 215; *CTB*, 3, pp. 389–90, 831, 1062.
[10] *CSPD 1675–76*, pp. 24, 25, 35; *1677–78*, p. 378; *Pepys's Diary*, VIII, eds Latham and Matthews, p. 363; LAOR, 8, p. 69.

agent, Carr could write confidently of 'my fenn men'.[11] We may also suggest that the country opposition recognized the need for a leader who maintained some useful court contacts, given the power deployed against them in Lincolnshire.

Robert Bertie, third earl of Lindsey (see Frontispiece) became lord lieutenant of Lincolnshire and a privy councillor on the death of his father in 1666. His loyalty to the court had not always been unquestioning: he had opposed Clarendon's ministry both in parliament and, by his lukewarm response to royal fiscal demands, in the county. But, with the rise of his brother-in-law, Sir Thomas Osbourne, later earl of Danby, to political eminence his court ties became closer — although, to his chagrin, he never enjoyed Charles's friendship or respect.[12] In August 1675 he wrote a fulsome letter of support for Danby's ministerial policies, concluding 'God hath raised you to this eminency of condition to save a tottering monarchy, which if your counsel is not followed, I am confident will be turned into an anarchy of confusion'. This apocalyptic vision led him to support Danby in parliament and to place his local power at the disposal of the ministry.[13]

In 1676 a bye-election occurred at Stamford, where 'the court party' supported the candidacy of Henry Noel, who was opposed by John Hatcher. Much of the pre-election period was taken up with in-fighting among those notables who believed they had an interest in the town — the earls of Exeter and Stamford, Lords Camden and Bridgewater — a process which left the corporation 'unhappy devided'. Lindsey placed his official influence at Henry Noel's disposal. 'In complement to Stamford' (and, presumably for the benefit of its shopkeepers) the earl ordered a muster of the Kesteven militia at the borough 'soon after the muster at Corby'. Noel's rival, John Hatcher, was struck from the commission of the peace upon the earl's personal complaint to the king and, to add insult to injury, was then nominated as sheriff of the county.[14]

---

[11] Browning, *Osbourne*, III, p. 109: see also p. 1. For Carr's personal friendships, see LAO, MON 7/12/40: for his court contacts, see SP 29/384/154: for his opposition to fen drainage, see *Milward's Diary*, ed. Robbins, pp. 128, 185, 246, 254; *CSPD 1671–72*, pp. 92, 600; E. Cust, *Records of the Cust Family . . . 1479–1700*, London, 1896, pp. 228–31.

[12] Browning, *Osbourne*, I, pp. 37–38, *CSPD 1666–67*, p. 320; LAO, 10 ANC 355/2; BL Egerton 3330, f. 28.

[13] HMC *14th Report*, App. 9, pp. 376–77; see also Browning, *Osbourne*, I, pp. 152–53.

[14] LAO, ASW 2/77/B; Holywell 97/14; SP 29/286/215; HMC *Buccleuch*, p. 325; HMC *Finch*, 2, p. 44; A. Trollope, 'Hatcher correspondence relating to Parliamentary elections', *AASR*, 23 (1895–96), pp. 136–42; BL Egerton 3330, f. 28.

In 1677 Lindsey's efforts to further the interest of the ministry within his lieutenancy twice brought about confrontations with Sir Robert Carr, now clearly identified as the organizer of the country opposition in the shire. The first incident, minor in itself, is of interest in that it drew from Lindsey a statement of his perception of local politics and of his role as Danby's satrap. Lindsey had backed the promotion as sergeant-at-law of the Stamford lawyer, Frances Wingfield, one of Danby's 'creatures and dependents' and 'a great card . . . in these parts to play in all affairs of importance'. In June he was dismayed to learn that the honour was being blocked at Carr's instigation by the lord chancellor. Lindsey informed Danby that his prior successes as the funnel of royal favour in Lincolnshire — 'that those who stick to me are preferred' — had been generally 'taken notice of' in the county, and was 'a very powerful and engaging argument for persons to adhere to our party, for the world will be governed by interest'. For Wingfield to fail to obtain the promised preferment through Carr's influence 'would be a strange retrogation in our affairs and nothing would more encourage the fanatic or Presbyterian party'; the king must be informed that 'it will discourage his whole party in this county and be the most acceptable news in the world to the commonwealthsmen'.[15]

The second conflict was a more public affair. The deaths of the 'very ancient' Sir William Thorold and of Henry Noel left seats vacant at Grantham and Stamford. At the latter Lindsey's alliance with Lord Camden, forged in the extended battle with Hatcher and the earl of Exeter's interest, proved its worth again, and the return of Charles Bertie, Lindsey's brother and Danby's most trusted aide, was secured without a struggle.[16] Grantham posed more of a problem. The vacancy had been anticipated for some time by Sir William Ellis, a political ally of Carr's and a patron of the dissenters. A year before Thorold's death Ellis had begun to conduct a series of extravagant entertainments in the town. In April 1677 he increased his investment: upon the suggestion of one of the town's governors that he should 'do some kindness for the town that he might oblige them', Ellis, with Carr's assistance, lent the town £1,000 interest free and promised to forget the debt if elected. To overcome his opponents' considerable start in canvassing votes, Lindsey determined that the corporation had to be fixed. Accordingly, in the summer of 1677, on the day of the annual election of borough officers, Lindsey summoned the militia to muster at Grantham. A

15 HMC *14th Report*, App. 9, p. 384.
16 Cust, *Records*, p. 228.

R

'tumultuous election' ensued, remarkable for the participation of freemen who had not lived in the borough for several years, in which Lindsey and his noble ally, Lord Roos, were victorious. The subsequent parliamentary election, in March 1678, was still vigorously contested: lampoons were exchanged and votes purchased, while Lindsey enhanced the highly charged political atmosphere by again ordering a muster of the militia at Grantham on polling day. Sir William Ellis finally polled 111 votes, while his court opponent, Sir Robert Markham, received 104. Lindsey's success in securing tame borough officers then proved its worth. The alderman disallowed some of Ellis's voters and declared Markham returned.

Carr had aided Ellis throughout the election campaign, but, when the return of Markham was challenged by petition to the house of commons, the limitations of his leadership of the Lincolnshire country party were revealed. Carr's strength was the court connections that enabled him, as in the Wingfield affair, to frustrate Lindsey's efforts to monopolize all patronage in the shire. But he feared that too outright an identification with the opposition might nip his court contacts and blight his political ambitions. So in June 1678, when the court and country parties in the Commons were both using the investigation of the Grantham bye-election as a litmus of their respective political strengths, and it was expected that Carr would 'rip up all that has passed in order to this election, for the overawing it by the Lord Lindsey', Sir Robert took fright and remained silent, 'thinking to merit at Whitehall'.

By June 1678 Lindsey was victorious both in the shire and in parliament. Carr's efforts were unsuccessful at Grantham, while his subsequent tortuous course during the investigation of the election left him 'a loser on all sides', experiencing both the anger of his erstwhile allies of the country party and the contempt of the king and his court. He was reported as being in a state of great mortification.[17]

Within a year the situation was reversed. In the autumn and winter of 1678 parliament and the nation were convulsed by the fictitious report of a popish plot manufactured by Oates and Tonge, and by the genuine revelations of Danby's secret negotiations with France. The Commons became completely unmanageable and in January Charles announced a dissolution; a new parliament was summoned to meet on 6 March. The general public fear of popery

[17] G. Davies, 'The By-Election at Grantham, 1678', *Huntingdon Library Quarterly*, 7 (1943–44), pp. 179–82; HMC *12th Report*, App. 5, pp. 43–45, 48, 50–52; HMC *Ormonde*, n.s. 4, pp. 429–34; Grantham Hall Book I, ff. 654v, 655, 656v; CSPD *1678*, p. 135; SP 29/398/149; 404/98.

and feeling against Danby's administration emerged in the ensuing elections in Lincolnshire. Sir Robert Carr toured the boroughs, 'liberally discoursing' of the evils of Danby's administration. His appeal for the return of 'patriots' failed only at Grimsby, which already enjoyed a dubious reputation for electoral venality, and returned an affiliate of the court party. The latter, the 'indigent papist', William Broxholme, was fearful of an investigation of his tangled operations as a collector of various taxes in Lincolnshire and dared not vote against the régime. Of all the Lincolnshire members only Broxholme was noted as 'vile' or 'base' when the whig leader, the earl of Shaftesbury, surveyed the election returns: Sir Richard Cust (Stamford) was 'doubtful', the remaining ten representatives were characterized as 'worthy' or 'honest'.[18] Carr and Lord Castleton remained as knights of the shire; their country party colleagues Meres (Lincoln), Irby (Boston), and Newton (Grantham) were also returned again. Irby's colleague at Boston was the eminent lawyer, Sergeant Sir William Ellis, who had been solicitor general to the Cromwellian régime; the latter's nephew, also Sir William Ellis, was returned for Grantham, where he had been defeated through Lindsey's machinations a year previously. The Stamford election must have been even more galling to Lindsey's *amour propre*: his brothers, Charles and Peregrine, were rejected. The election of Sir Richard Cust and William Hyde has been attributed to the decision of the earl of Exeter, 'the virtual proprietor, to use his influence' against the Berties. Cust and Hyde *were* supported by Exeter, but the latter's influence had been unavailing in 1676 and 1678 against Lindsey and Camden. The Cust family correspondence suggests that Exeter was successful in 1679 in part because the Bertie brothers were thought to have been insufficiently solicitous of the borough's concerns at Westminster, but partly because there was considerable popular feeling against men so closely connected with the Danby régime.[19] In September 1679 Lincolnshire was said to be 'alarm'd and dissatisfied' by the king's treatment of the duke of Monmouth, and public fears of popery and suspicion of the court were equally apparent in the election returns. All the members of the first Exclusion Parliament

[18] BL Egerton 3331, f. 101: For Grimsby, see LAO, HILL 30/1A/9; *Milward's Diary*, ed. Robbins, p. 134: for Broxholme, see Browning, *Osbourne*, III, pp. 59, 66, 91, 109, 115; *CSPD 1679–80*, pp. 213, 257; *1660–85*, p. 108; E 134 24 Charles II Mich. 25; *CTB*, 2, pp. 222, 231, 233, 248, 268, 495; 3, pp. 84, 361, 383, 1094, 1189, 1282; 4, p. 564; J. R. Jones, 'Shaftesbury's "Worthy Men": A Whig view of the Parliament of 1679', *Bull. IHR*, 30 (1957), p. 238.

[19] HMC *13th Report*, App. 6, p. 13; J. R. Jones, *The First Whigs*, London, 1961, p. 41; Cust, *Records*, pp. 233–36.

R*

were again returned, save Sergeant Ellis who had been made a judge: he was replaced by Sir William Yorke, whose house at Leasingham was a haven for nonconformist divines.[20] The elections to the third Exclusion Parliament in the spring of 1681 saw only one change — Sir Thomas Hussey for Henry Monson at Lincoln: clearly the county remained generally satisfied with the men Shaftsbury had thought honest or worthy in 1679. Popular feeling would appear to have been predominantly 'whig' — suspicious of the executive, fearful of popery, favouring some scheme for the exclusion of, or limitations upon, the duke of York, the Catholic heir to the throne. Yet the county does not appear to have participated in the nation-wide campaign of petitions which the whigs organized — demanding the assembly of parliament in the winter of 1679–80 and again in early 1681; insisting upon the exclusion of the duke of York in instructions to the members of the Oxford Parliament in 1681.[21] The reason again may be the ambiguous position of the most influential opposition leader in the shire, Sir Robert Carr. Ambitious for court office and favour, he feared too close an identification with the whig leaders. Typically, he absented himself from the Commons in May 1679 when the first Exclusion Bill was debated. In the following November, as the duke of York passed through Kesteven *en route* for Scotland, the earl of Lindsey endeavoured to 'give as publick a demonstration as I could' of his personal devotion to the duke: the latter stayed at Grimsthorpe, and the corporations of Stamford and Grantham, despite 'opposition from the factious party', were persuaded to provide suitable entertainment. Incongruously Carr, alone of the local exclusionists, felt obliged to wait upon the duke — and was snubbed for his pains. Lindsey noted the same ambiguity in Carr's attitude upon this occasion that had emerged during the Commons' investigation of the Grantham election: Sir Robert 'was very uneasy betwixt doing something the duke should take kindly and yett should not expose him to his party'.[22] Yet Carr's efforts to maintain his court affiliations, while they may have weakened his local leadership during the Exclusion Crisis, did benefit his supporters

[20] HMC *14th Report*, App. 9, p. 416: for Yorke, see Edmund Calamy, *An abridgement of Mr Baxter's History . . . with an account of the ministers . . . who were ejected*, II, London, 1713, p. 548; Edmund Calamy, *A continuation of the Account*, London, 1727, pp. 549, 606.
[21] Jones, *The First Whigs*, pp. 116–19, 166–73.
[22] A. Browning and D. J. Milne, 'An exclusion bill division list', *Bull. IHR*, 23 (1930), p. 213; LAO, CRAGG 2/30, f. 2; HMC *Ormonde*, n.s. 5, p. 234.

during the reaction that followed Charles's dissolution of the Oxford Parliament.

The king, his financial position secured by French gold, resolved to govern without parliament, and to exploit the growing public feeling that the whig leaders were fanatical insurrectionaries who would not scruple to plunge the nation into renewed civil war in pursuit of their subversive goals. This was an ideology and policy to which the earl of Lindsey could whole-heartedly subscribe. He had been bitterly resentful of the treatment accorded Danby, his family, and himself during the crisis. He had been dismissed from the Privy Council, and his authority in Lincolnshire had been whittled away when Charles 'putt out some of my friends' from the commission of the peace 'and added those who have very little respect for mee'. 'The king', he wrote indignantly, 'hath been pleased to lay a new indignity upon mee'; the king was 'not the most constant prince in the world'. Yet in 1681 Lindsey threw himself behind Charles's anti-whig policy. In the 1670s the earl's political rhetoric invariably recalled the restoration: Carr's allies were 'the fanatic or Presbyterian party'; the 'commonwealthsmen'. Now, it seemed, the king had come to recognize the truth of this analysis: the whigs were the direct descendants of the Levellers and Diggers. The point was driven home in a number of tory petitions backed by the earl. The freeholders of Lindsey and Kesteven prefaced their thanks to Charles for his public declaration upon the dissolution of the Oxford Parliament with a reference to 'the late unnatural war, with the horrid mischiefs attending on it': the Elloe tories accused the whigs of 'designing . . . to throw us back again into the same miseries and confusions we were lately delivered from, by your majestie's happy and miraculous restauration'.[23] The identification of the exclusionists with the civil war radicals also entailed, for Lindsey, a policy consequence for local government: a purge of all whose loyalty was not demonstrated and unqualified.

In July 1681 Lindsey organized an entertainment for the gentry at Grantham, to procure signatures to an address from the country lauding the king for his declaration setting out the motives for the dissolution of parliament: a spectator remarked ironically of this affair, that 'if good meat and drinke will make men loyall . . . my lord spares no cost to effect it'. Yet the address fizzled out. Many

---

[23] BL Egerton 3331, f. 126; 3334, f. 116; HMC *14th Report*, App. 9, pp. 419–20, 432–34; *The London Gazette*, nos 1640, 1642, 1706.

leading gentlemen refused to have anything to do with it, the grand jury at the summer assizes would not subscribe to it, and it was 'endeavoured by the fanatic party to be turned into ridicule'. This humiliation provoked Lindsey to demand a total purge of those deputy lieutenants, justices and militia officers in any way associated with the whigs during the Exclusion Crisis or who had refused to subscribe to the address. He asked,

what probability it there that those who have refused to give the king thanks for the most gracious declaration that ever prince put out, should in tyme of danger assist him with theire lifes and fortunes? And then how unsafe is itt for a prince to have dependance upon such persons who in all human probability shall make use of his authority against himselfe?

Charles gave Lindsey lavish thanks for his loyalty and assiduity and promised all assistance. The earl's nominees were appointed as justices and deputy lieutenants, and one was picked as sheriff, a choice which resulted in a packed grand jury at the Easter assizes, claiming to be 'the representative body' of the county, expressing their public abhorrence of the proposed whig association which had been produced in evidence at Shaftesbury's trial. Yet Lindsey's insistent demands for the displacing of whigs from local office were not gratified, and when Lindsey employed his authority as lord lieutenant to dismiss William Hyde, member for Stamford in all three Exclusion Parliaments, from his militia captaincy he was ordered to explain his actions to the king. Lindsey had no doubts as to why his whig opponents continued in office. Despite his loyalty he did not enjoy Charles's full confidence while Sir Robert Carr, despite his exclusionist associates and, Lindsey hinted, his treasonable intentions, 'hath too much credit with his majesty who according to his usual method seems to cut a feather between us'.[24]

Through 1682 Lindsey continued to complain of Carr's malign backstairs influence, which kept on the commission of the peace magistrates who supported nonconformists and would 'obstruct the election of honest men' should parliament be summoned. However, in 1683 the premature death of Sir Robert Carr and the scare engendered by the Rye House Plot gave him a better opportunity to pursue his vendetta with the whigs. Upon the report of the plot Lindsey mustered the militia, and raided the houses of three exclusionist members, Sir William Ellis ('head of all

---

[24] *The Memoirs of Sir John Reresby*, ed. A. Browning, London, 1936, pp. 227–28; SP 29/416/107; 418/147, 163; *CSPD 1680–81*, pp. 354, 376, 442, 466, 506, 529–30, 558, 581; HMC *14th Report*, App. 9, p. 437.

the Presbyterians in the county'), Cust, and Yorke, and of the old Cromwellian, 'active in the late war', Sir Drayner Massingberd: his disappointment when no significant caches of arms were turned up was very apparent. Lindsey also launched a renewed persecution of nonconformists, making unprecedented personal appearances, presumably to add the weight of his authority to the proceedings, at the Bourne quarter sessions in July 1683, when the prosecution of dissenters, moribund for a decade, was renewed, and again in April 1684.[25] Perhaps most gratifying to Lindsey, given his emphasis upon securing a loyalist monopoly of local office, was the king's new policy towards the corporations. Charles could temporarily govern without parliament by virtue of a French subvention, but if he aspired to an independent foreign policy or to significant domestic reforms, clearly the Commons and Lords would have to be summoned. Charles was determined that any future parliament would be of a far more tractable temper than those of 1679 to 1681, and to secure the election of a subservient Commons he resolved to pack the governing bodies of the parliamentary boroughs. A series of *quo warranto* investigations was begun, challenging the boroughs' exercise of their corporate privileges, and most corporations, rather than fight an expensive and futile lawsuit, promptly surrendered their charters to the crown. The new charters normally contained a purged slate of urban officers, and a provision that any officer might be removed by an order of the Privy Council.

In Lincolnshire only Grimsby avoided royal interference. None of the other four boroughs chose to contest the *quo warranto*: Grantham agreed to surrender its charter in June 1684, followed by Lincoln in July, Boston in November, and Stamford in January. The new charters had all taken effect by the spring of 1685. The royal purge was most drastic at Boston, where the mayor, all ten aldermen and thirteen of the eighteen common council men were displaced: their successors included as mayor Sir Henry Heron, a man noted by Lindsey as of 'Church of England and the old cavalier principles'; and as aldermen three members of the Bertie family and a number of other local gentlemen. Peregrine and Charles Bertie were also added to the corporation of Stamford. At Grantham, where of the twenty-five officers of the borough thirteen were displaced, the governing body was afforced by three local gentlemen headed by Thomas Harrington, who had been chosen by

25 SP 29/425/129; 429/96; LAO, MM VI/10/11, nos 1, 2, 6–11; S. A. Peyton, 'The Religious Census of 1676', *EHR*, 48 (1933), p. 110; Peyton, ed., *Minutes of Quarter Sessions for Kesteven*, pp. 155, 167.

Lindsey to present the anti-Shaftesbury petition from the grand jury in 1683.[26]

The new charters often contained sops to the economic interest or corporate pride of the borough (Stamford was granted the right to hold an additional fair; at Grantham the alderman was 'gloriously changed into a mayor'), and they were received with appropriate rejoicing and professions of loyalty. Yet they represented the triumph of the tory gentry over the traditional governors of the boroughs. In Lincolnshire they also represented the triumph of the earl of Lindsey over the ghost of Sir Robert Carr. The earl's nominees from among his own family and his political coterie had displaced the urban officers who had supervised the elections of the exclusionists in 1679 to 1681.

The triumph of the tory faction and of the earl of Lindsey was short-lived: within four years the Lincolnshire tories were joining their exclusionist opponents in support of the invasion of William of Orange.

Charles had undertaken the remodelling of the corporations with an eye to future parliamentary elections. Upon his death in February 1685, his brother, the Catholic James II, became the beneficiary of his policy: in the spring the purged corporations returned a house of commons dominated by tory gentlemen. The election results in Lincolnshire were typical of those throughout England. The Bertie family monopolized Boston and Stamford and were joined in the Commons by four close adherents of Lindsey's — Sir Thomas Hussey (Lincolnshire), Sir Edward Ayscough (Grimsby), and Thomas Harrington and John Thorold (Grantham). The Grantham election clearly demonstrated the value of the new charter. The whig members, from 1679 to 1681 Sir William Ellis and Sir John Newton, were defeated ('the exclusion of the excluder', crowed Lindsey, an 'honourable revenge') by the wholesale creation of new freemen by the mayor and recorder; eighty-three freemen were made, twenty-nine of them local gentry and a further twenty clergymen. Three exclusionists were returned — Lord Castleton (Lincolnshire), and Sir Henry Monson and Sir Thomas Meres (Lincoln): but Meres (and possibly his colleague)

---

[26] For Lincoln, see Hill, *Tudor and Stuart Lincoln*, pp. 188–89; SP 44/335, pp. 224–25: for Boston, *CSPD 1685*, p. 49; Boston Common Council Minute Book 4, ff. 107v–112v: for Stamford, *CSPD 1684–85*, p. 292; *1685*, p. 39; Stamford Hall Book 2, ff. 112–14: for Grantham, SP 44/335, p. 387; Grantham Hall Book 1, ff. 693–693v; G. H. Martin, *The Royal Charters of Grantham*, Leicester, 1963, pp. 173–81. For the ties of Heron and Harrington to Lindsey, see *CSPD 1680–81*, p. 376; *1682*, pp. 137–38.

had repented, probably frightened off by the unyielding policies of the whig leaders and by the threat that they posed to his beloved Church of England.[27]

In the summer of 1685 the canard that the tories had so assiduously disseminated concerning their whig opponents, that they were prepared to plunge the nation into civil war, received some measure of confirmation with Monmouth's rebellion. The revolt had no adherents in Lincolnshire, although the scare that it aroused did enable Lindsey, in a not untypical display of paranoia compounded by petty meanness, to order the imprisonment of a number of dissenting ministers and gentlemen who had been associated with the interregnum régimes. As Sir Drayner Massingberd, one of his victims, protested, it was scarcely credible that men now seventy years of age would engage in such a 'mad rebellion'. Yet Lindsey kept his prisoners in Hull longer than did any of the other lord lieutenants, because they were not 'more mannerly' in requesting their release.[28]

Royal manipulation of the corporations gave James II a solidly tory house of commons whose loyalty was enhanced by Monmouth's rebellion. Yet in November 1685 the king prorogued parliament, and it did not meet again. A majority of the loyal members had balked at the direction of James's policy that emerged in the short second session: the proposal for an increased standing army, in part officered by Catholics, was resisted, and in consequence the king resolved to govern without parliament.

In 1686 James endeavoured to assert his co-religionists' rights to enjoy complete religious freedom and to proselytize actively. In Lincolnshire this resulted in the suspension of the prosecution of Catholics, and in orders for the release of a popish bookseller of Lincoln, and the return of his stock. Lincoln also became the centre of a small Jesuit mission and school. James was determined to permit Catholics the same political and civil opportunities as members of the Church of England. In Lincolnshire in December 1685 ten Catholic gentlemen were added to the commission of the peace.[29]

---

[27] HMC *12th Report*, App. 5, pp. 86–88; LAO, MON 7/23/43a; Grantham Hall Book I, ff. 693v sqq.: for Meres, see Browning, *Osbourne*, I, pp. 357–58; Jones, *The First Whigs*, p. 178.

[28] *CSPD 1685*, p. 212; LAO, MM VI/10/11, nos 4–6; Calamy, *Account*, II, pp. 448, 456; Calamy, *Continuation*, pp. 600–1.

[29] SP 44/336, pp. 388–91; *CSPD 1685*, p. 295; *1686–87*, p. 100; *LNQ*, I (1893), pp. 146–47; PC 2/71, p. 369.

In 1685 a loyalist parliament had displayed considerable uneasiness at the direction of James's policies: when privately approached in 1686 tory leaders, both clerical and lay, continued to express their reluctance to accede to the king's pro-Catholic efforts. Accordingly in 1687–88 James undertook a major policy shift which represented a seismic transformation of English politics. He sought to establish a new base of support for his policies, offering toleration and the cessation of civil disabilities upon the dissenters upon the condition that they would support similar rights for the Catholic minority. James, by the Declaration of Indulgence of April 1687 and his subsequent efforts to guarantee a parliament that would repeal the penal laws and the Test Act, was wooing the men whom Charles had purged from all positions of local power in the aftermath of the Exclusion Crisis.

The royal *volte-face* split the tories. In Lincolnshire Bishop Barlow supported the king's policy, and with a body of his clergy, forwarded a declaration asserting both their satisfaction with the royal promises to maintain the established church and their loyalty 'as becomes the true sons of the Church of England'. But other ministers refused to join Barlow or, in 1668, to obey his order to publish the Declaration of Indulgence from their pulpits.[30] The divisions among the tory gentry appeared most clearly at a meeting at Sleaford in November 1687, where the king's 'three questions' were presented to the assembled county élite. A few gentlemen who had been associated with Lindsey from 1681 joined with the Catholic recruits to the commission of the peace, and declared their readiness if returned to parliament to rescind the penal laws and the Test Act or to work for the election of those associated with the king's policy. The bulk of the gentry present, however, refused to support repeal and would promise no more than that they would give their votes for honest, loyal men 'who . . . will faythfully serve His Majesty and theire country'. This answer, it was suggested, would have been given by those gentlemen who had not attended the meeting.[31]

Having refused to identify themselves with James's policy, the recalcitrant tories saw their monopoly of local office dissolved. The militia was placed in the charge of a group of ten Catholics and five pro-Indulgence tory deputy lieutenants. A further purge of the commission of the peace was contemplated, involving the addition

[30] *The London Gazette*, no. 2256; HMC *14th Report*, App. 2, p. 409.

[31] *CSPD 1687–79*, pp. 82, 88; G. Duckett, *Penal Laws and Test Act: Questions touching their repeal propounded . . . by James II to the Deputy Lieutenants and Magistrates of. . . Cumberland, Westmoreland*, London, 1882, pp. 152–57.

of more Catholic gentlemen, some whig exclusionists, and even the ancient Cromwellian, Sir Drayner Massingberd. Seeking to guarantee the return of a house of commons that would advance his programme James also tampered with the parliamentary boroughs. At Boston (twice) and Grantham corporate officers were displaced by Order in Council before, in September, new charters which included a thoroughly revised slate of officers were issued for both boroughs, and for Grimsby.[32]

The tories during and in the aftermath of the Exclusion Crisis had affirmed their absolute devotion to the crown, the established system of law and property relationships and the church of England. They also accused their whig opponents of rabble-rousing tactics that could easily plunge the nation into civil war, with the same unthinkably radical social, political and religious consequences that followed 1642. This tory ideology could not survive the experience of James II's government. Few tories could accept Bishop Barlow's premise, that loyalty 'such as becomes the true sons of the Church of England' required an unquestioning acceptance of royal policies since it was unthinkable that the king would act contrary to the welfare of the Church or the provisions of the constitution. It was too obvious that James challenged both. Worse, he threatened the same subversive consequences that tories had attributed to whig machinations. James like Cromwell maintained a standing army. James like Cromwell ousted the natural rulers of society from local office. James like Cromwell favoured the 'insolent Phanaticks'. In May 1688 the king received a petition expressing 'the sense of satisfaction' at the Declaration of Indulgence of the 'old dissenting officers and soldiers' of Lincolnshire, who, somewhat tactlessly, reminded James that they had once 'been driven into arms to obtain that by force which now your majesty hath so mercifully condescended to'.[33] In the eyes of the tory faction of the country gentry, reared on 'the Church of England and the old cavalier principles', the praise of so tainted a group was a damning indictment of the thrust of James's policies.

The king's programme depended upon the active support of an incongruous congeries of Catholics, dissenters, and the splinter group of tories. It was also predicated upon a belief that the principles of non–resistance so frequently articulated by the majority of the tories would keep them from vigorous opposition.

[32] *CSPD 1687–89*, pp. 132, 261, 263, 264, 269, 275; Duckett, *Penal Laws and Test Act*, pp. 149–51; Boston Common Council Minute Book 4, ff. 134, 134v, 137; Martin, *Royal Charters of Grantham*, pp. 214–27.
[33] *The London Gazette*, nos 2256, 2344.

In the autumn of 1688, with the invasion of William of Orange, the futility of James's political calculations was starkly revealed. The Catholic element lacked public credibility, administrative experience, and even the inclination to take up offices from which they had been so long excluded: only William Thorold of the ten Catholics added to the Kesteven commission of the peace in 1685 actually attended quarter sessions.[34] The dissenters, though grateful for the opportunity to worship freely, distrusted James's broader, pro-Catholic, policies. No substantial assistance was forthcoming from either quarter. The tory doctrine on non-resistance proved a broken reed. A number of tory leaders invited William's intervention and then actively assisted his cause. One was Lindsey's heir, Lord Willoughby, whose opposition to James's programme in 1685 had led to his dismissal from his military posts and local offices. In 1687 Willoughby had communicated with William of Orange, and on 22 November 1688 he and two of his brothers joined their uncle, Danby, in seizing control of York. Willoughby was somewhat embarrassed by his involvement in the revolt, but argued that the maintenance of the other planks of the tory creed made action against James imperative: 'it was the first time any Bertie was ever engaged against the crown . . . but there was a necessity either to part with our religion and properties or doe it'.[35] The bulk of the tory gentry more scrupulously refused to resist, but, equally, felt no obligation to aid their king. In 1688 only eight justices, half the average for the years 1683–85, were involved in local administration in Kesteven: one was a Catholic, four were tories who supported the Declaration of Indulgence. None raised a finger to aid James in 1688. Nor did their lord lieutenant, the earl of Lindsey, whose actions from 1686 had been extremely ambiguous. The earl agreed to vote for the repeal of the penal laws and the Test Act, yet he had also ostentatiously displayed his hostility to 'the papists' — even though his wife was a Catholic. From 1686 he had punctually obeyed the king's orders, yet with obvious reservations: in November 1687 he had carried out the king's instructions to put the 'three questions' to the local gentry, but he made no attempt to proselytize for James's policy, and little effort even to ensure a good attendance at the Sleaford meeting. His cool loyalty was equally apparent in 1688. He offered James his personal service against William; when ordered, he mustered the local militia. Yet he

---

[34] Peyton, ed., *Minutes of Quarter Sessions for Kesteven*, pp. 253–345.
[35] HMC *12th Report*, App. 5, p. 97; PC 2/71, p. 369; K. H. D. Haley, 'A list of the English peers, c.May 1687', *EHR*, 69 (1954), pp. 302–6; *Reresby's Memoirs*, ed. Browning, p. 529.

reported that the military effectiveness of the trained bands was questionable, while the only royal action that won his unfeigned enthusiasm was the proclamation restoring the pre-1684 charters to the parliamentary boroughs. He made absolutely no attempt to interfere with the proceedings at Nottingham, York and Hull by William's adherents.[36]

During the crisis of late November and early December 1688 fears of popular insurrection and civil strife — 'amazeing rumours of warrs' — convulsed Lincolnshire. The Berties prepared to defend Grimsthorpe from a body of 1,500 cavalry reported to be at Northampton, where 'they fire all, and put everie one to the sword'. Such alarming fictions derived some credibility from the outbreak of mob violence against the Catholics: 'the rabble plunder and affront our neighbour Catholics every day' it was reported from Stroxton.[37] In the face of social dislocation the Lincolnshire gentry papered over their differences to present a unanimous front, a process eased by James's panicked flight to the continent. 'All the gentry of the county' at a meeting at Sleaford in mid December agreed upon an address to William,

purporting their unanimous thanks for his protection and assistance of the true Protestant interest and giving him full assurance of their ready concurrence to the makeing . . . such sure and solid lawes for confirming and establishing the same as no power whatsoever for the future shall be able to shake or subvert.[38]

[36] D. H. Hosford, 'The Peerage and the Test Act: a list of c.November 1687', *Bull. IHR*, 42 (1969), p. 119; HMC *14th Report*, App. 9, pp. 446–47; Duckett, *Penal Laws and Test Act*, pp. 152–56; *CSPD 1687–89*, pp. 334, 338; SP 31/4/78; BL Add. 41805, ff. 85, 146, 188.
[37] HMC *11th Report*, App. 7, p. 28; LAO, MON 7/12/61, 62; Hill, *Tudor and Stuart Lincoln*, p. 191.
[38] HMC *14th Report*, App. 9, p. 452; HMC *11th Report*, App. 7, p. 28; LAO, MON 7/12/62.

CHAPTER 15

THE REVOLUTION
SETTLEMENT: TRIUMPH OF
THE COUNTY COMMUNITY?

W HIG historians have traditionally argued that the Glorious Revolution was a constitutional parousia which guaranteed liberty and property: more recently it has been suggested that 1689 was also a watershed for local government, as the county gentry finally succeeded in guaranteeing their hegemony. 'After the Revolution', writes Dr Carter

there was a distinct, though not complete, withdrawal of central authority from controlling local affairs, and the typical eighteenth-century situation of gentry . . . independence in the localities took shape.

Dr Clark characterizes the period 1660–1720 as that of 'the triumph of the county community'.[1]

Much *had* been achieved by the local gentry. The assault on property rights represented in Charles I's unparliamentary taxation and his drainage projects had been repelled. So had the military despotism which loomed between 1647 and 1660. So had James II's efforts (in the pursuit of his pro-Catholic mirage) to re-model the corporations and purge the agencies of local government. Yet the localities were not hermetically sealed from the central government either politically or administratively from 1689.

The apparent administrative irresponsibility of the local magistracy is often an optical illusion induced by a shift in the agency which exercised oversight. Prior to the civil war fen drainage was controlled by the Privy Council. As we have seen, after 1660 those undertaking major drainage projects had to seek legislative authorization — a point driven home in 1700 when another attempt by the earl of Lindsey to secure an act of parliament to enable him to

[1] J. Carter, 'The Revolution and the Constitution', p. 53, in *Britain after the Glorious Revolution, 1689–1714*, ed. G. Holmes, London, 1969; P. Clark, *English Provincial Society from the Reformation to the Revolution*, Hassocks, 1977, p. 398.

recommence work in his Level was scythed by the Commons: the proposal 'invades the properties of thousands of people', thundered an opponent. If parliament had replaced the Privy Council as the major agency of innovation, the judges replaced it for purposes of direction and review. The judges had the authority, invoked by the writs of *mandamus* and *certiorari*, both to compel the commissioners to act and to test the legality of their actions: so in the 1670s the judges struck down the attempt by the commissioners of sewers to extend their competence to cover the drainage of marshy lowlands in the wolds. The judges also arbitrated conflicts among or within the various commissions of sewers. At the end of the century, in a case very reminiscent of the 1618–24 Boston sluice controversy which had ultimately been adjudicated by the Privy Council, it was the judges who sought to settle the complex Wainfleet Haven dispute which had reduced to impotence the local commissioners of sewers, divided between those representing the interests of the soke of Bolingbroke and those from the 'Level towns'.[2]

The county was not insulated from administrative direction. Nor was it isolated from central politics. Parliament's status as sovereign legislative and sole tax-granting body was reinforced by the Revolution. Yet many of the paradoxes of parliament's position which had emerged in the first decades of Charles II's reign remained. Unless the king was prepared to accept the role of a doge of Venice — and William III was certainly not — parliament had to be managed. And the structure of parliament, and the resources still available to the crown ensured that it was manageable.

In the aftermath of the Exclusion Crisis Charles and James had sought to pack the Commons by wholesale interference with the governing bodies of the parliamentary boroughs. After the Revolution such naked tactics were unavailable to William. Yet the more modest operation on behalf of royal control undertaken during the sessions of the Cavalier Parliament was still feasible. The king could rely on the votes of those royal officers with seats in the Commons. He could build up a majority by negotiation with aristocratic political leaders, buying their support, and that of those groups of members bound to them by ties of family or patronage, with offers of positions of influence and profit in the government. The cadet members of the Bertie clan were one element in the extensive *clientela* organized by their relative and old political mentor Thomas Osbourne, now duke of Leeds. Their votes were solidly for the government when Leeds was working in tandem with the 'junto'

---

[2] HMC *House of Lords*, n.s. 4, pp. 215–19; LAO, MM 6/7; MG 6/7/1, nos 12, 16.

leaders: in 1696 as Leeds grew disillusioned with his ministerial allies, the Berties followed his convoluted course, now with, now against, the administration in divisions of the House. In March 1697 William expressed exasperation with Leeds and 'the whole family of Berties', and Lord Willoughby and Philip Bertie paid for their patron's tergiversations with the loss of their own offices.

The creed of such men, dedicated to the quest for power and patronage at Westminster, was expressed in a series of letters from Peregrine Bertie approving a nephew's intention to stand for parliament in 1694: 'it will be of great advantage to him, and make the court look upon him with better eyes'; a seat in the Commons 'will helpe on his businesse at court'; finally, and most revealing, 'courtiers must venture their fortunes, and they can have no better lottery than our House to push their fortunes in'.[3]

The existence of placemen and political connections was in part predicated upon peculiarities in the electoral structure of parliament, which undercut its function as a representative assembly. Stamford, the constituency for which Peregrine's nephew was standing, was close to becoming a pocket borough. The town had witnessed some fierce contests in 1675–81, but a major factor in the vigorous campaigns of these years had been a dispute for control of Stamford's governing body between the traditional patron, the earl of Exeter, and the interlopers, Lindsey and Lord Camden. After the Revolution, the Cecils and the Berties arrived at a *modus vivendi* and split the representation of the borough: they controlled the civic government and were prepared to spend heavily to maintain their hegemony. The ambitions of the local whig gentleman, Sir Pury Cust, were defeated by the machinations of the aristocratic tandem in 1688 and again in 1695. Cust did not challenge his noble opponents a third time having been warned off with the threat that 'he must expect, if he stood, to spend £500 to £600'.[4]

Stamford was virtually a pocket borough: by the end of the seventeenth century. Grimsby was a rotten borough, its small yet venal electorate ready to be cajoled by the highest bidder. Since 1660 Grimsby had been buyable — the going rate in 1667 was £300 in ale and £52 in buttered ale — but the constituency had been procured by local gentlemen. In the last decade of the seventeenth

[3] I. F. Burton, P. W. J. Riley, and E. Rowlands, *Political Parties in the Reigns of William III and Anne: the evidence of division lists*, Bull. IHR Special Suplmt, 7 (1968), pp. 28–29, 45; H. Horwitz, *Parliament, policy and politics in the reign of William III*, Newark, 1977, p. 193; HMC *13th Report*, App. 6, p. 250.

[4] LAO, 3 ANC 8/1/17; E. Cust, *Records of the Cust Family . . . 1479–1700*, London, 1898, pp. 359, 375, 399.

century one seat was still held by a representative of this group, Sir Edward Ayscough, a lay vicar of Bray who graduated from being one of Lindsey's trusted adherents during the Exclusion Crisis, to one of King James's few gentry supporters, to a completely reliable placeman of the whig junto. But, in 1690, outside wealth had already been tempted by the notorious corruptability of the Grimsby electorate, and by the end of the century the aspirants consisted of two heirs to London-made fortunes, a director of the Old East India Company, and a director of the rival new company: the latter had emerged as a candidate only after a couple of Grimsby freemen had hawked the representation of their borough in London 'to such as would give most money'.[5]

The connection; pocket boroughs; rotten boroughs: these made the management of parliament by the executive possible and, equally, detracted from parliament's pure representative function. The co-optation of the Houses by the crown was bitterly resented by many country gentlemen after 1689. Sir Edward Hussey, member for Lincoln in the 1689 convention, in 1690–95 and in 1698 was a whig: he sympathized with the dissenters; he voted for the 'Sacheveral clause' excluding from local office all who had co-operated with the crown in the purges of the corporations from 1681 to 1688; he occasionally permitted himself a sardonic jibe at the expense of the Anglican Church. Hussey was a whig. Yet the arguments of later 'whig historians' that 1689 guaranteed liberty and property, or that it represented the triumph of the county community would have been incomprehensible to him. He was deeply suspicious of William's rule. He questioned demands for the upkeep of the army, opposing additional taxation and pushing for investigation of government waste and mismanagement. He led the resistance to royal interference in the Commons: he favoured annual parliaments and, noting how 'some men by preferment have their mouths gagged up against the interest of the people', he was the sponsor of a bill for the exclusion of those holding crown offices or pensions from the Commons.[6]

Politics at Westminster as the interplay of factions hungry for office; local elections little more than a procession of tamed or venal

---

[5] E. Gillett, *A history of Grimsby*, London, 1970, pp. 133–51; A. Weston, 'Lincolnshire Politics in the reign of Queen Anne, 1702–14', *LHA*, 6 (1971), pp. 90–92, 96–99.
[6] *The Parliamentary Diary of Narcissus Luttrell, 1691–93*, ed. H. Horwitz, Oxford, 1972, pp. 55, 144, 256, 263, 276, 284, 336, 360, 407, 415, 497; A. G. Matthews, *Calamy Revised*, London, 1934, pp. 58–59; Horwitz, *Parliament, policy and politics*, pp. 109–10, 124, 127, 200, 212.

voters giving (or, more usually, selling) their franchises to those eager to play the court roulette: this is the political world of the mid eighteenth century as described by Sir Lewis Namier. Even Hussey fits: a member of that small group of country gentlemen, fiercely independent, immune to the lure of office, and, in Sir Lewis's opinion, 'fortunately' insufficient in numbers to disturb the 'everyday work' of parliament.[7]

The 1690s were not the 1750s, however. The executive had not yet tapped the full range of resources available for wooing members — that was to be Sir Robert Walpole's achievement. The independent element in parliament, Hussey and men of his ilk, were numerous and vocal. In consequence the situation at the centre was extremely unstable and general elections were frequent and hotly contested. Not only did national concerns galvanize the localities on these occasions, they were the subject of intense discussion throughout the last decade of the century. It is in this respect that the localities are not politically isolated from events at Westminster.

Abraham de la Pryme, curate of Broughton from 1695, made frequent forays from his rural backwater to the neighbouring market towns, Brigg and Caistor, 'to hear what news there was stirring' and to discuss it with his fellow clerics, minor gentlemen and merchants of the area. Two issues particularly exercised de la Pryme and his companions. First, the progress of the war with Louis XIV: martial successes and the restoration of national prestige were gratifying, but had to be set against heavy taxation and inflation. The local results of the government's programme of recoinage designed to handle the latter problem were of particular concern to de la Pryme. In March 1696 he was hopeful of the success of the deflationary scheme, but in the early summer he reported its disastrous consequences in Lincolnshire — the stoppage of trade, subsistence riots and popular disillusionment with the government and its policies. De la Pryme's own loyalty to the régime wavered: he speculated that the recoinage was a subtle plot devised by the French to force England out of the war; he intimated that parliament was morally responsible for the suicide of a poor pedlar of Ferriby who killed herself when she found that her painfully hoarded cache of money was worthless.[8]

The war and its consequences was one issue of public discussion in Lincolnshire in the 1690s: religion was the other. In 1688–89 the

[7] L. Namier, *The structure of politics at the accession of George III*, London, 1961, pp. 4–7.
[8] *The diary of Abraham de la Pryme*, ed. C. Jackson, Surtees Soc., 54, 1870, pp. 60, 61, 64, 66, 79, 84, 93, 95–98, 110, 136.

Anglican clergy were invited to disavow the themes that had dominated their preaching for thirty years — divine right, non-resistance, hereditary succession — and to swallow the oaths they had sworn to James II. Twelve Lincolnshire ministers refused and lost their livings. The majority accepted William, but with grave conscientious scruples that appear in de la Pryme's comment that it was easier for him to acknowledge William as 'rightful and lawful king' than it was for many of his colleagues, since 'I was not bound with any oath or tye of allegiance to King James'. Similar uncertainties underlie Samuel Wesley of Epworth's extraordinary reaction to his wife's refusal to join in the prayers for William:

he immediately kneeled down and imprecated the divine vengeance upon himself and all his posterity if ever he touched me more or came into a bed with me before I had begged God's pardon and his, for not saying Amen to the prayer for the [king].

Troubled by the uncomfortable moral quandary into which they had been forced by the events of 1688–89, the clergy were deeply suspicious and resentful of the movers of the Revolution and of its nonconformist beneficiaries. De la Pryme was a supporter of William's title, as of his foreign policy. He was also perfectly aware that the dissenters were no longer frenzied radicals:

the Quakers now are nothing like what they were formerly. They are now the most reformed that ever was seen. They now were fine cloathes, and learns all sorts of sempstry and behavour, as others do that are not of their opinions . . . They do not now quake, and howl, and foam with their mouths, as they did formerly, but modestly and devoutly behave themselves.

Yet consideration of the ecclesiastical policy of the 1689 Convention Parliament — the Toleration Act, the attempted Comprehension Bill — caused the curate of Broughton to gibber with rage. The Convention 'had the impudencie to meddle with the holy things of the Church', he wrote and went on to pen a blistering attack upon the ecclesiastical interventions of the Commons in general: the House was invariably made up of

a company of irreligious wretches who cares not . . . what becomes of the Church . . . if they can but get their hawkes, houndes and whores, and the sacred possessions of the Church.

The king, de la Pryme believed, should be bound by his coronation oath never to change the established government of the Church; this would prevent any further assaults by the Commons, 'who vallues the weal politic above the ecclesiastic, and their own wordly ends above their own salvation'. De la Pryme was not the only

Lincolnshire clergyman to be enraged by the attempts of the whigs to meddle with ecclesiastical affairs. 'Good God!', thundered the vicar of Uffington, John Evans, in 1689

how will this look to the reformed churches abroad, to thousands hear at home and to future ages that a parliament should reforme our liturgie, expunge creeds, tell us what we must not believe and what wee must without advising with a convocation . . . what shall wee reply . . . to our old adversaries at Rome when they affirme our religion is meerly parliamentary, that our church hath noe power nor authority but is derived from the law of the land.

Like de la Pryme, Evans was also suspicious of William's credentials as a defender of the Church: 'the Church of England men must never hope to be courted and relyed on by the crowne any longer then their interest prooves the most considerable'.[9]

Fears of the ecclesiastical consequences of the Revolution and scruples concerning William's title to the throne were not peculiar to the clergy. Both troubled the Lincolnshire gentry. In 1689 Sir Henry Monson would not swear the oaths to the new king and lost his seat in parliament and his local offices in consequence. In 1696 Sir John Bolles of Scampton (who in 1699 was to denounce the assize judges who 'came down with the king's commission to enslave the people') refused to sign the Association, with its affirmation that William was 'rightful and lawful king'. Five Lincolnshire justices, headed by Sir John Oldfield, also failed to sign and were dismissed from the commission of the peace.[10]

As with the clergy, gentry martyrs were few but they represented the tip of an iceberg of tory doubt and concern about the Revolution and its consequences. The latter emerges in the occasional outburst, fired by drink, as that at Caistor in 1690 when a number of gentlemen, including Matthew Lister of Burwell, one of the few Lincolnshire gentry who had participated actively in the Revolution, compelled a soldier to drink the health of King James. It is apparent, in a more constructive form, in the victory at the Grantham bye-election in 1697 of Sir John Thorold, whose 'party' included a sizeable clerical element. Such tory sentiment was certainly fostered by the earl of Lindsey, who employed his position as lord lieutenant both to protect those gentlemen rash enough to denounce the régime openly, and to hound the most

[9] VCH, Lincs., II, p. 69; J. A. Newton, Susanna Wesley, London, 1968, pp. 87–93; Diary of de la Pryme, ed. Jackson, pp. 53, 150; BL Egerton 3337, f. 2.
[10] L. K. J. Glassey, Politics and the Appointment of Justices of the Peace, 1675–1720, Oxford, 1979, pp. 114, 119; PC 2/76, p. 543; Narcissus Luttrell, A brief historical relation, IV, Oxford, 1857, p. 545.

active whigs: so in 1691 Lindsey removed from their positions in the Lincolnshire militia his old enemies from the Exclusion crisis period, Lord Castleton and Sir William Ellis, and the influential whig spokesman, Sir Edward Hussey.[11]

In the reign of Anne, freed from the constraints induced by the moral ambiguity of their allowance of William's dubious title, the tories became more active and with their battlecry of 'the Church in danger' and with Doctor Sacheverell as their totem, fired the rage of party at the centre and in the localities. In Lincolnshire party strife was intense and the belligerents sought allies outside the ruling class. During the 1705 election the whigs encouraged the jeers and petty assaults of the mob against Samuel Wesley, vicar of Epworth, who had published a tract against their candidate. In 1710 the sermons of the clergy, seconded by the efforts of the tory gentry (such as distributing loaves inscribed 'Sacheverell 1710' to the poor) whipped up a popular 'frenzy' to which the whigs attributed their defeat in the shire election.[12]

The events of the quarter century following the Revolution of 1689 hardly display an unqualified 'triumph of the county community'. Local office was still hostage to central politics as both the tory Sir John Oldfield and the whig Sir Edward Hussey discovered. The Lincolnshire gentry were divided about constitutional and religious issues and invited the participation of the lower orders in their conflicts. The county was forking out taxes, duly sanctioned by parliament to maintain a standing army, by comparison with which the sums raised by Charles I during the 'eleven years tyranny' or the 'unheard-of TAXES' of the Cromwellian Protectorate pale into insignificance. Professor Alan Everitt has suggested that the political concerns of the gentry focused upon the locality. They watched central politics with suspicion and distaste, alert for, and ready to act upon, those occasions when 'the gyrations of politicians became more than ordinarily demented, and threatened the structure of their own local and largely self-centred world'.[13] If we accept this argument, we must also concede that the local gentry's essential ignorance of central politics extended to an ignorance of how to control the gyrations of Westminster effectively. Three times in the seventeenth century the Lincolnshire

[11] BL Egerton 3337, ff. 175–181b; LAO, MON 7/12/94; 7/14/88; BL Loan 29/185, f. 86; Glassey, *Justices of the Peace*, pp. 107, 109.
[12] HMC *Kenyon*, p. 435; G. Holmes, *The Trial of Doctor Sacheverell*, London, 1973, pp. 240, 251–52.
[13] A. Everitt, *Change in the Provinces: the Seventeenth Century*, Leicester, 1969, p. 47.

gentry had stood in serried opposition to the central government, and in each case, in 1640, in 1660, again in 1688, the régime had challenged their local hegemony. Yet in each case the moment of gentry unity was ephemeral, and did not result in the establishment of any mechanism which would guarantee local independence from central interference. But were Star Chamber, the major-generals, and James II's commissioners for regulating the corporations the only foci of local hostility? In each case Westminster had *also* assailed religious prejudices by, respectively, hounding the godly, patronizing sectaries, and advancing the papists. National constitutional principles were also clearly at issue during the three climacterics. In 1660 the Lincolnshire gentry excoriated the flagrant assaults upon 'our known established lawes and fundamentall liberties' by the interregnum governments: their statement echoes the rhetoric of 1640, which was to resound again in 1688–89. It was the rhetoric of a political culture which the governors of Lincolnshire shared with gentlemen throughout England. And, I would argue, the divisions among the gentry which followed their momentary solidarity and their failure to insulate the localities from Westminster demonstrate that constitutional and religious issues were not subordinated to the defence of their 'local world'. County boundaries did not circumscribe the interests of the local élite.

I do not wish to revert to a crude 'whig' historiography with its unidimensional orientation to central institutions and politics. The organization of local government was of major concern to the Lincolnshire gentry and their exercise of the authority deputed to them in the locality was frequently contrary to the aims of their principals at Westminster: that has surely been demonstrated in this study. But the gentry's acceptance of a national ideology of a centralized state under a common law is equally apparent. It emerges in the failure of their uncertain efforts to neutralize the shire in 1642. It explains why so little was done to provide structural guarantees of local independence in 1640, in 1660 or even in 1688: as emerges in the reigns of William and Anne, local independence was hardly furthered by the Revolution's assertion of the sovereignty of parliament and its failure to change the internal structure of the institution to prevent its manipulation by the executive.

The Lincolnshire gentry were part of a national class, with whom, as I argued in the first part of this work, they intermarried, with whom they socialized at London, with whom they shared an educational system and a common administrative experience. And, crucially, with whom they shared religious and political concerns and ideals. Local sentiment was strong, but, lacking any formal institutional focus, it was subordinated to the national ideology of a centralized polity and a common law. Cromwell, who in his less ecstatic moments embodied the prejudices of the English gentry, contemplated the confusion of local autonomy with horror:

would it not make England like the Switzerland country, one canton of the Swiss against another, and one county against another? . . . And if so, what would that produce but an absolute desolation — an absolute desolation to the nation. [14]

Lincolnshire was not a canton, not a semi-autonomous 'county commonwealth' in the seventeenth century. Like the villages and towns within it, the county was tied in by a complex series of interactions to the 'nation', and national consciousness was strong — but that fact does not, I believe, detract from the interest of its history.

[14] A. S. P. Woodhouse, *Puritanism and Liberty*, London, 1974, pp. 7–8.

S*

INDEX

Places are in the ancient county of Lincoln unless otherwise specified.